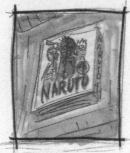

岸本斉史

Quite a few dearly missed characters appear in this volume. I had to keep checking past volumes while drawing them because I'd forgotten some of their specs, which ended up taking way too long. Argh!!

—Masashi Kishimoto, 2011

...as born in 1974 in rural ...pending time in art college, ...ew manga artists with his ...shimoto decided to base his ...culture. His first version of **Naruto**, drawn in ~~1997~~, ...e-shot story about fox spirits; his final version, which debuted in **Weekly Shonen Jump** in 1999, quickly became the most popular ninja manga in Japan.

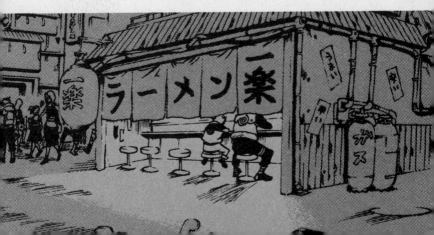

NARUTO VOL. 55
SHONEN JUMP Manga Edition

This graphic novel contains material that was originally published in English
in SHONEN JUMP #105–108. Artwork in the magazine may have been
slightly altered from that presented here.

STORY AND ART BY MASASHI KISHIMOTO

Translation/Mari Morimoto
English Adaptation/Joel Enos
Touch-up Art & Lettering/Inori Fukuda Trant, Sabrina Heep
Design/Sam Elzway
Editor/Megan Bates

NARUTO © 1999 by Masashi Kishimoto. All rights reserved. First
published in Japan in 1999 by SHUEISHA Inc., Tokyo. English translation
rights arranged by SHUEISHA Inc.

Printed in the U.S.A.

Published by VIZ Media, LLC
P.O. Box 77010
San Francisco, CA 94107

10 9 8 7 6 5 4 3 2 1
First printing, March 2012

www.viz.com

THE WORLD'S
MOST POPULAR MANGA

www.shonenjump.com

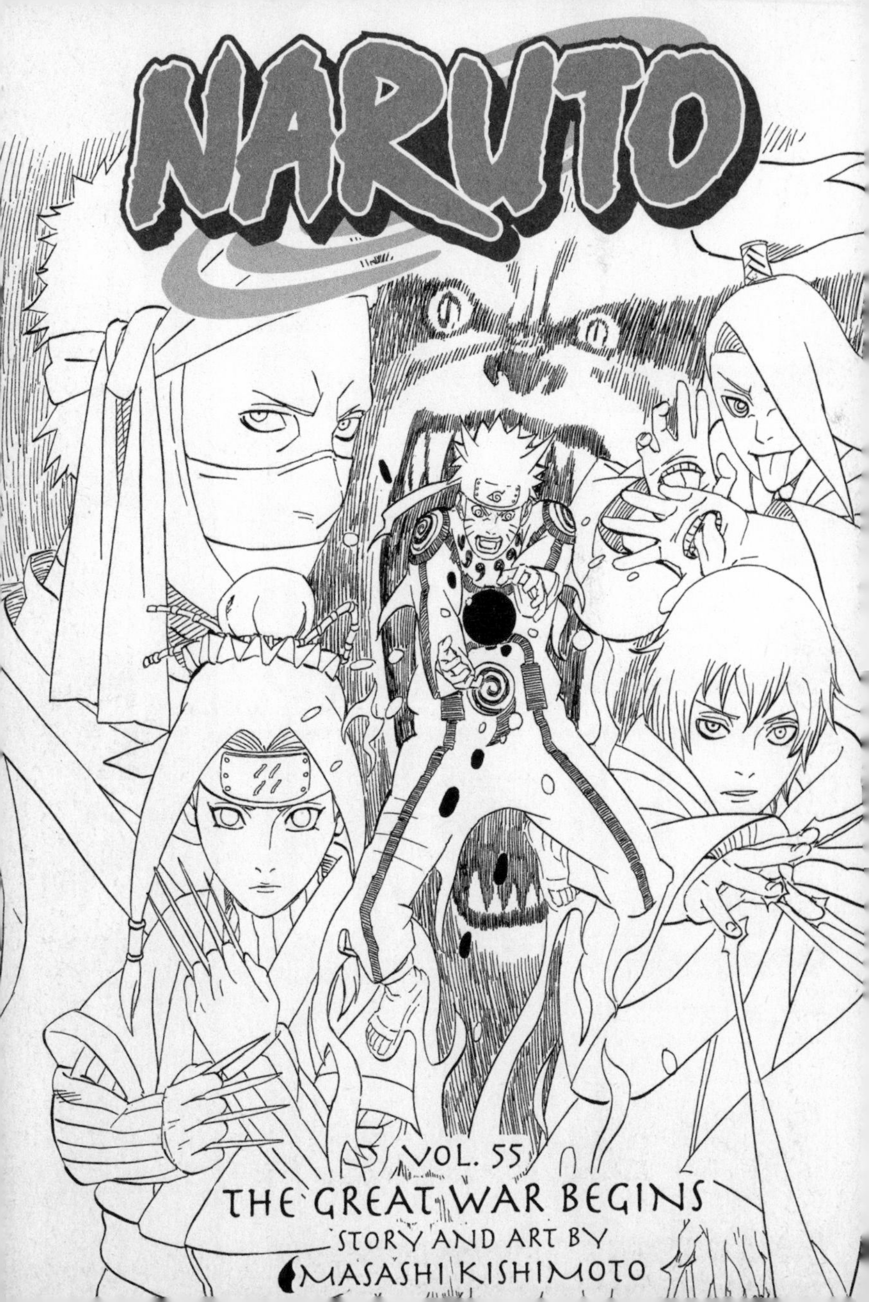
NARUTO
VOL. 55
THE GREAT WAR BEGINS
STORY AND ART BY
MASASHI KISHIMOTO

CHARACTERS

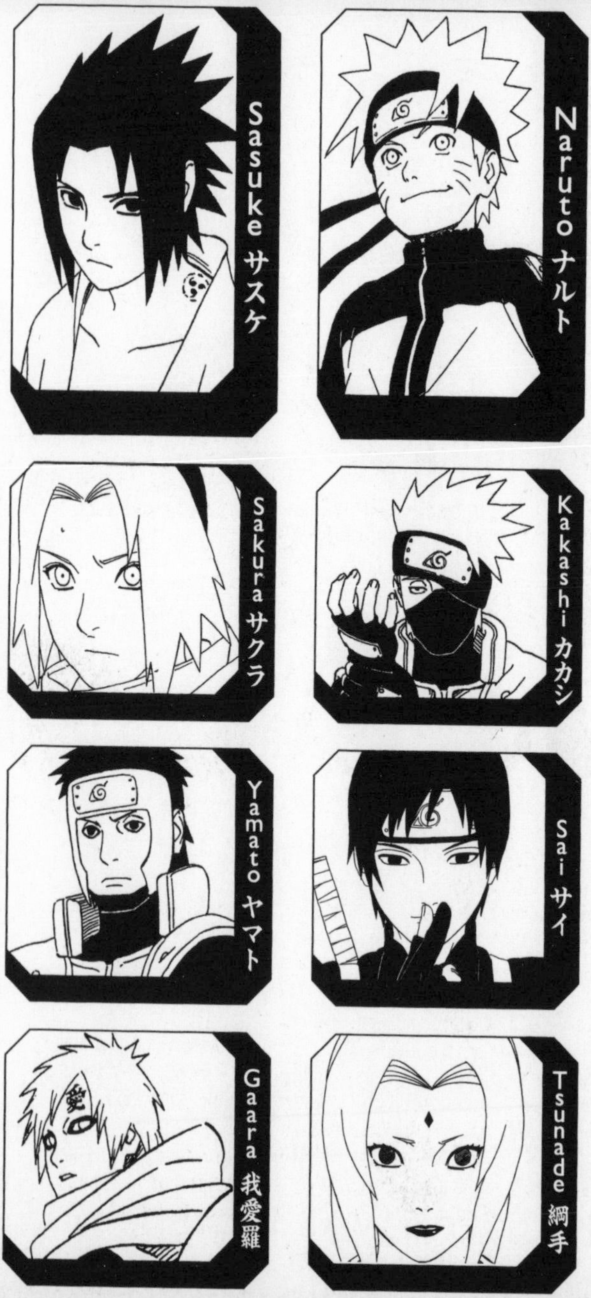

Naruto ナルト
Sasuke サスケ
Kakashi カカシ
Sakura サクラ
Sai サイ
Yamato ヤマト
Tsunade 綱手
Gaara 我愛羅

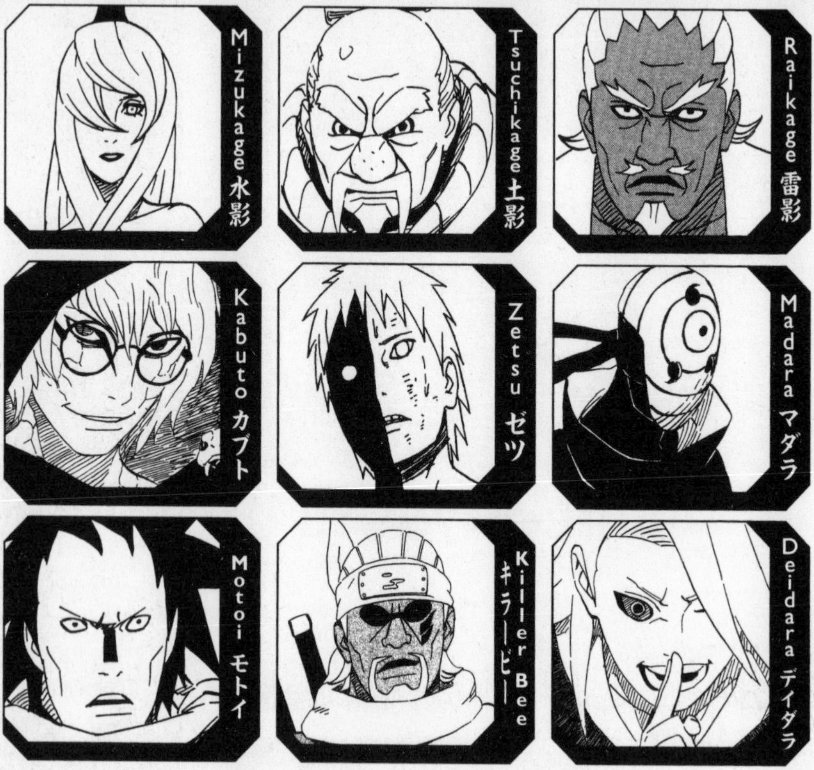
Raikage 雷影
Tsuchikage 土影
Mizukage 水影
Madara マダラ
Zetsu ゼツ
Kabuto カブト
Deidara デイダラ
Killer Bee キラービー
Motoi モトイ

THE STORY SO FAR...

Naruto, the biggest troublemaker at the Ninja Academy in the Village of Konohagakure, finally becomes a ninja along with his classmates Sasuke and Sakura. They grow and mature through countless trials and battles. However, Sasuke, unable to give up his quest for vengeance, leaves Konohagakure to seek Orochimaru and his power…

Two years pass. Naruto grows up and engages in fierce battles against the Tailed Beast-targeting Akatsuki. Elsewhere, after winning the heroic battle against Itachi and learning his older brother's true intentions, Sasuke allies with the Akatsuki and sets out to destroy Konoha.

Upon Madara's declaration of war, an Allied Shinobi Force is formed. As tensions rise in both camps, the Akatsuki pinpoint Naruto's location. Madara directs Kabuto to capture Nine Tails. Yamato heads out to intercept Kabuto and protect Naruto, but is captured instead!

NARUTO

VOL. 55
THE GREAT WAR BEGINS

CONTENTS

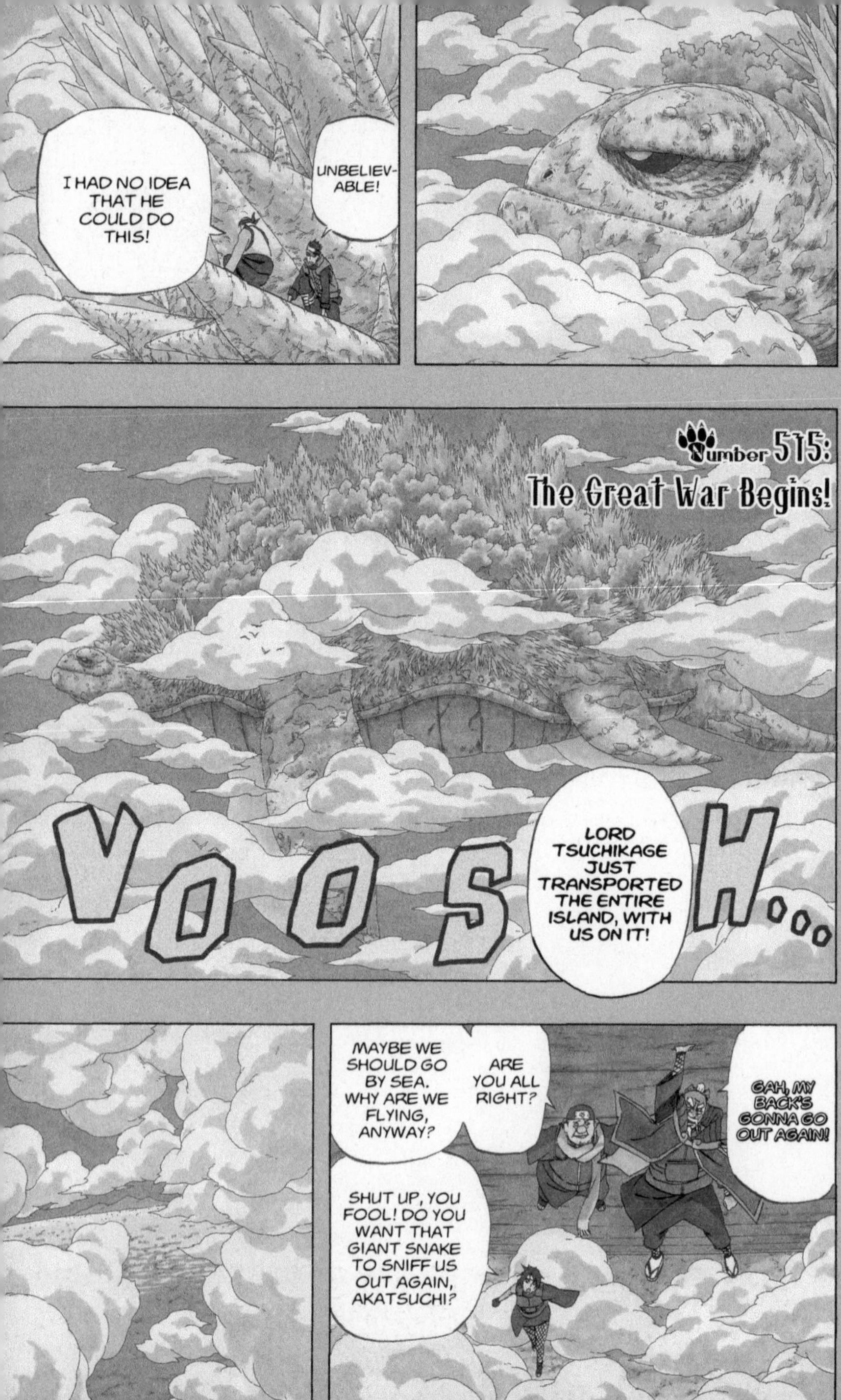
UNBELIEV-ABLE!
I HAD NO IDEA THAT HE COULD DO THIS!
Number 515:
The Great War Begins!
VOOSH...
LORD TSUCHIKAGE JUST TRANSPORTED THE ENTIRE ISLAND, WITH US ON IT!
GAH, MY BACK'S GONNA GO OUT AGAIN!
ARE YOU ALL RIGHT?
MAYBE WE SHOULD GO BY SEA. WHY ARE WE FLYING, ANYWAY?
SHUT UP, YOU FOOL! DO YOU WANT THAT GIANT SNAKE TO SNIFF US OUT AGAIN, AKATSUCHI?

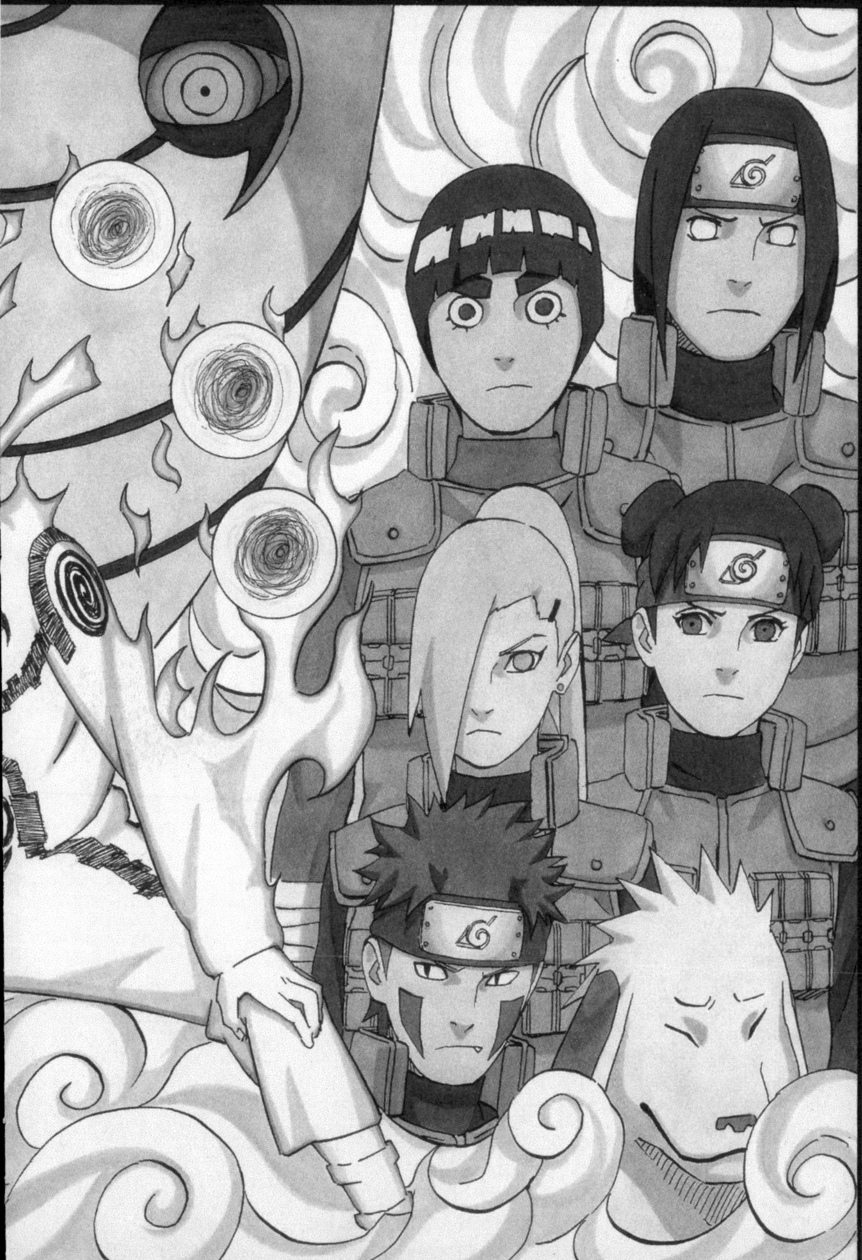

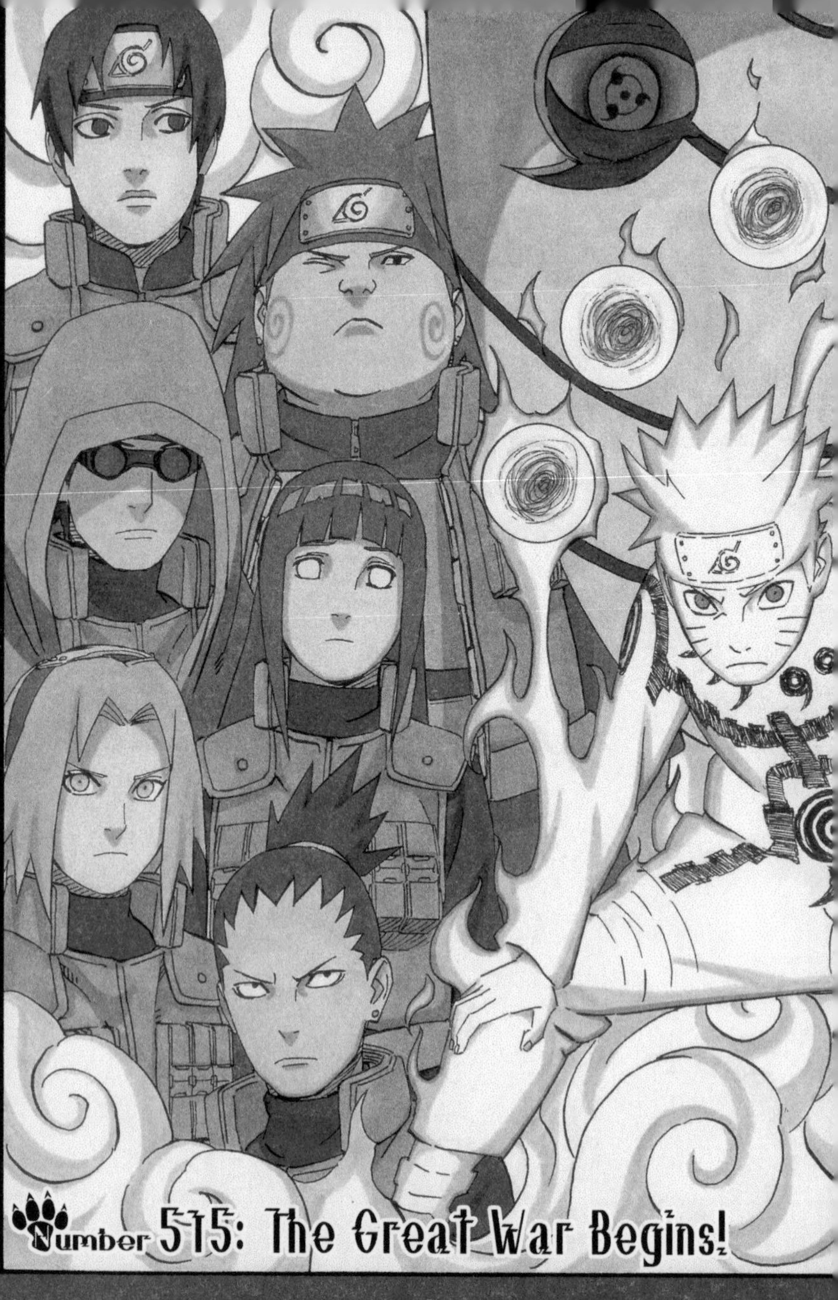

Number 515: The Great War Begins!

NARUTO

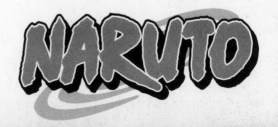

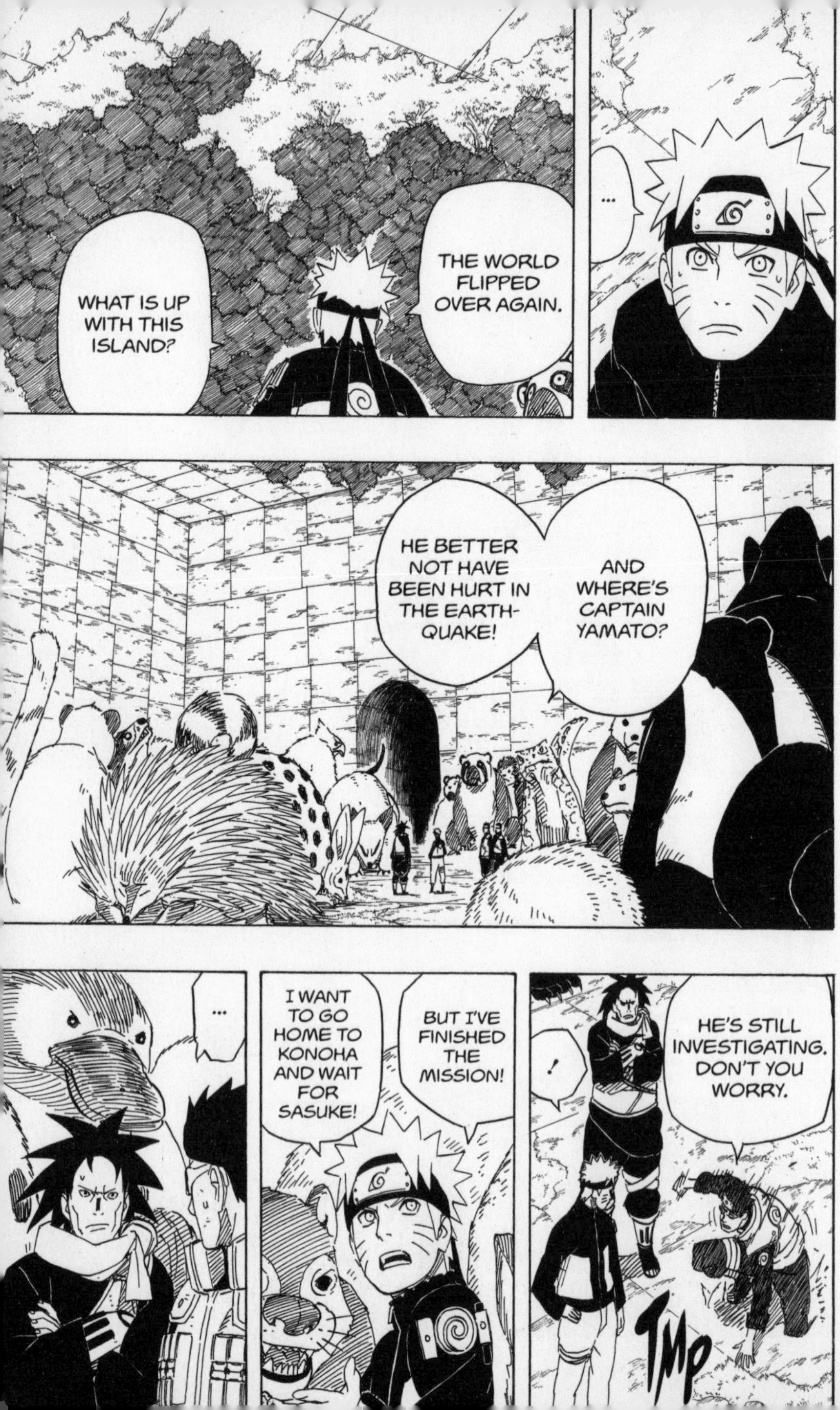
...
THE WORLD FLIPPED OVER AGAIN.
WHAT IS UP WITH THIS ISLAND?
AND WHERE'S CAPTAIN YAMATO?
HE BETTER NOT HAVE BEEN HURT IN THE EARTH-QUAKE!
HE'S STILL INVESTIGATING. DON'T YOU WORRY.
!
TMP
BUT I'VE FINISHED THE MISSION!
I WANT TO GO HOME TO KONOHA AND WAIT FOR SASUKE!
...

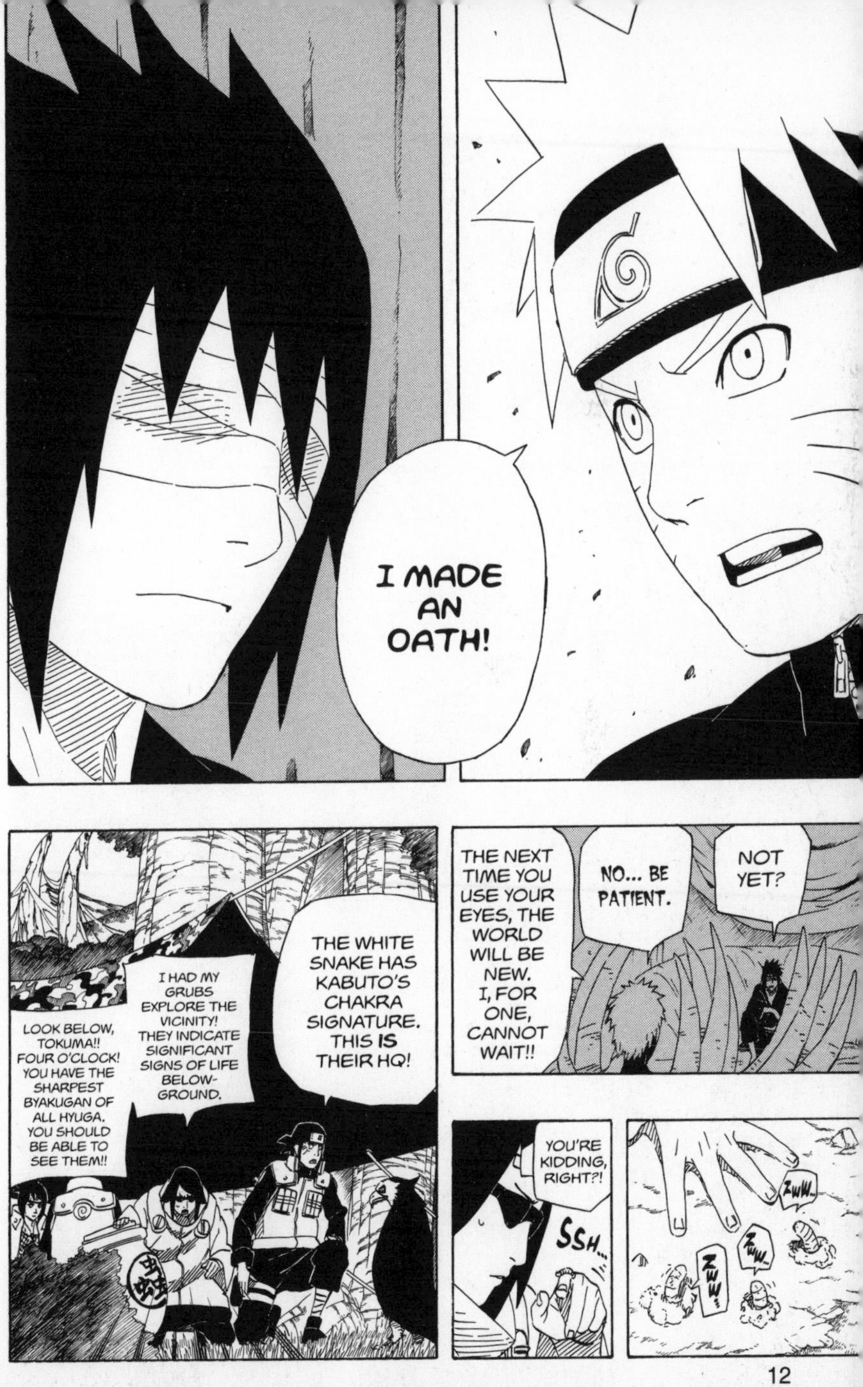
I MADE AN OATH!
NOT YET?
NO... BE PATIENT.
THE NEXT TIME YOU USE YOUR EYES, THE WORLD WILL BE NEW. I, FOR ONE, CANNOT WAIT!!
ZWW...
ZWW...
ZWW...
YOU'RE KIDDING, RIGHT?!
SSH...
THE WHITE SNAKE HAS KABUTO'S CHAKRA SIGNATURE. THIS **IS** THEIR HQ!
I HAD MY GRUBS EXPLORE THE VICINITY! THEY INDICATE SIGNIFICANT SIGNS OF LIFE BELOW-GROUND.
LOOK BELOW, TOKUMA!! FOUR O'CLOCK! YOU HAVE THE SHARPEST BYAKUGAN OF ALL HYUGA. YOU SHOULD BE ABLE TO SEE THEM!!

READ THIS WAY

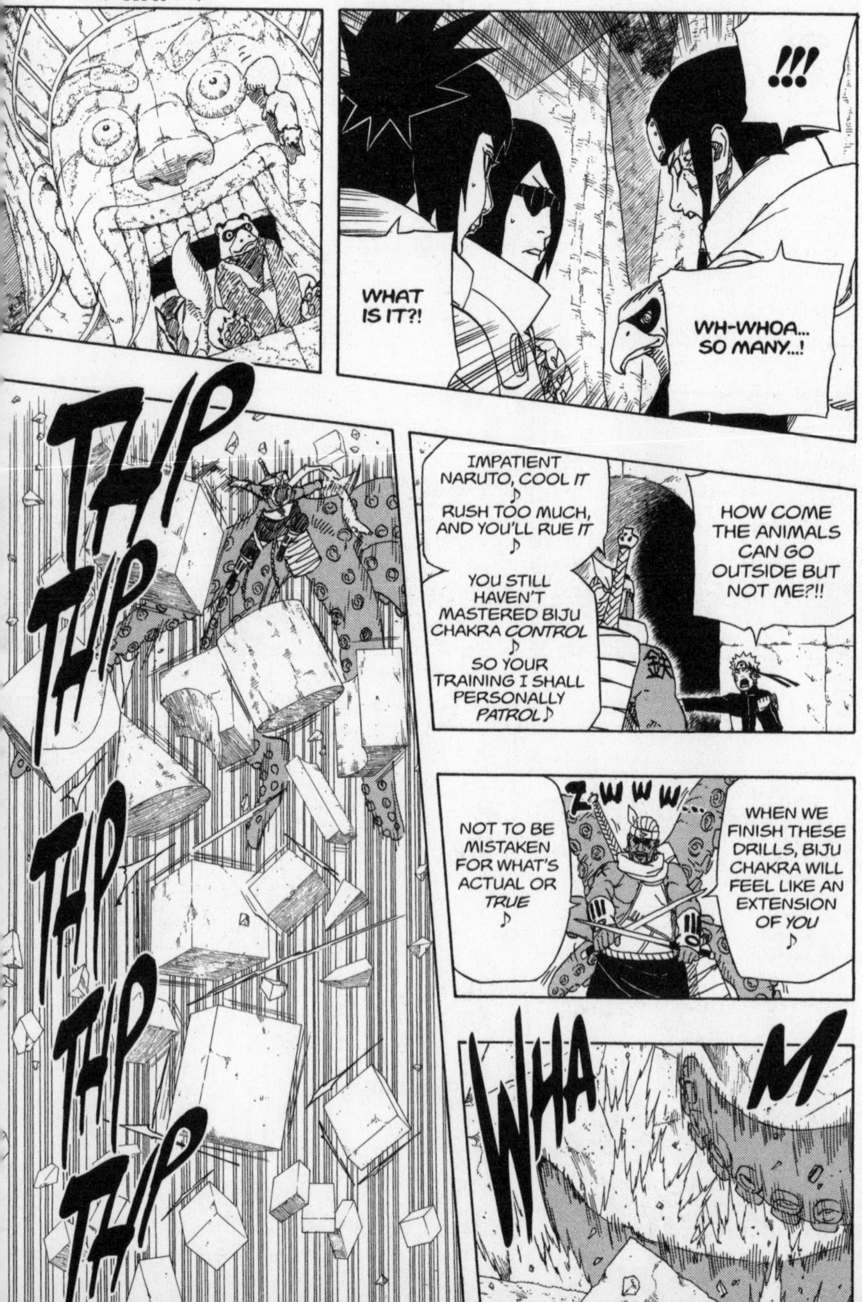
!!!
WH-WHOA... SO MANY...!
WHAT IS IT?!
HOW COME THE ANIMALS CAN GO OUTSIDE BUT NOT ME?!!
IMPATIENT NARUTO, COOL IT ♪ RUSH TOO MUCH, AND YOU'LL RUE IT ♪
YOU STILL HAVEN'T MASTERED BIJU CHAKRA CONTROL ♪ SO YOUR TRAINING I SHALL PERSONALLY PATROL♪
WHEN WE FINISH THESE DRILLS, BIJU CHAKRA WILL FEEL LIKE AN EXTENSION OF YOU ♪
ZWWW
NOT TO BE MISTAKEN FOR WHAT'S ACTUAL OR TRUE ♪
WHAM
THP THP THP THP THP THP THP

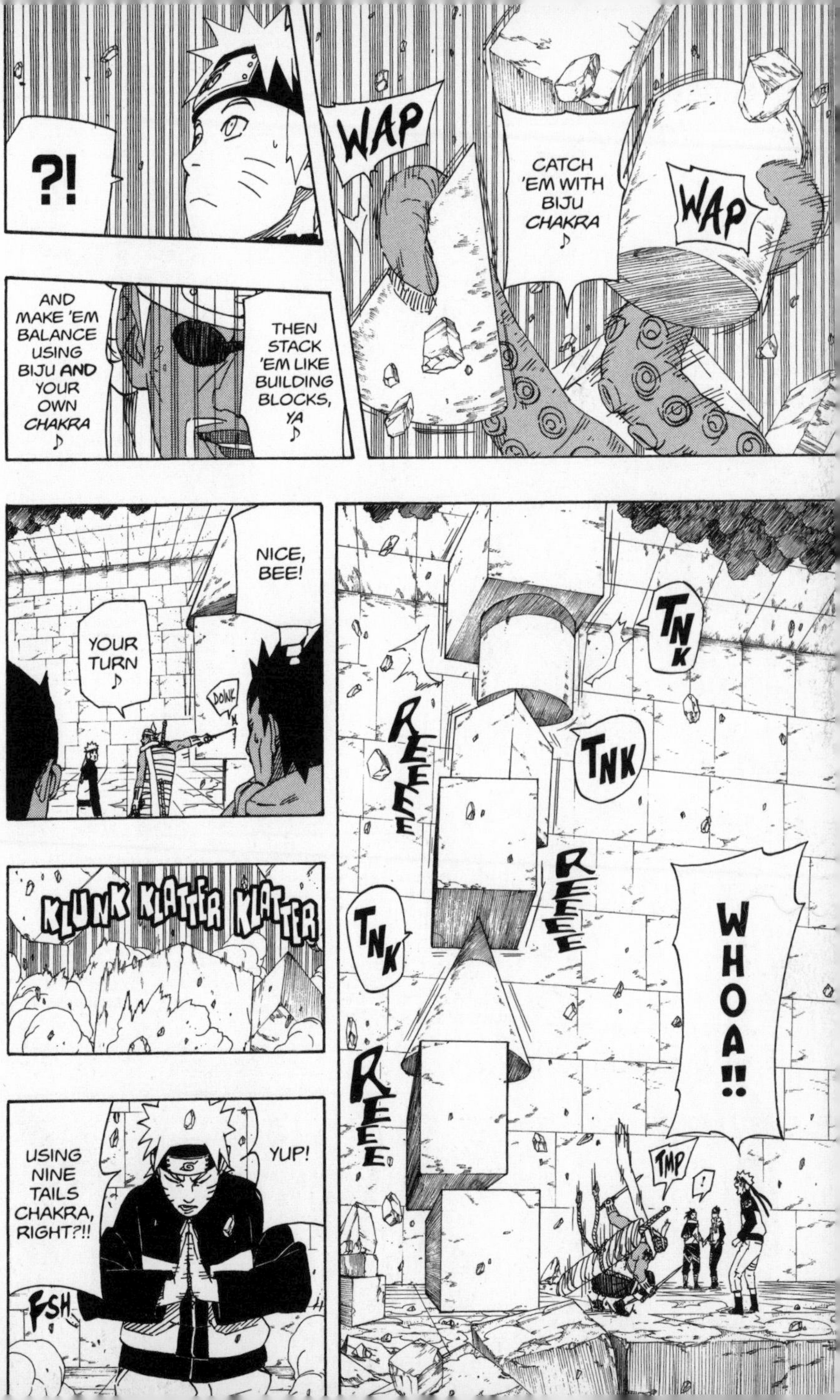
WAP
CATCH 'EM WITH BIJU CHAKRA ♪
WAP
?!
THEN STACK 'EM LIKE BUILDING BLOCKS, YA ♪
AND MAKE 'EM BALANCE USING BIJU AND YOUR OWN CHAKRA ♪
TNK
REEE
TNK
REEE
WHOA!!
TNK
REEE
TMP
!
NICE, BEE!
YOUR TURN ♪
DOINK
KLUNK KLATTER KLATTER
YUP!
USING NINE TAILS CHAKRA, RIGHT?!!
FSH

READ THIS WAY

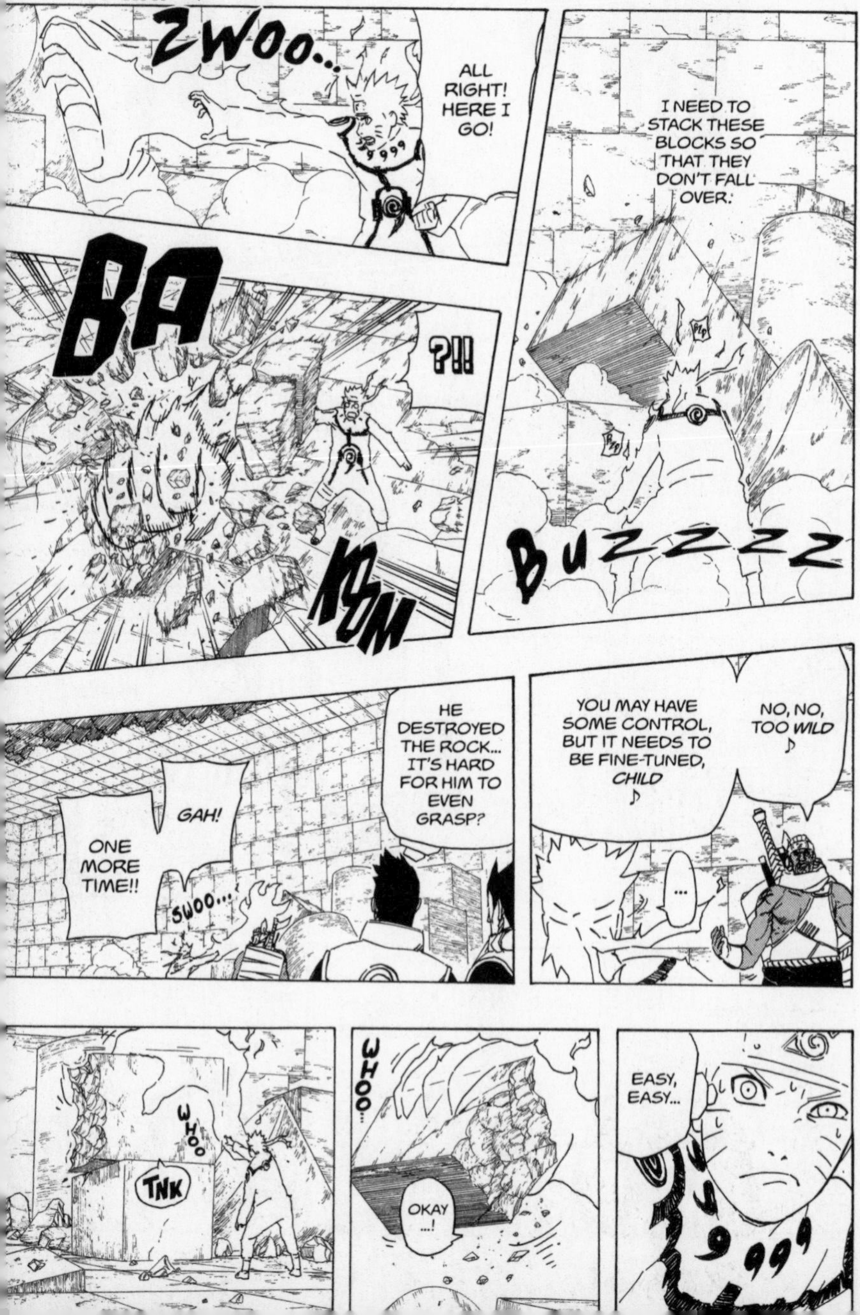
I NEED TO STACK THESE BLOCKS SO THAT THEY DON'T FALL OVER.
BUZZZZZ
ZWOO...
ALL RIGHT! HERE I GO!
BA
KBOM
?!!
NO, NO, TOO WILD ♪
YOU MAY HAVE SOME CONTROL, BUT IT NEEDS TO BE FINE-TUNED, CHILD ♪
...
HE DESTROYED THE ROCK... IT'S HARD FOR HIM TO EVEN GRASP?
GAH!
ONE MORE TIME!!
SWOO...
EASY, EASY...
WHOO...
OKAY ...!
WHOO
TNK

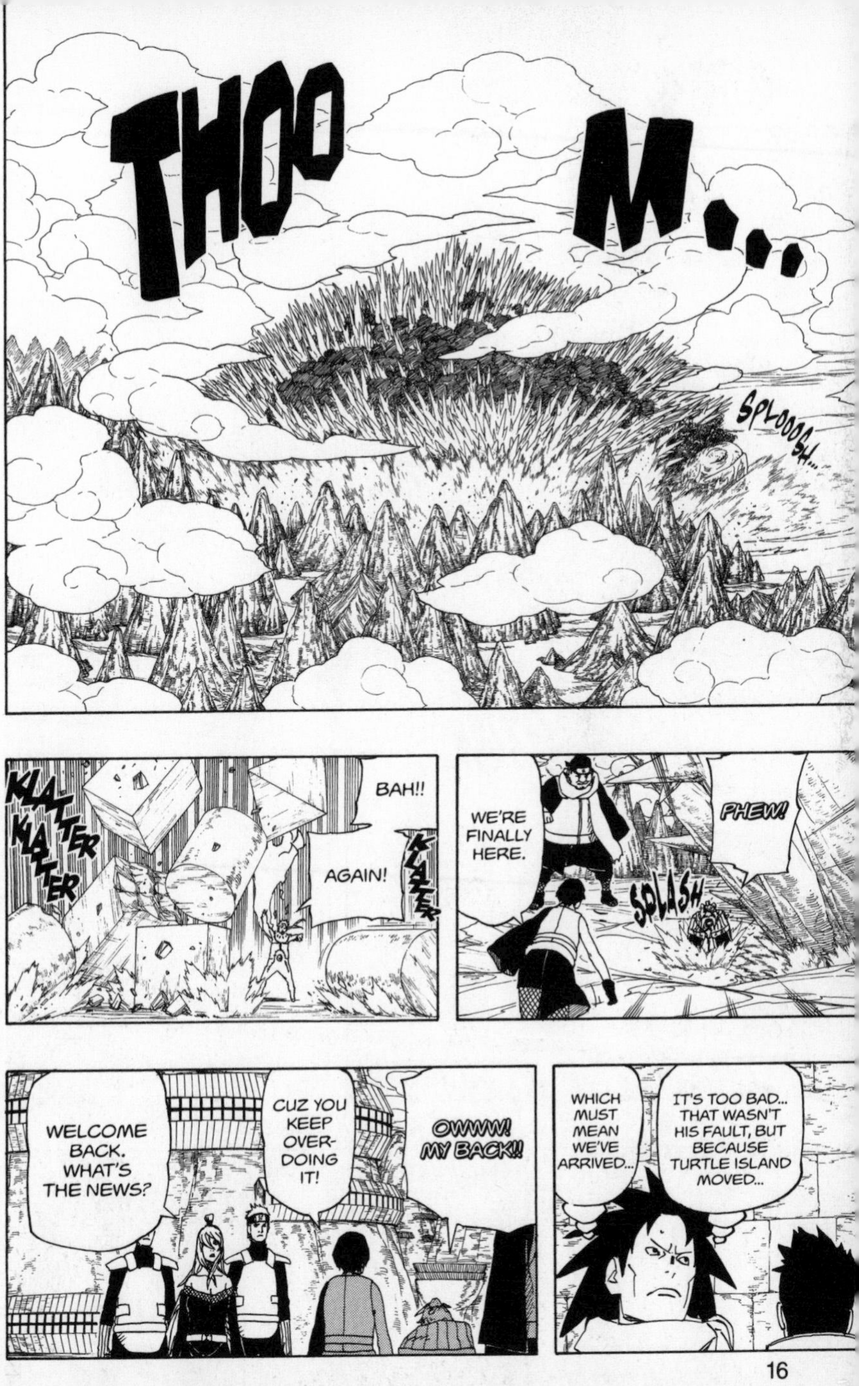
THOOM...
SPLOOOSH...
PHEW!
WE'RE FINALLY HERE.
SPLASH
KLATTER
BAH!!
AGAIN!
KLATTER KLATTER
IT'S TOO BAD... THAT WASN'T HIS FAULT, BUT BECAUSE TURTLE ISLAND MOVED...
WHICH MUST MEAN WE'VE ARRIVED...
OWWW! MY BACK!!
CUZ YOU KEEP OVER-DOING IT!
WELCOME BACK. WHAT'S THE NEWS?

READ THIS WAY

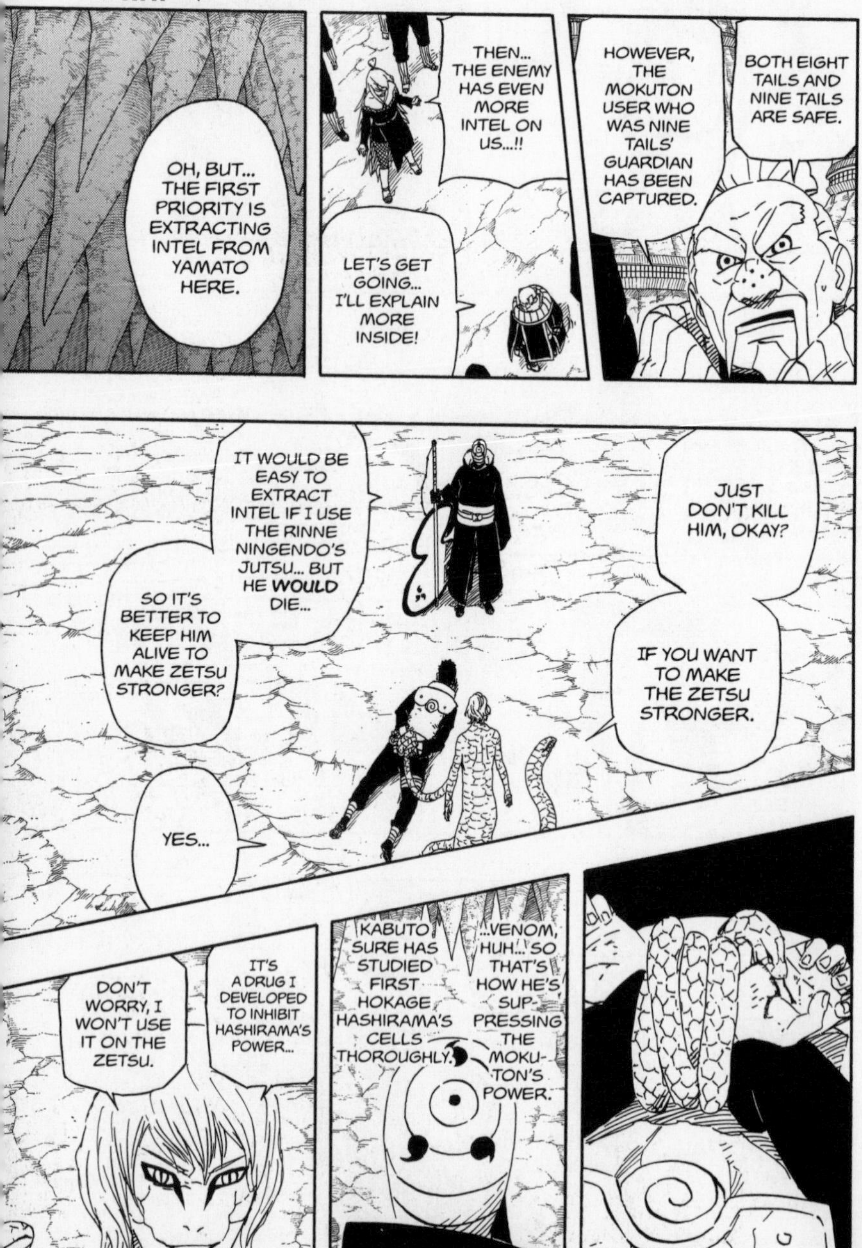
BOTH EIGHT TAILS AND NINE TAILS ARE SAFE.
HOWEVER, THE MOKUTON USER WHO WAS NINE TAILS' GUARDIAN HAS BEEN CAPTURED.
THEN... THE ENEMY HAS EVEN MORE INTEL ON US...!!
LET'S GET GOING... I'LL EXPLAIN MORE INSIDE!
OH, BUT... THE FIRST PRIORITY IS EXTRACTING INTEL FROM YAMATO HERE.
JUST DON'T KILL HIM, OKAY?
IF YOU WANT TO MAKE THE ZETSU STRONGER.
IT WOULD BE EASY TO EXTRACT INTEL IF I USE THE RINNE NINGENDO'S JUTSU... BUT HE **WOULD** DIE...
SO IT'S BETTER TO KEEP HIM ALIVE TO MAKE ZETSU STRONGER?
YES...
...VENOM, HUH... SO THAT'S HOW HE'S SUPPRESSING THE MOKUTON'S POWER.
KABUTO SURE HAS STUDIED FIRST HOKAGE HASHIRAMA'S CELLS THOROUGHLY.
IT'S A DRUG I DEVELOPED TO INHIBIT HASHIRAMA'S POWER...
DON'T WORRY, I WON'T USE IT ON THE ZETSU.

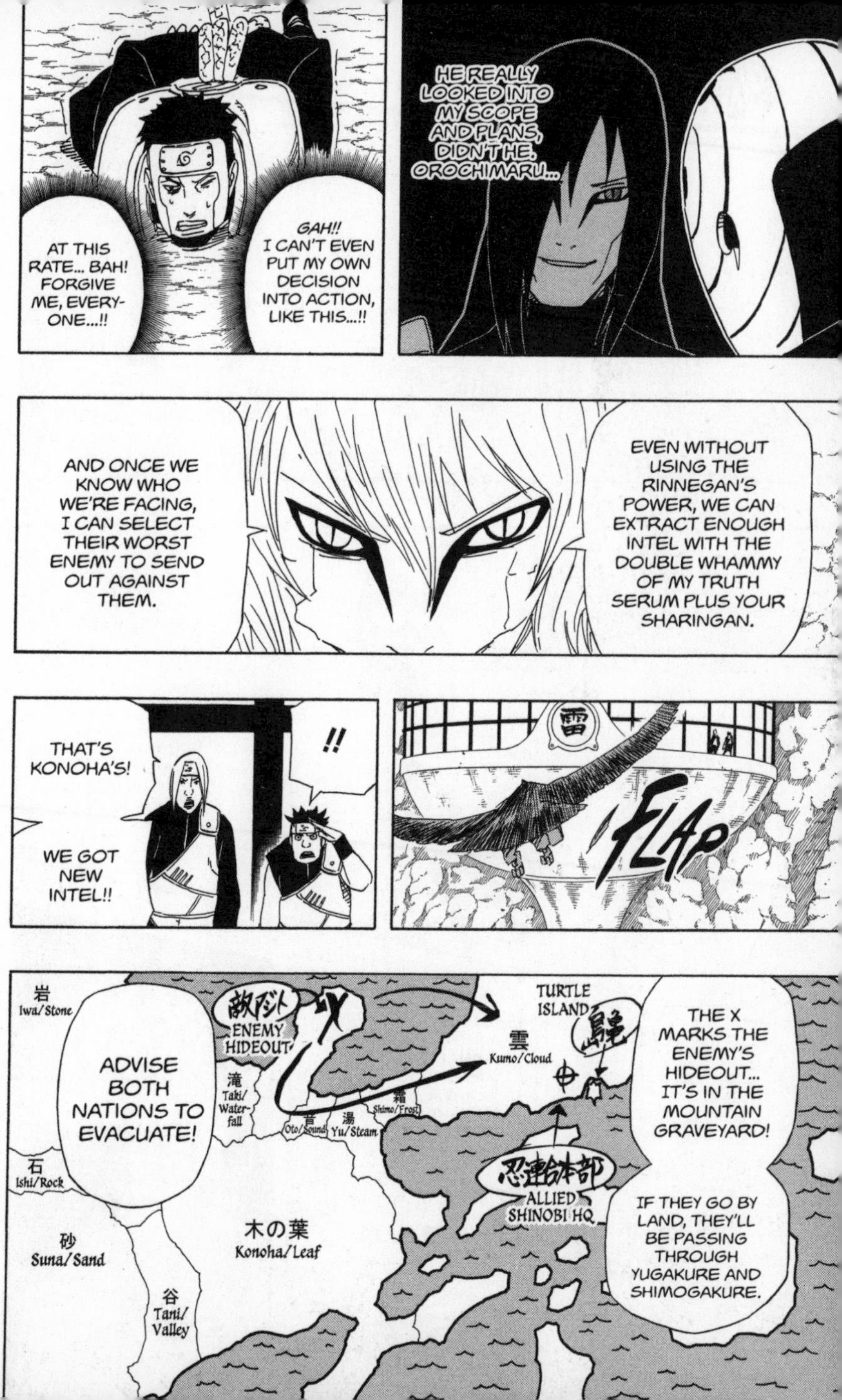
HE REALLY LOOKED INTO MY SCOPE AND PLANS, DIDN'T HE. OROCHIMARU...
GAH!! I CAN'T EVEN PUT MY OWN DECISION INTO ACTION, LIKE THIS...!!
AT THIS RATE... BAH! FORGIVE ME, EVERY-ONE...!!
EVEN WITHOUT USING THE RINNEGAN'S POWER, WE CAN EXTRACT ENOUGH INTEL WITH THE DOUBLE WHAMMY OF MY TRUTH SERUM PLUS YOUR SHARINGAN.
AND ONCE WE KNOW WHO WE'RE FACING, I CAN SELECT THEIR WORST ENEMY TO SEND OUT AGAINST THEM.
FLAP
!!
THAT'S KONOHA'S!
WE GOT NEW INTEL!!
THE X MARKS THE ENEMY'S HIDEOUT... IT'S IN THE MOUNTAIN GRAVEYARD!
IF THEY GO BY LAND, THEY'LL BE PASSING THROUGH YUGAKURE AND SHIMOGAKURE.
TURTLE ISLAND
雲 Kumo/Cloud
忍連合本部 ALLIED SHINOBI HQ
敵アジト ENEMY HIDEOUT
岩 Iwa/Stone
滝 Taki/Waterfall
霜 Shimo/Frost
音 Oto/Sound
湯 Yu/Steam
石 Ishi/Rock
木の葉 Konoha/Leaf
砂 Suna/Sand
谷 Tani/Valley
ADVISE BOTH NATIONS TO EVACUATE!

READ THIS WAY

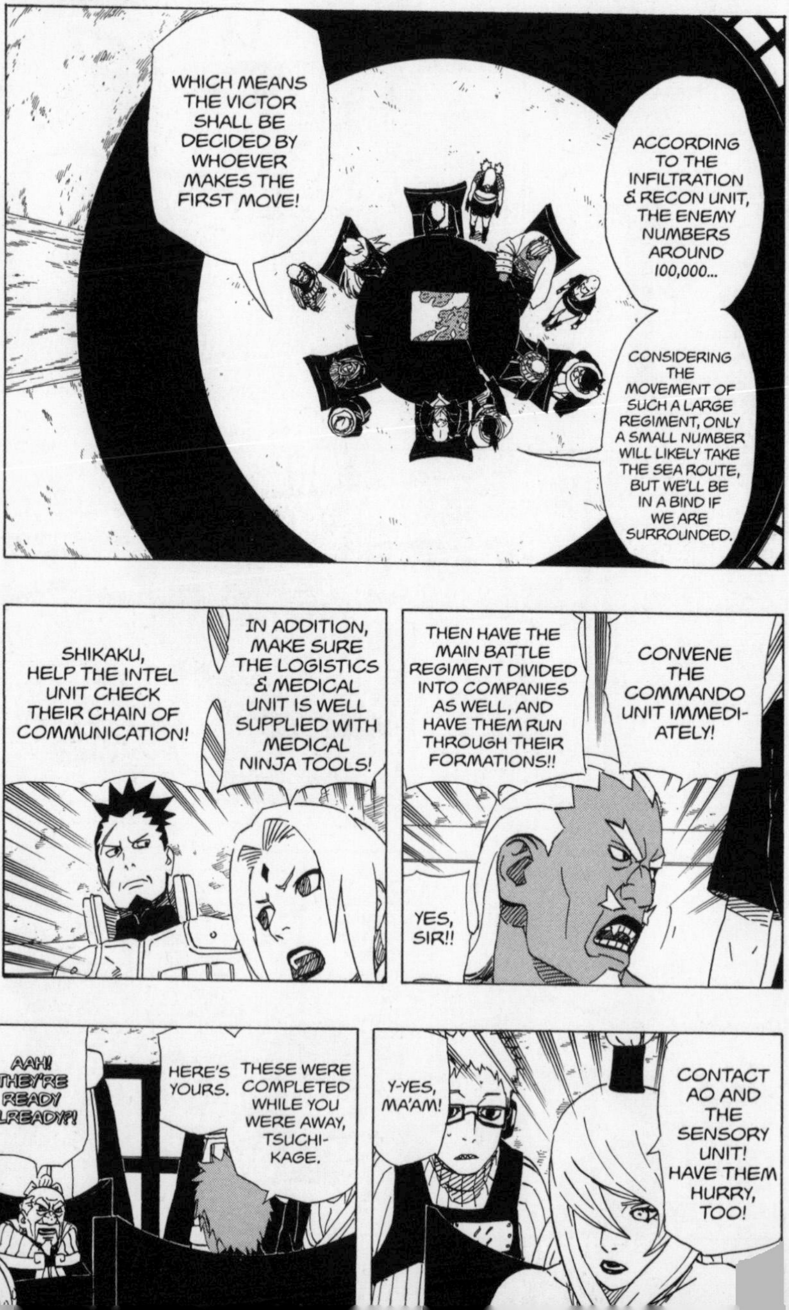
ACCORDING TO THE INFILTRATION & RECON UNIT, THE ENEMY NUMBERS AROUND 100,000...
CONSIDERING THE MOVEMENT OF SUCH A LARGE REGIMENT, ONLY A SMALL NUMBER WILL LIKELY TAKE THE SEA ROUTE, BUT WE'LL BE IN A BIND IF WE ARE SURROUNDED.
WHICH MEANS THE VICTOR SHALL BE DECIDED BY WHOEVER MAKES THE FIRST MOVE!
CONVENE THE COMMANDO UNIT IMMEDIATELY!
THEN HAVE THE MAIN BATTLE REGIMENT DIVIDED INTO COMPANIES AS WELL, AND HAVE THEM RUN THROUGH THEIR FORMATIONS!!
YES, SIR!!
IN ADDITION, MAKE SURE THE LOGISTICS & MEDICAL UNIT IS WELL SUPPLIED WITH MEDICAL NINJA TOOLS!
SHIKAKU, HELP THE INTEL UNIT CHECK THEIR CHAIN OF COMMUNICATION!
CONTACT AO AND THE SENSORY UNIT! HAVE THEM HURRY, TOO!
Y-YES, MA'AM!
THESE WERE COMPLETED WHILE YOU WERE AWAY, TSUCHIKAGE.
HERE'S YOURS.
AAH! THEY'RE READY ALREADY?!

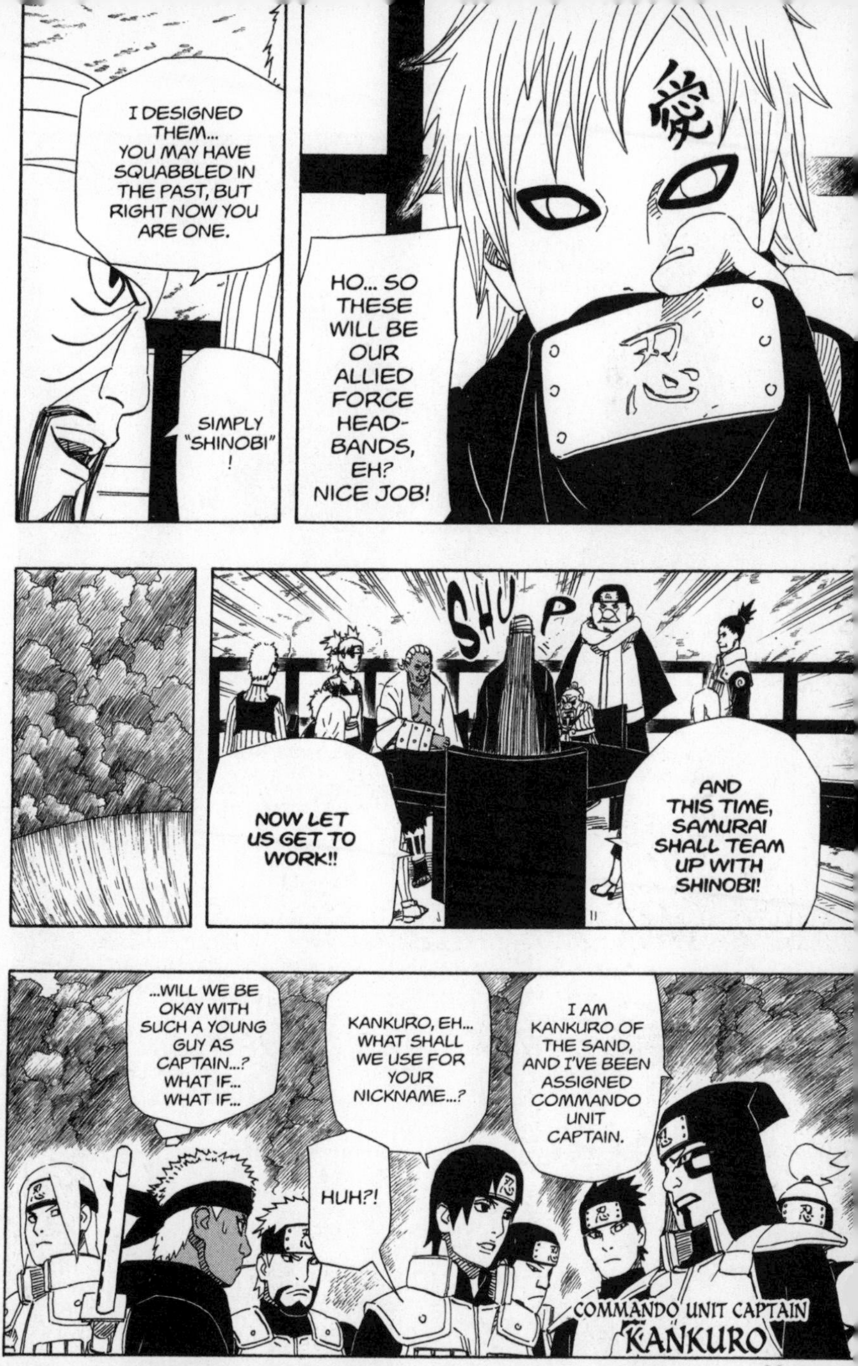
HO... SO THESE WILL BE OUR ALLIED FORCE HEAD-BANDS, EH? NICE JOB!
I DESIGNED THEM... YOU MAY HAVE SQUABBLED IN THE PAST, BUT RIGHT NOW YOU ARE ONE.
SIMPLY "SHINOBI"!
SHUP
AND THIS TIME, SAMURAI SHALL TEAM UP WITH SHINOBI!
NOW LET US GET TO WORK!!
I AM KANKURO OF THE SAND, AND I'VE BEEN ASSIGNED COMMANDO UNIT CAPTAIN.
KANKURO, EH... WHAT SHALL WE USE FOR YOUR NICKNAME...?
...WILL WE BE OKAY WITH SUCH A YOUNG GUY AS CAPTAIN...? WHAT IF... WHAT IF...
HUH?!
COMMANDO UNIT CAPTAIN
KANKURO

READ THIS WAY

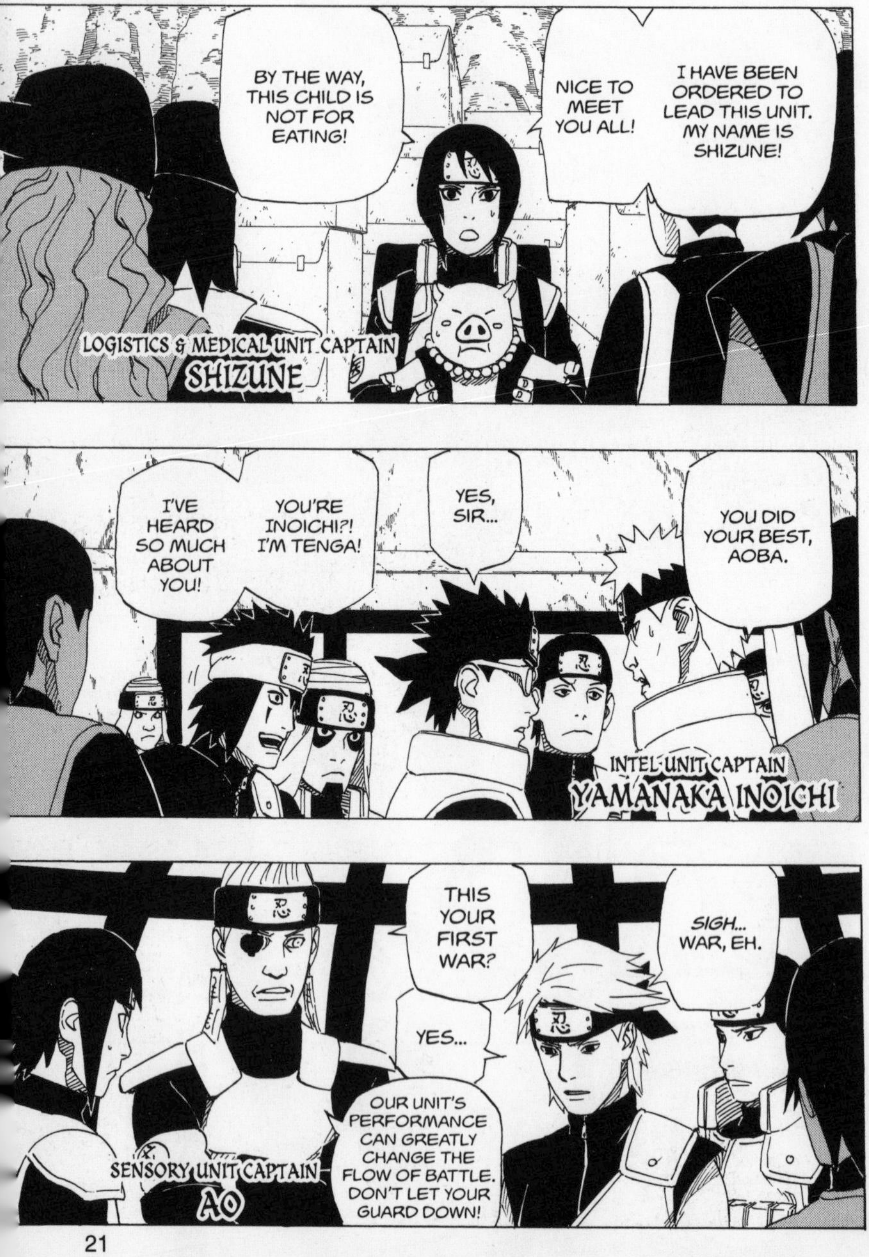
I HAVE BEEN ORDERED TO LEAD THIS UNIT. MY NAME IS SHIZUNE!
NICE TO MEET YOU ALL!
BY THE WAY, THIS CHILD IS NOT FOR EATING!
LOGISTICS & MEDICAL UNIT CAPTAIN SHIZUNE
YOU DID YOUR BEST, AOBA.
YES, SIR...
YOU'RE INOICHI?! I'M TENGA!
I'VE HEARD SO MUCH ABOUT YOU!
INTEL UNIT CAPTAIN YAMANAKA INOICHI
SIGH... WAR, EH.
THIS YOUR FIRST WAR?
YES...
OUR UNIT'S PERFORMANCE CAN GREATLY CHANGE THE FLOW OF BATTLE. DON'T LET YOUR GUARD DOWN!
SENSORY UNIT CAPTAIN AO

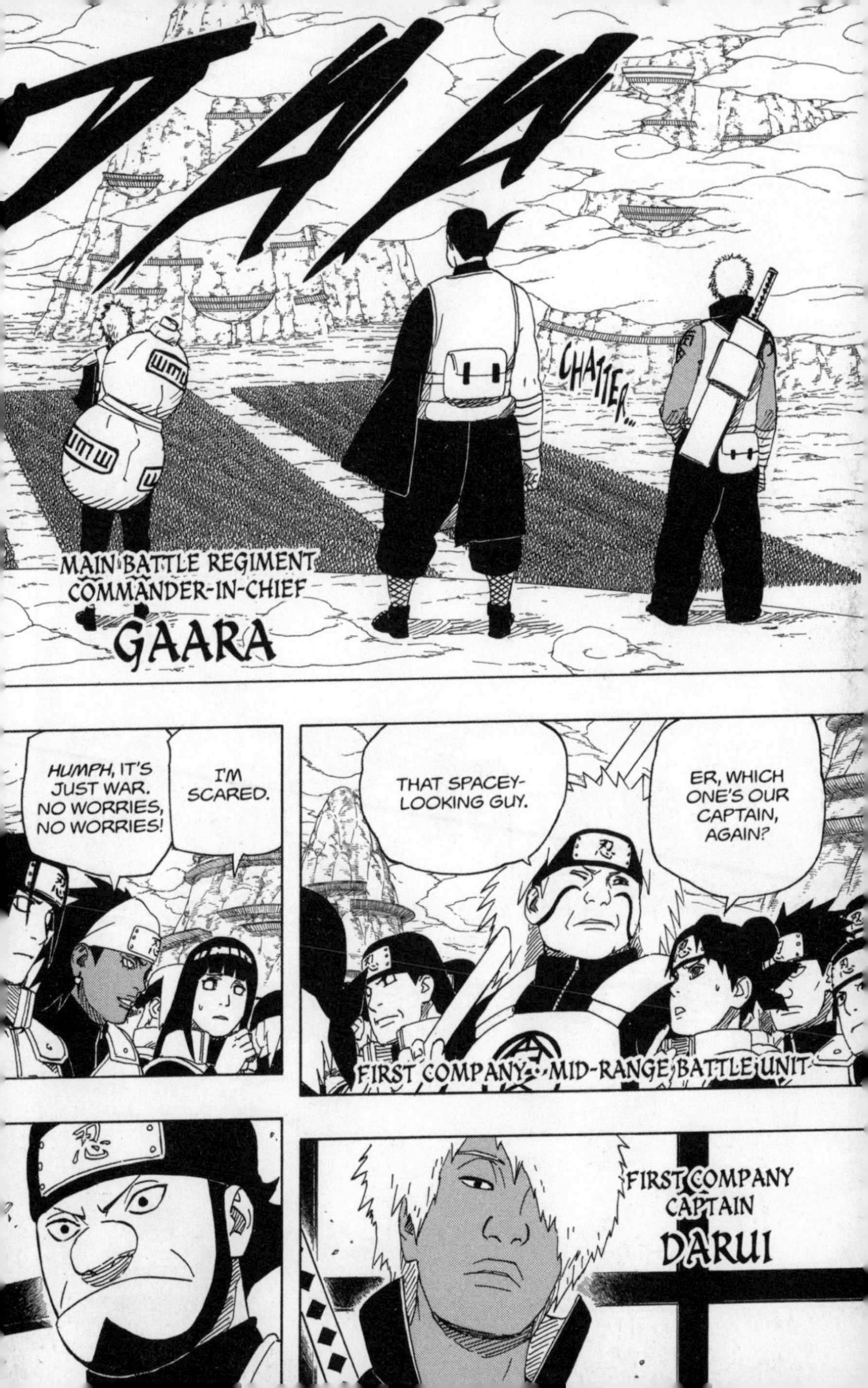
CHATTER...
MAIN BATTLE REGIMENT
COMMANDER-IN-CHIEF
GAARA
ER, WHICH ONE'S OUR CAPTAIN, AGAIN?
THAT SPACEY-LOOKING GUY.
FIRST COMPANY · MID-RANGE BATTLE UNIT
I'M SCARED.
HUMPH, IT'S JUST WAR. NO WORRIES, NO WORRIES!
FIRST COMPANY
CAPTAIN
DARUI

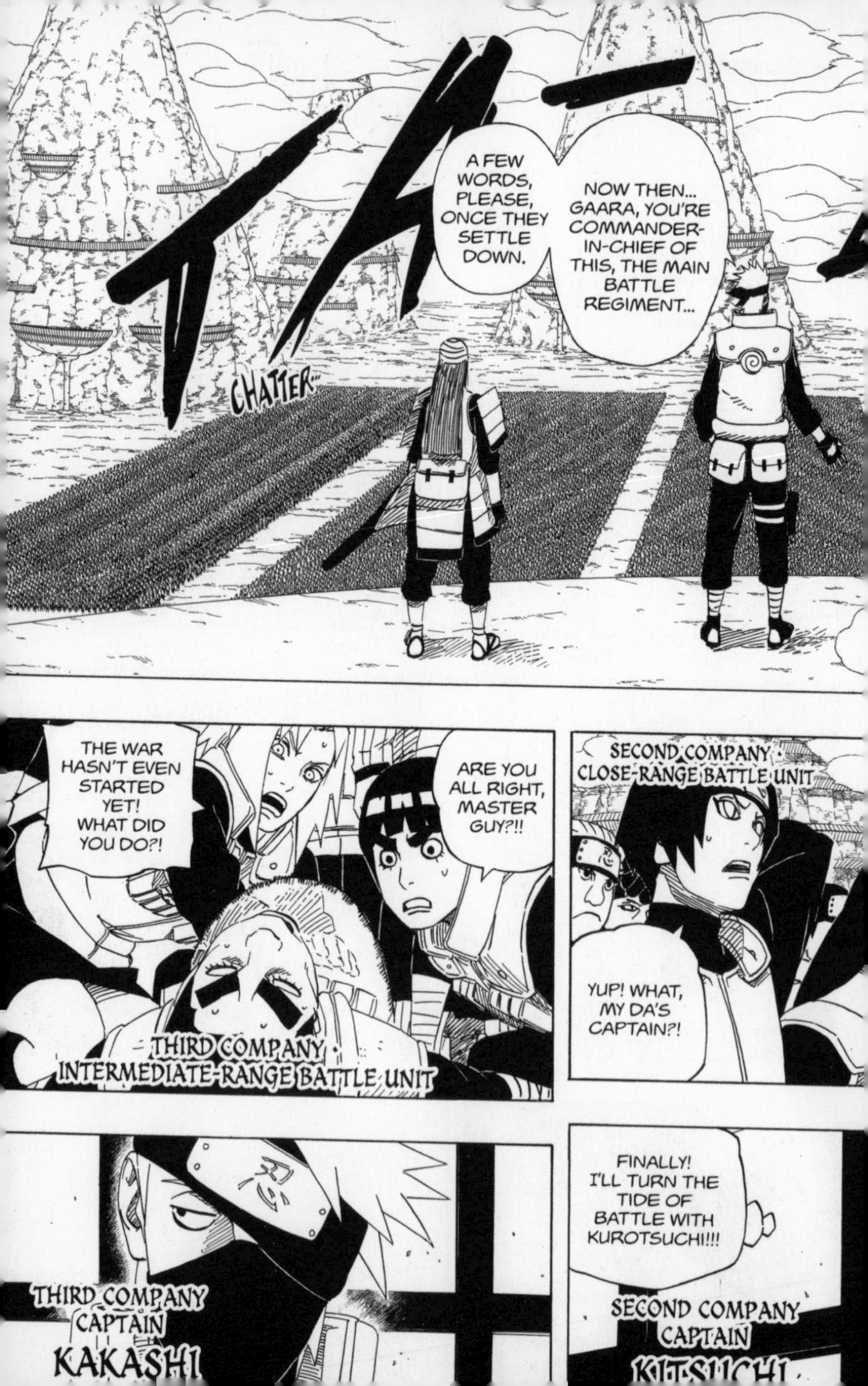
NOW THEN... GAARA, YOU'RE COMMANDER-IN-CHIEF OF THIS, THE MAIN BATTLE REGIMENT...
A FEW WORDS, PLEASE, ONCE THEY SETTLE DOWN.
CHATTER...
SECOND COMPANY · CLOSE-RANGE BATTLE UNIT
YUP! WHAT, MY DA'S CAPTAIN?!
ARE YOU ALL RIGHT, MASTER GUY?!!
THE WAR HASN'T EVEN STARTED YET! WHAT DID YOU DO?!
THIRD COMPANY · INTERMEDIATE-RANGE BATTLE UNIT
FINALLY! I'LL TURN THE TIDE OF BATTLE WITH KUROTSUCHI!!!
SECOND COMPANY CAPTAIN
THIRD COMPANY CAPTAIN KAKASHI

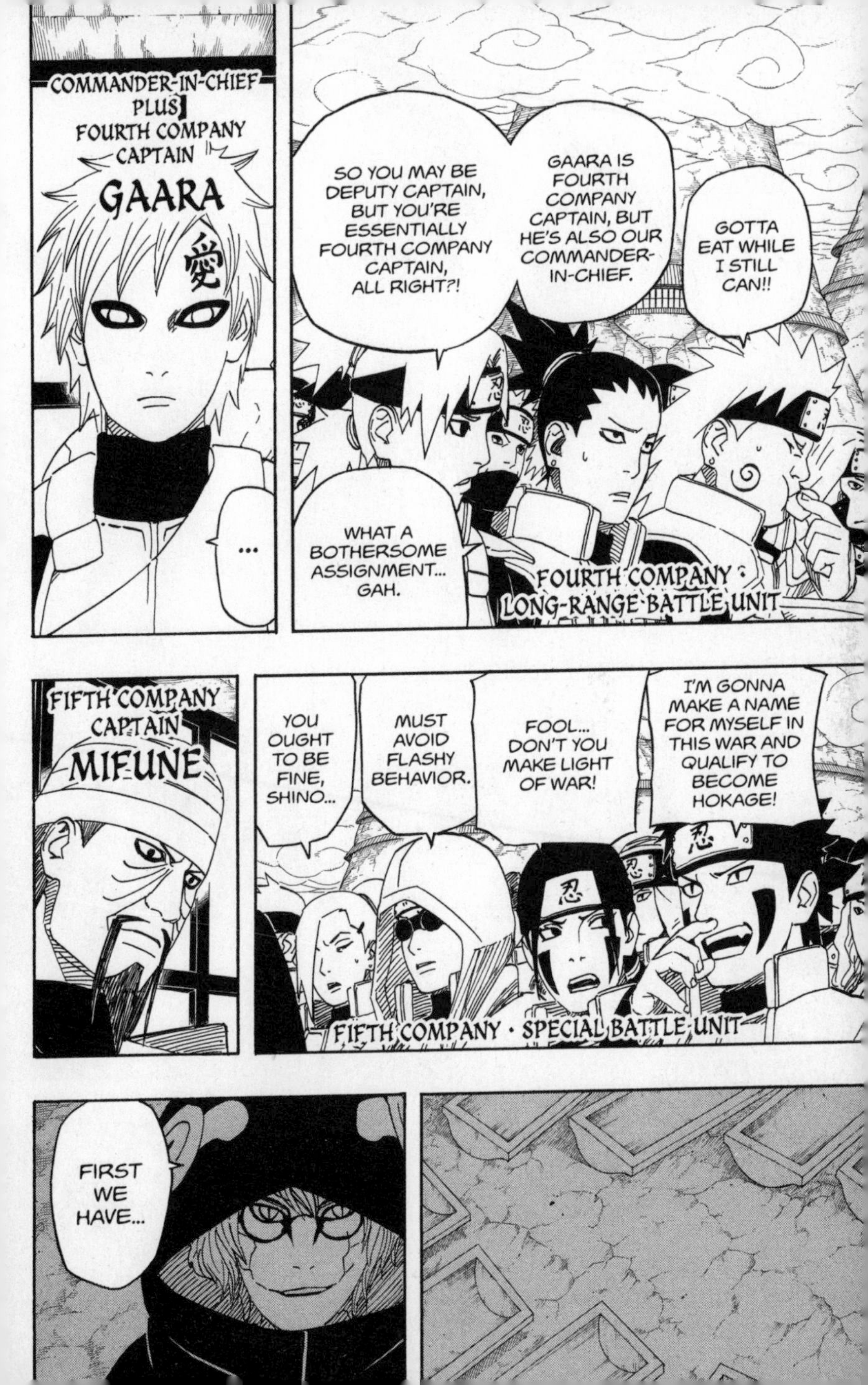
GOTTA EAT WHILE I STILL CAN!!
GAARA IS FOURTH COMPANY CAPTAIN, BUT HE'S ALSO OUR COMMANDER-IN-CHIEF.
SO YOU MAY BE DEPUTY CAPTAIN, BUT YOU'RE ESSENTIALLY FOURTH COMPANY CAPTAIN, ALL RIGHT?!
WHAT A BOTHERSOME ASSIGNMENT... GAH.
FOURTH COMPANY · LONG-RANGE BATTLE UNIT
COMMANDER-IN-CHIEF PLUS FOURTH COMPANY CAPTAIN
GAARA
...
I'M GONNA MAKE A NAME FOR MYSELF IN THIS WAR AND QUALIFY TO BECOME HOKAGE!
FOOL... DON'T YOU MAKE LIGHT OF WAR!
MUST AVOID FLASHY BEHAVIOR.
YOU OUGHT TO BE FINE, SHINO...
FIFTH COMPANY · SPECIAL BATTLE UNIT
FIFTH COMPANY CAPTAIN
MIFUNE
FIRST WE HAVE...

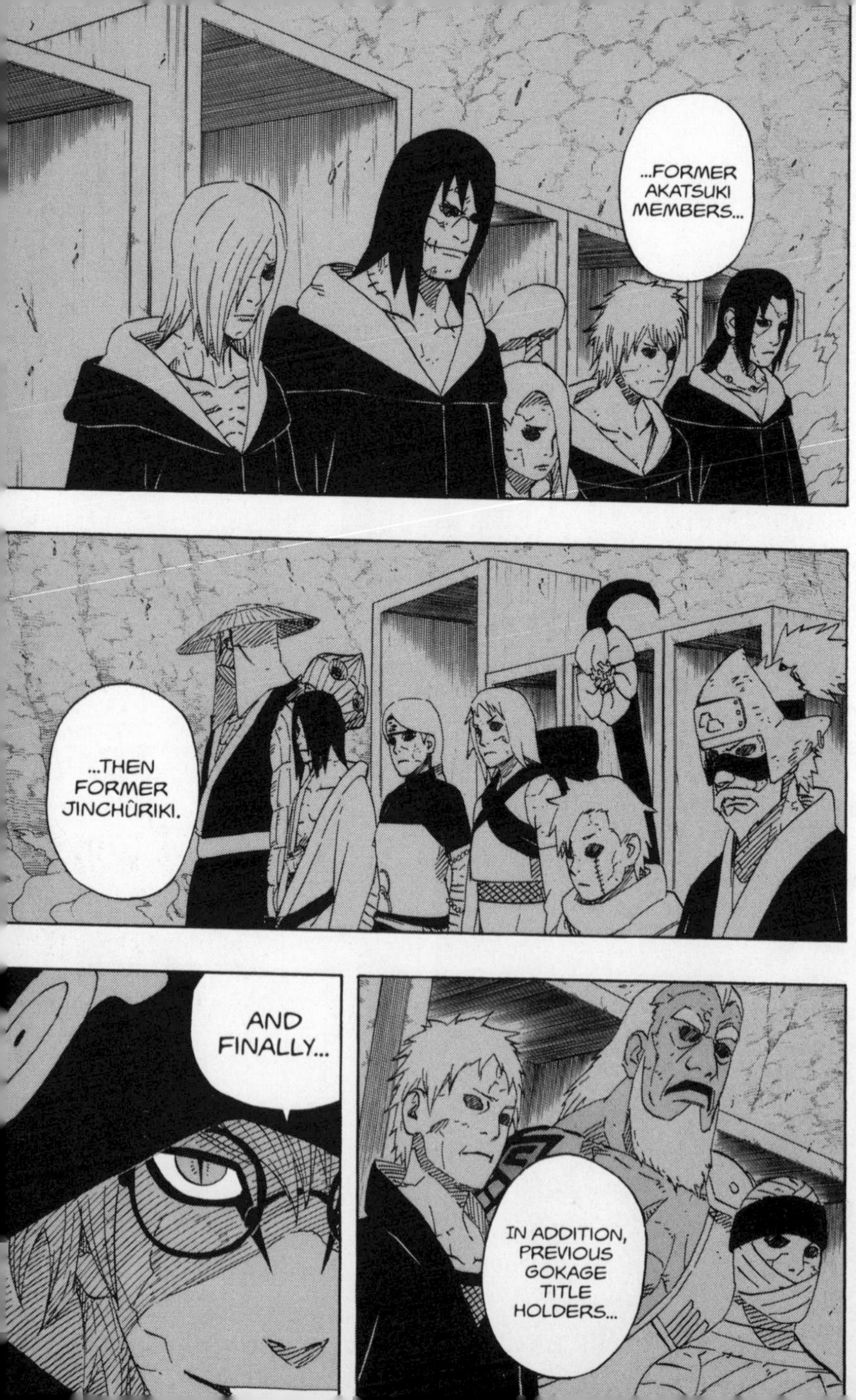
...FORMER AKATSUKI MEMBERS...
...THEN FORMER JINCHÛRIKI.
IN ADDITION, PREVIOUS GOKAGE TITLE HOLDERS...
AND FINALLY...

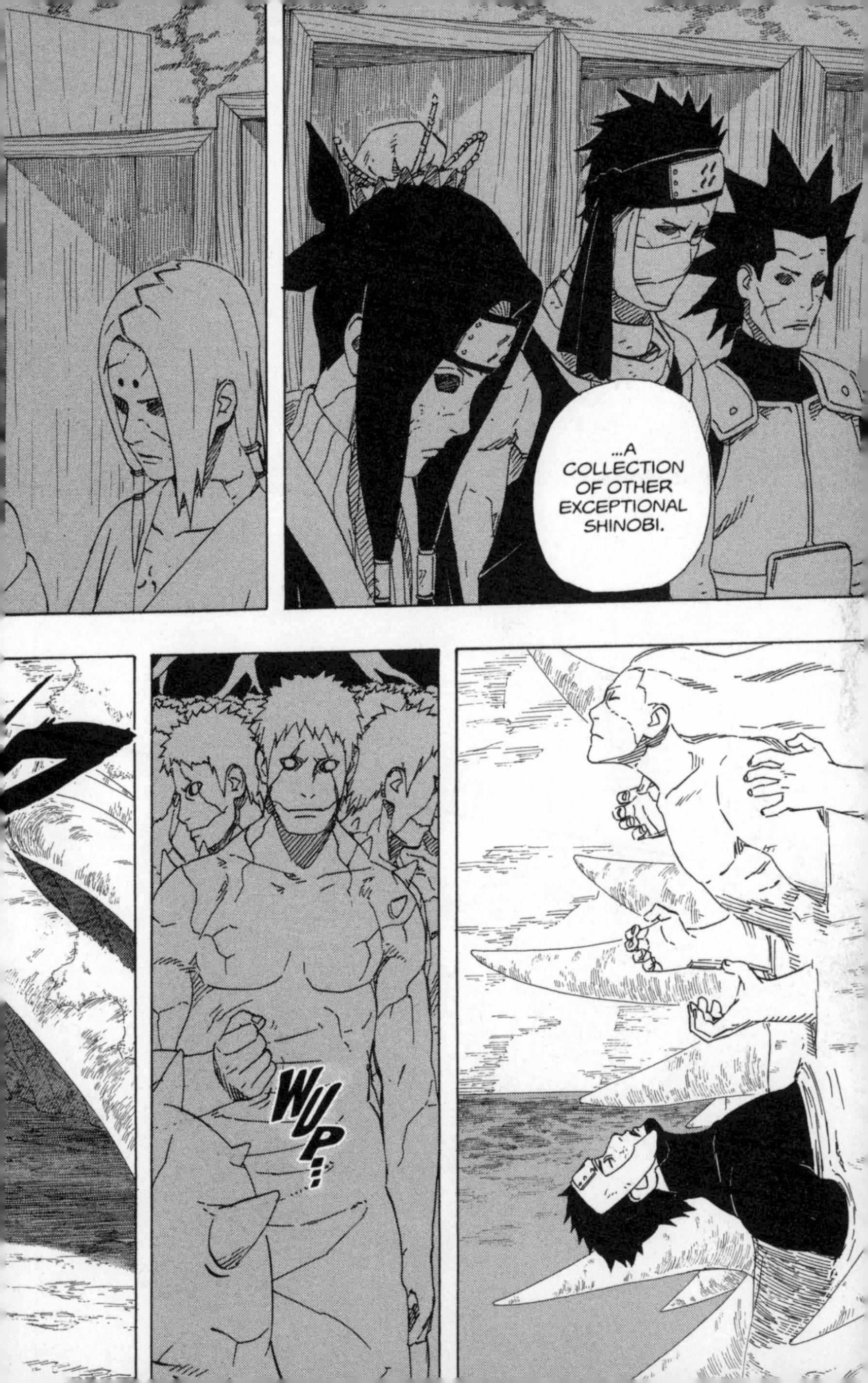
...A COLLECTION OF OTHER EXCEPTIONAL SHINOBI.
WUP...

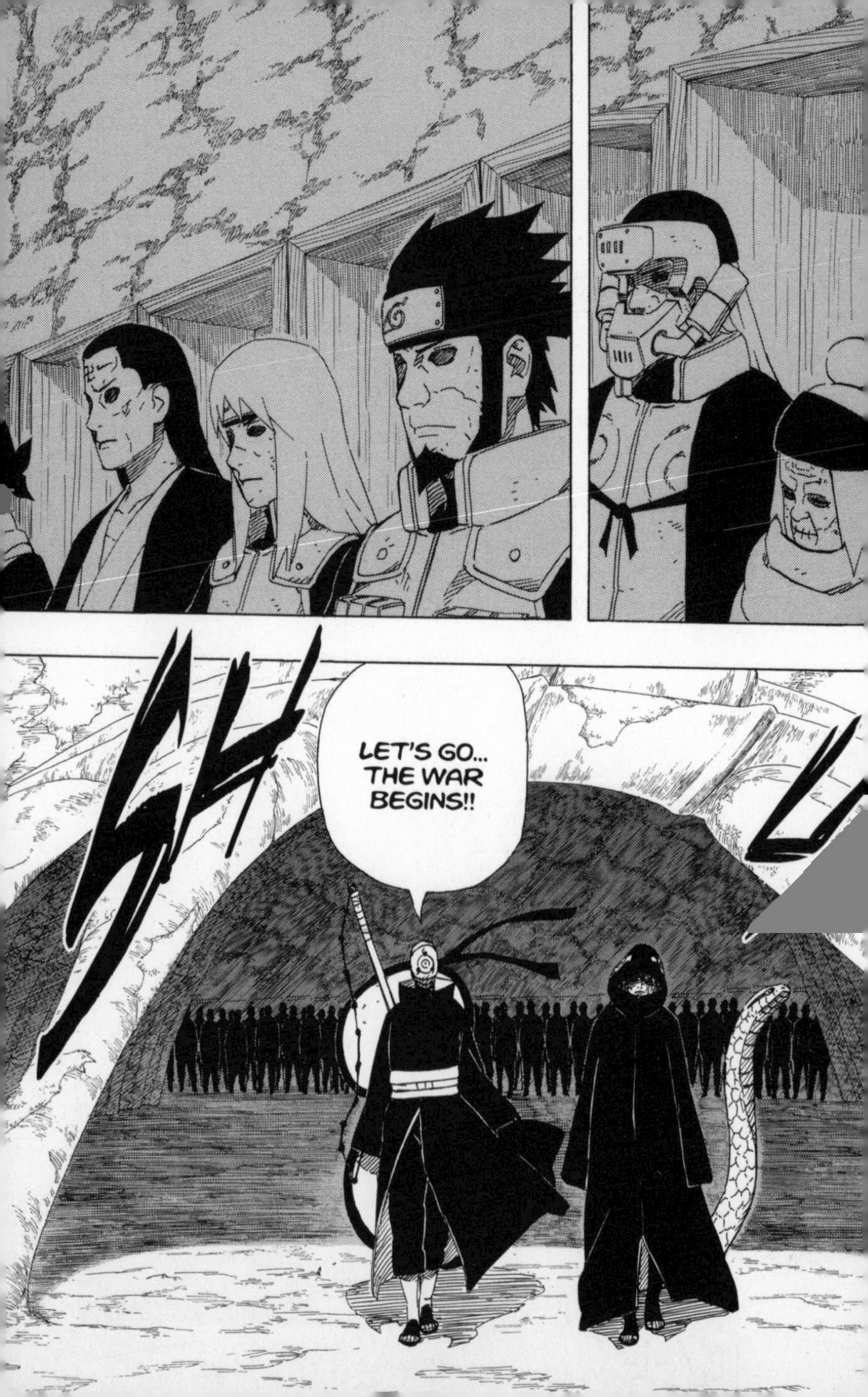
LET'S GO... THE WAR BEGINS!!

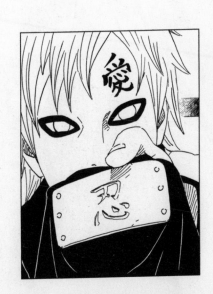

Number 516: Gaara's Speech

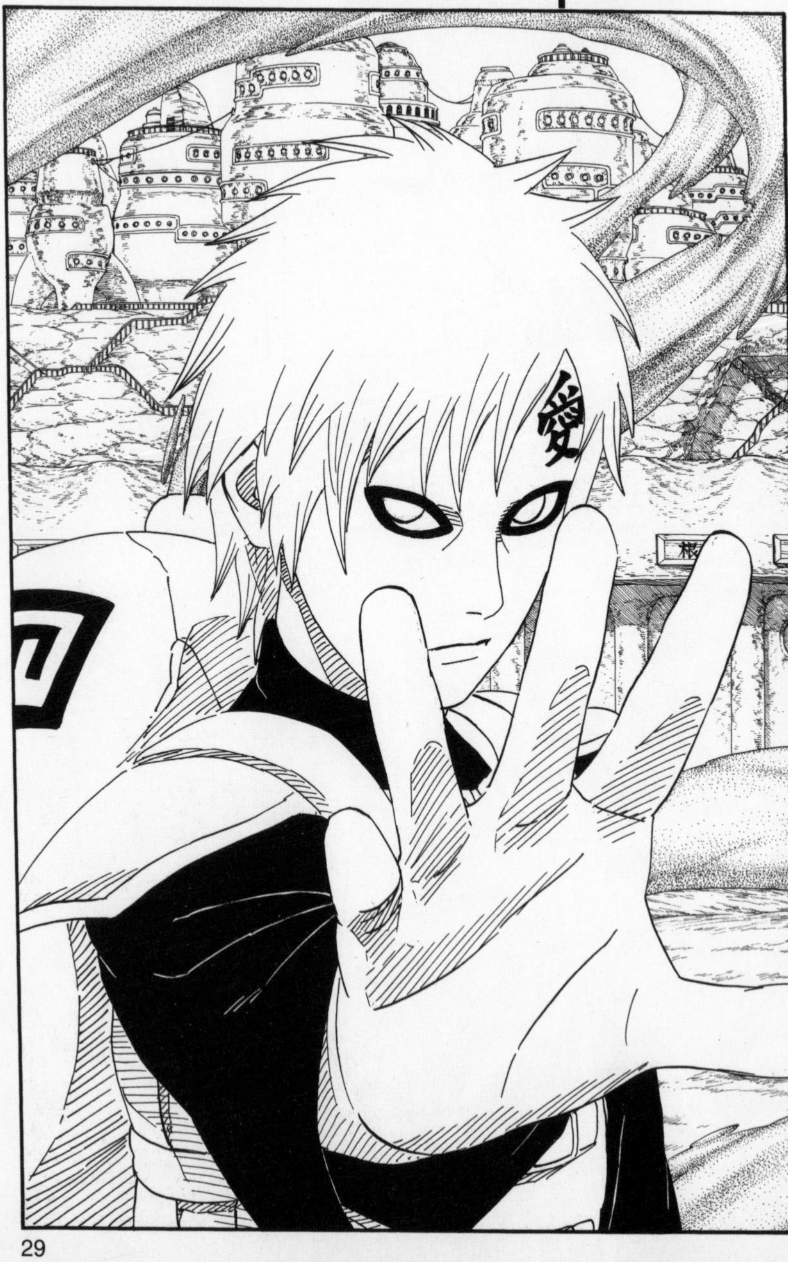
愛

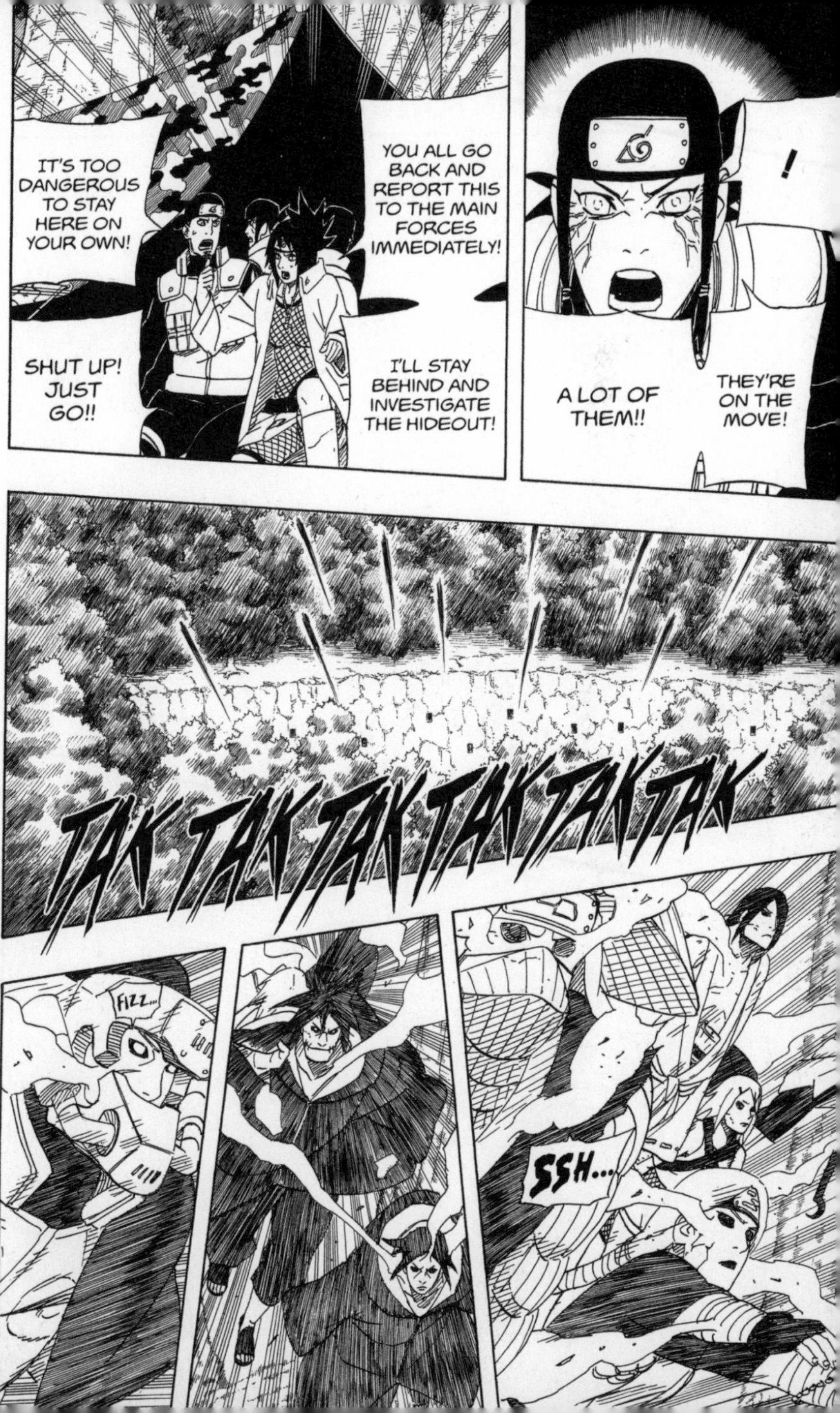
!
THEY'RE ON THE MOVE!
A LOT OF THEM!!
YOU ALL GO BACK AND REPORT THIS TO THE MAIN FORCES IMMEDIATELY!
IT'S TOO DANGEROUS TO STAY HERE ON YOUR OWN!
I'LL STAY BEHIND AND INVESTIGATE THE HIDEOUT!
SHUT UP! JUST GO!!
TAK TAK TAK TAK TAK TAK
SSH...
FIZZ...

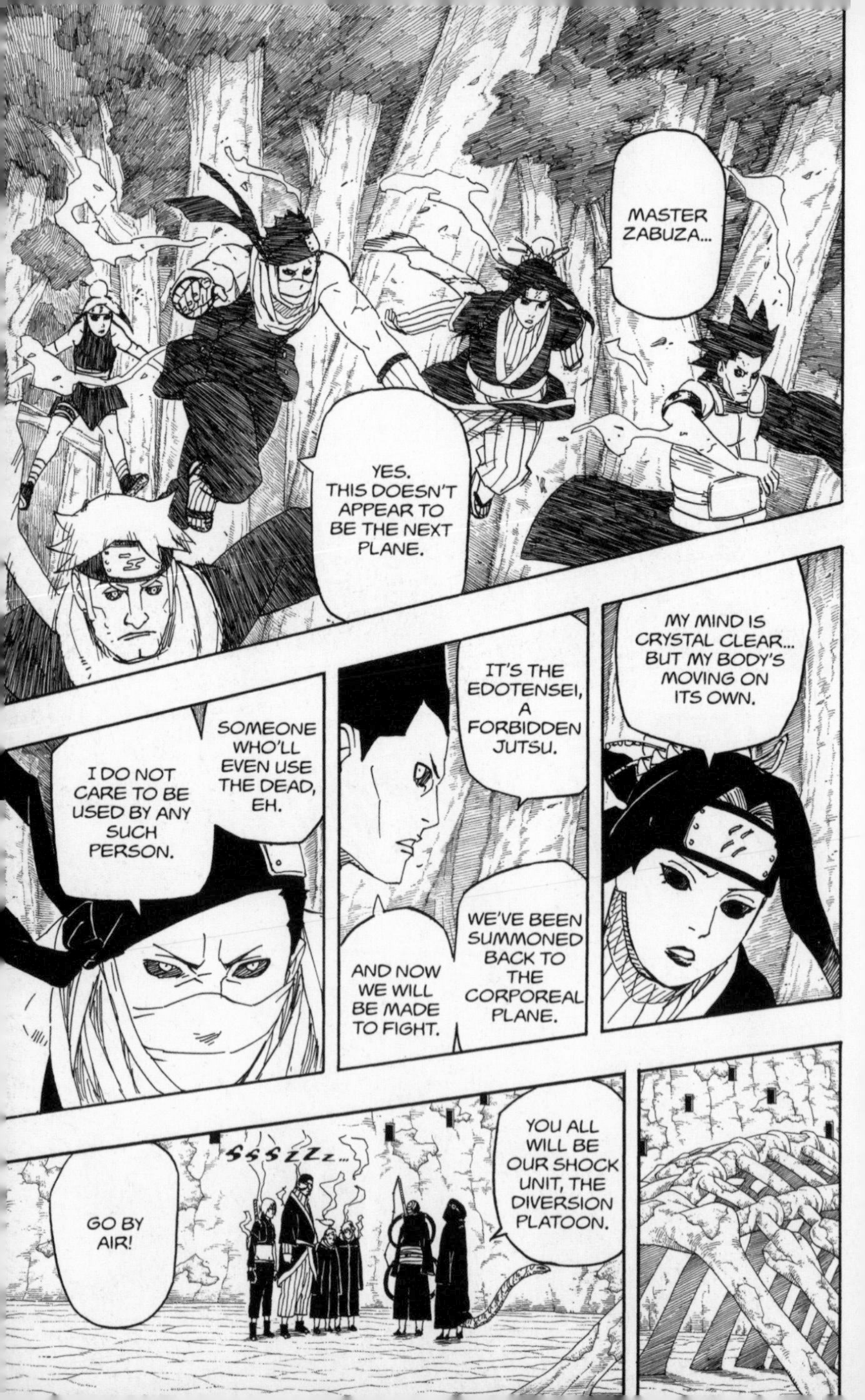
MASTER ZABUZA...
YES. THIS DOESN'T APPEAR TO BE THE NEXT PLANE.
MY MIND IS CRYSTAL CLEAR... BUT MY BODY'S MOVING ON ITS OWN.
IT'S THE EDOTENSEI, A FORBIDDEN JUTSU.
WE'VE BEEN SUMMONED BACK TO THE CORPOREAL PLANE.
AND NOW WE WILL BE MADE TO FIGHT.
SOMEONE WHO'LL EVEN USE THE DEAD, EH.
I DO NOT CARE TO BE USED BY ANY SUCH PERSON.
YOU ALL WILL BE OUR SHOCK UNIT, THE DIVERSION PLATOON.
SSSZZz...
GO BY AIR!

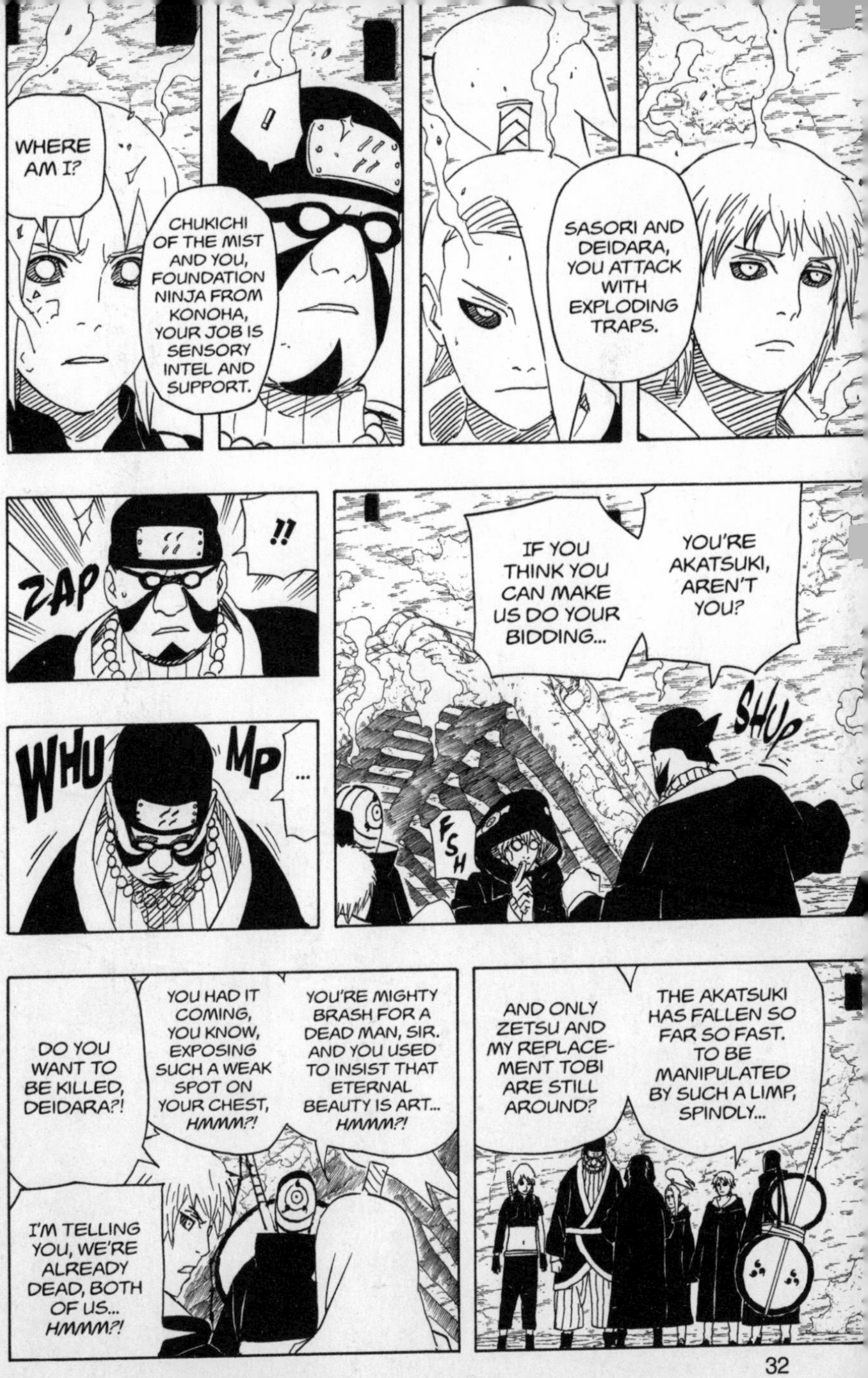
SASORI AND DEIDARA, YOU ATTACK WITH EXPLODING TRAPS.
!
CHUKICHI OF THE MIST AND YOU, FOUNDATION NINJA FROM KONOHA, YOUR JOB IS SENSORY INTEL AND SUPPORT.
WHERE AM I?
YOU'RE AKATSUKI, AREN'T YOU?
IF YOU THINK YOU CAN MAKE US DO YOUR BIDDING...
SHUP
FSH
!!
ZAP
WHUMP
...
THE AKATSUKI HAS FALLEN SO FAR SO FAST. TO BE MANIPULATED BY SUCH A LIMP, SPINDLY...
AND ONLY ZETSU AND MY REPLACEMENT TOBI ARE STILL AROUND?
YOU'RE MIGHTY BRASH FOR A DEAD MAN, SIR. AND YOU USED TO INSIST THAT ETERNAL BEAUTY IS ART... *HMMM?!*
YOU HAD IT COMING, YOU KNOW, EXPOSING SUCH A WEAK SPOT ON YOUR CHEST, *HMMM?!*
DO YOU WANT TO BE KILLED, DEIDARA?!
I'M TELLING YOU, WE'RE ALREADY DEAD, BOTH OF US... *HMMM?!*

READ THIS WAY

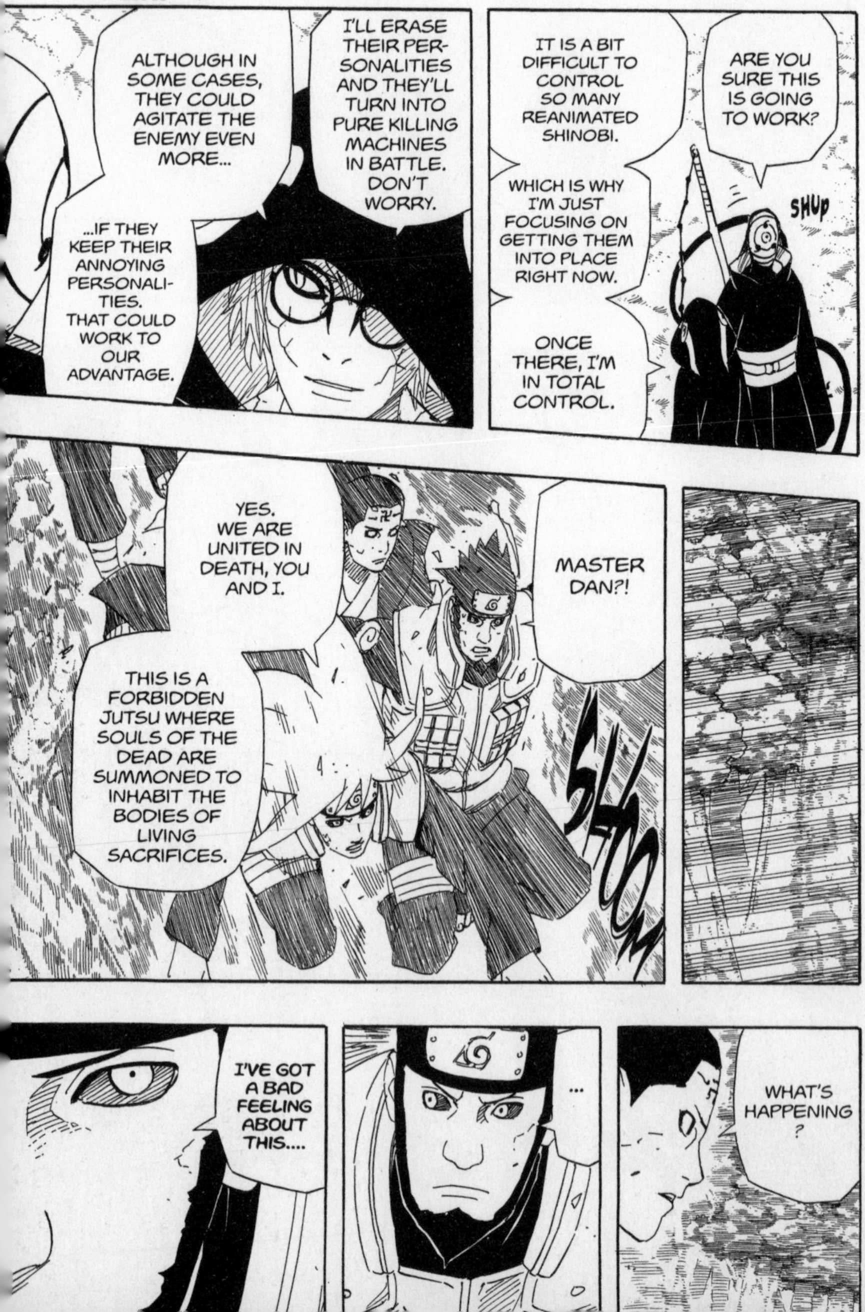

ARE YOU SURE THIS IS GOING TO WORK?
SHUP
IT IS A BIT DIFFICULT TO CONTROL SO MANY REANIMATED SHINOBI.
WHICH IS WHY I'M JUST FOCUSING ON GETTING THEM INTO PLACE RIGHT NOW.
ONCE THERE, I'M IN TOTAL CONTROL.
I'LL ERASE THEIR PERSONALITIES AND THEY'LL TURN INTO PURE KILLING MACHINES IN BATTLE. DON'T WORRY.
ALTHOUGH IN SOME CASES, THEY COULD AGITATE THE ENEMY EVEN MORE...
...IF THEY KEEP THEIR ANNOYING PERSONALITIES. THAT COULD WORK TO OUR ADVANTAGE.
MASTER DAN?!
SHOOM
YES. WE ARE UNITED IN DEATH, YOU AND I.
THIS IS A FORBIDDEN JUTSU WHERE SOULS OF THE DEAD ARE SUMMONED TO INHABIT THE BODIES OF LIVING SACRIFICES.
WHAT'S HAPPENING ?
...
I'VE GOT A BAD FEELING ABOUT THIS....

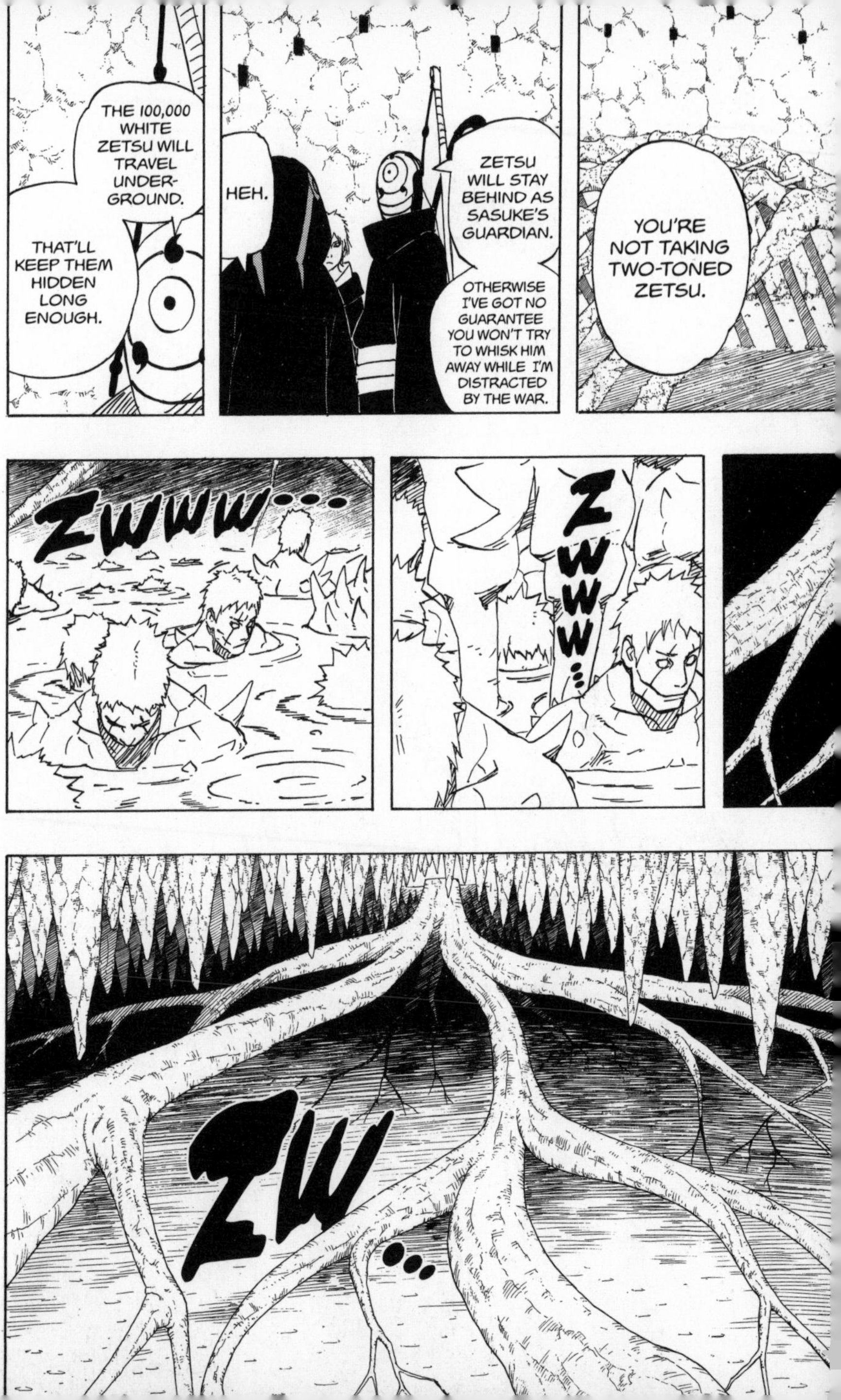
YOU'RE NOT TAKING TWO-TONED ZETSU.
ZETSU WILL STAY BEHIND AS SASUKE'S GUARDIAN.
OTHERWISE I'VE GOT NO GUARANTEE YOU WON'T TRY TO WHISK HIM AWAY WHILE I'M DISTRACTED BY THE WAR.
HEH.
THE 100,000 WHITE ZETSU WILL TRAVEL UNDER-GROUND.
THAT'LL KEEP THEM HIDDEN LONG ENOUGH.
ZWWW...
ZWWWW...
ZW...

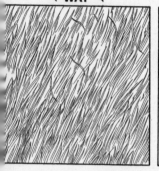

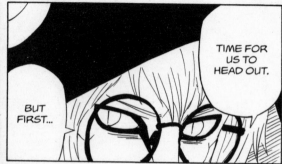

TIME FOR US TO HEAD OUT.

BUT FIRST...

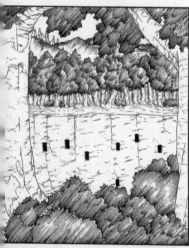

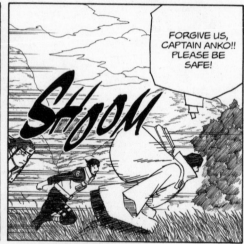

FORGIVE US, CAPTAIN ANKO!! PLEASE BE SAFE!

SHOOM

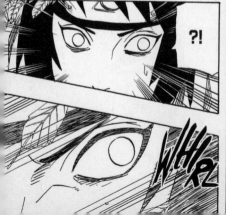

?!

WHIRL

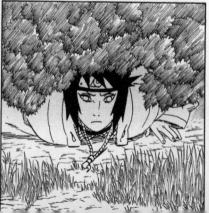

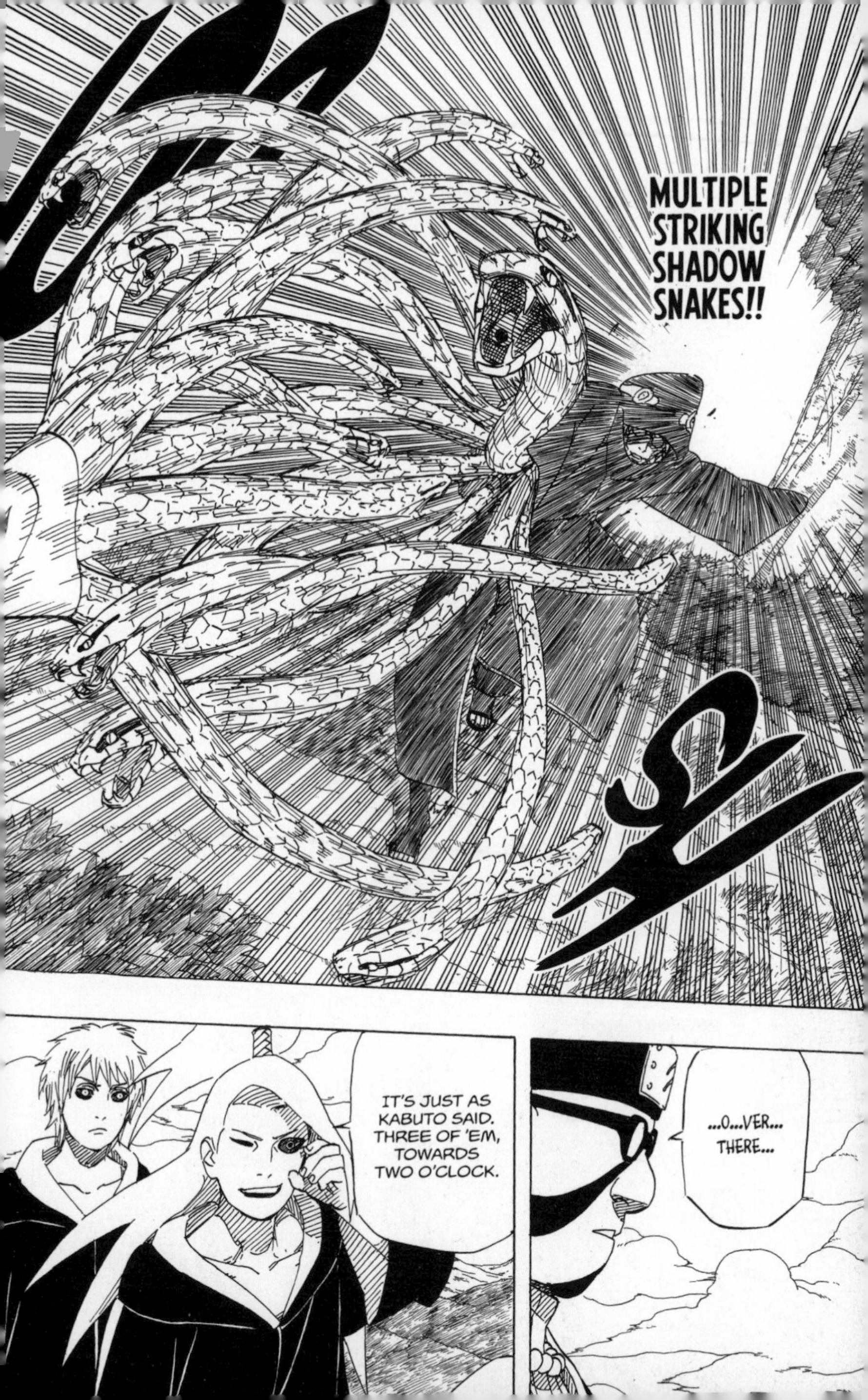
MULTIPLE STRIKING SHADOW SNAKES!!
...O...VER... THERE...
IT'S JUST AS KABUTO SAID. THREE OF 'EM, TOWARDS TWO O'CLOCK.

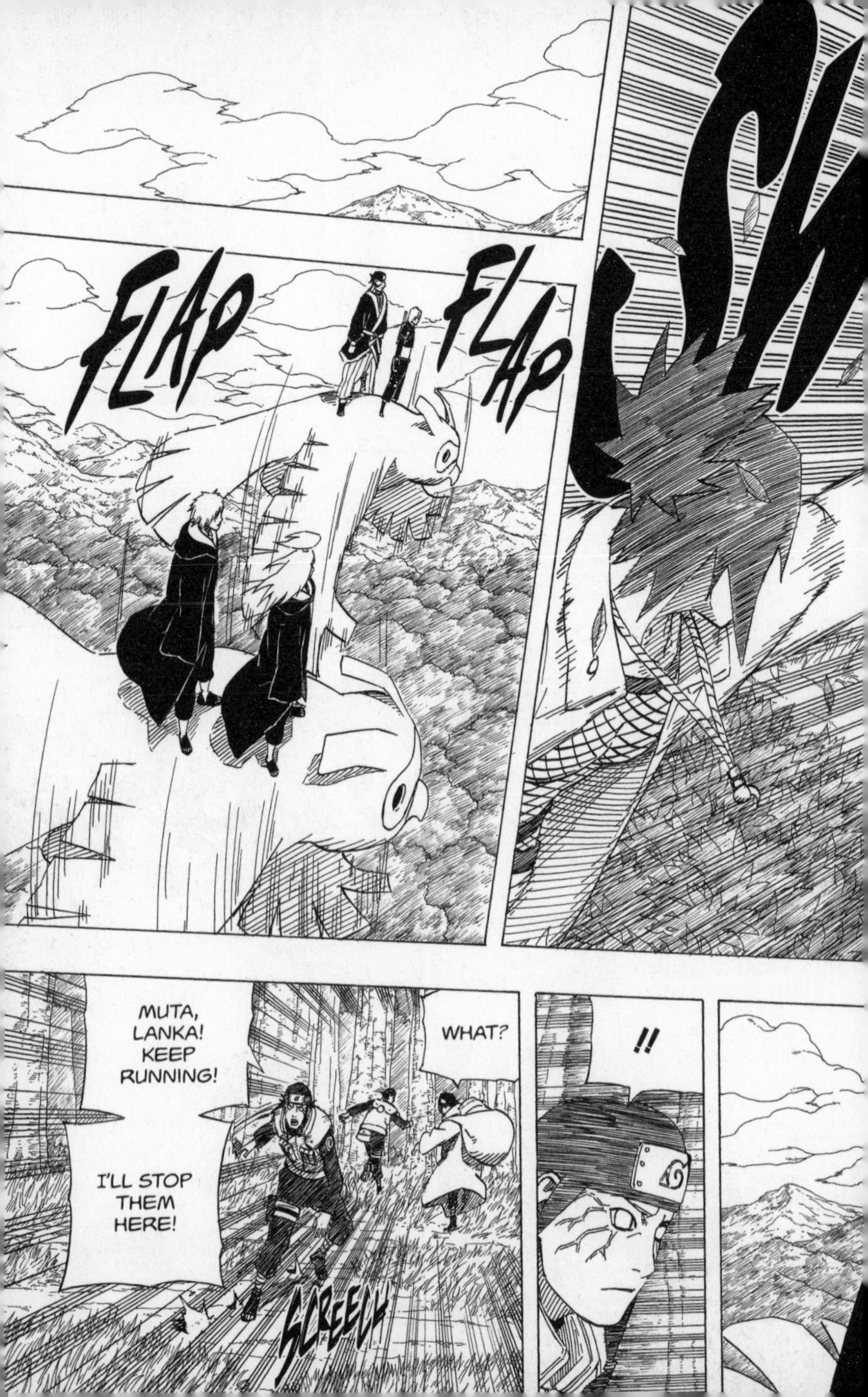
SH
FLAP
FLAP
!!
MUTA, LANKA! KEEP RUNNING!
WHAT?
I'LL STOP THEM HERE!
SCREECH

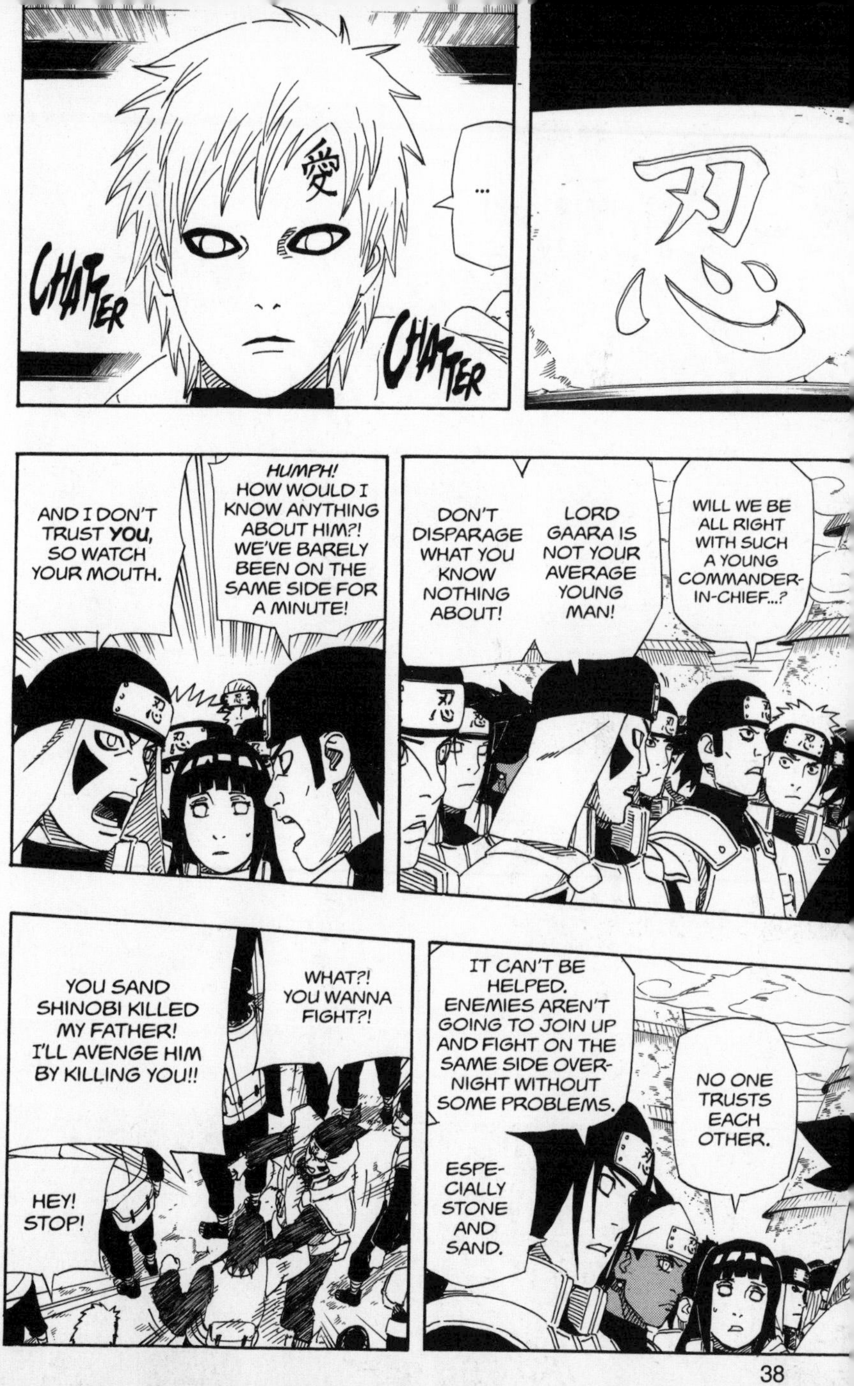
...
CHATTER
CHATTER
WILL WE BE ALL RIGHT WITH SUCH A YOUNG COMMANDER-IN-CHIEF...?
LORD GAARA IS NOT YOUR AVERAGE YOUNG MAN!
DON'T DISPARAGE WHAT YOU KNOW NOTHING ABOUT!
HUMPH! HOW WOULD I KNOW ANYTHING ABOUT HIM?! WE'VE BARELY BEEN ON THE SAME SIDE FOR A MINUTE!
AND I DON'T TRUST **YOU**, SO WATCH YOUR MOUTH.
NO ONE TRUSTS EACH OTHER.
IT CAN'T BE HELPED. ENEMIES AREN'T GOING TO JOIN UP AND FIGHT ON THE SAME SIDE OVER-NIGHT WITHOUT SOME PROBLEMS.
ESPE-CIALLY STONE AND SAND.
WHAT?! YOU WANNA FIGHT?!
YOU SAND SHINOBI KILLED MY FATHER! I'LL AVENGE HIM BY KILLING YOU!!
HEY! STOP!

READ THIS WAY

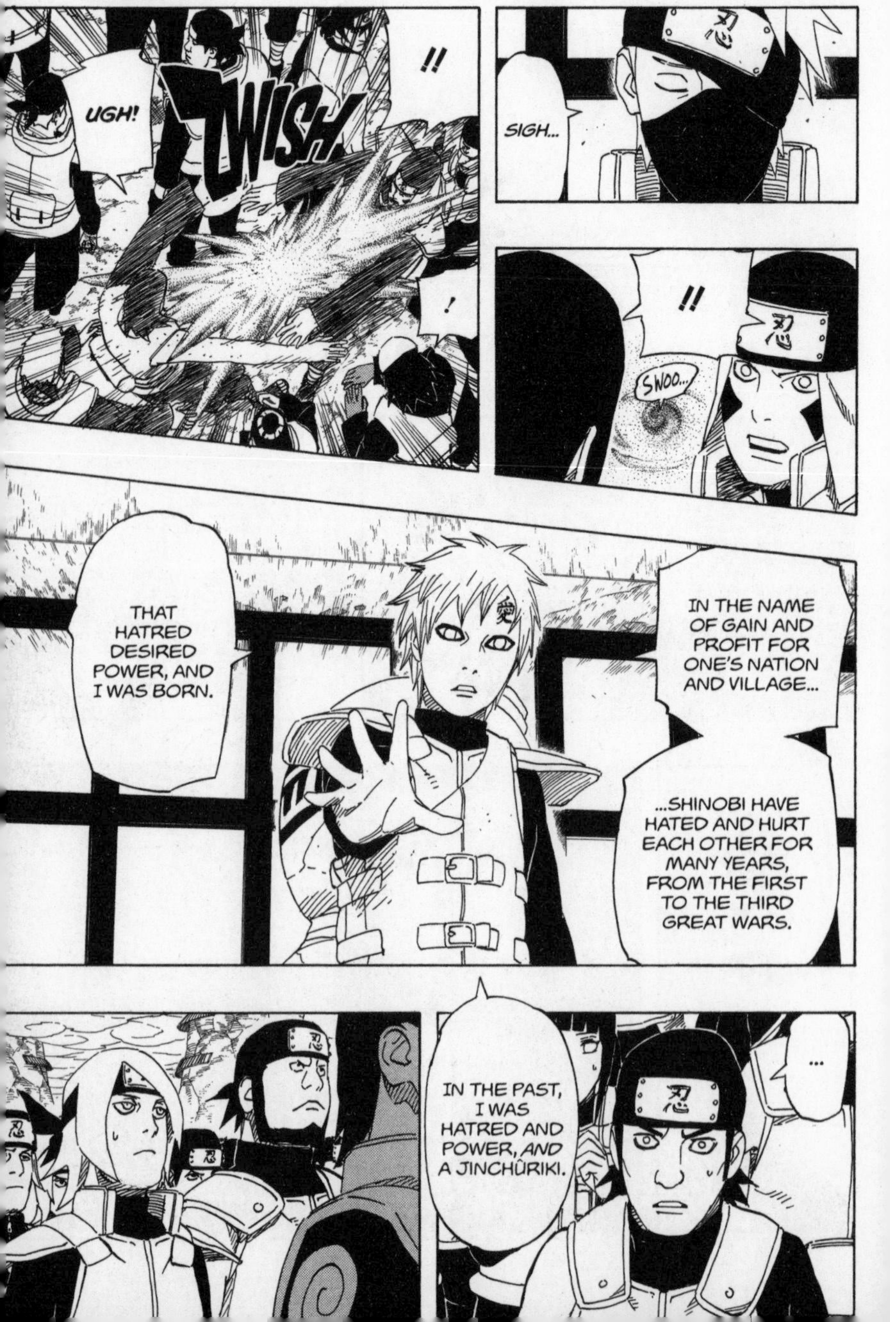
SIGH...
!!
SWOO...
!!
ZWISH
UGH!
!
IN THE NAME OF GAIN AND PROFIT FOR ONE'S NATION AND VILLAGE...
...SHINOBI HAVE HATED AND HURT EACH OTHER FOR MANY YEARS, FROM THE FIRST TO THE THIRD GREAT WARS.
THAT HATRED DESIRED POWER, AND I WAS BORN.
...
IN THE PAST, I WAS HATRED AND POWER, AND A JINCHÛRIKI.

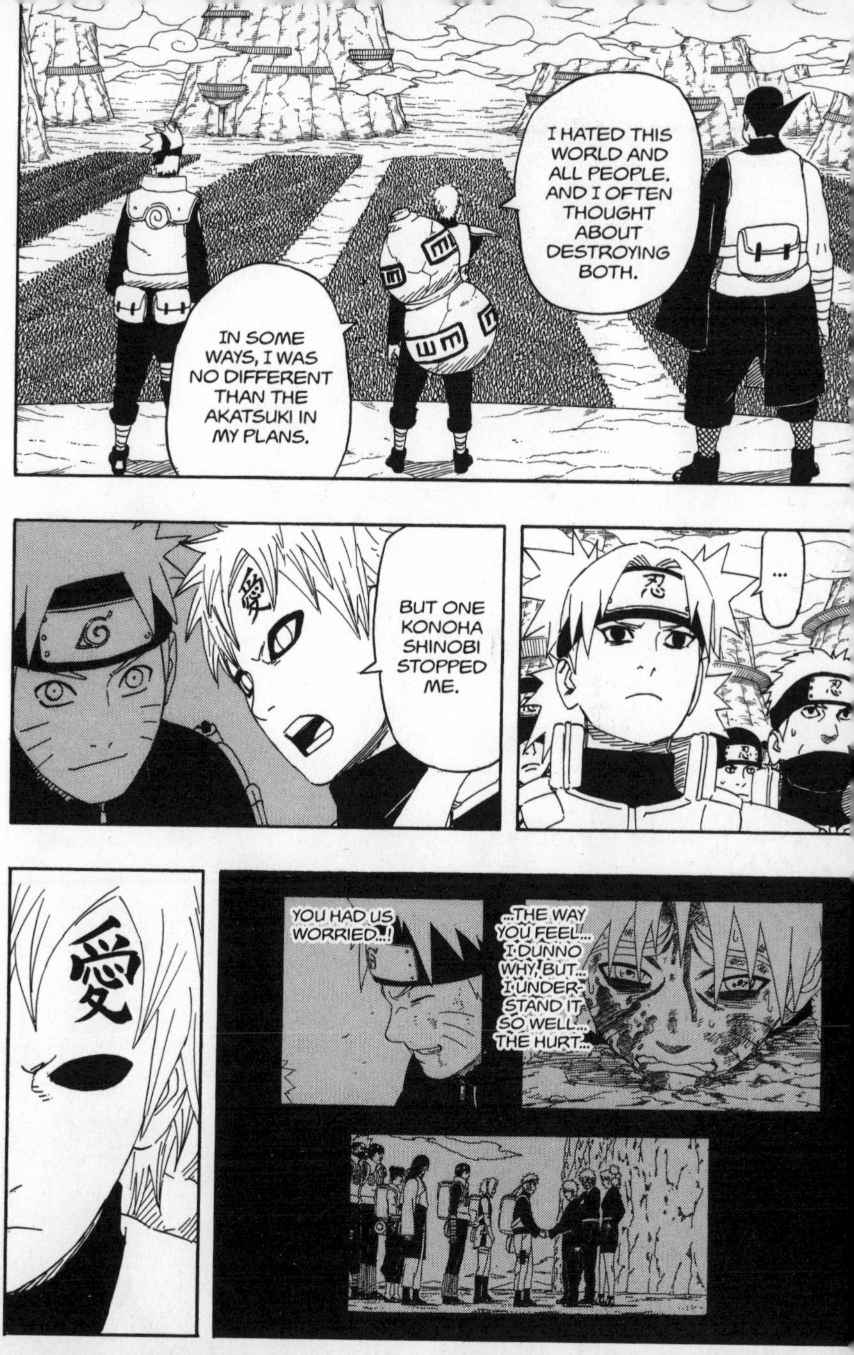
I HATED THIS WORLD AND ALL PEOPLE. AND I OFTEN THOUGHT ABOUT DESTROYING BOTH.
IN SOME WAYS, I WAS NO DIFFERENT THAN THE AKATSUKI IN MY PLANS.
...
BUT ONE KONOHA SHINOBI STOPPED ME.
...THE WAY YOU FEEL... I DUNNO WHY, BUT... I UNDERSTAND IT SO WELL... THE HURT...
YOU HAD US WORRIED...!

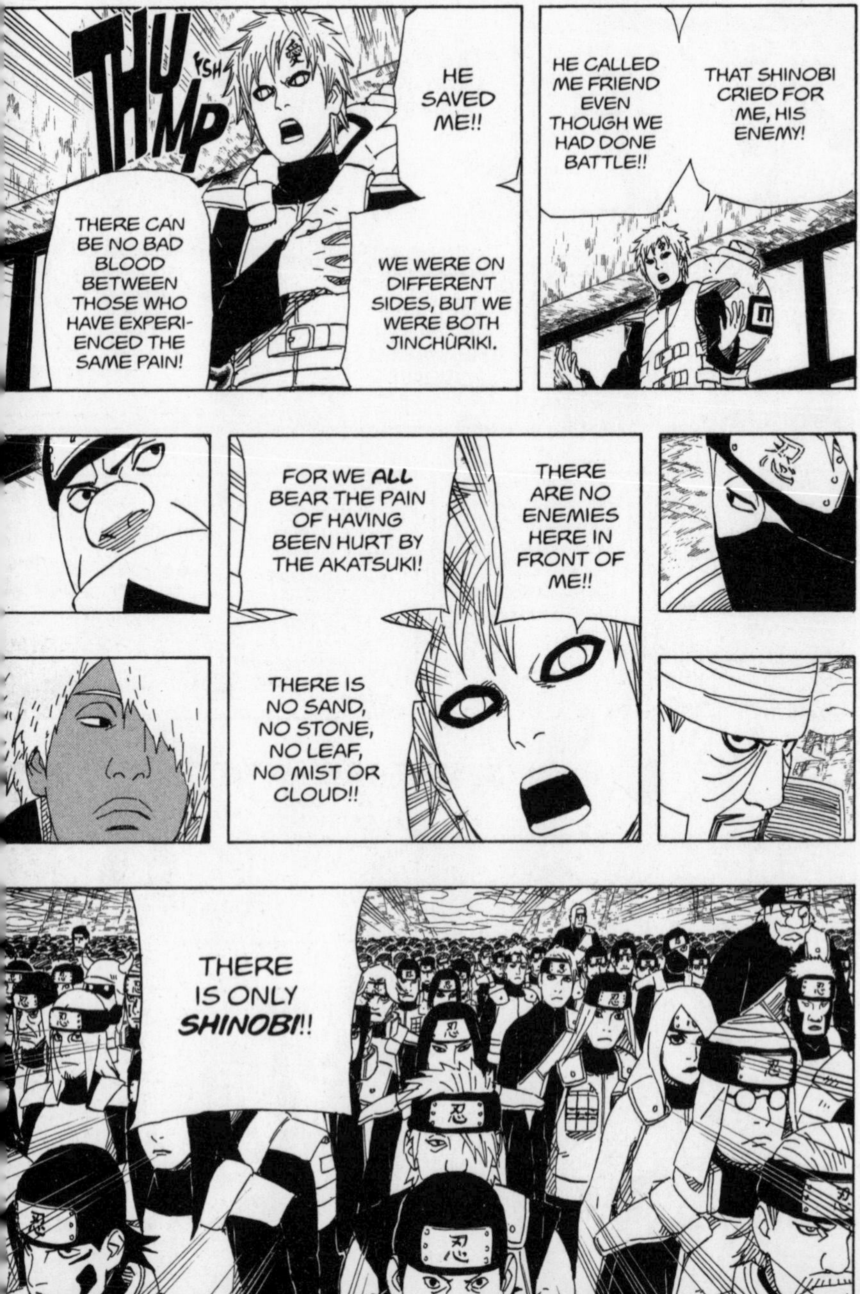
THAT SHINOBI CRIED FOR ME, HIS ENEMY!
HE CALLED ME FRIEND EVEN THOUGH WE HAD DONE BATTLE!!
HE SAVED ME!!
THUMP
FSH
WE WERE ON DIFFERENT SIDES, BUT WE WERE BOTH JINCHÛRIKI.
THERE CAN BE NO BAD BLOOD BETWEEN THOSE WHO HAVE EXPERIENCED THE SAME PAIN!
THERE ARE NO ENEMIES HERE IN FRONT OF ME!!
FOR WE ALL BEAR THE PAIN OF HAVING BEEN HURT BY THE AKATSUKI!
THERE IS NO SAND, NO STONE, NO LEAF, NO MIST OR CLOUD!!
THERE IS ONLY SHINOBI!!

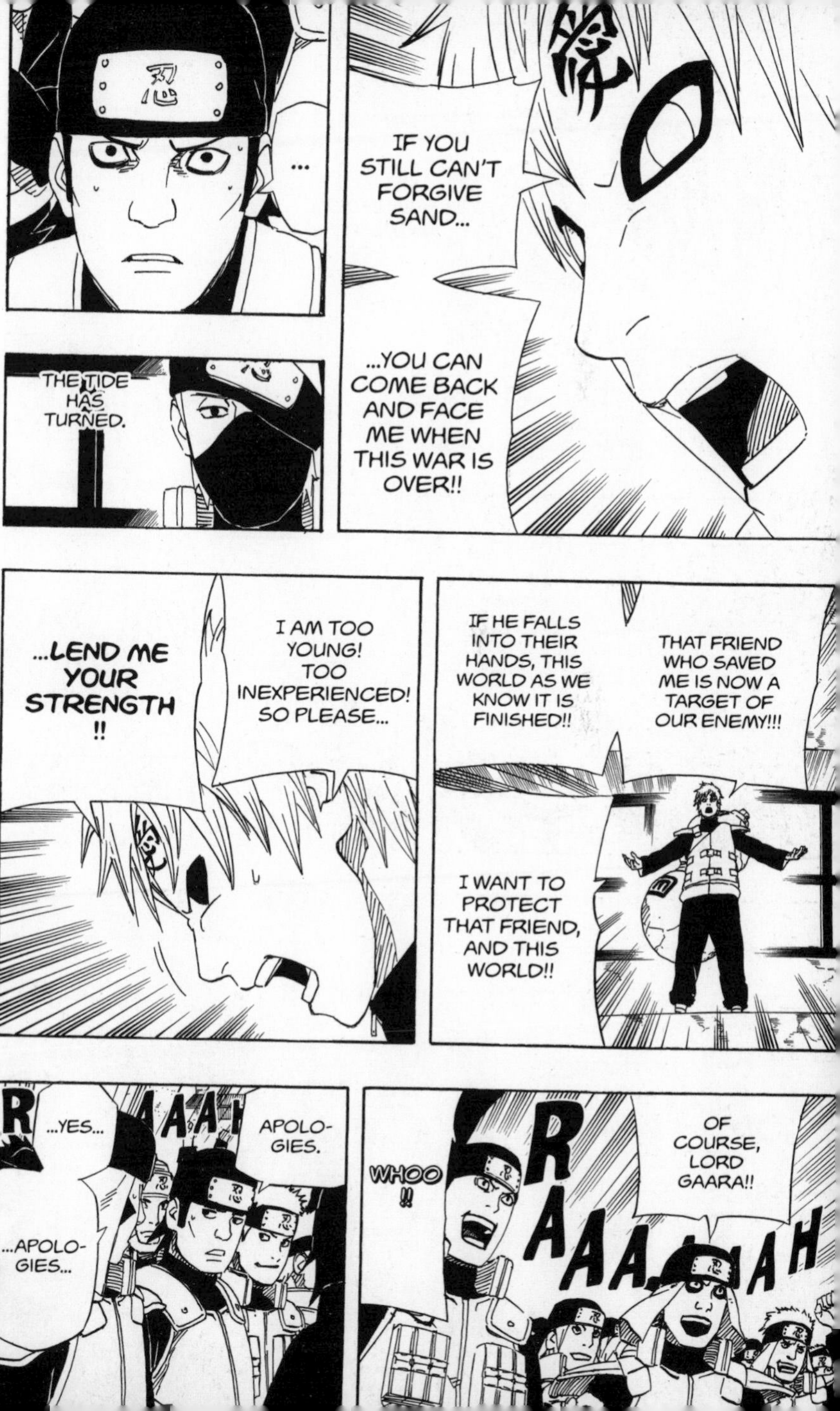
IF YOU STILL CAN'T FORGIVE SAND...
...YOU CAN COME BACK AND FACE ME WHEN THIS WAR IS OVER!!
...
THE TIDE HAS TURNED.
THAT FRIEND WHO SAVED ME IS NOW A TARGET OF OUR ENEMY!!!
IF HE FALLS INTO THEIR HANDS, THIS WORLD AS WE KNOW IT IS FINISHED!!
I WANT TO PROTECT THAT FRIEND, AND THIS WORLD!!
I AM TOO YOUNG! TOO INEXPERIENCED! SO PLEASE...
...LEND ME YOUR STRENGTH !!
OF COURSE, LORD GAARA!!
RAAAAAAH
WHOO !!
APOLOGIES.
...YES...
...APOLOGIES...

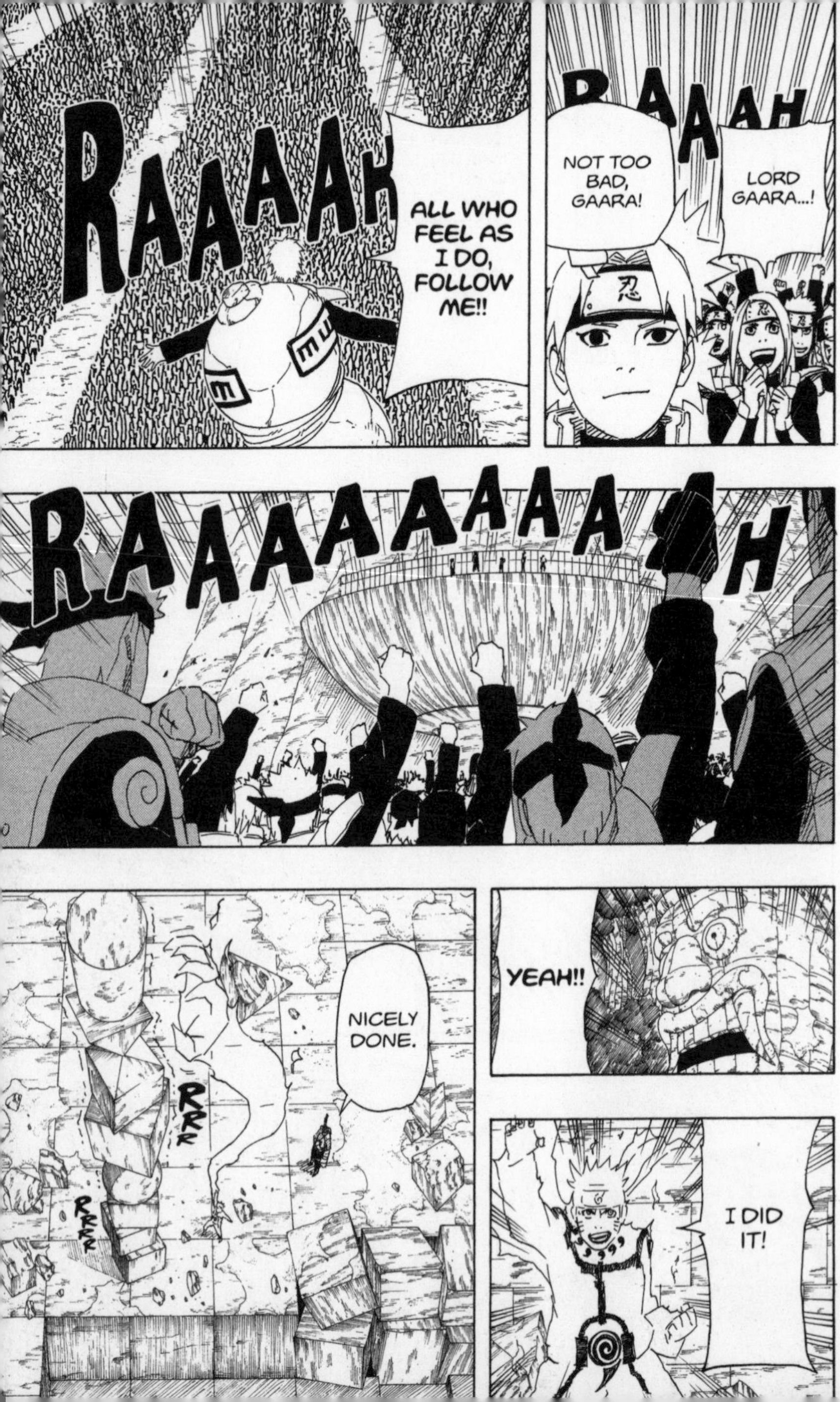
ALL WHO FEEL AS I DO, FOLLOW ME!!
RAAAAK
RAAAH
LORD GAARA...!
NOT TOO BAD, GAARA!
RAAAAAAAAAH
YEAH!!
I DID IT!
NICELY DONE.
RRR
RRRR

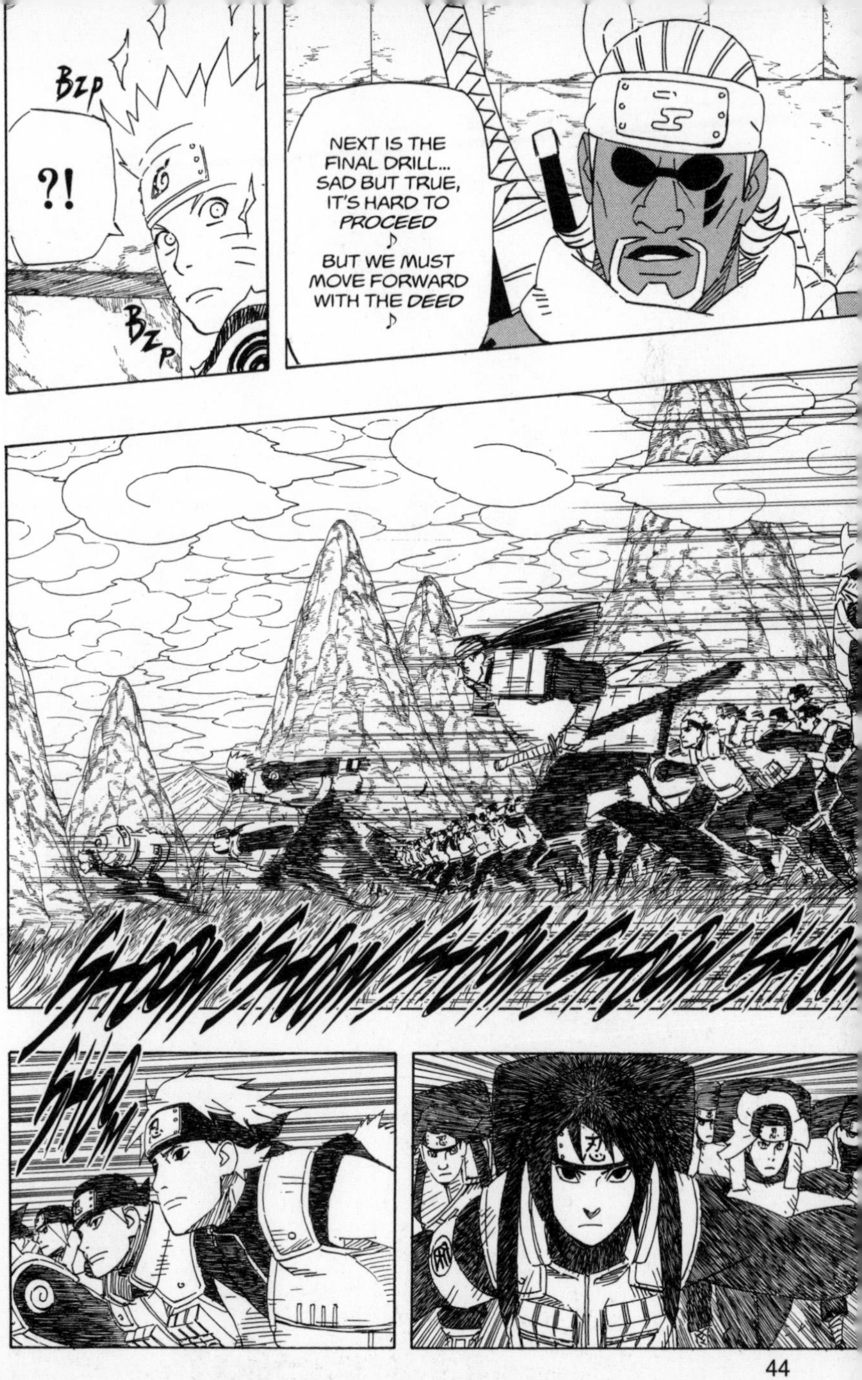
NEXT IS THE FINAL DRILL... SAD BUT TRUE, IT'S HARD TO *PROCEED* ♪ BUT WE MUST MOVE FORWARD WITH THE *DEED* ♪
BZP
?!
BZP

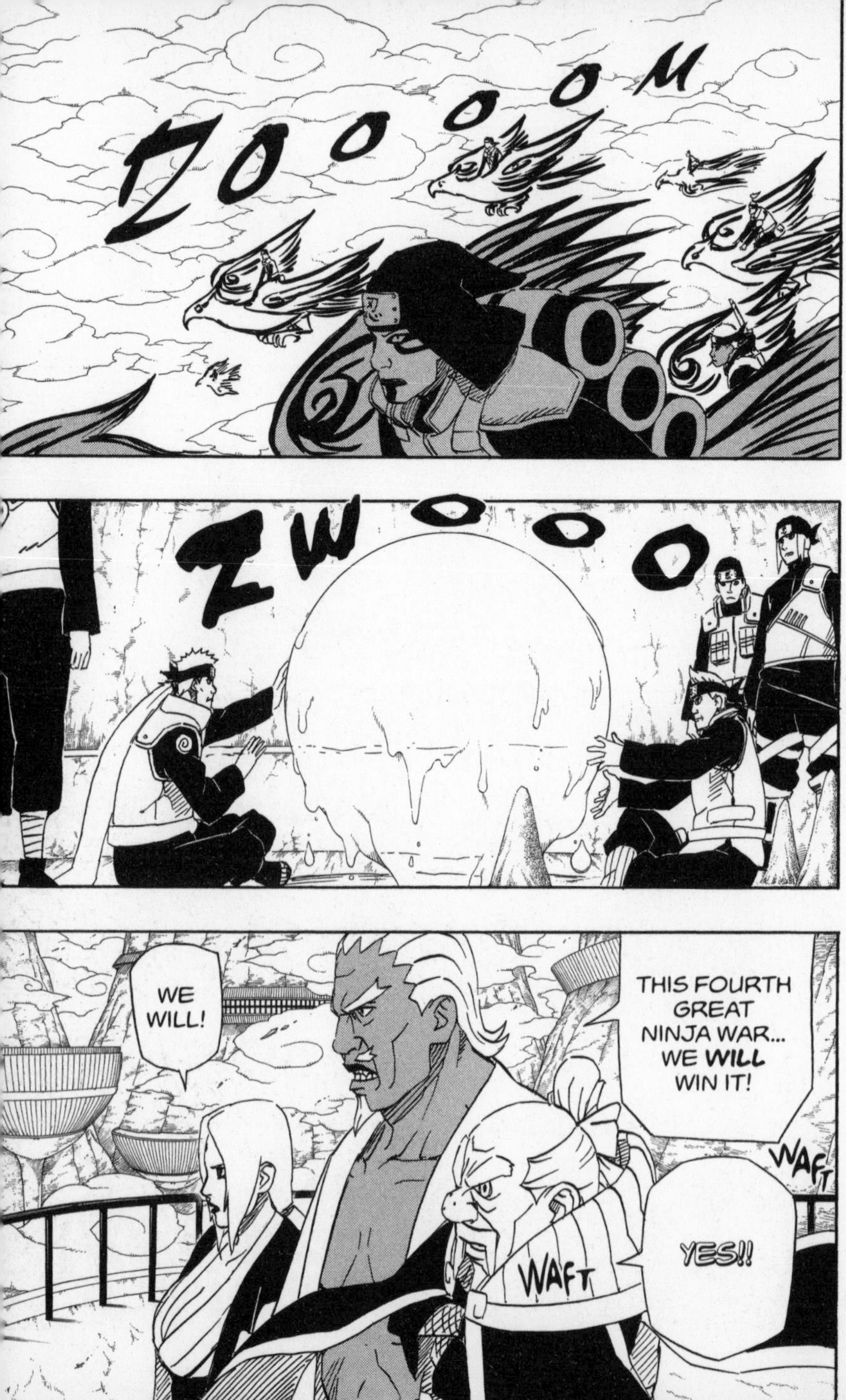
ZOOOOOM
OOOO
ZWOOOO
THIS FOURTH GREAT NINJA WAR... WE **WILL** WIN IT!
WE WILL!
WAFT
YES!!
WAFT

NARUTO

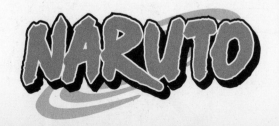

Number 517: Omoi's War!!

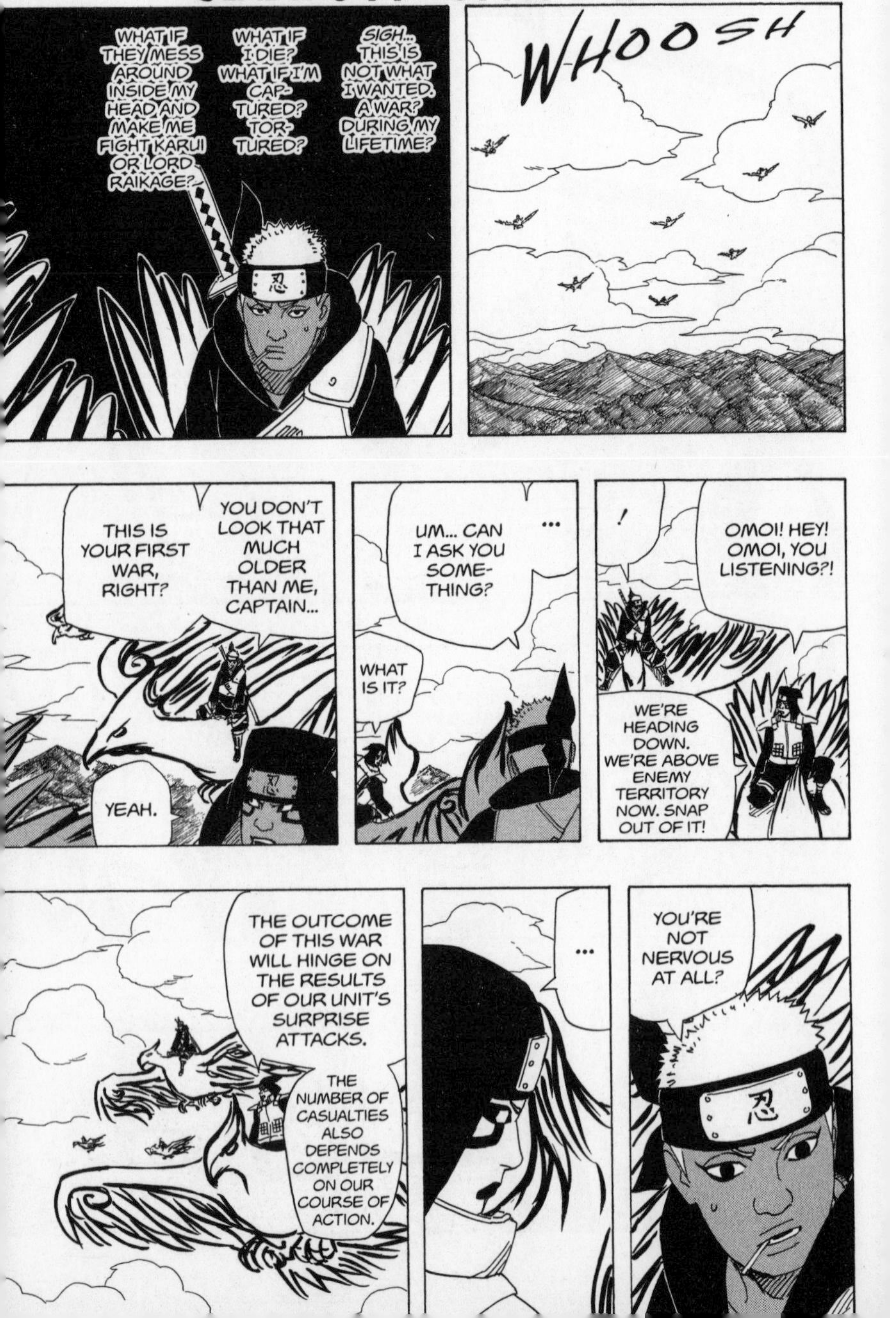
WHOOSH
SIGH... THIS IS NOT WHAT I WANTED. A WAR? DURING MY LIFETIME?
WHAT IF I DIE? WHAT IF I'M CAPTURED? TORTURED?
WHAT IF THEY MESS AROUND INSIDE MY HEAD AND MAKE ME FIGHT KARUI OR LORD RAIKAGE?
OMOI! HEY! OMOI, YOU LISTENING?!
!
WE'RE HEADING DOWN. WE'RE ABOVE ENEMY TERRITORY NOW. SNAP OUT OF IT!
...
UM... CAN I ASK YOU SOMETHING?
WHAT IS IT?
YOU DON'T LOOK THAT MUCH OLDER THAN ME, CAPTAIN...
THIS IS YOUR FIRST WAR, RIGHT?
YEAH.
YOU'RE NOT NERVOUS AT ALL?
...
THE OUTCOME OF THIS WAR WILL HINGE ON THE RESULTS OF OUR UNIT'S SURPRISE ATTACKS.
THE NUMBER OF CASUALTIES ALSO DEPENDS COMPLETELY ON OUR COURSE OF ACTION.

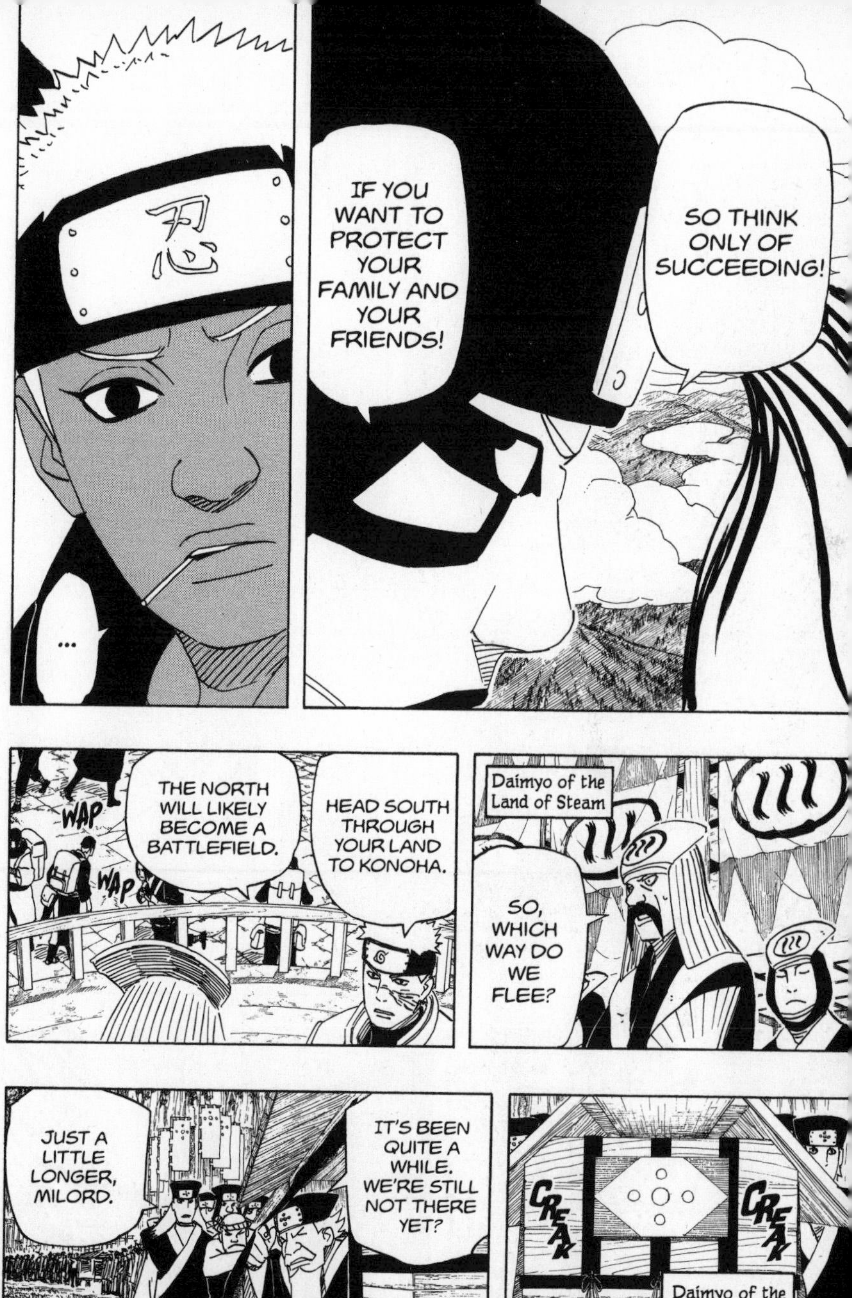
SO THINK ONLY OF SUCCEEDING!
IF YOU WANT TO PROTECT YOUR FAMILY AND YOUR FRIENDS!
...
Daimyo of the Land of Steam
SO, WHICH WAY DO WE FLEE?
HEAD SOUTH THROUGH YOUR LAND TO KONOHA.
THE NORTH WILL LIKELY BECOME A BATTLEFIELD.
WAP
WAP
CREAK
CREAK
Daimyo of the Land of Frost
IT'S BEEN QUITE A WHILE. WE'RE STILL NOT THERE YET?
JUST A LITTLE LONGER, MILORD.

READ THIS WAY

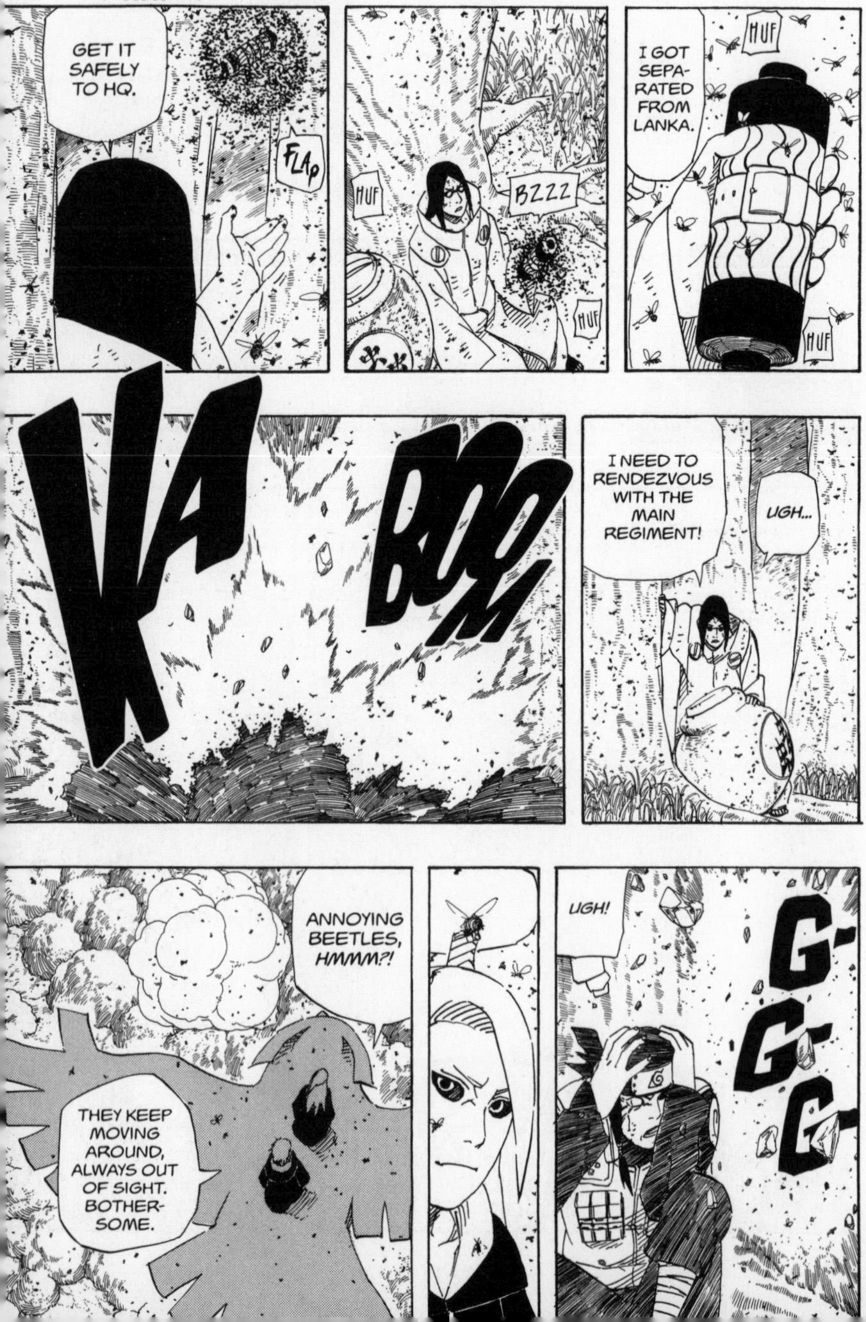
HUF
I GOT SEPARATED FROM LANKA.
HUF
HUF
BZZZ
HUF
GET IT SAFELY TO HQ.
FLAP
I NEED TO RENDEZVOUS WITH THE MAIN REGIMENT!
UGH...
KA BOOM
UGH!
G-G-G
ANNOYING BEETLES, HMMM?!
THEY KEEP MOVING AROUND, ALWAYS OUT OF SIGHT. BOTHERSOME.

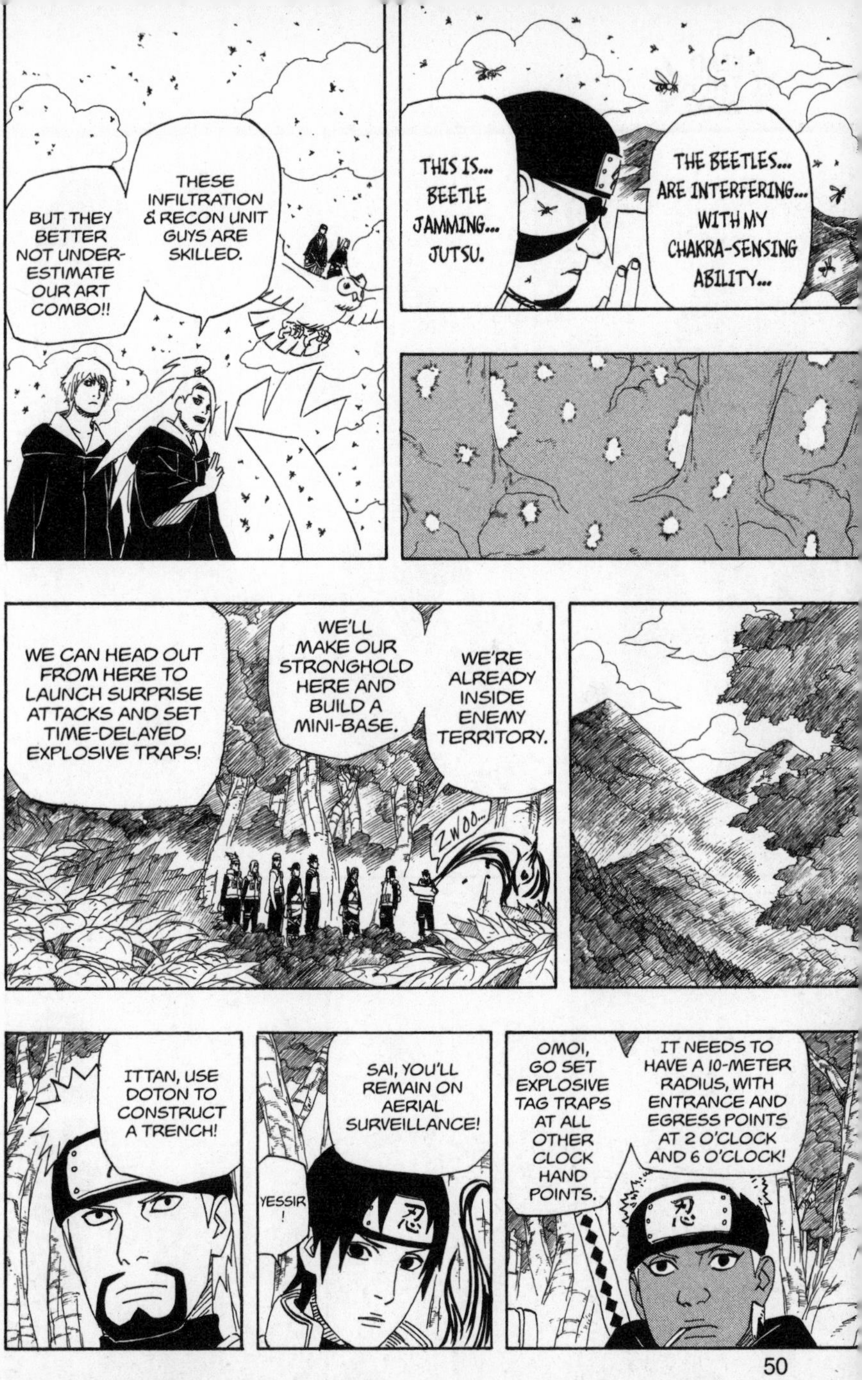
THE BEETLES... ARE INTERFERING... WITH MY CHAKRA-SENSING ABILITY...
THIS IS... BEETLE JAMMING... JUTSU.
THESE INFILTRATION & RECON UNIT GUYS ARE SKILLED.
BUT THEY BETTER NOT UNDERESTIMATE OUR ART COMBO!!
WE'RE ALREADY INSIDE ENEMY TERRITORY.
WE'LL MAKE OUR STRONGHOLD HERE AND BUILD A MINI-BASE.
WE CAN HEAD OUT FROM HERE TO LAUNCH SURPRISE ATTACKS AND SET TIME-DELAYED EXPLOSIVE TRAPS!
ZWOO...
IT NEEDS TO HAVE A 10-METER RADIUS, WITH ENTRANCE AND EGRESS POINTS AT 2 O'CLOCK AND 6 O'CLOCK!
OMOI, GO SET EXPLOSIVE TAG TRAPS AT ALL OTHER CLOCK HAND POINTS.
SAI, YOU'LL REMAIN ON AERIAL SURVEILLANCE!
YESSIR!
ITTAN, USE DOTON TO CONSTRUCT A TRENCH!

READ THIS WAY

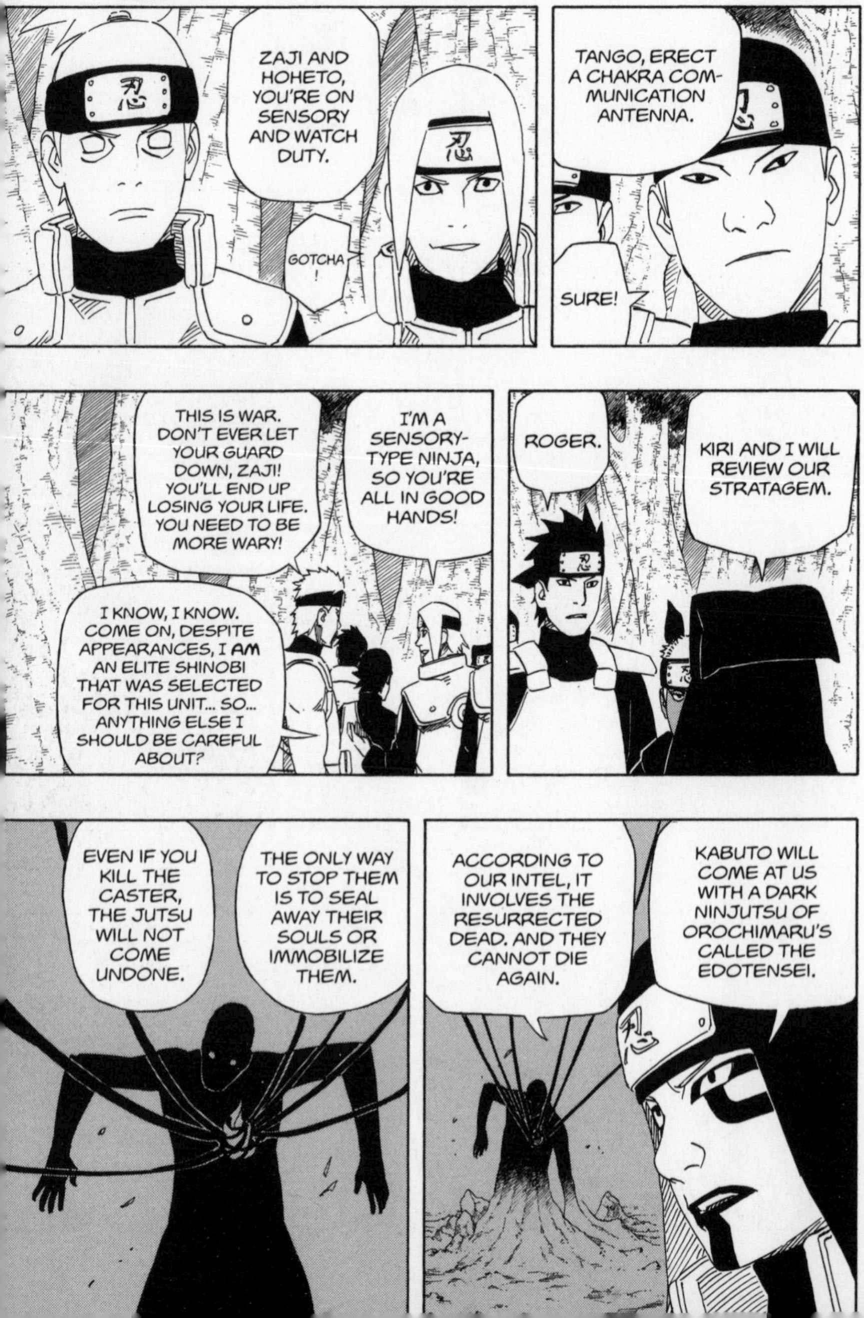

TANGO, ERECT A CHAKRA COM-MUNICATION ANTENNA.
SURE!
ZAJI AND HOHETO, YOU'RE ON SENSORY AND WATCH DUTY.
GOTCHA!
KIRI AND I WILL REVIEW OUR STRATAGEM.
ROGER.
I'M A SENSORY-TYPE NINJA, SO YOU'RE ALL IN GOOD HANDS!
THIS IS WAR. DON'T EVER LET YOUR GUARD DOWN, ZAJI! YOU'LL END UP LOSING YOUR LIFE. YOU NEED TO BE MORE WARY!
I KNOW, I KNOW. COME ON, DESPITE APPEARANCES, I AM AN ELITE SHINOBI THAT WAS SELECTED FOR THIS UNIT... SO... ANYTHING ELSE I SHOULD BE CAREFUL ABOUT?
KABUTO WILL COME AT US WITH A DARK NINJUTSU OF OROCHIMARU'S CALLED THE EDOTENSEI.
ACCORDING TO OUR INTEL, IT INVOLVES THE RESURRECTED DEAD. AND THEY CANNOT DIE AGAIN.
THE ONLY WAY TO STOP THEM IS TO SEAL AWAY THEIR SOULS OR IMMOBILIZE THEM.
EVEN IF YOU KILL THE CASTER, THE JUTSU WILL NOT COME UNDONE.

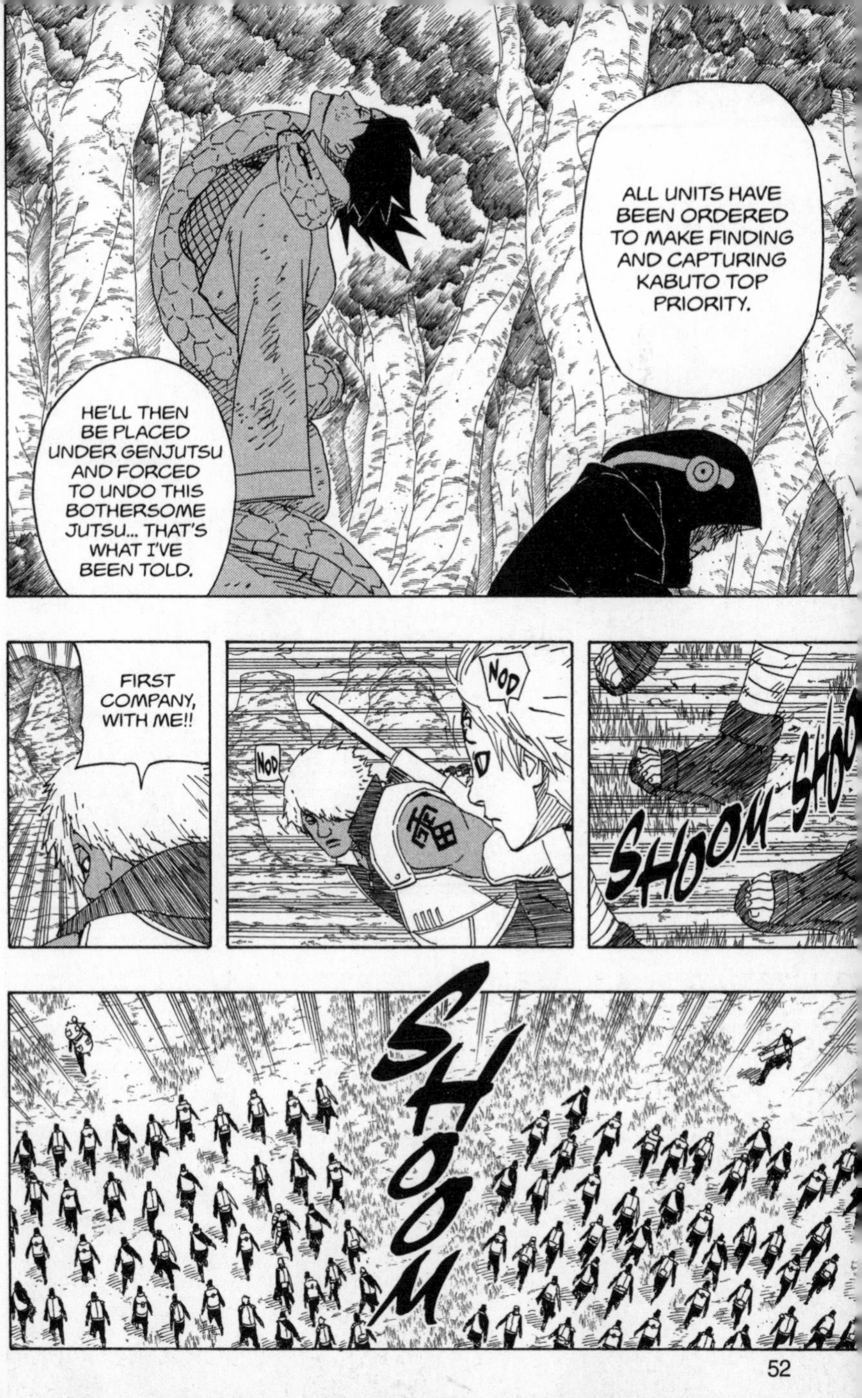
ALL UNITS HAVE BEEN ORDERED TO MAKE FINDING AND CAPTURING KABUTO TOP PRIORITY.
HE'LL THEN BE PLACED UNDER GENJUTSU AND FORCED TO UNDO THIS BOTHERSOME JUTSU... THAT'S WHAT I'VE BEEN TOLD.
SHOOM
SHOO
NOD
NOD
FIRST COMPANY, WITH ME!!
SHOOM

READ THIS WAY

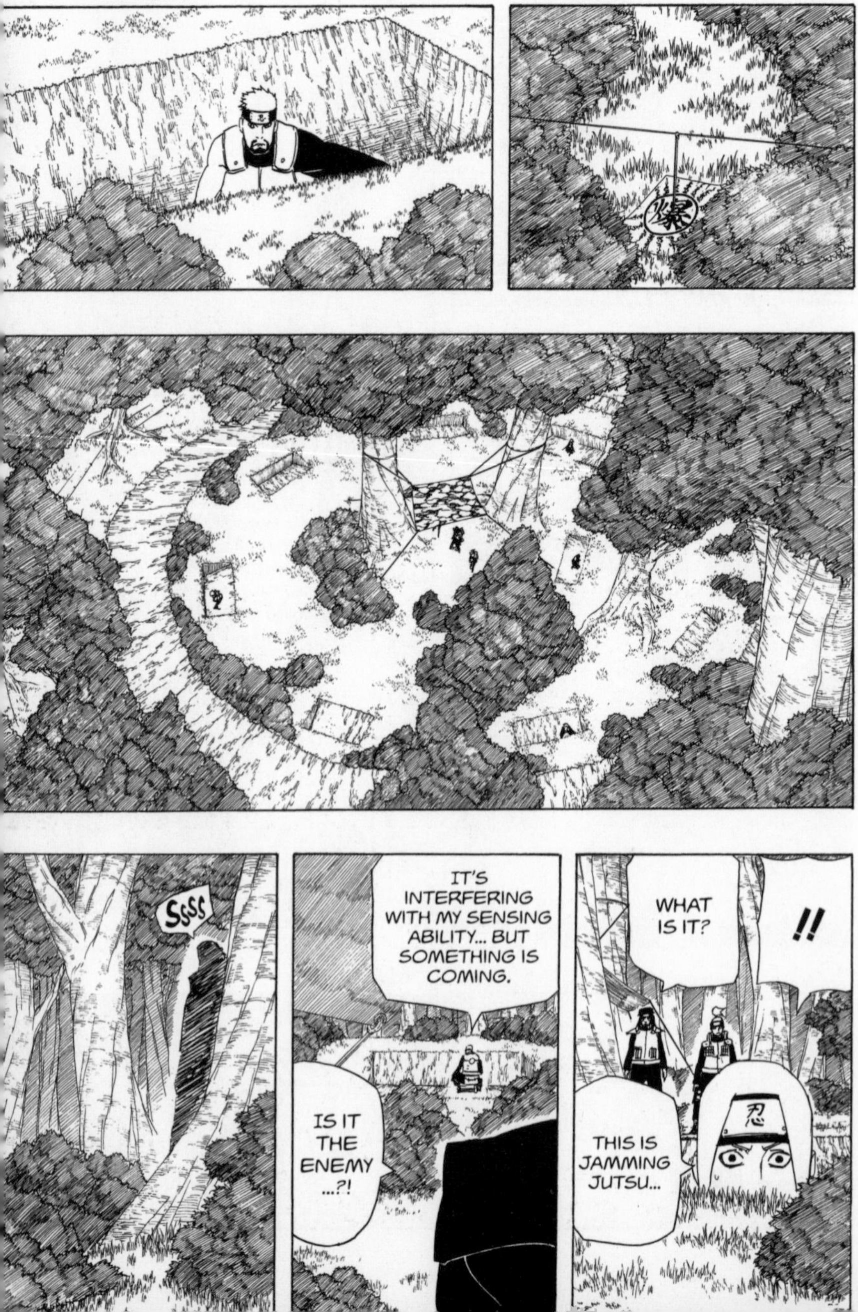
爆
!!
WHAT IS IT?
THIS IS JAMMING JUTSU...
IT'S INTERFERING WITH MY SENSING ABILITY... BUT SOMETHING IS COMING.
IS IT THE ENEMY ...?!
Ssss

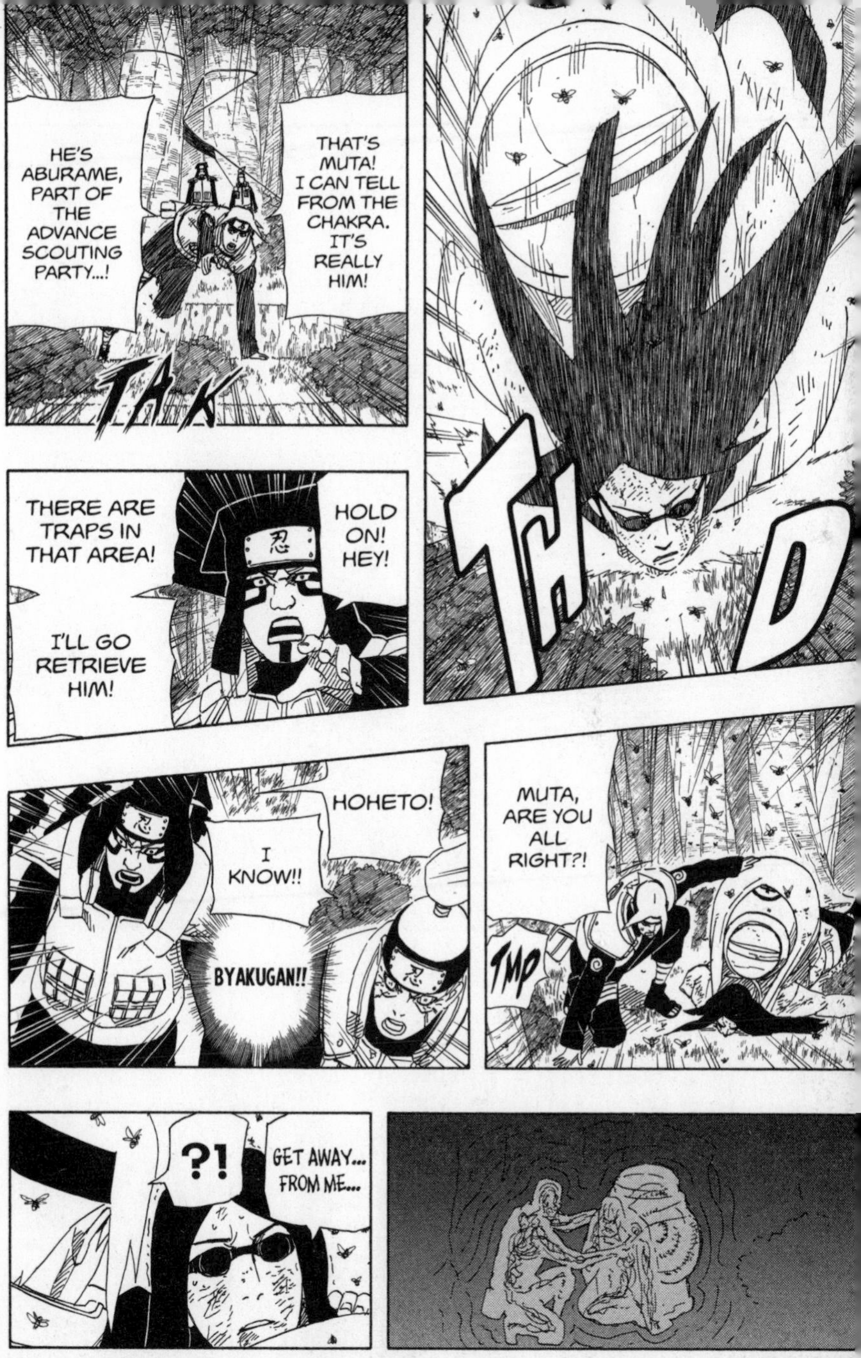
THD
THAT'S MUTA! I CAN TELL FROM THE CHAKRA. IT'S REALLY HIM!
HE'S ABURAME, PART OF THE ADVANCE SCOUTING PARTY...!
TAK
HOLD ON! HEY!
THERE ARE TRAPS IN THAT AREA!
I'LL GO RETRIEVE HIM!
MUTA, ARE YOU ALL RIGHT?!
TMP
HOHETO!
I KNOW!!
BYAKUGAN!!
GET AWAY... FROM ME...
?!

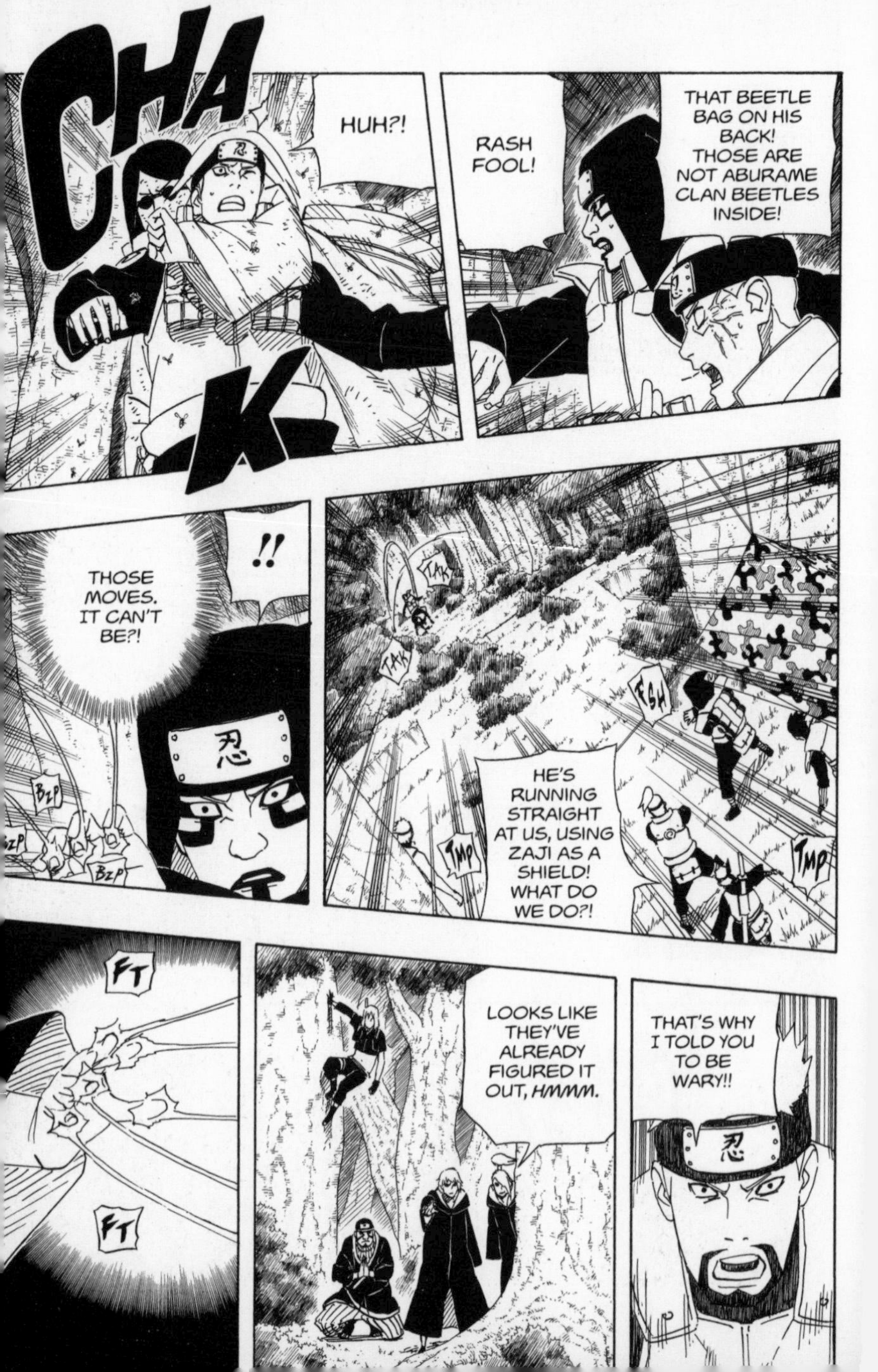
THAT BEETLE BAG ON HIS BACK! THOSE ARE NOT ABURAME CLAN BEETLES INSIDE!
RASH FOOL!
HUH?!
CHACK
TAK
TAK
FSH
TMP
HE'S RUNNING STRAIGHT AT US, USING ZAJI AS A SHIELD! WHAT DO WE DO?!
TMP
!!
THOSE MOVES. IT CAN'T BE?!
BZP
BZP
BZP
THAT'S WHY I TOLD YOU TO BE WARY!!
LOOKS LIKE THEY'VE ALREADY FIGURED IT OUT, HMMM.
FT
FT

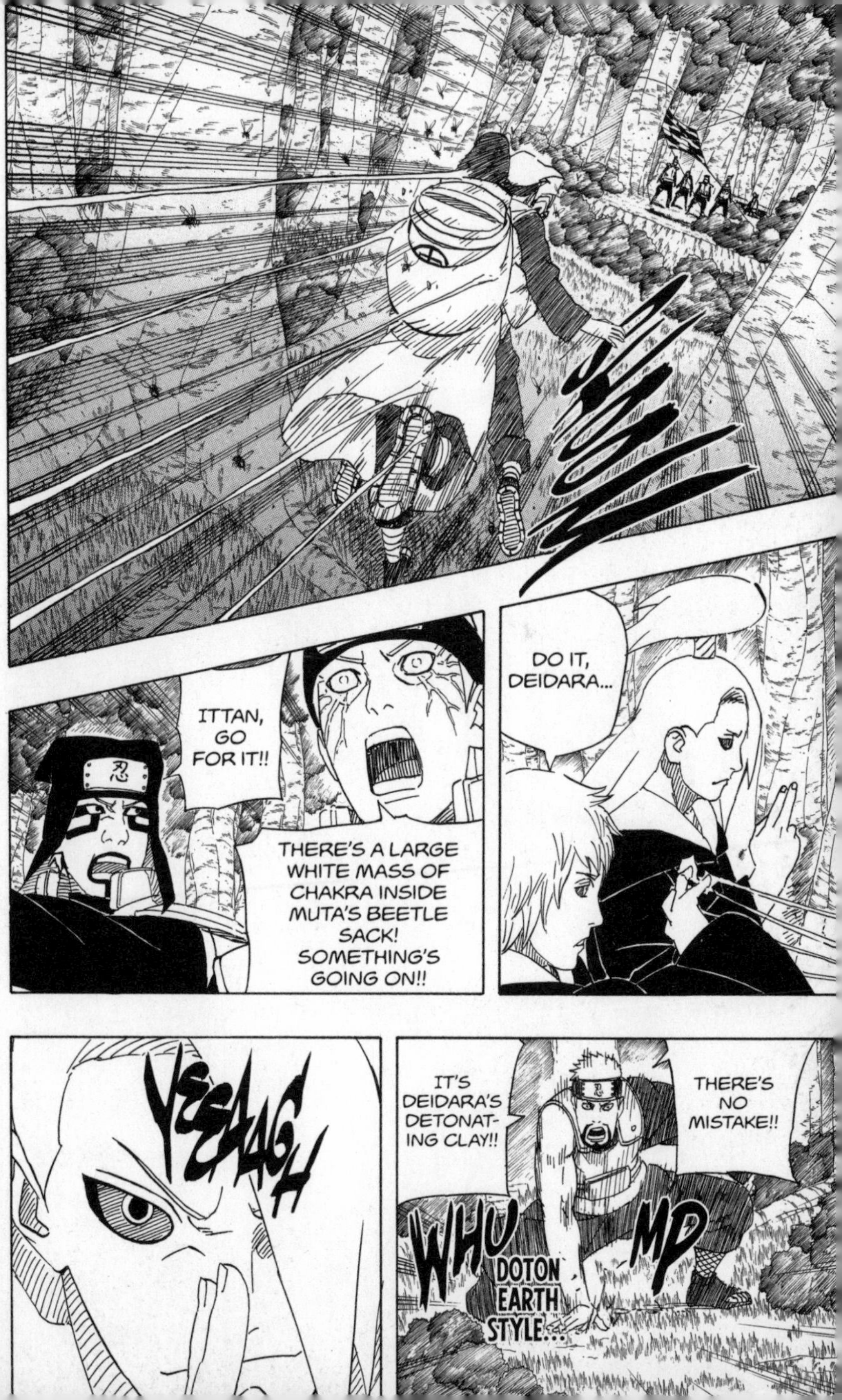
DO IT, DEIDARA...
THERE'S A LARGE WHITE MASS OF CHAKRA INSIDE MUTA'S BEETLE SACK! SOMETHING'S GOING ON!!
ITTAN, GO FOR IT!!
THERE'S NO MISTAKE!!
IT'S DEIDARA'S DETONAT-ING CLAY!!
WHUMP
DOTON EARTH STYLE...
YEEAAGH

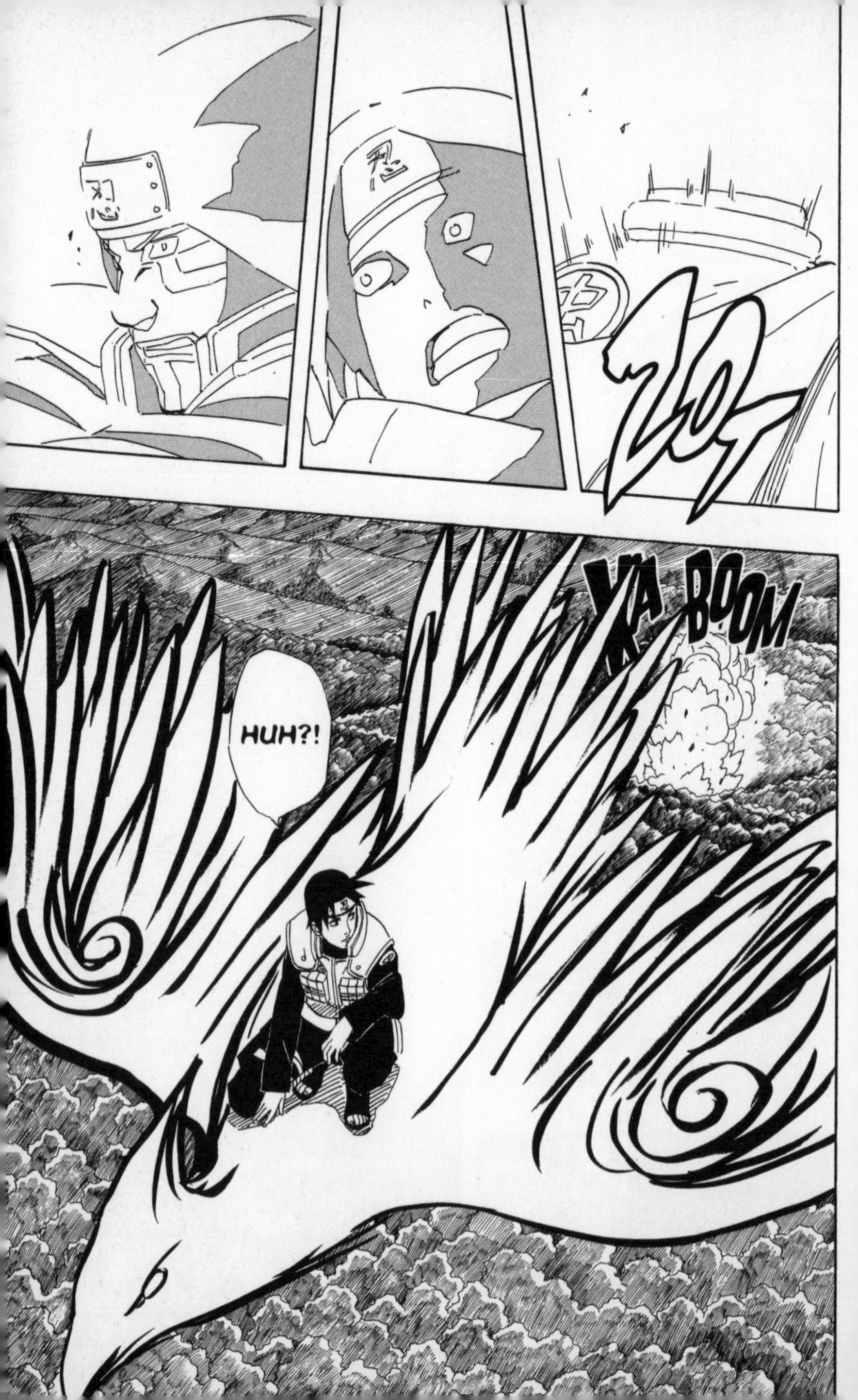
KA BOOM
HUH?!

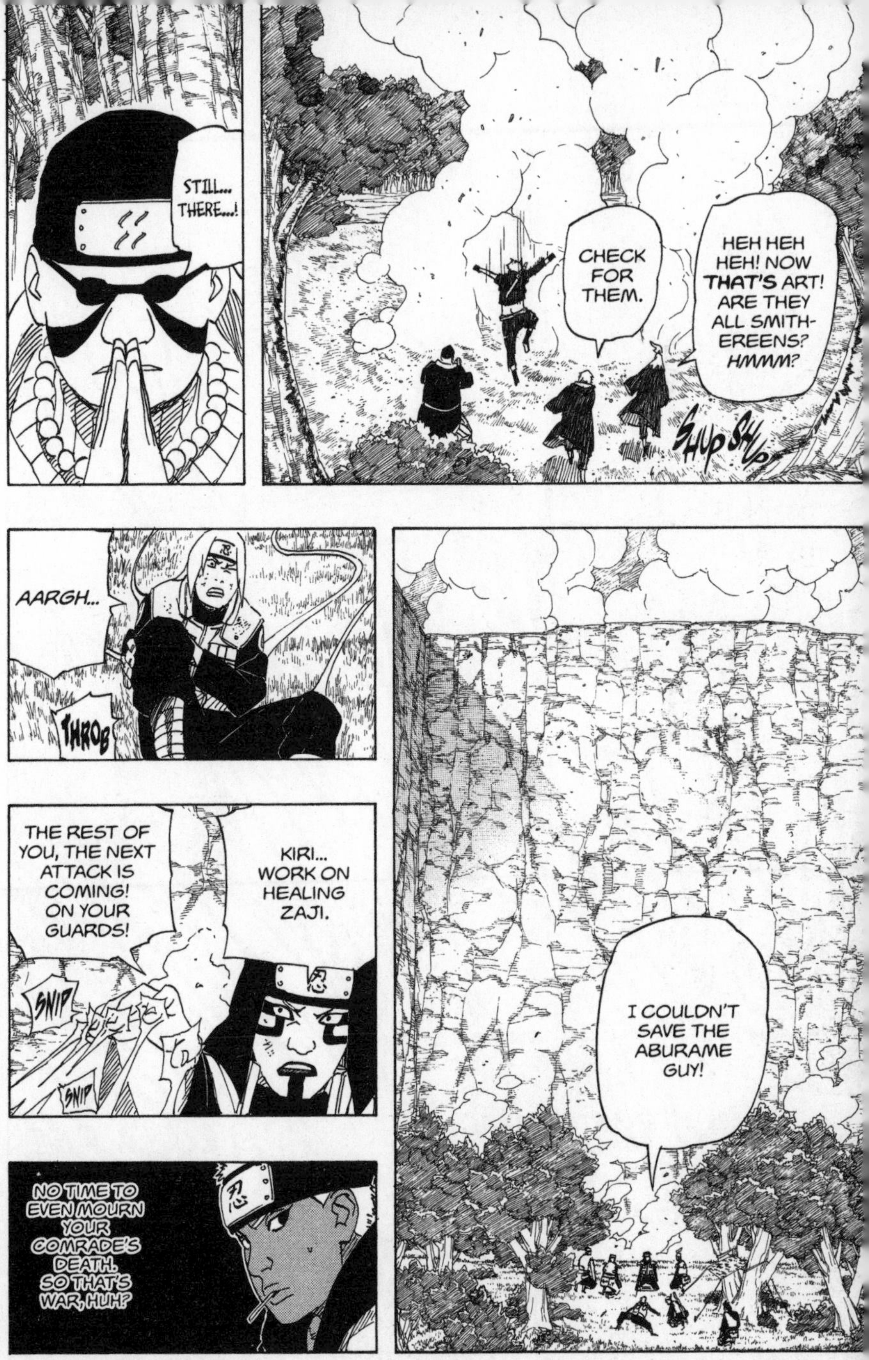
HEH HEH HEH! NOW THAT'S ART! ARE THEY ALL SMITHEREENS? HMMM?
CHECK FOR THEM.
SHUP SHUP
STILL... THERE...!
I COULDN'T SAVE THE ABURAME GUY!
AARGH...
THROB
KIRI... WORK ON HEALING ZAJI.
THE REST OF YOU, THE NEXT ATTACK IS COMING! ON YOUR GUARDS!
SNIP
SNIP
NO TIME TO EVEN MOURN YOUR COMRADE'S DEATH. SO THAT'S WAR, HUH?

READ THIS WAY

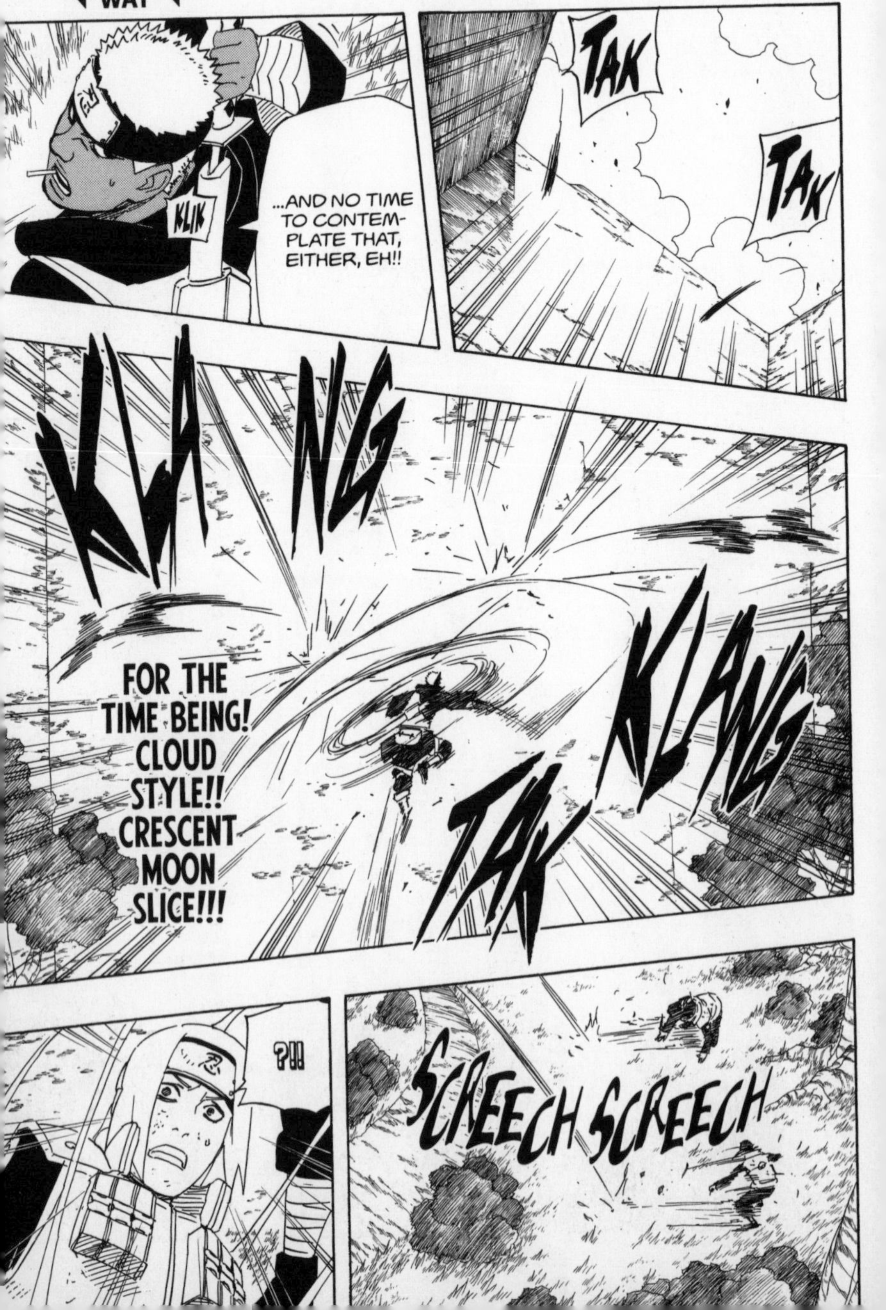
TAK
TAK
KLIK
...AND NO TIME TO CONTEMPLATE THAT, EITHER, EH!!
KLANG
FOR THE TIME BEING! CLOUD STYLE!! CRESCENT MOON SLICE!!!
KLANG
TAK
SCREECH SCREECH
?!!

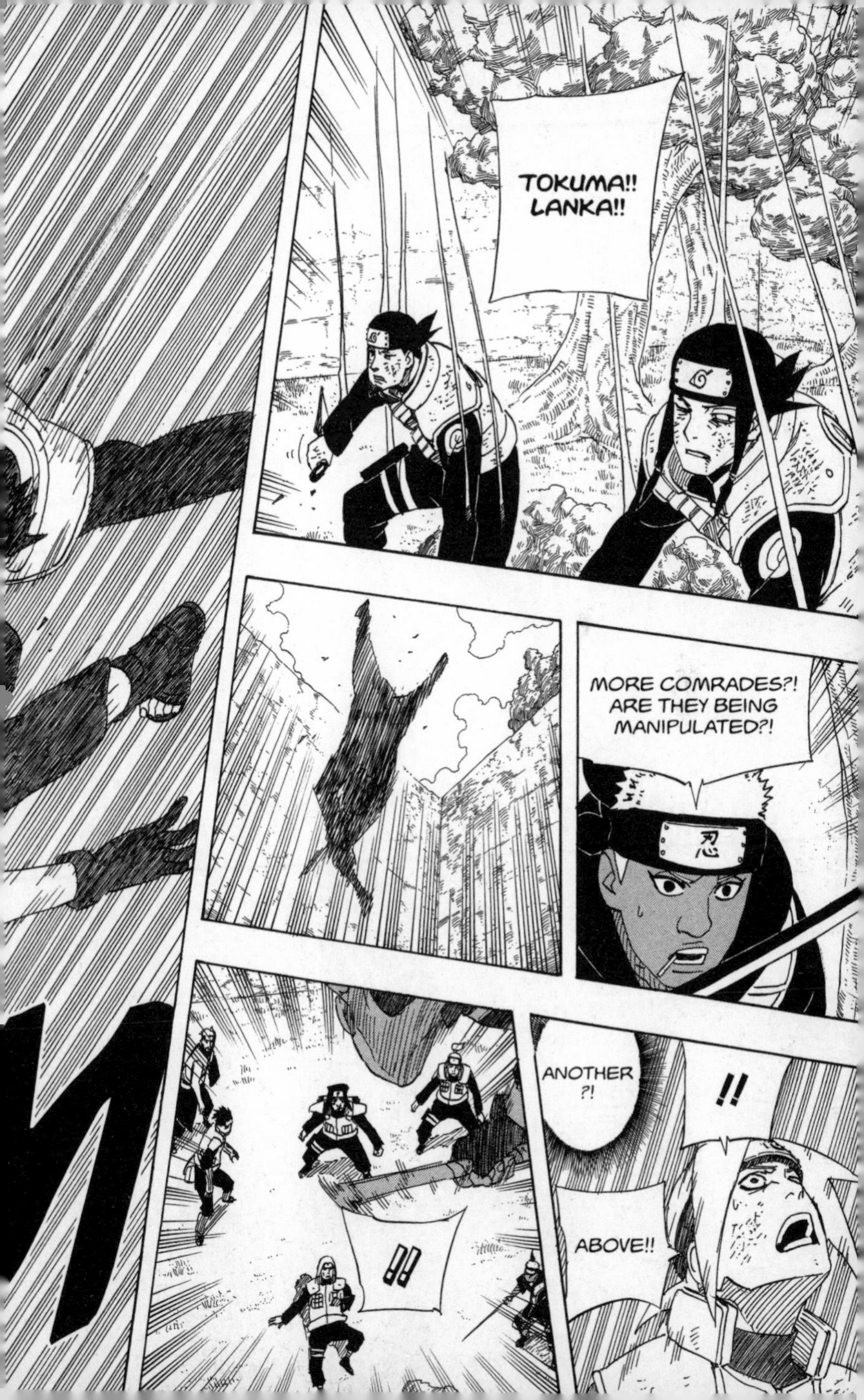
TOKUMA!! LANKA!!
MORE COMRADES?! ARE THEY BEING MANIPULATED?!
!!
ANOTHER ?!
ABOVE!!
!!

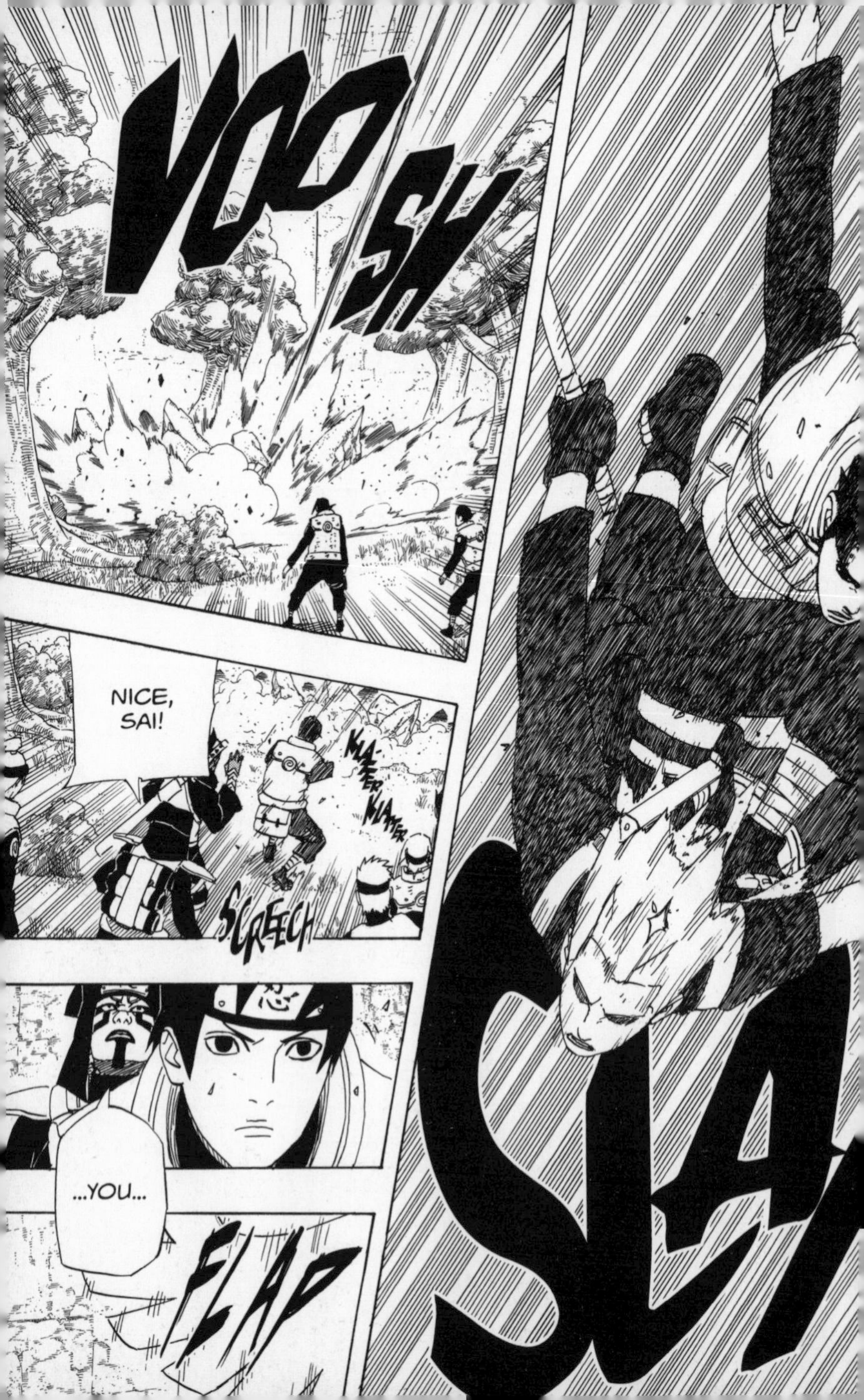
SLA
VOOSH
NICE, SAI!
KLATTER KLATTER
SCREECH
...YOU...
FLAP

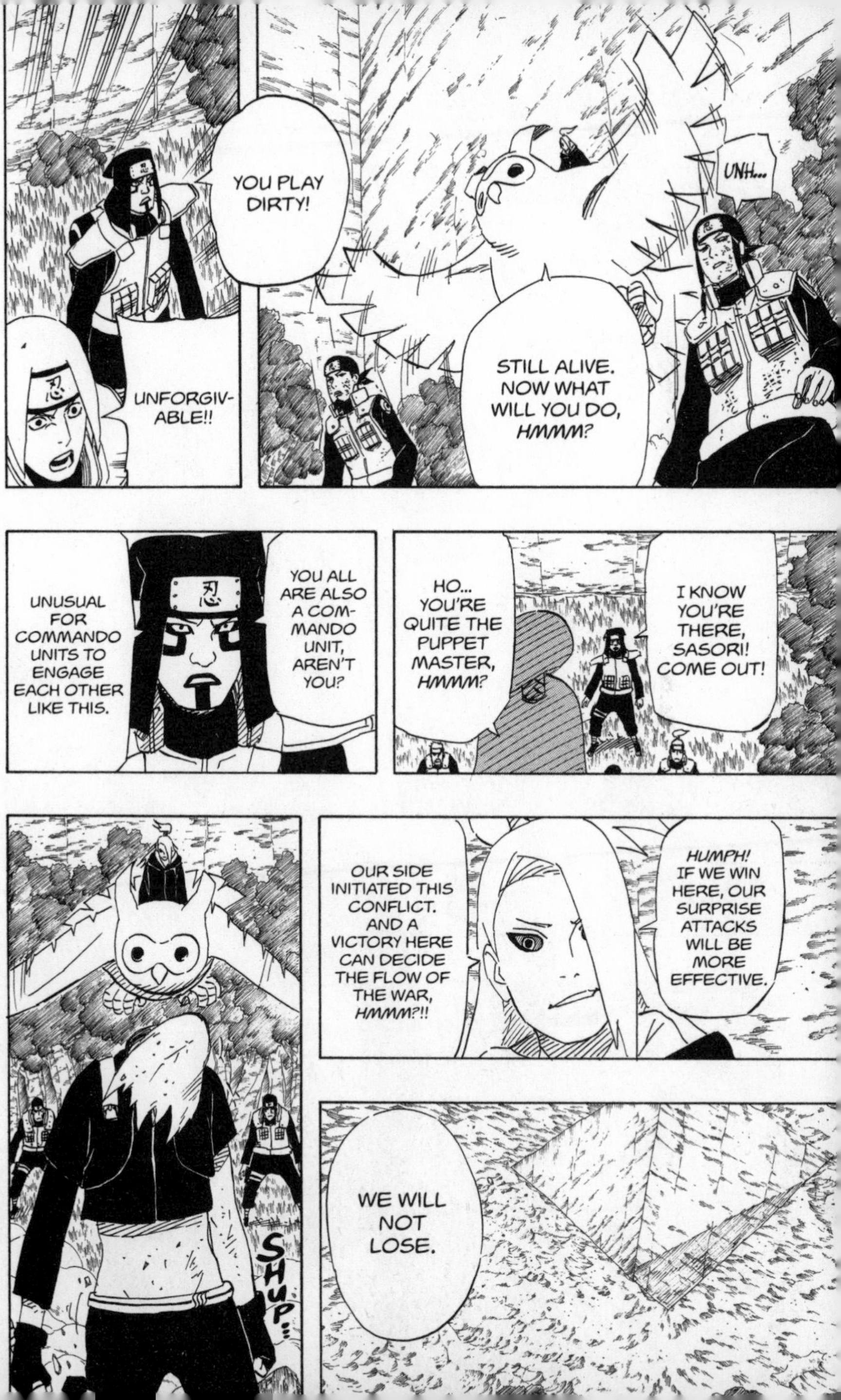
UNH...
STILL ALIVE. NOW WHAT WILL YOU DO, *HMMM?*
YOU PLAY DIRTY!
UNFORGIV-ABLE!!
I KNOW YOU'RE THERE, SASORI! COME OUT!
HO... YOU'RE QUITE THE PUPPET MASTER, *HMMM?*
YOU ALL ARE ALSO A COM-MANDO UNIT, AREN'T YOU?
UNUSUAL FOR COMMANDO UNITS TO ENGAGE EACH OTHER LIKE THIS.
HUMPH! IF WE WIN HERE, OUR SURPRISE ATTACKS WILL BE MORE EFFECTIVE.
OUR SIDE INITIATED THIS CONFLICT. AND A VICTORY HERE CAN DECIDE THE FLOW OF THE WAR, *HMMM?!!*
WE WILL NOT LOSE.
SHUP...

READ THIS WAY

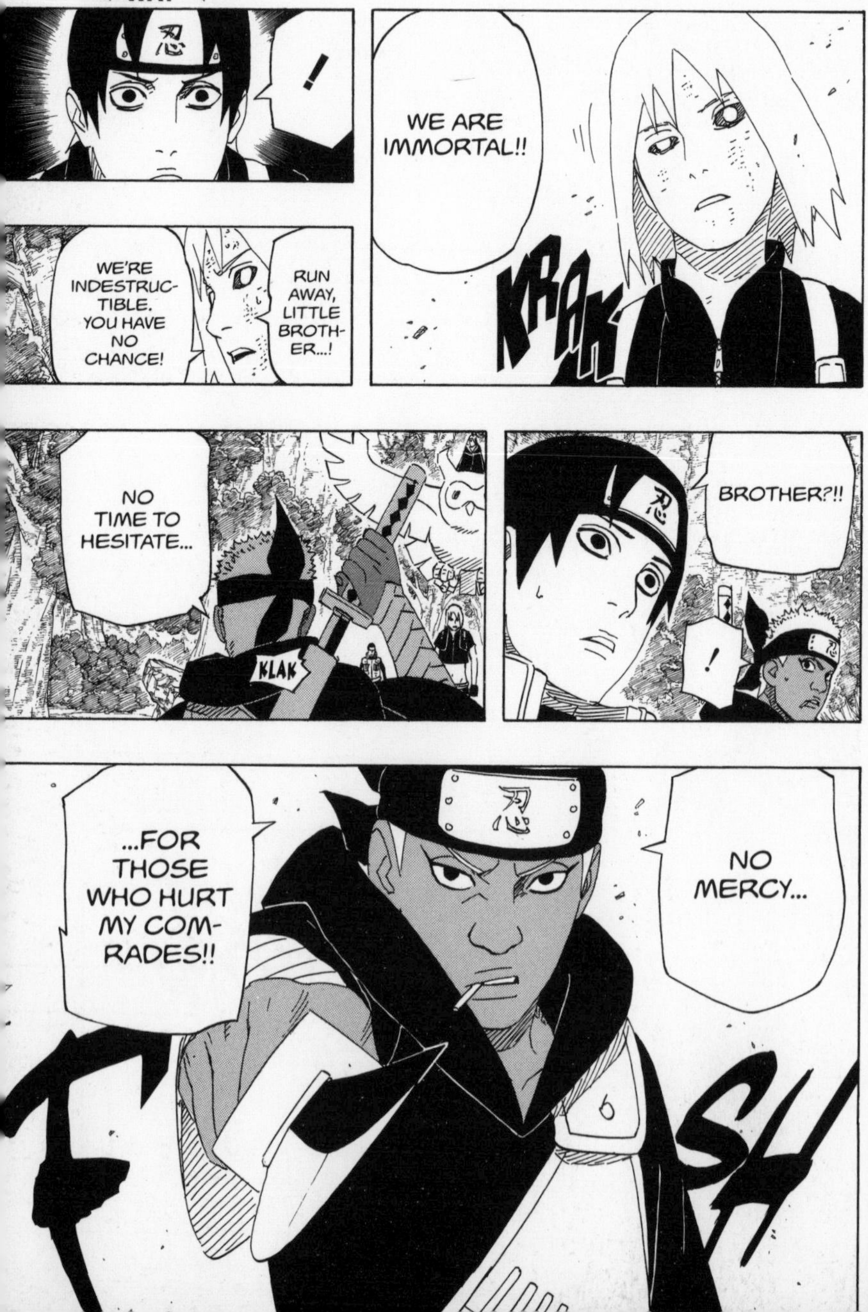

WE ARE IMMORTAL!!
KRAK
!
RUN AWAY, LITTLE BROTH-ER...!
WE'RE INDESTRUC-TIBLE. YOU HAVE NO CHANCE!
BROTHER?!!
!
NO TIME TO HESITATE...
KLAK
NO MERCY...
...FOR THOSE WHO HURT MY COM-RADES!!
SH

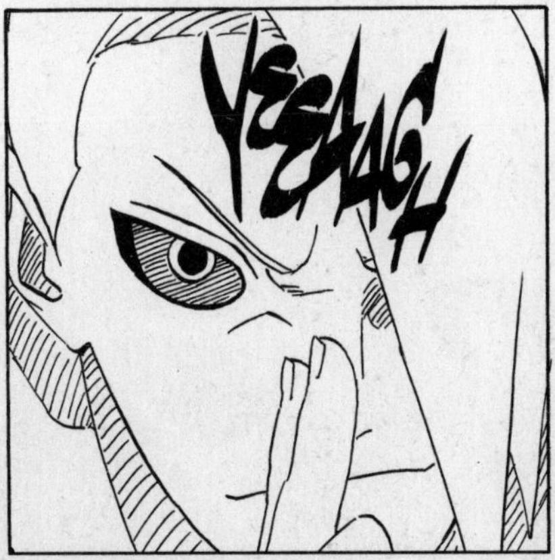
YEEAAGH

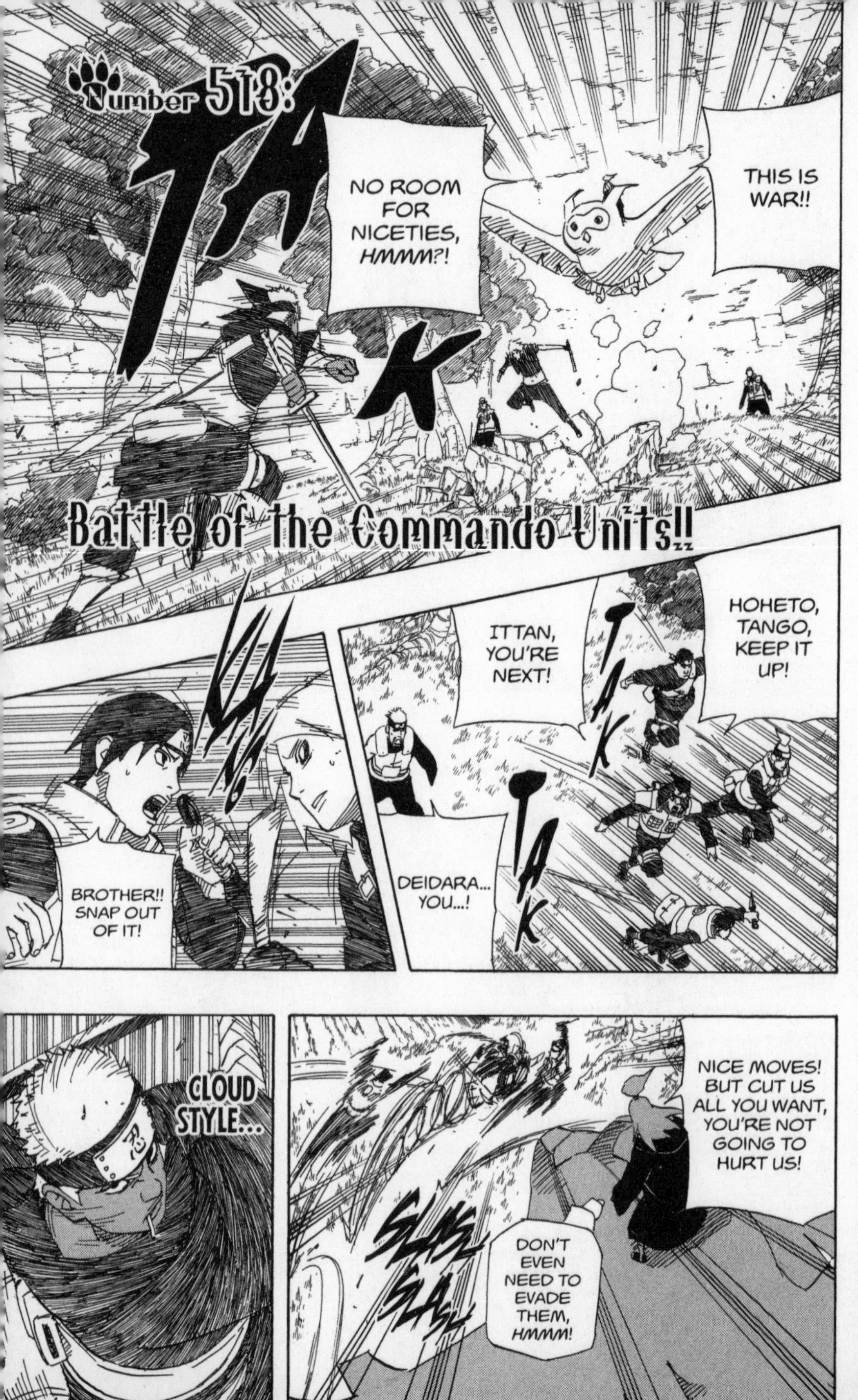
Number 518:
Battle of the Commando Units!!
THIS IS WAR!!
NO ROOM FOR NICETIES, HMMM?!
HOHETO, TANGO, KEEP IT UP!
ITTAN, YOU'RE NEXT!
TAK
TAK
DEIDARA... YOU...!
BROTHER!! SNAP OUT OF IT!
NICE MOVES! BUT CUT US ALL YOU WANT, YOU'RE NOT GOING TO HURT US!
SLASH
SLASH
DON'T EVEN NEED TO EVADE THEM, HMMM!
CLOUD STYLE...

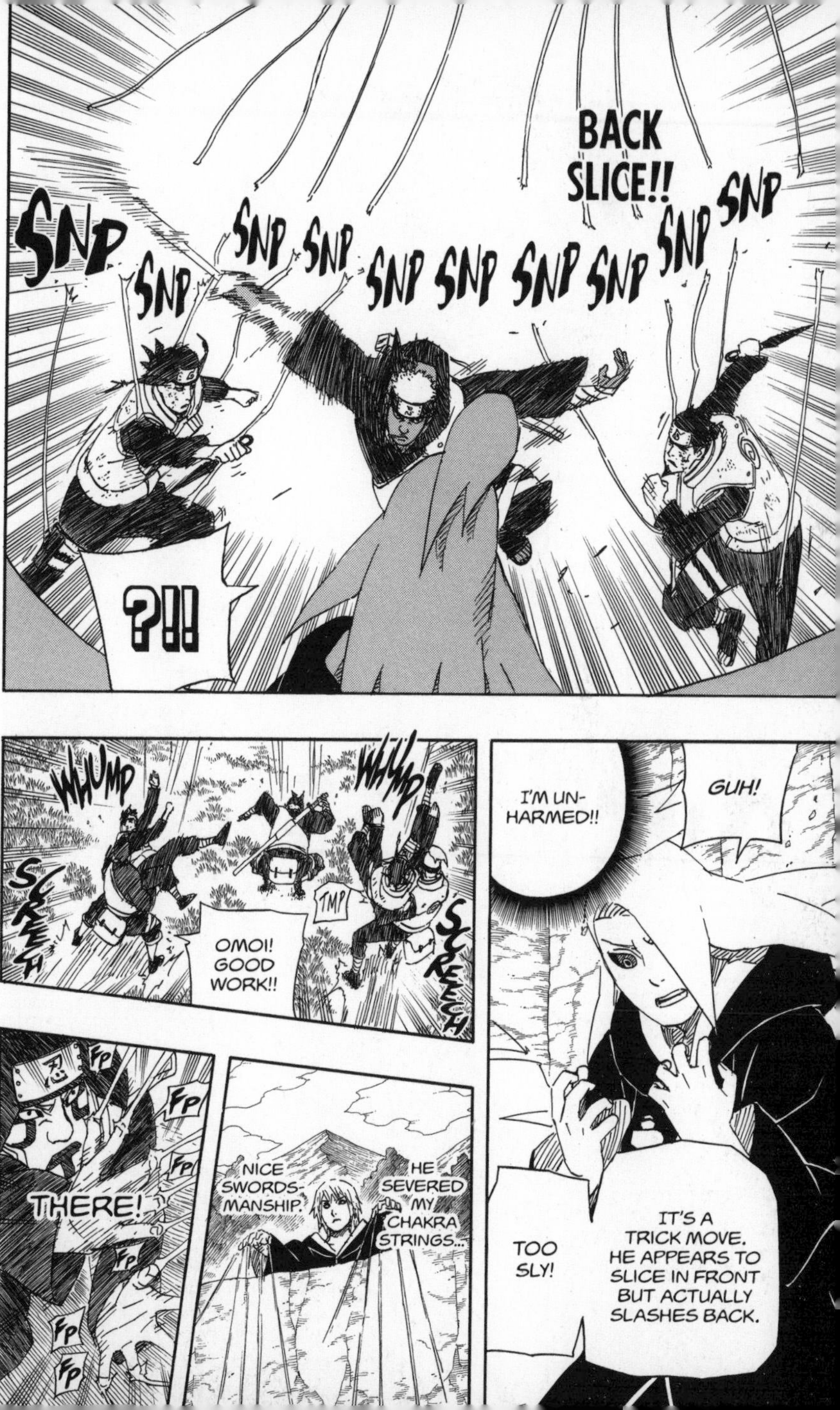
SNP
SNP
BACK SLICE!!
SNP
SNP
SNP
SNP
SNP
SNP
SNP
SNP
?!!
GUH!
I'M UN-HARMED!!
IT'S A TRICK MOVE. HE APPEARS TO SLICE IN FRONT BUT ACTUALLY SLASHES BACK.
TOO SLY!
WHUMP
SCREECH
TMP
OMOI! GOOD WORK!!
WHUMP
SCREECH
HE SEVERED MY CHAKRA STRINGS...
NICE SWORDS-MANSHIP.
FP
FP
FP
THERE!
FP
FP
FP

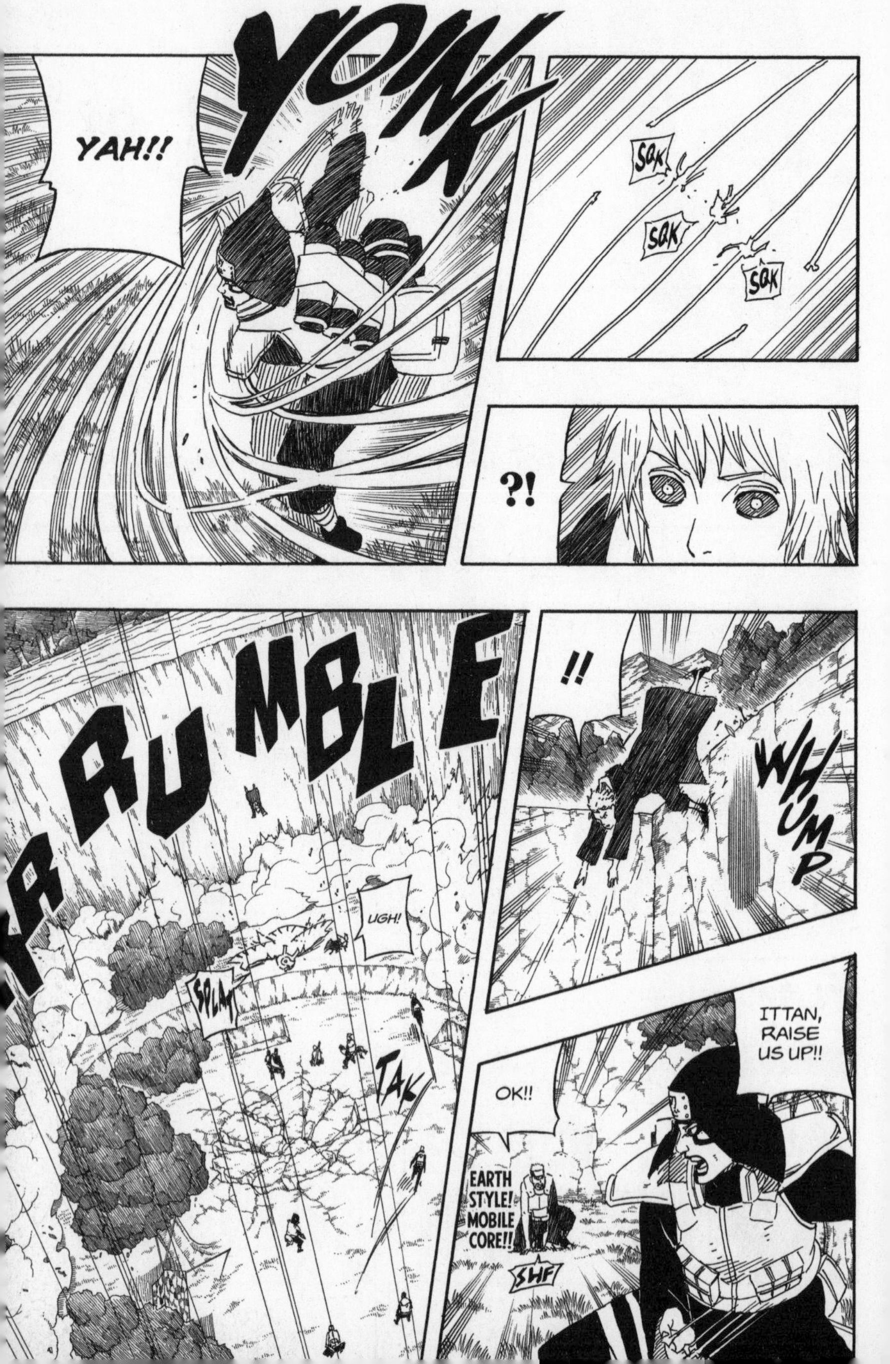
SQK
SQK
SQK
?!
YONK
YAH!!
!!
WHUMP
ITTAN, RAISE US UP!!
OK!!
EARTH STYLE! MOBILE CORE!!
SHF
RRUMBLE
UGH!
SPLAT
TAK

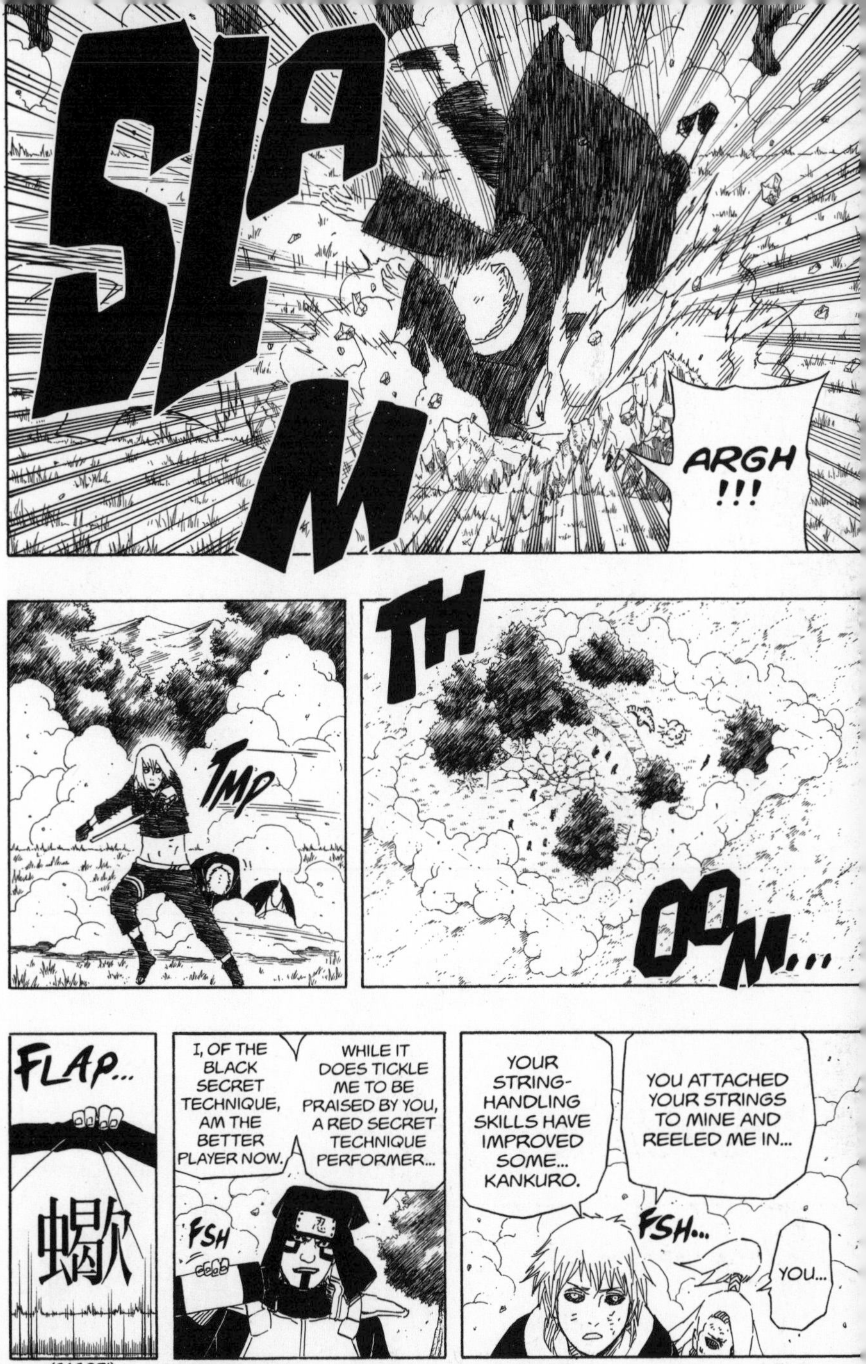
SLAM
ARGH!!!
THOOM...
TMP
YOU ATTACHED YOUR STRINGS TO MINE AND REELED ME IN...
YOUR STRING-HANDLING SKILLS HAVE IMPROVED SOME... KANKURO.
FSH...
YOU...
WHILE IT DOES TICKLE ME TO BE PRAISED BY YOU, A RED SECRET TECHNIQUE PERFORMER...
I, OF THE BLACK SECRET TECHNIQUE, AM THE BETTER PLAYER NOW.
FSH
FLAP...
蠍
(SASORI)

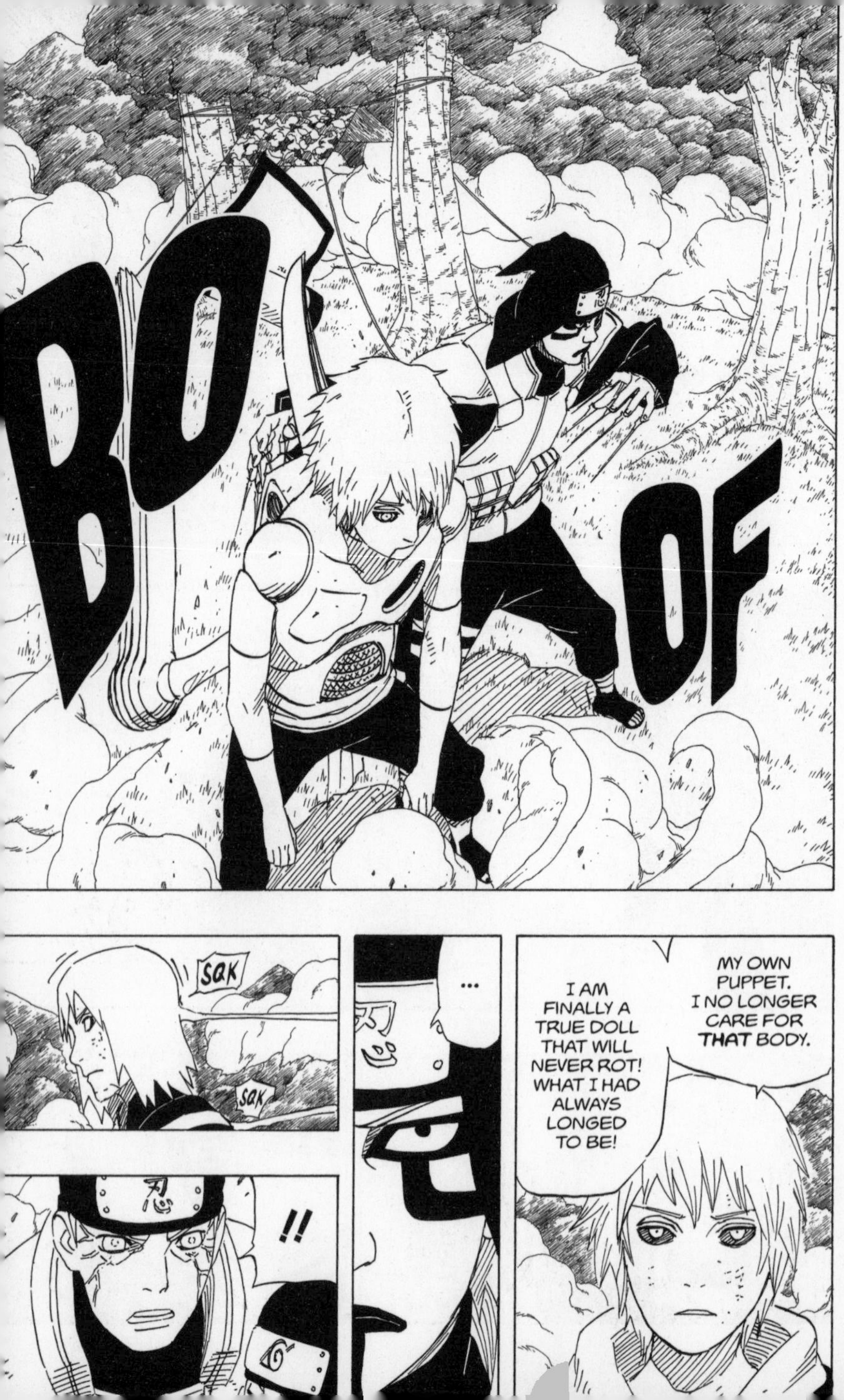

BOOF
MY OWN PUPPET. I NO LONGER CARE FOR THAT BODY.
I AM FINALLY A TRUE DOLL THAT WILL NEVER ROT! WHAT I HAD ALWAYS LONGED TO BE!
...
SQK
SQK
!!

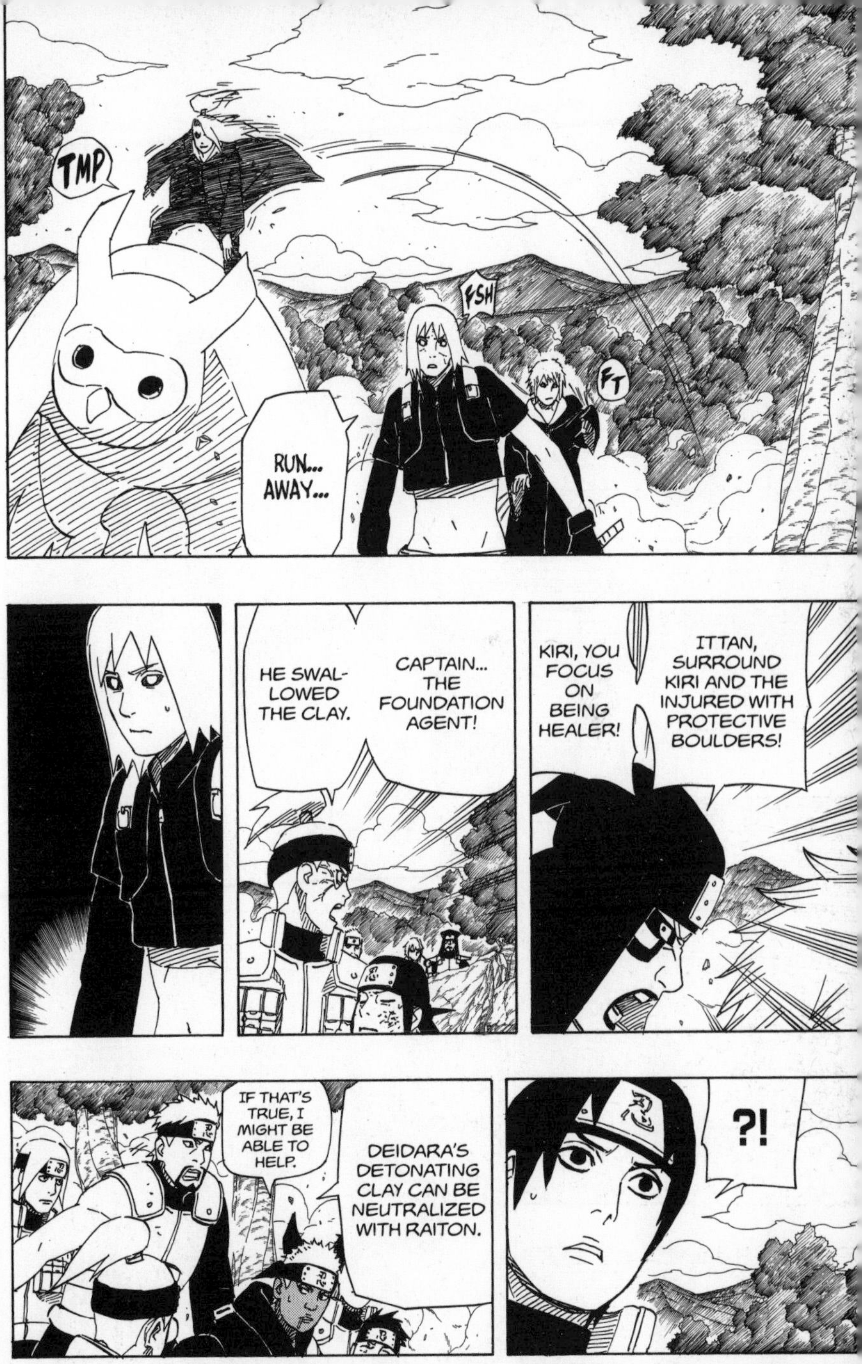
TMP
FSH
FT
RUN... AWAY...
ITTAN, SURROUND KIRI AND THE INJURED WITH PROTECTIVE BOULDERS!
KIRI, YOU FOCUS ON BEING HEALER!
CAPTAIN... THE FOUNDATION AGENT!
HE SWAL-LOWED THE CLAY.
?!
DEIDARA'S DETONATING CLAY CAN BE NEUTRALIZED WITH RAITON.
IF THAT'S TRUE, I MIGHT BE ABLE TO HELP.

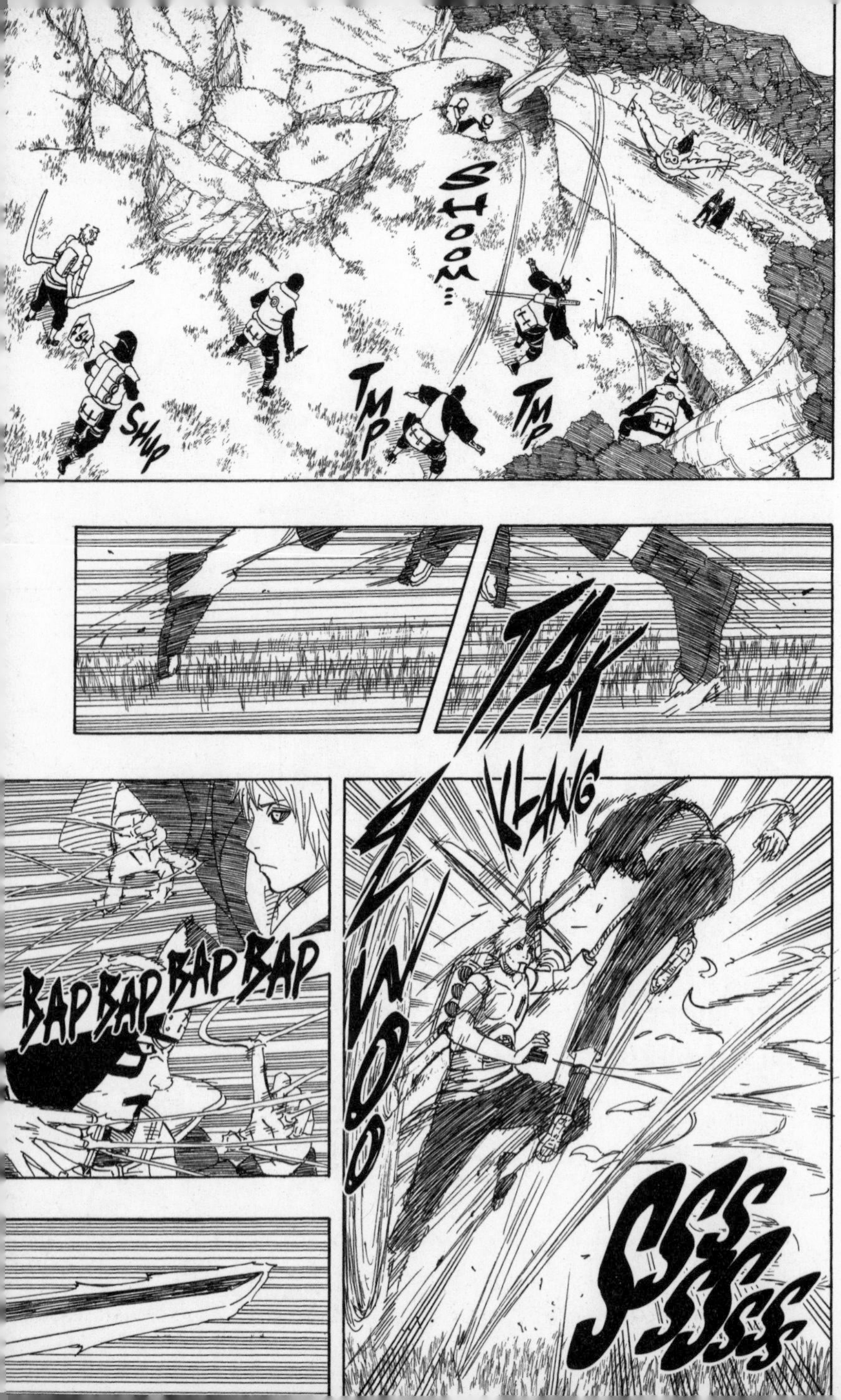
SHOOM...
TMP
TMP
FSH
SHUP
TAK
KLANG
ZWOOO
SSSSSS
BAP BAP BAP BAP

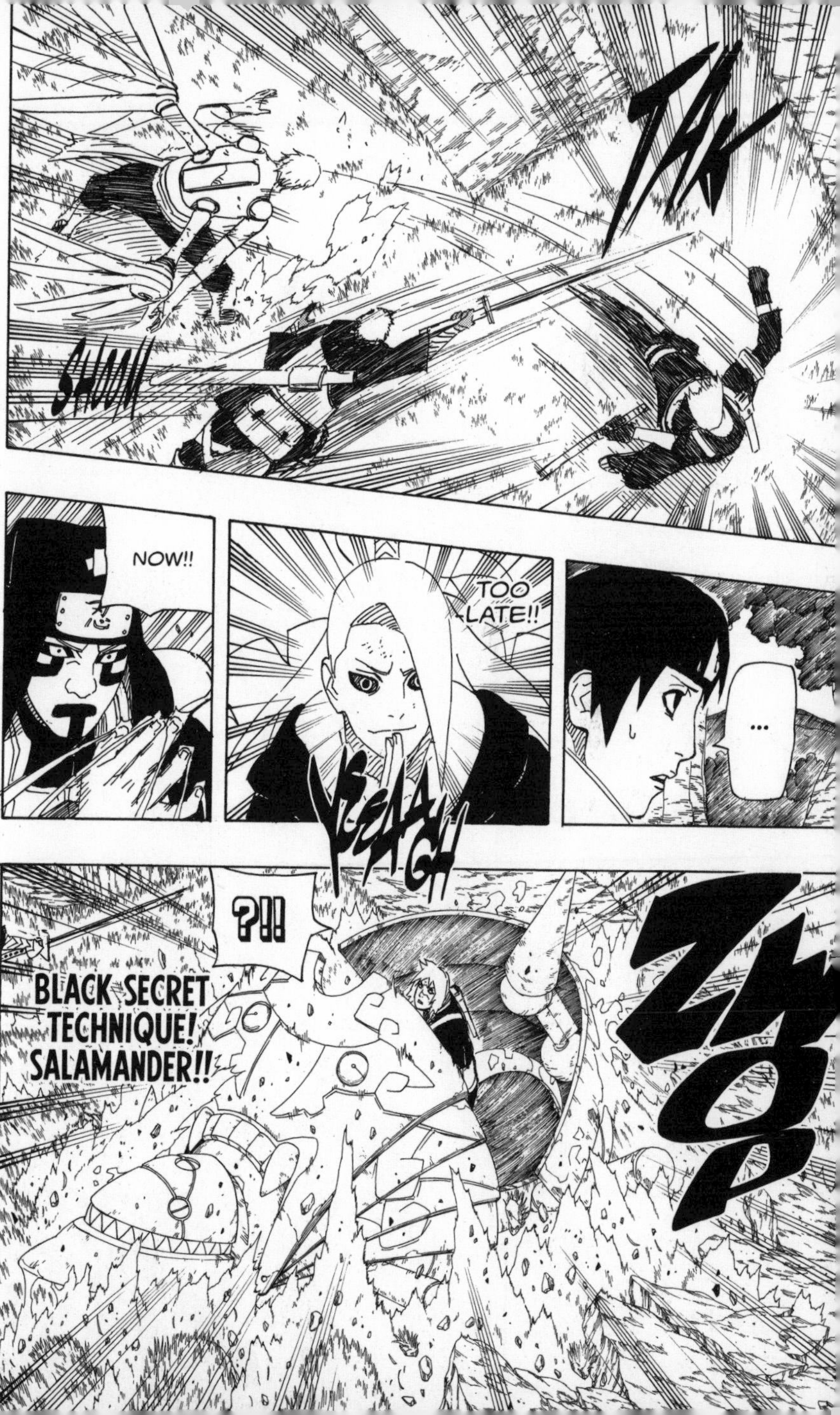
TAK
SHUUN
...
TOO LATE!!
NOW!!
YEAAAGH
?!!
BLACK SECRET TECHNIQUE! SALAMANDER!!

READ THIS WAY

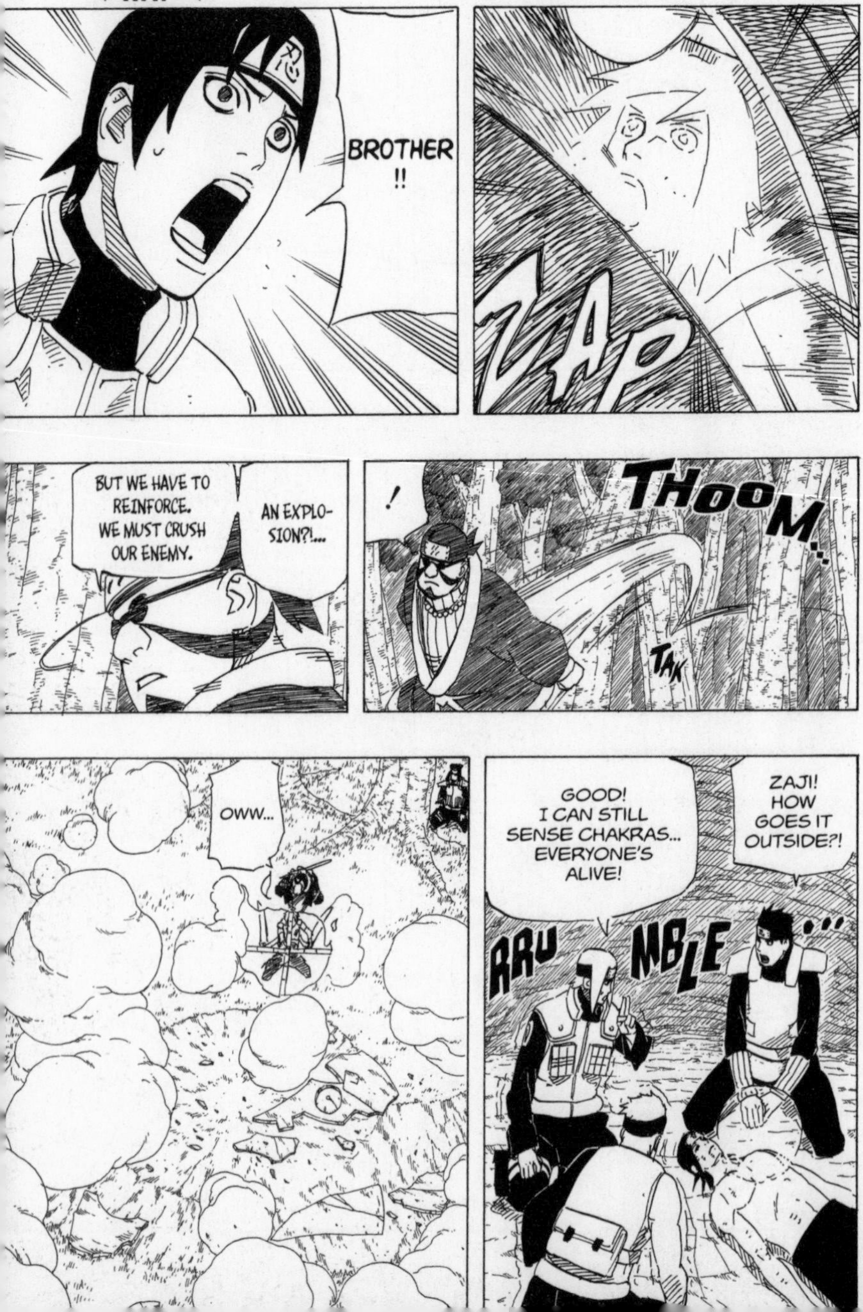
ZAP
BROTHER!!
THOOM...
!
TAK
AN EXPLOSION?!...
BUT WE HAVE TO REINFORCE. WE MUST CRUSH OUR ENEMY.
ZAJI! HOW GOES IT OUTSIDE?!
GOOD! I CAN STILL SENSE CHAKRAS... EVERYONE'S ALIVE!
RRUMBLE...
OWW...

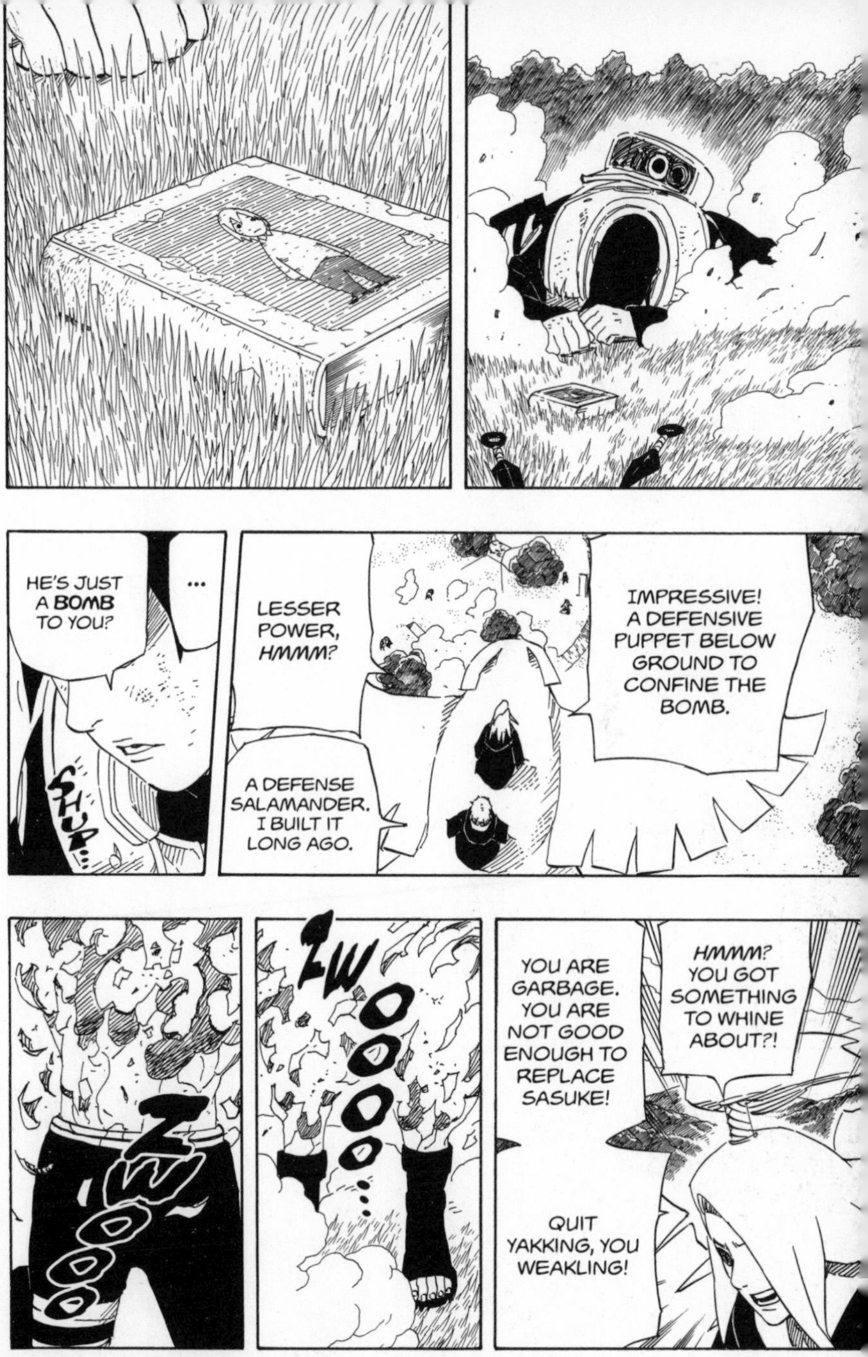
IMPRESSIVE! A DEFENSIVE PUPPET BELOW GROUND TO CONFINE THE BOMB.
LESSER POWER, HMMM?
A DEFENSE SALAMANDER. I BUILT IT LONG AGO.
...
HE'S JUST A **BOMB** TO YOU?
SHUP...
HMMM? YOU GOT SOMETHING TO WHINE ABOUT?!
YOU ARE GARBAGE. YOU ARE NOT GOOD ENOUGH TO REPLACE SASUKE!
QUIT YAKKING, YOU WEAKLING!
ZWOOOOOO...
ZWOOOO

READ THIS WAY

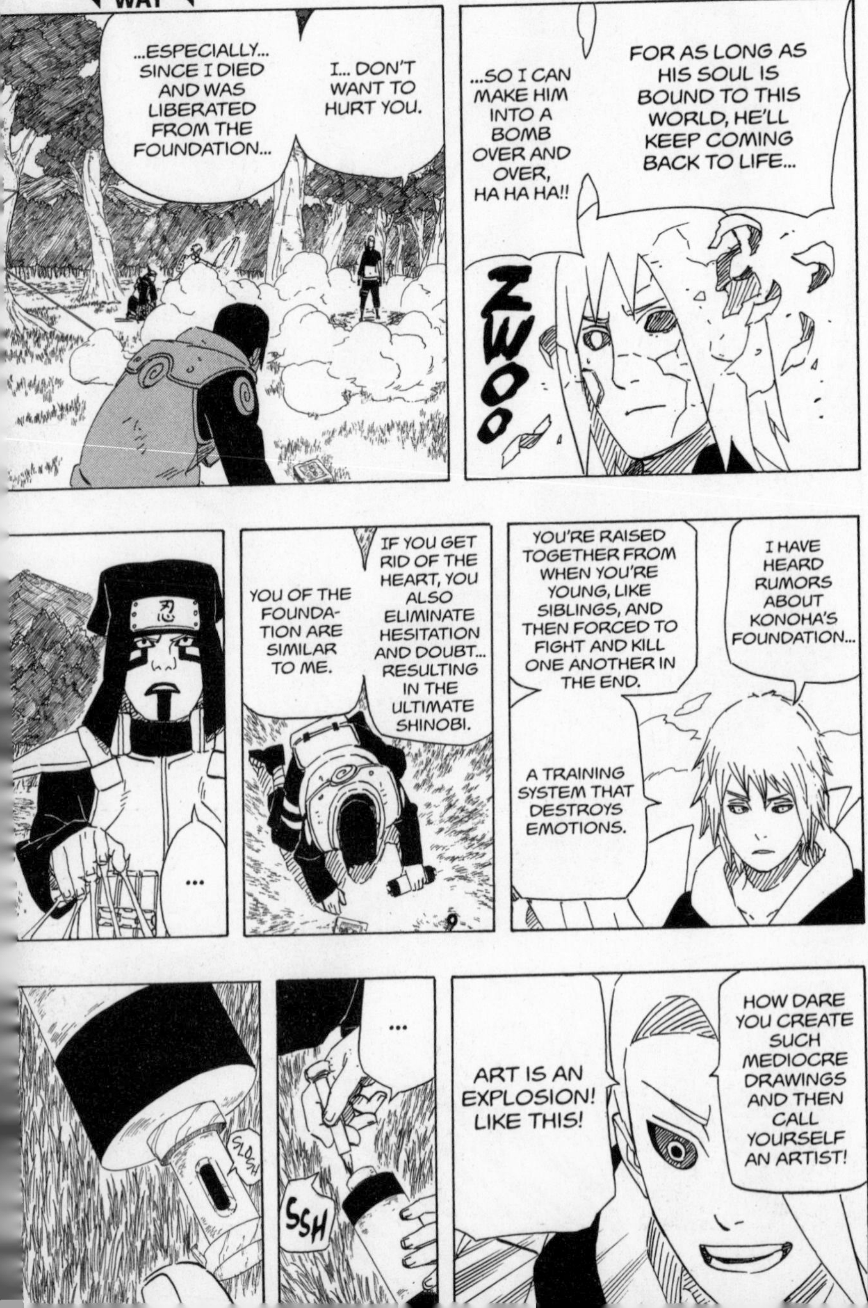
FOR AS LONG AS HIS SOUL IS BOUND TO THIS WORLD, HE'LL KEEP COMING BACK TO LIFE...
...SO I CAN MAKE HIM INTO A BOMB OVER AND OVER, HA HA HA!!
ZWOO
I... DON'T WANT TO HURT YOU.
...ESPECIALLY... SINCE I DIED AND WAS LIBERATED FROM THE FOUNDATION...
I HAVE HEARD RUMORS ABOUT KONOHA'S FOUNDATION...
YOU'RE RAISED TOGETHER FROM WHEN YOU'RE YOUNG, LIKE SIBLINGS, AND THEN FORCED TO FIGHT AND KILL ONE ANOTHER IN THE END.
A TRAINING SYSTEM THAT DESTROYS EMOTIONS.
IF YOU GET RID OF THE HEART, YOU ALSO ELIMINATE HESITATION AND DOUBT... RESULTING IN THE ULTIMATE SHINOBI.
YOU OF THE FOUNDATION ARE SIMILAR TO ME.
...
HOW DARE YOU CREATE SUCH MEDIOCRE DRAWINGS AND THEN CALL YOURSELF AN ARTIST!
ART IS AN EXPLOSION! LIKE THIS!
...
SSH
SLOSH

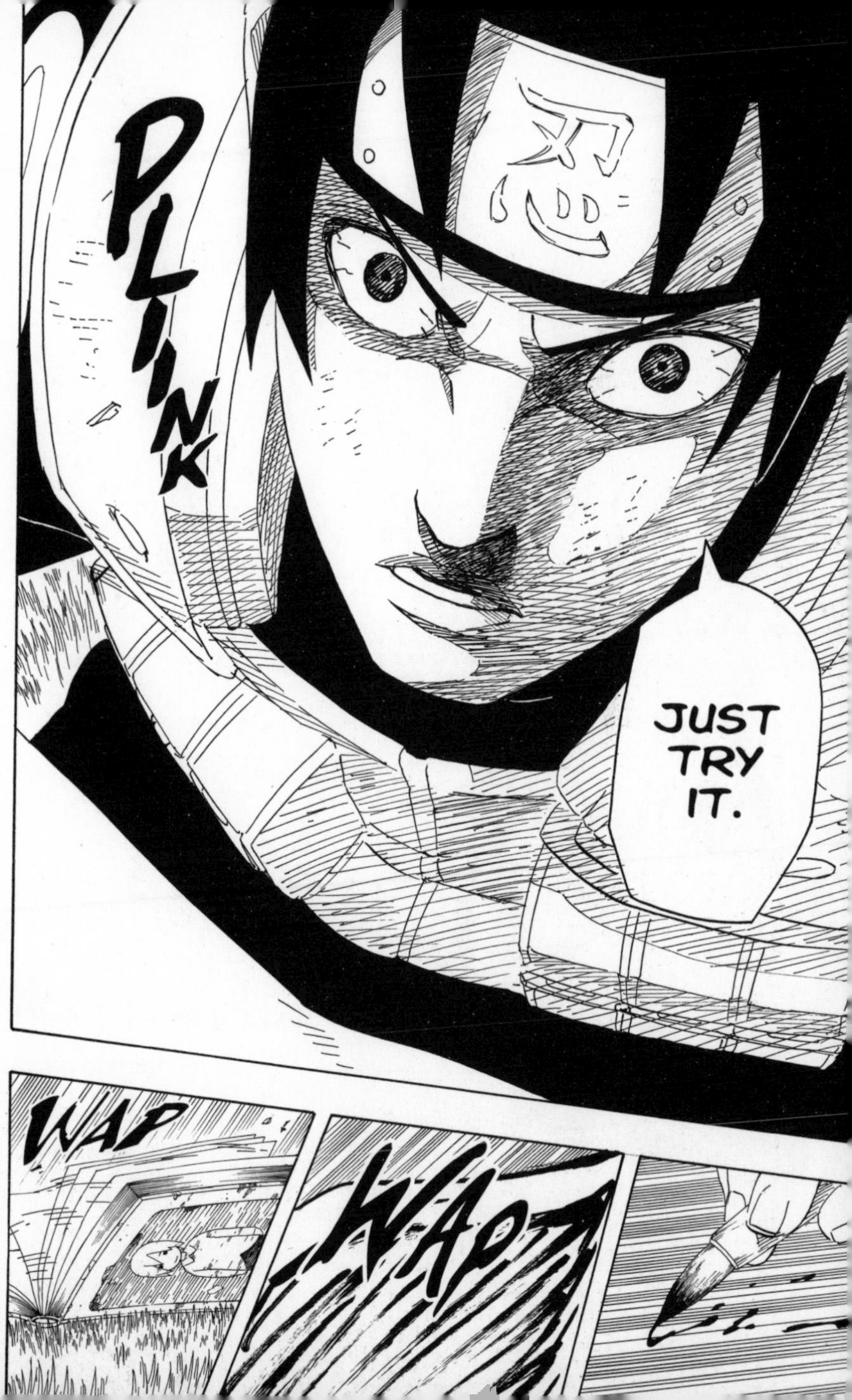
PLINK
JUST TRY IT.
WAP
WAP

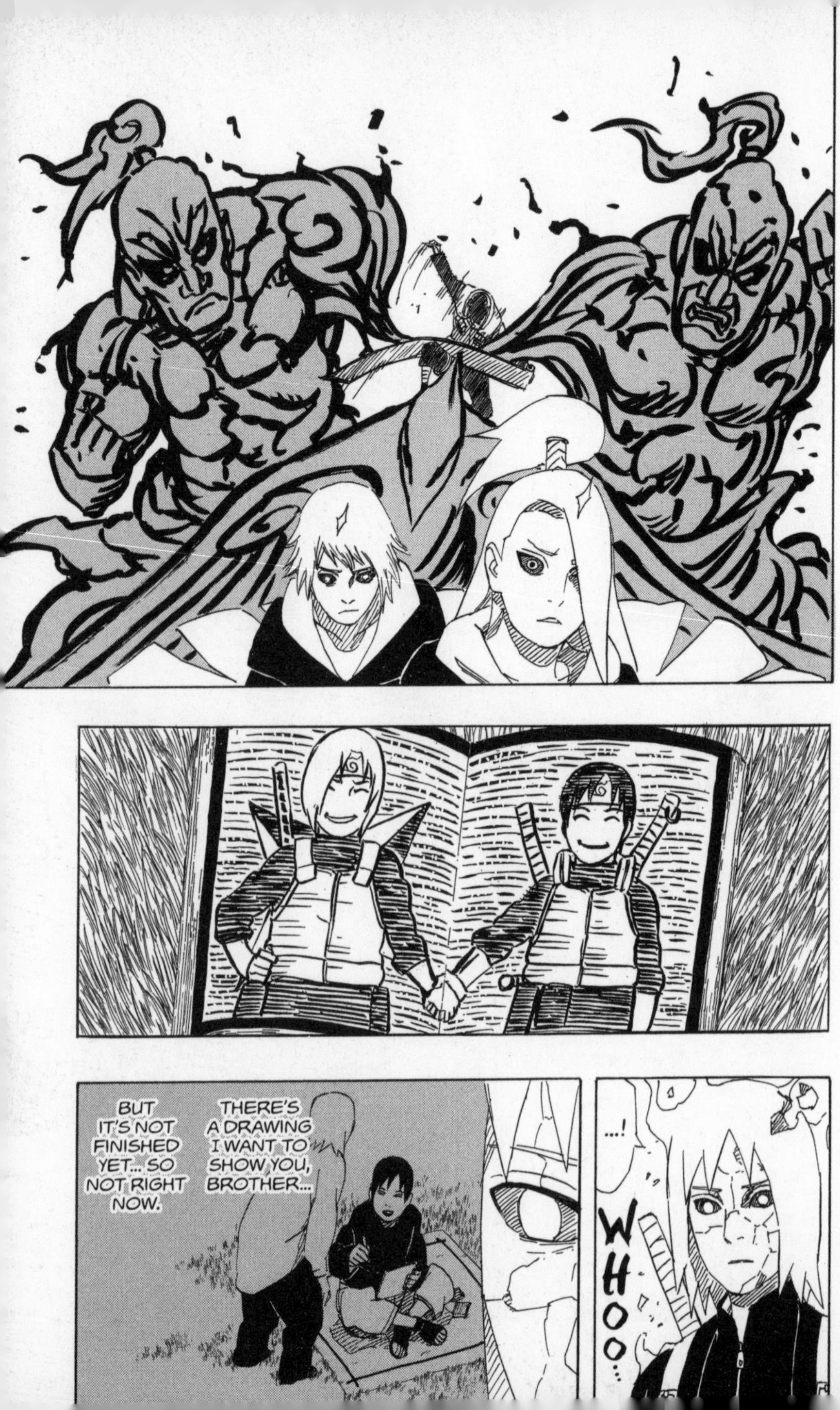
...!
WHOOO...
THERE'S A DRAWING I WANT TO SHOW YOU, BROTHER...
BUT IT'S NOT FINISHED YET... SO NOT RIGHT NOW.

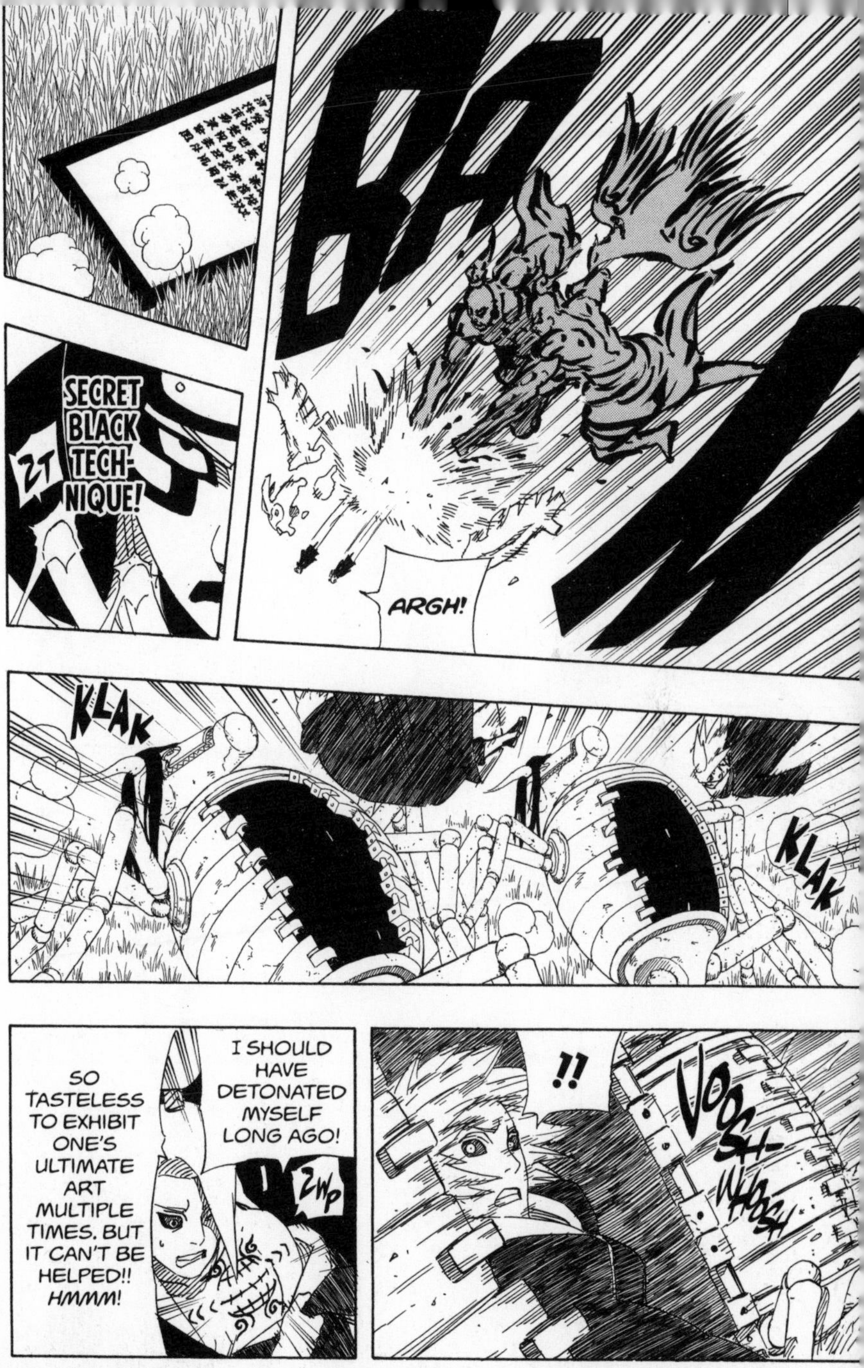
BAM
ARGH!
SECRET BLACK TECH-NIQUE!
ZT
KLAK
KLAK
!!
VOOSH
WHOOSH
I SHOULD HAVE DETONATED MYSELF LONG AGO!
SO TASTELESS TO EXHIBIT ONE'S ULTIMATE ART MULTIPLE TIMES. BUT IT CAN'T BE HELPED!! HMMM!
ZWP

READ THIS WAY

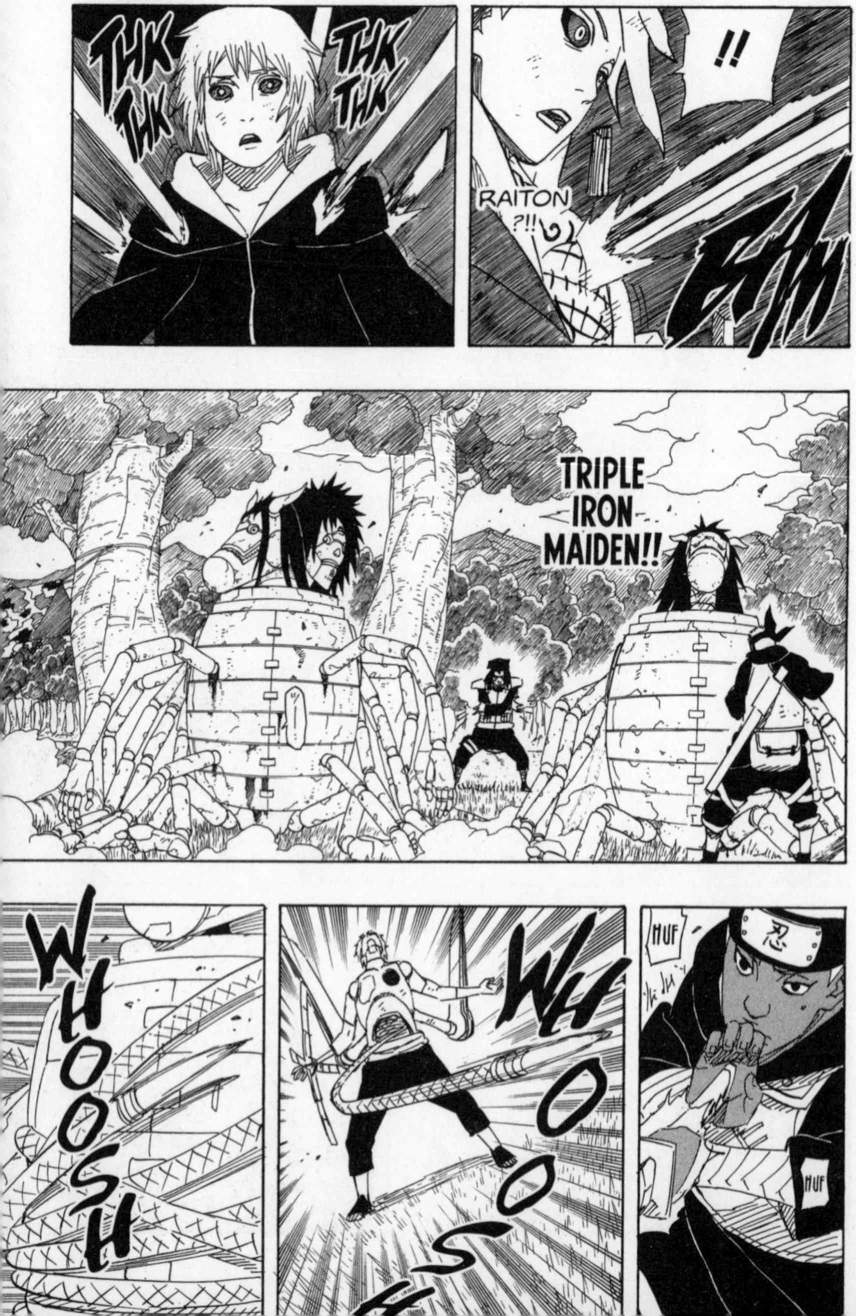
!!
RAITON ?!!
THK THK
THK THK
TRIPLE IRON MAIDEN!!
HUF
HUF
WHOOSH
WHOOSH

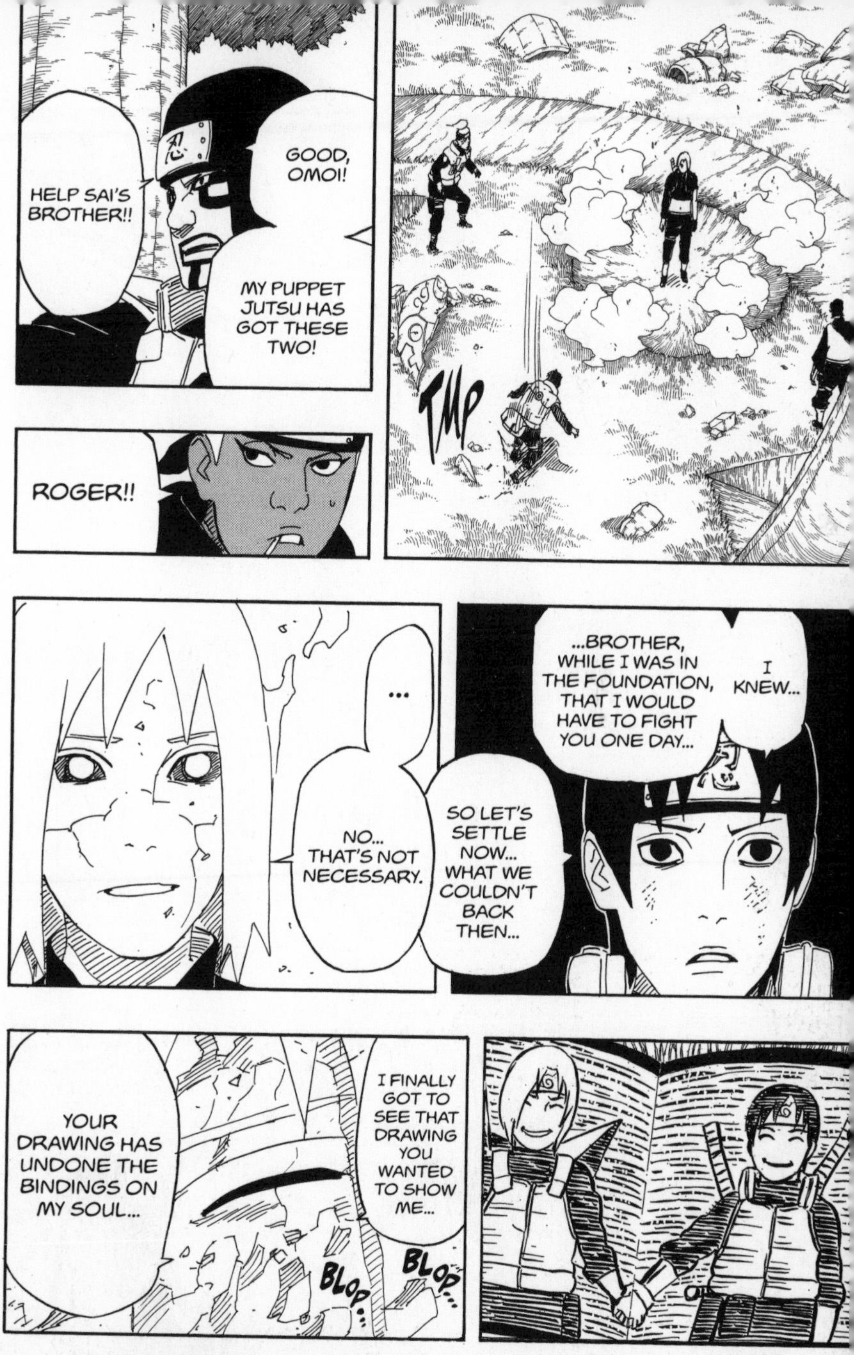
TMP
GOOD, OMOI!
MY PUPPET JUTSU HAS GOT THESE TWO!
HELP SAI'S BROTHER!!
ROGER!!
I KNEW...
...BROTHER, WHILE I WAS IN THE FOUNDATION, THAT I WOULD HAVE TO FIGHT YOU ONE DAY...
SO LET'S SETTLE NOW... WHAT WE COULDN'T BACK THEN...
...
NO... THAT'S NOT NECESSARY.
I FINALLY GOT TO SEE THAT DRAWING YOU WANTED TO SHOW ME...
BLOP...
BLOP...
YOUR DRAWING HAS UNDONE THE BINDINGS ON MY SOUL...

READ THIS WAY

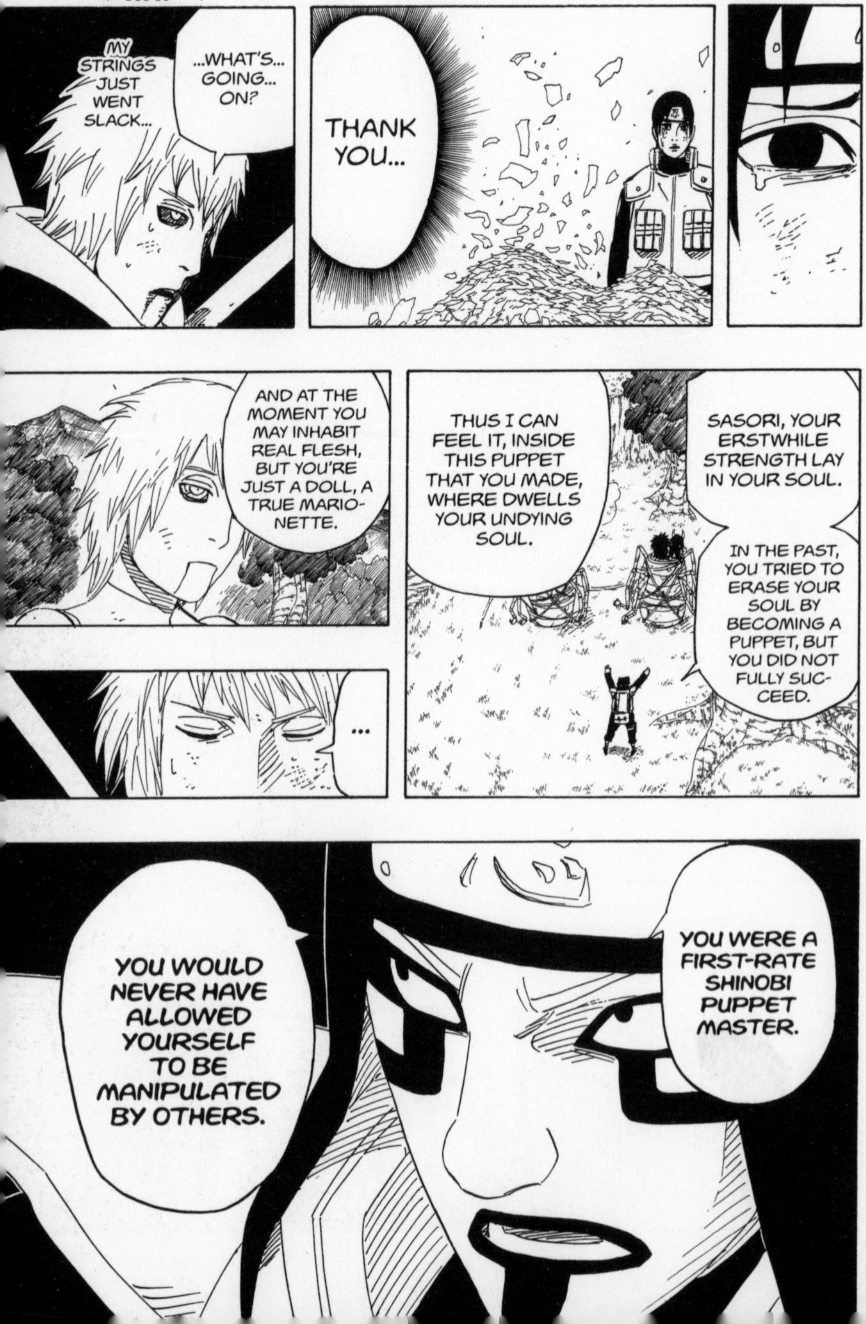
THANK YOU...
...WHAT'S... GOING... ON?
MY STRINGS JUST WENT SLACK...
SASORI, YOUR ERSTWHILE STRENGTH LAY IN YOUR SOUL.
IN THE PAST, YOU TRIED TO ERASE YOUR SOUL BY BECOMING A PUPPET, BUT YOU DID NOT FULLY SUC-CEED.
THUS I CAN FEEL IT, INSIDE THIS PUPPET THAT YOU MADE, WHERE DWELLS YOUR UNDYING SOUL.
AND AT THE MOMENT YOU MAY INHABIT REAL FLESH, BUT YOU'RE JUST A DOLL, A TRUE MARIO-NETTE.
...
YOU WERE A FIRST-RATE SHINOBI PUPPET MASTER.
YOU WOULD NEVER HAVE ALLOWED YOURSELF TO BE MANIPULATED BY OTHERS.

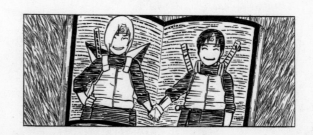

Number 519: The Biju Bomb

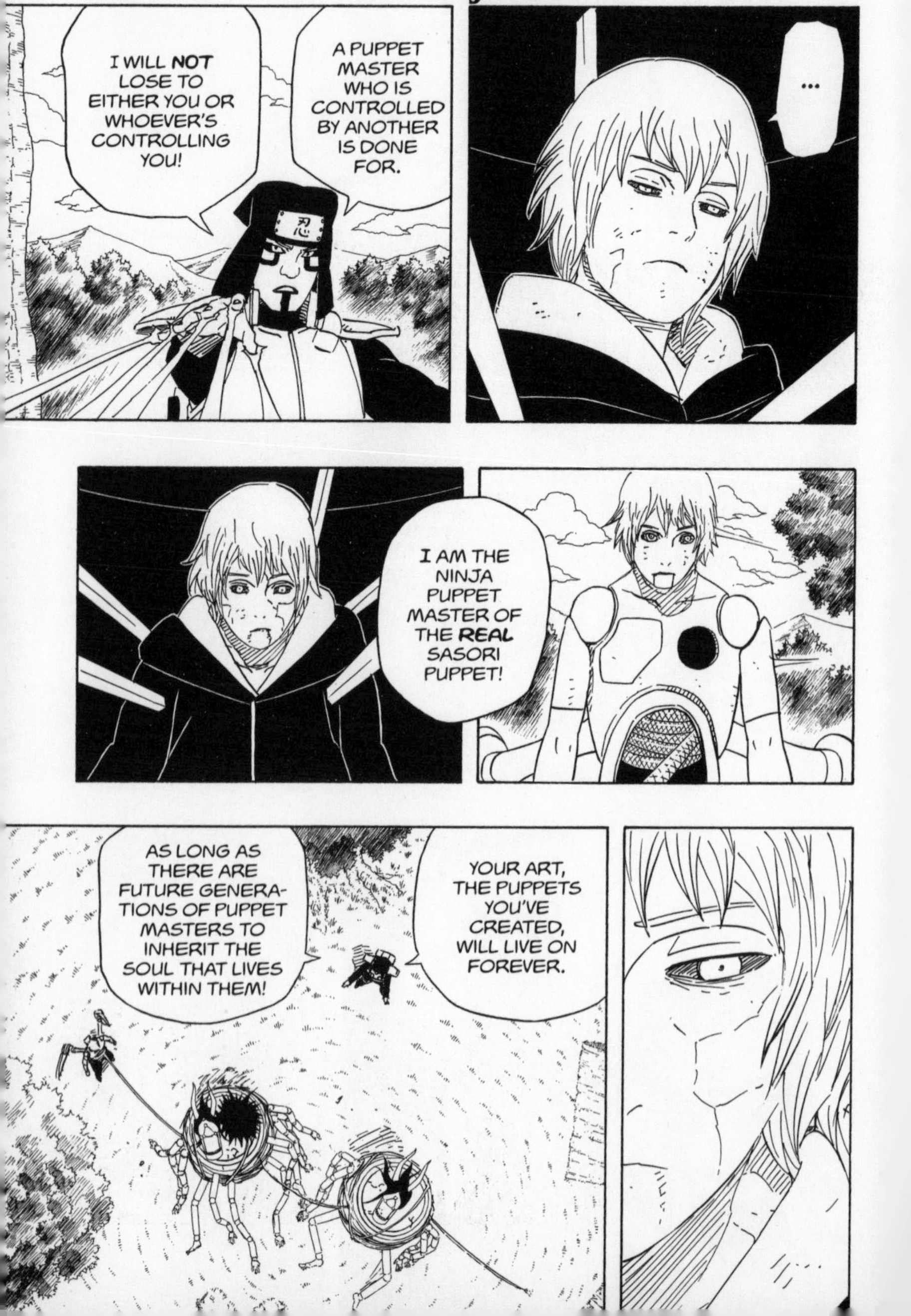
...
A PUPPET MASTER WHO IS CONTROLLED BY ANOTHER IS DONE FOR.
I WILL NOT LOSE TO EITHER YOU OR WHOEVER'S CONTROLLING YOU!
I AM THE NINJA PUPPET MASTER OF THE REAL SASORI PUPPET!
YOUR ART, THE PUPPETS YOU'VE CREATED, WILL LIVE ON FOREVER.
AS LONG AS THERE ARE FUTURE GENERA-TIONS OF PUPPET MASTERS TO INHERIT THE SOUL THAT LIVES WITHIN THEM!

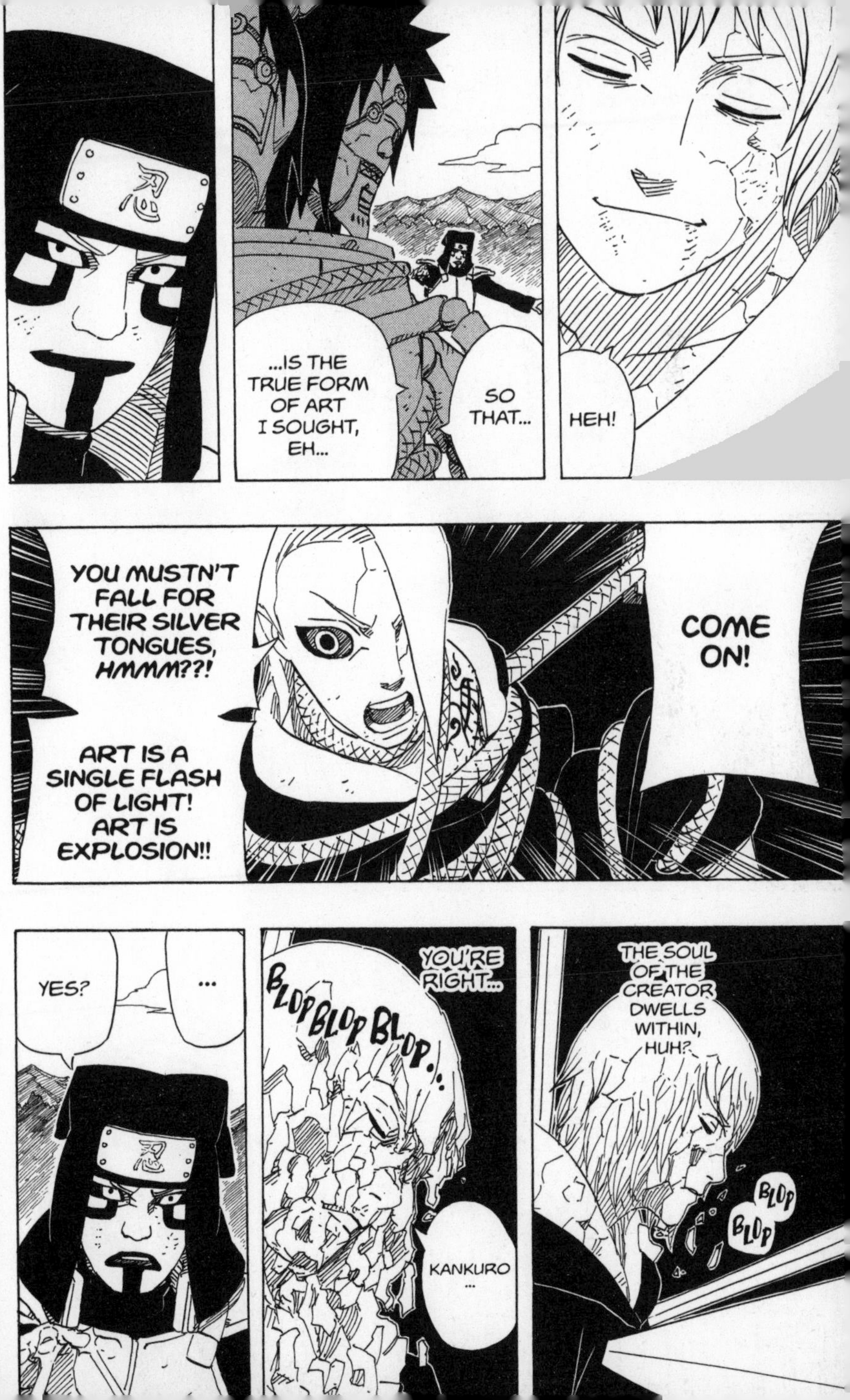
HEH!
SO THAT...
...IS THE TRUE FORM OF ART I SOUGHT, EH...
COME ON!
YOU MUSTN'T FALL FOR THEIR SILVER TONGUES, HMMM??!
ART IS A SINGLE FLASH OF LIGHT! ART IS EXPLOSION!!
THE SOUL OF THE CREATOR DWELLS WITHIN, HUH?
BLOP BLOP
YOU'RE RIGHT...
BLOP BLOP BLOP...
KANKURO ...
...
YES?

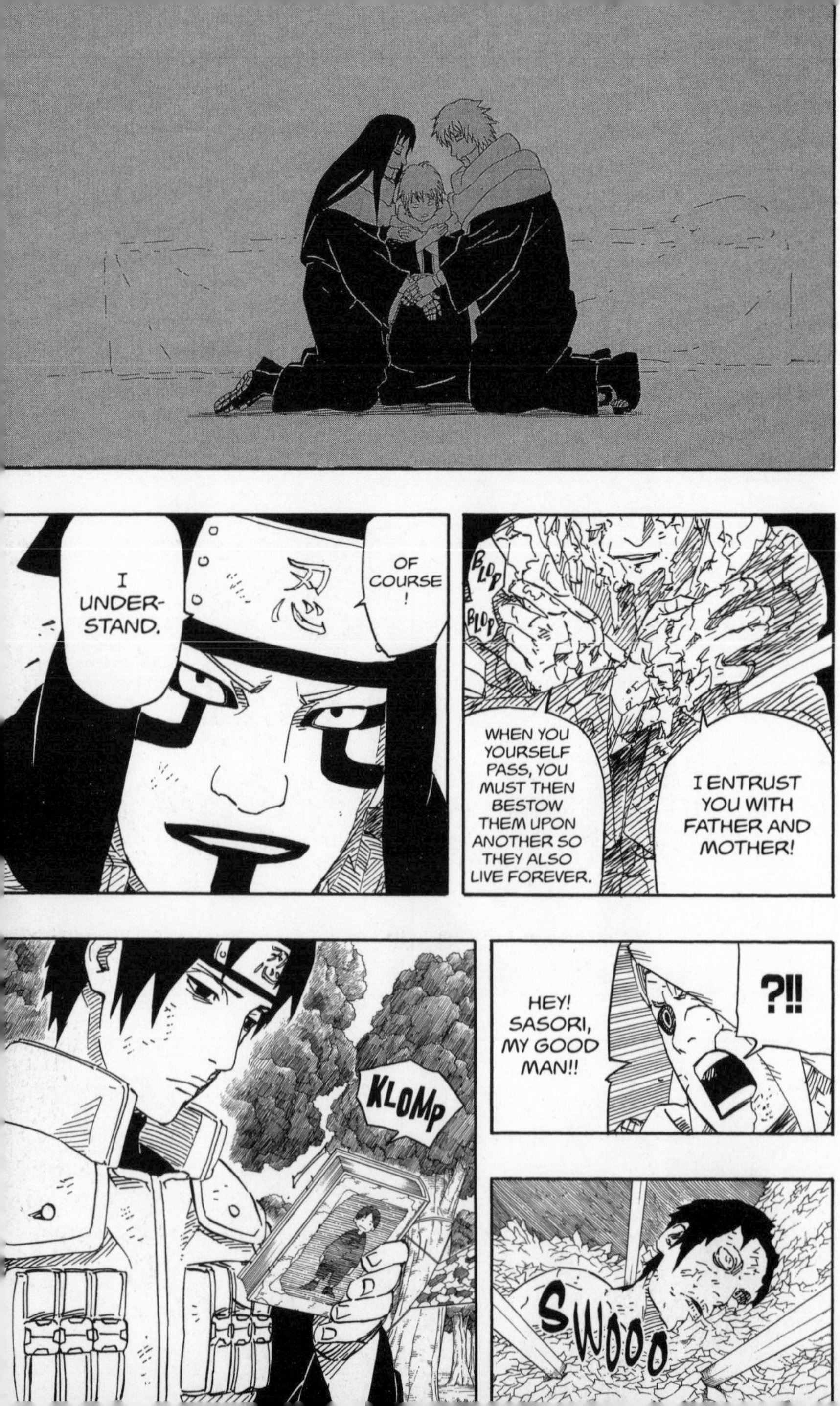
BLOP
BLOP
I ENTRUST YOU WITH FATHER AND MOTHER!
WHEN YOU YOURSELF PASS, YOU MUST THEN BESTOW THEM UPON ANOTHER SO THEY ALSO LIVE FOREVER.
OF COURSE!
I UNDERSTAND.
?!!
HEY! SASORI, MY GOOD MAN!!
SWOOO
KLOMP

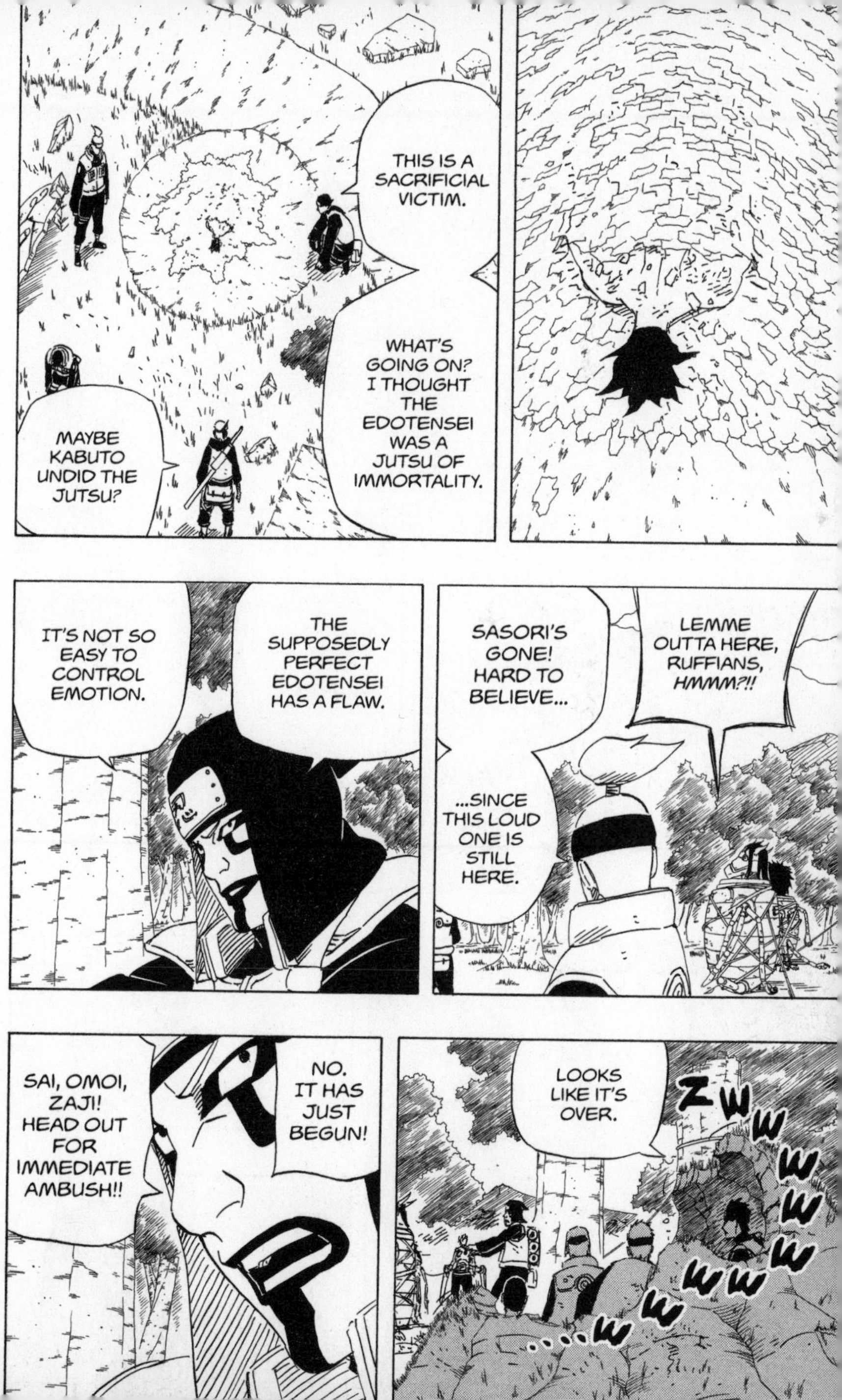
THIS IS A SACRIFICIAL VICTIM.
WHAT'S GOING ON? I THOUGHT THE EDOTENSEI WAS A JUTSU OF IMMORTALITY.
MAYBE KABUTO UNDID THE JUTSU?
LEMME OUTTA HERE, RUFFIANS, *HMMM?!!*
SASORI'S GONE! HARD TO BELIEVE...
...SINCE THIS LOUD ONE IS STILL HERE.
THE SUPPOSEDLY PERFECT EDOTENSEI HAS A FLAW.
IT'S NOT SO EASY TO CONTROL EMOTION.
LOOKS LIKE IT'S OVER.
ZWWWWWWWWWWW...
NO. IT HAS JUST BEGUN!
SAI, OMOI, ZAJI! HEAD OUT FOR IMMEDIATE AMBUSH!!

READ THIS WAY

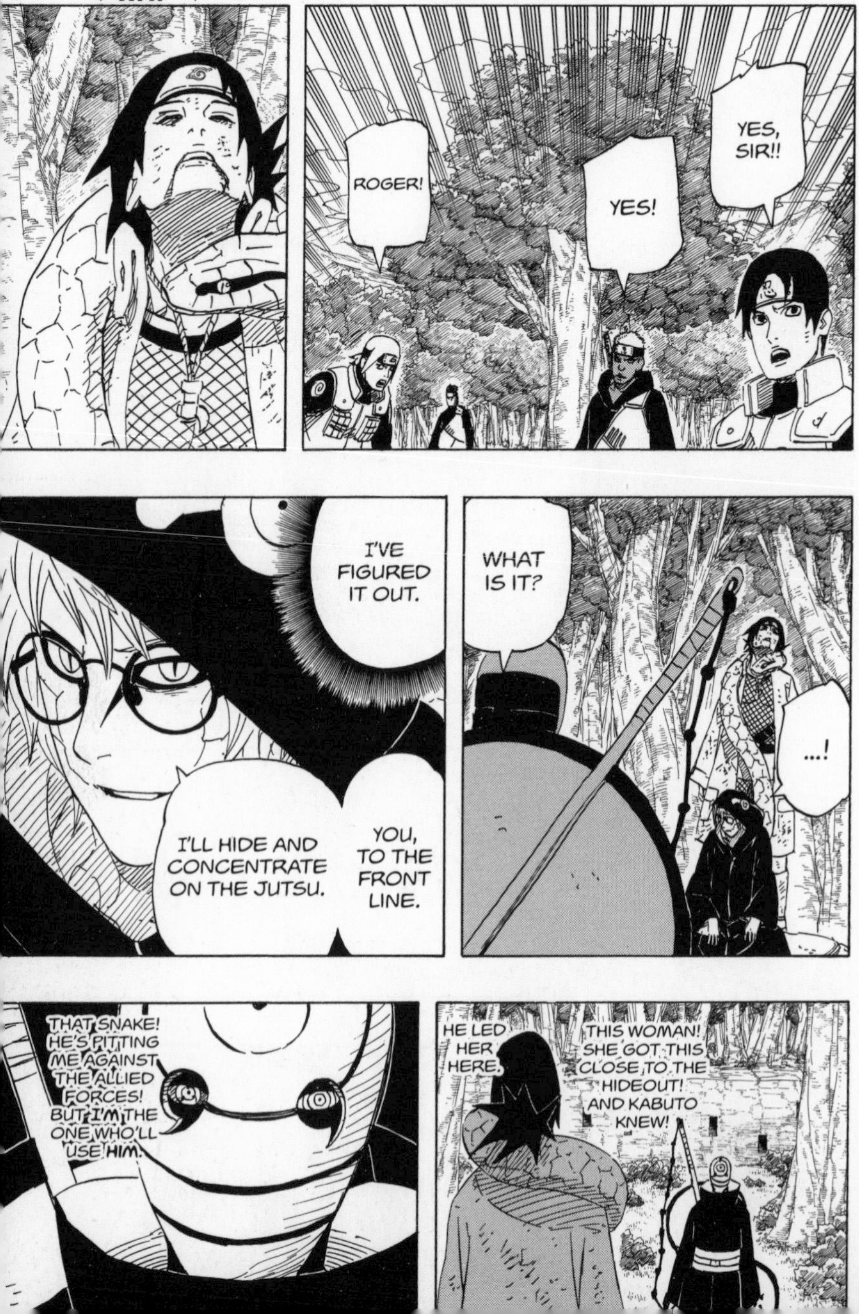
YES, SIR!!
YES!
ROGER!
WHAT IS IT?
...!
I'VE FIGURED IT OUT.
YOU, TO THE FRONT LINE.
I'LL HIDE AND CONCENTRATE ON THE JUTSU.
THIS WOMAN! SHE GOT THIS CLOSE TO THE HIDEOUT! AND KABUTO KNEW!
HE LED HER HERE.
THAT SNAKE! HE'S PITTING ME AGAINST THE ALLIED FORCES! BUT I'M THE ONE WHO'LL USE HIM.

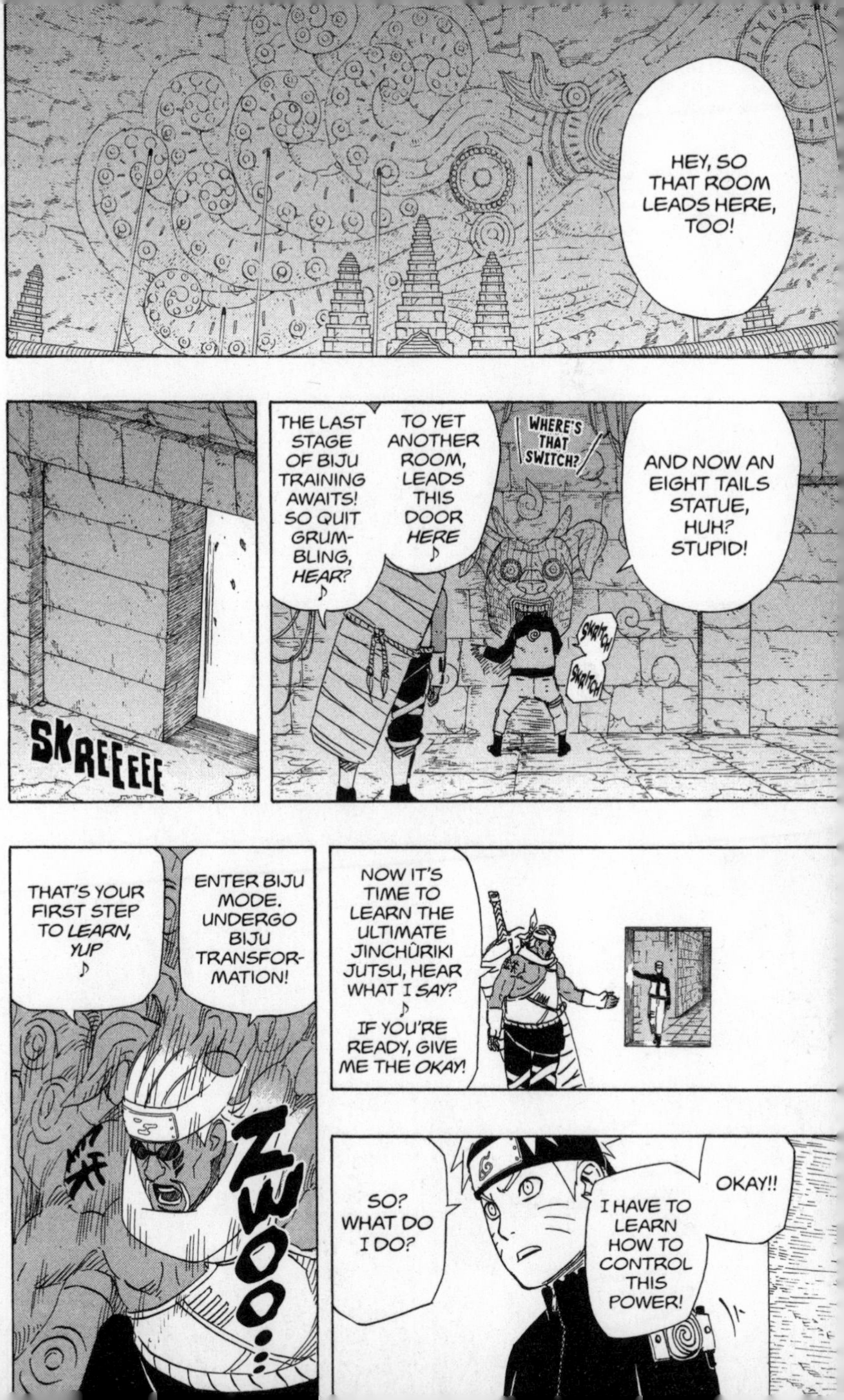
HEY, SO THAT ROOM LEADS HERE, TOO!
AND NOW AN EIGHT TAILS STATUE, HUH? STUPID!
WHERE'S THAT SWITCH?
SKRITCH
SKRITCH
TO YET ANOTHER ROOM, LEADS THIS DOOR HERE ♪
THE LAST STAGE OF BIJU TRAINING AWAITS! SO QUIT GRUM-BLING, HEAR? ♪
SKREEEEE
NOW IT'S TIME TO LEARN THE ULTIMATE JINCHÛRIKI JUTSU, HEAR WHAT I SAY? ♪
IF YOU'RE READY, GIVE ME THE OKAY!
OKAY!!
I HAVE TO LEARN HOW TO CONTROL THIS POWER!
SO? WHAT DO I DO?
ENTER BIJU MODE. UNDERGO BIJU TRANSFOR-MATION!
THAT'S YOUR FIRST STEP TO LEARN, YUP ♪
ZWOO...

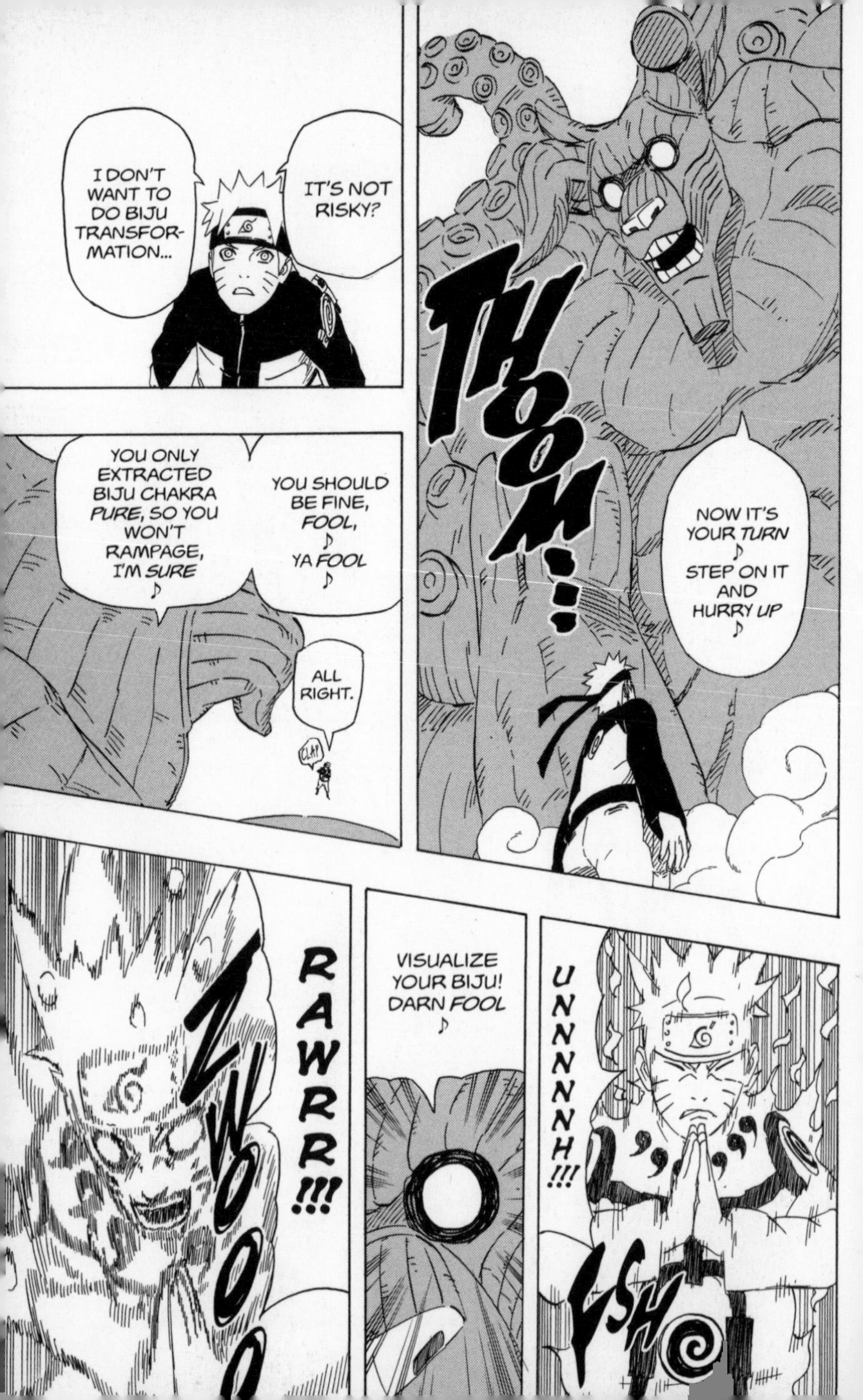
THOOM!!!
NOW IT'S YOUR TURN ♪ STEP ON IT AND HURRY UP ♪
IT'S NOT RISKY?
I DON'T WANT TO DO BIJU TRANSFORMATION...
YOU SHOULD BE FINE, FOOL, ♪ YA FOOL ♪
YOU ONLY EXTRACTED BIJU CHAKRA PURE, SO YOU WON'T RAMPAGE, I'M SURE ♪
ALL RIGHT.
CLAP
UNNNNNH!!!
VSH
VISUALIZE YOUR BIJU! DARN FOOL ♪
RAWRR!!!

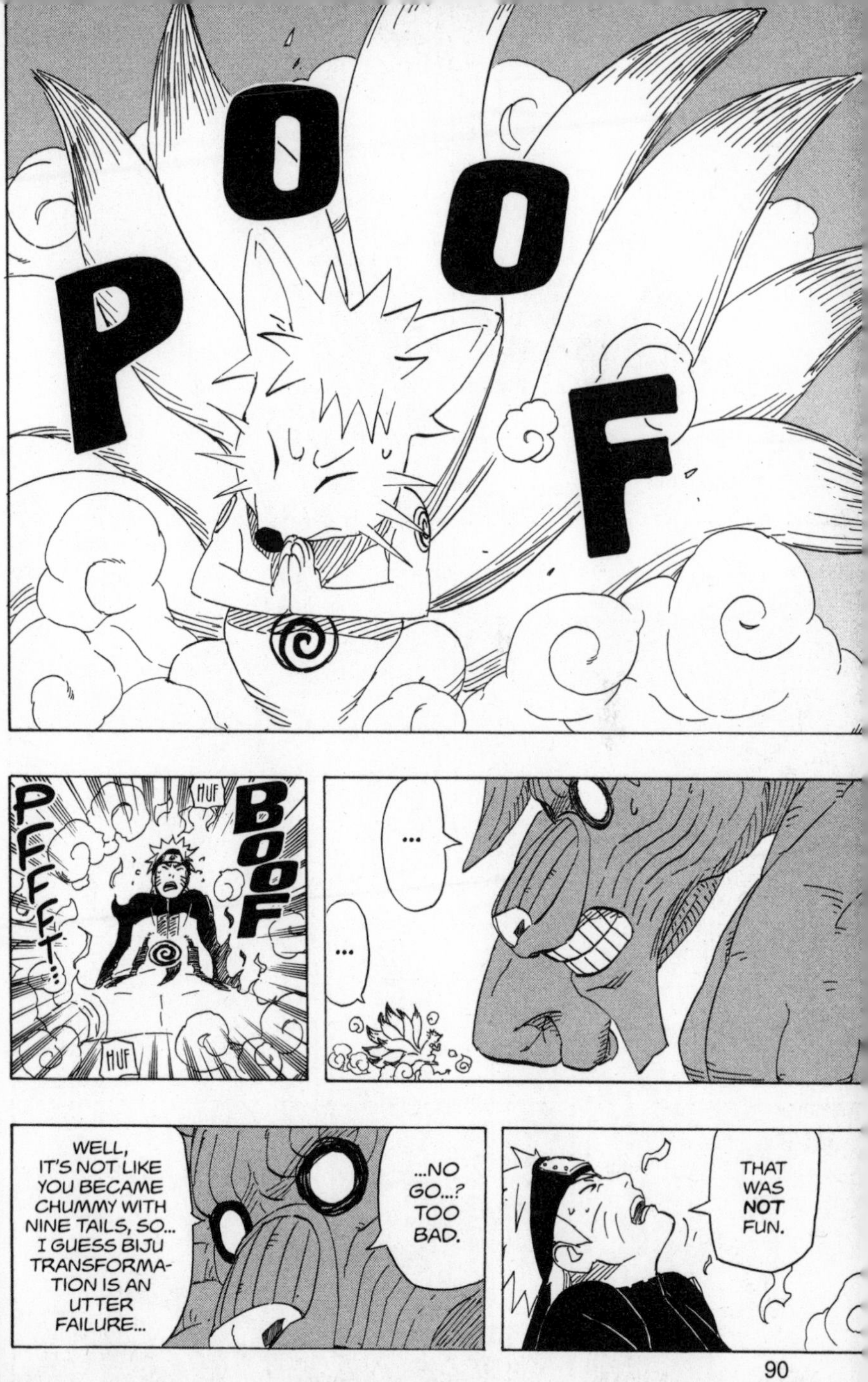
POOF
...
...
PFFFT...
BOOF
HUF
HUF
THAT WAS **NOT** FUN.
...NO GO...? TOO BAD.
WELL, IT'S NOT LIKE YOU BECAME CHUMMY WITH NINE TAILS, SO... I GUESS BIJU TRANSFORMATION IS AN UTTER FAILURE...

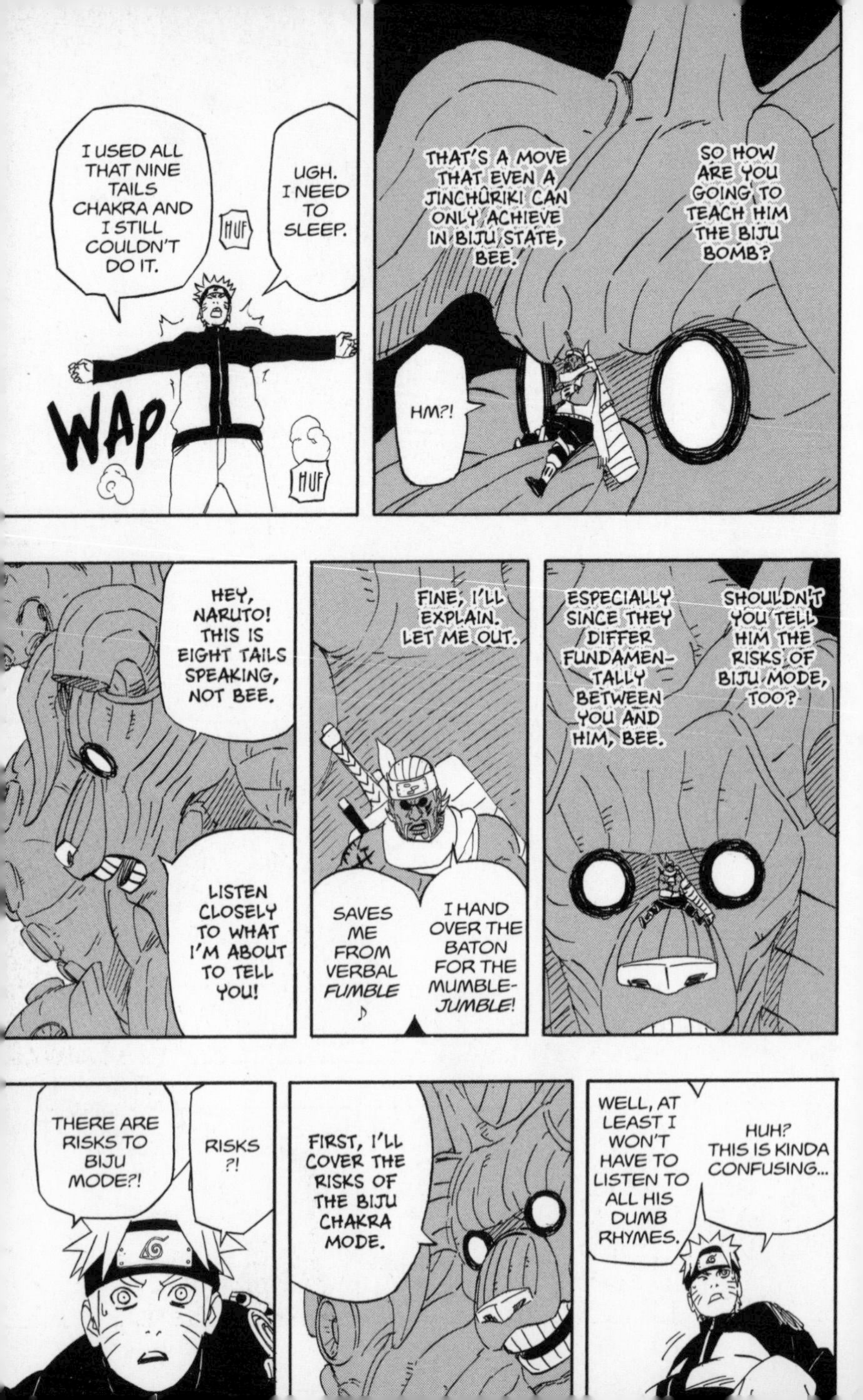
SO HOW ARE YOU GOING TO TEACH HIM THE BIJU BOMB?
THAT'S A MOVE THAT EVEN A JINCHÛRIKI CAN ONLY ACHIEVE IN BIJU STATE, BEE.
HM?!
UGH. I NEED TO SLEEP.
I USED ALL THAT NINE TAILS CHAKRA AND I STILL COULDN'T DO IT.
HUF
WAP
HUF
SHOULDN'T YOU TELL HIM THE RISKS OF BIJU MODE, TOO?
ESPECIALLY SINCE THEY DIFFER FUNDAMENTALLY BETWEEN YOU AND HIM, BEE.
FINE, I'LL EXPLAIN. LET ME OUT.
I HAND OVER THE BATON FOR THE MUMBLE-JUMBLE!
SAVES ME FROM VERBAL *FUMBLE* ♪
HEY, NARUTO! THIS IS EIGHT TAILS SPEAKING, NOT BEE.
LISTEN CLOSELY TO WHAT I'M ABOUT TO TELL YOU!
HUH? THIS IS KINDA CONFUSING...
WELL, AT LEAST I WON'T HAVE TO LISTEN TO ALL HIS DUMB RHYMES.
FIRST, I'LL COVER THE RISKS OF THE BIJU CHAKRA MODE.
RISKS?!
THERE ARE RISKS TO BIJU MODE?!

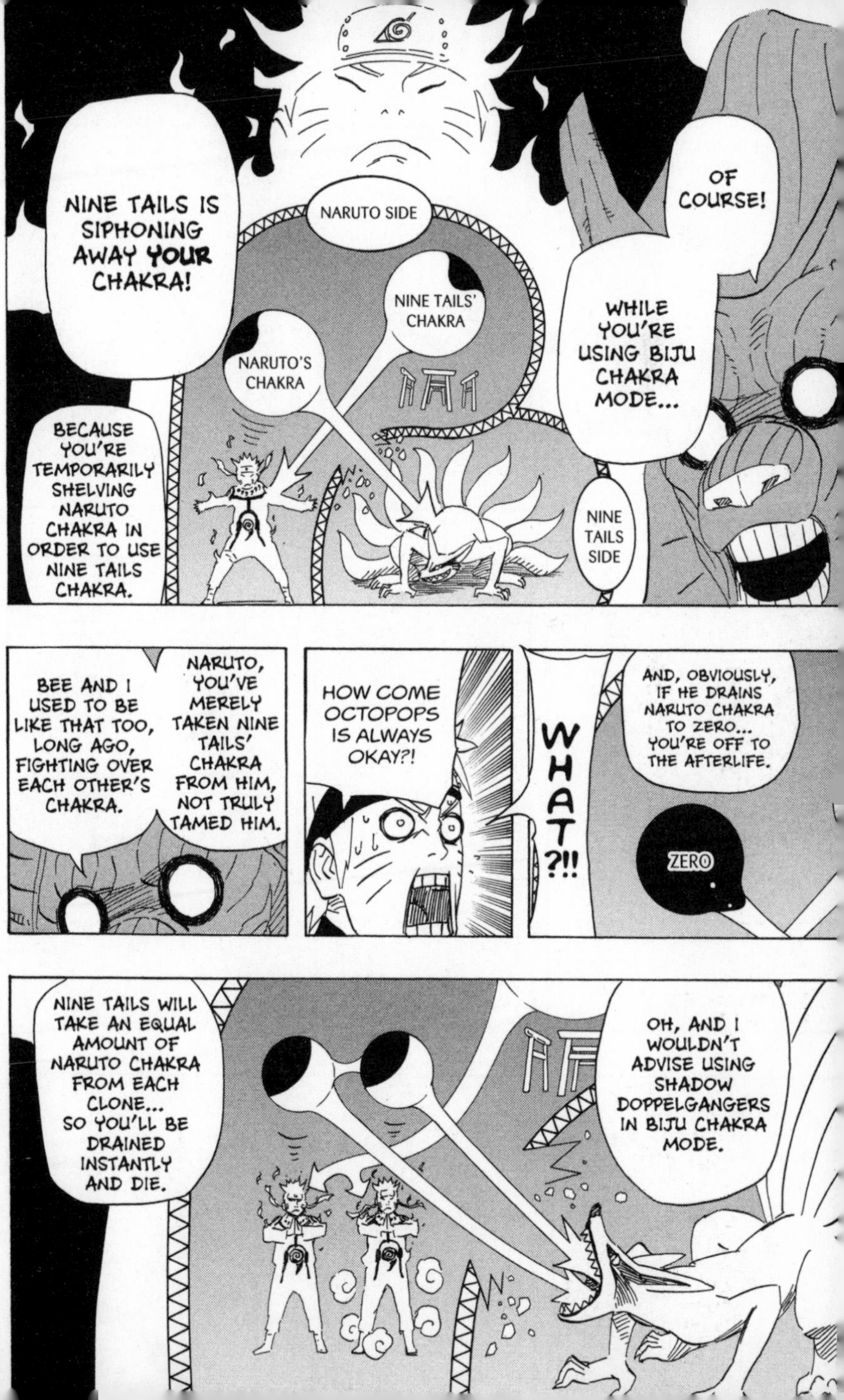
OF COURSE!
WHILE YOU'RE USING BIJU CHAKRA MODE...
NINE TAILS SIDE
NARUTO SIDE
NINE TAILS' CHAKRA
NARUTO'S CHAKRA
NINE TAILS IS SIPHONING AWAY YOUR CHAKRA!
BECAUSE YOU'RE TEMPORARILY SHELVING NARUTO CHAKRA IN ORDER TO USE NINE TAILS CHAKRA.
AND, OBVIOUSLY, IF HE DRAINS NARUTO CHAKRA TO ZERO... YOU'RE OFF TO THE AFTERLIFE.
ZERO
WHAT?!!
HOW COME OCTOPOPS IS ALWAYS OKAY?!
NARUTO, YOU'VE MERELY TAKEN NINE TAILS' CHAKRA FROM HIM, NOT TRULY TAMED HIM.
BEE AND I USED TO BE LIKE THAT TOO, LONG AGO, FIGHTING OVER EACH OTHER'S CHAKRA.
OH, AND I WOULDN'T ADVISE USING SHADOW DOPPELGANGERS IN BIJU CHAKRA MODE.
NINE TAILS WILL TAKE AN EQUAL AMOUNT OF NARUTO CHAKRA FROM EACH CLONE... SO YOU'LL BE DRAINED INSTANTLY AND DIE.

READ THIS WAY

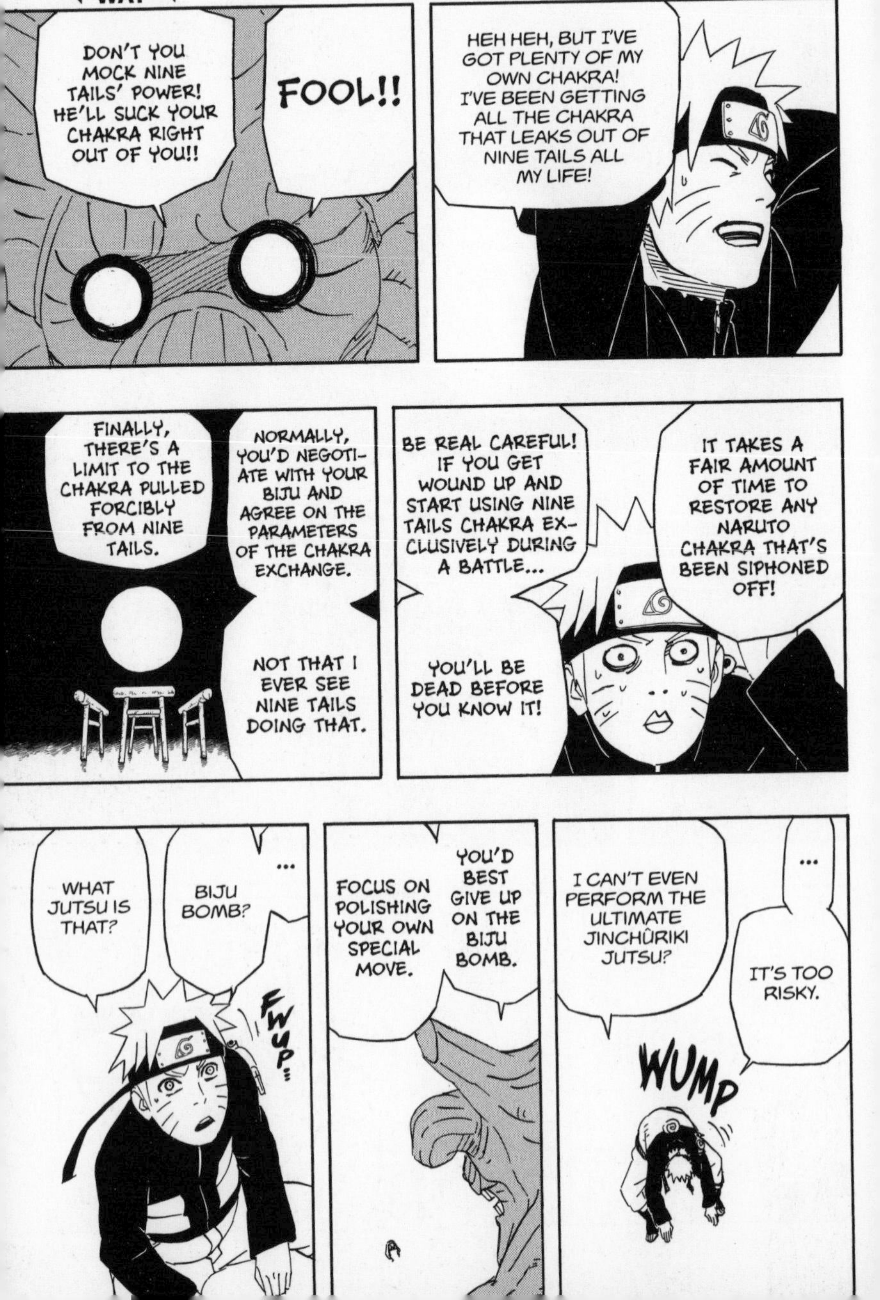

HEH HEH, BUT I'VE GOT PLENTY OF MY OWN CHAKRA! I'VE BEEN GETTING ALL THE CHAKRA THAT LEAKS OUT OF NINE TAILS ALL MY LIFE!
FOOL!!
DON'T YOU MOCK NINE TAILS' POWER! HE'LL SUCK YOUR CHAKRA RIGHT OUT OF YOU!!
IT TAKES A FAIR AMOUNT OF TIME TO RESTORE ANY NARUTO CHAKRA THAT'S BEEN SIPHONED OFF!
BE REAL CAREFUL! IF YOU GET WOUND UP AND START USING NINE TAILS CHAKRA EXCLUSIVELY DURING A BATTLE...
YOU'LL BE DEAD BEFORE YOU KNOW IT!
NORMALLY, YOU'D NEGOTIATE WITH YOUR BIJU AND AGREE ON THE PARAMETERS OF THE CHAKRA EXCHANGE.
NOT THAT I EVER SEE NINE TAILS DOING THAT.
FINALLY, THERE'S A LIMIT TO THE CHAKRA PULLED FORCIBLY FROM NINE TAILS.
...
I CAN'T EVEN PERFORM THE ULTIMATE JINCHÛRIKI JUTSU?
IT'S TOO RISKY.
WUMP
YOU'D BEST GIVE UP ON THE BIJU BOMB.
FOCUS ON POLISHING YOUR OWN SPECIAL MOVE.
...
BIJU BOMB?
WHAT JUTSU IS THAT?
FWUP

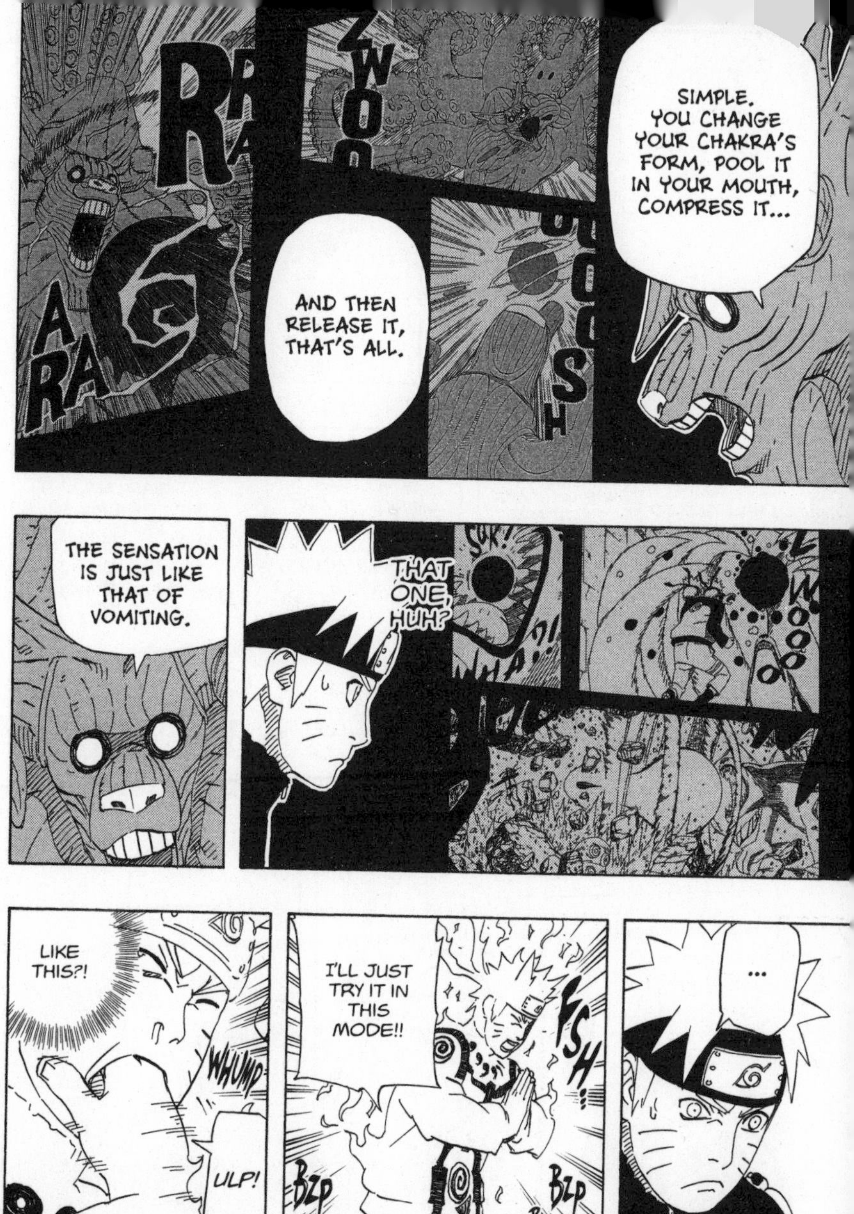
SIMPLE. YOU CHANGE YOUR CHAKRA'S FORM, POOL IT IN YOUR MOUTH, COMPRESS IT...
AND THEN RELEASE IT, THAT'S ALL.
ZWOO
SH
THE SENSATION IS JUST LIKE THAT OF VOMITING.
THAT ONE, HUH?
WHA?!
...
I'LL JUST TRY IT IN THIS MODE!!
FSH
BZP
BZP
BZP
LIKE THIS?!
WHUMP
ULP!

READ THIS WAY

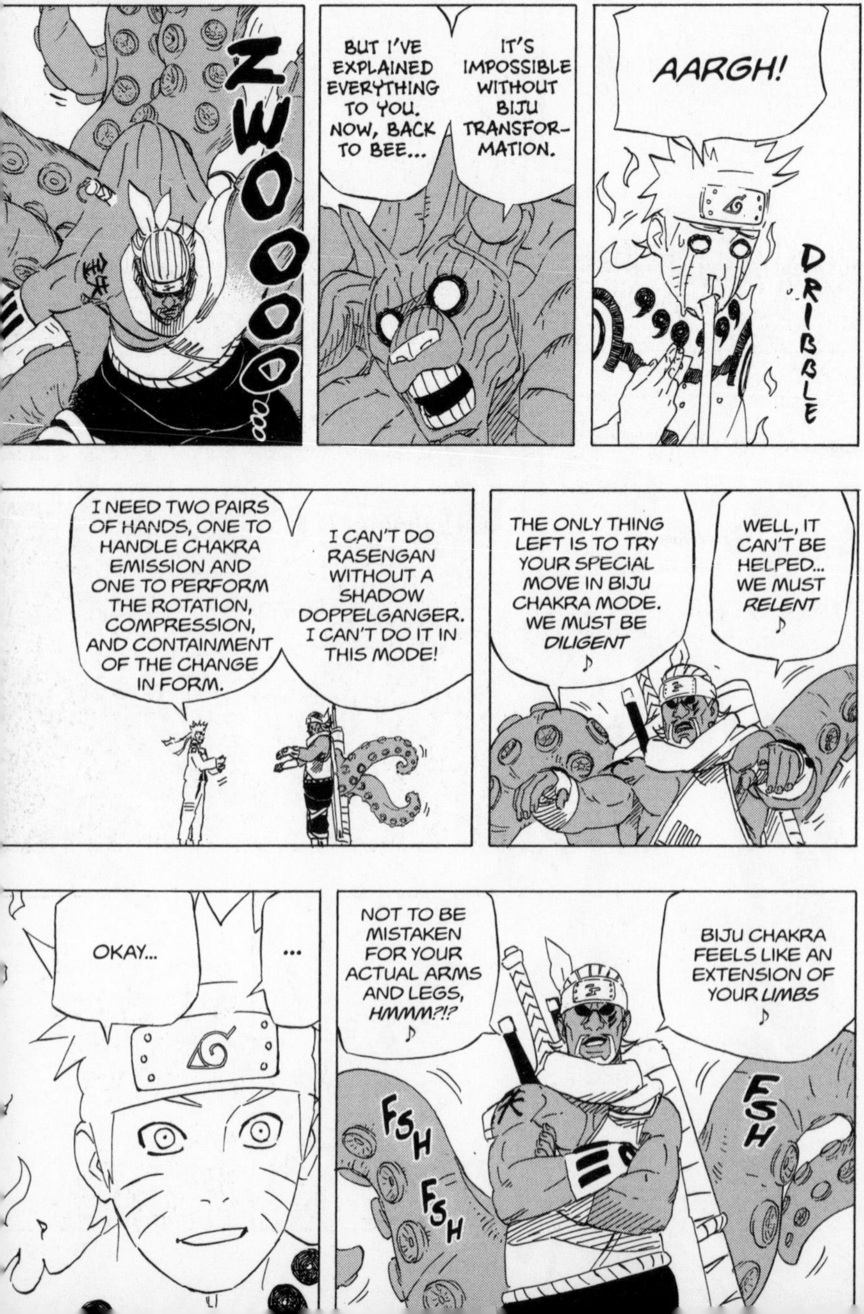
AARGH!
DRIBBLE
IT'S IMPOSSIBLE WITHOUT BIJU TRANSFORMATION.
BUT I'VE EXPLAINED EVERYTHING TO YOU. NOW, BACK TO BEE...
ZWOOOOOooo
WELL, IT CAN'T BE HELPED... WE MUST *RELENT* ♪
THE ONLY THING LEFT IS TO TRY YOUR SPECIAL MOVE IN BIJU CHAKRA MODE. WE MUST BE *DILIGENT* ♪
I CAN'T DO RASENGAN WITHOUT A SHADOW DOPPELGANGER. I CAN'T DO IT IN THIS MODE!
I NEED TWO PAIRS OF HANDS, ONE TO HANDLE CHAKRA EMISSION AND ONE TO PERFORM THE ROTATION, COMPRESSION, AND CONTAINMENT OF THE CHANGE IN FORM.
BIJU CHAKRA FEELS LIKE AN EXTENSION OF YOUR *LIMBS* ♪
NOT TO BE MISTAKEN FOR YOUR ACTUAL ARMS AND LEGS, *HMMM?!?* ♪
FSH
FSH
FSH
...
OKAY...

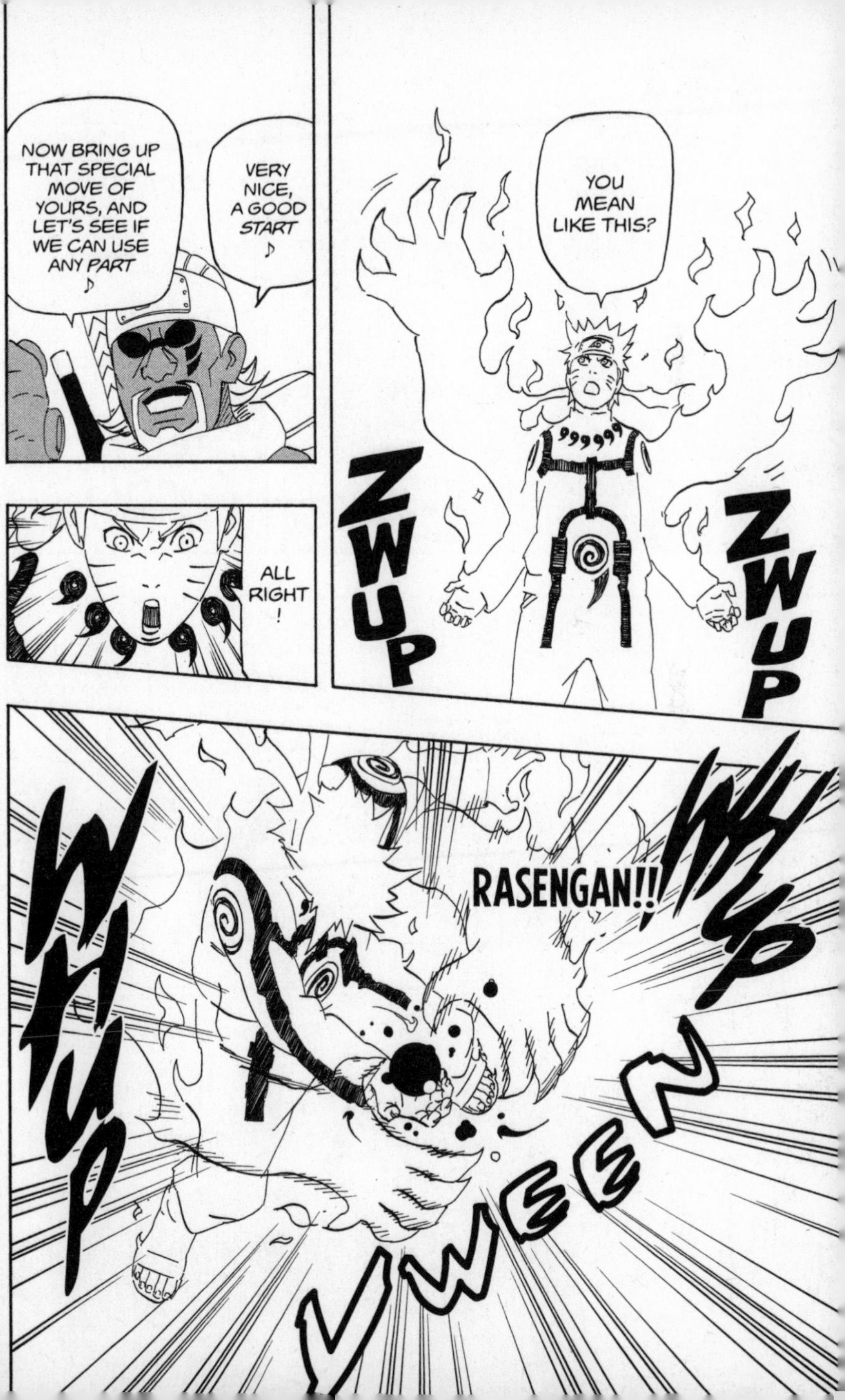
YOU MEAN LIKE THIS?
ZWUP
ZWUP
VERY NICE, A GOOD START ♪
NOW BRING UP THAT SPECIAL MOVE OF YOURS, AND LET'S SEE IF WE CAN USE ANY PART ♪
ALL RIGHT!
WHUP
RASENGAN!!
VWEEN
WHUP

READ THIS WAY

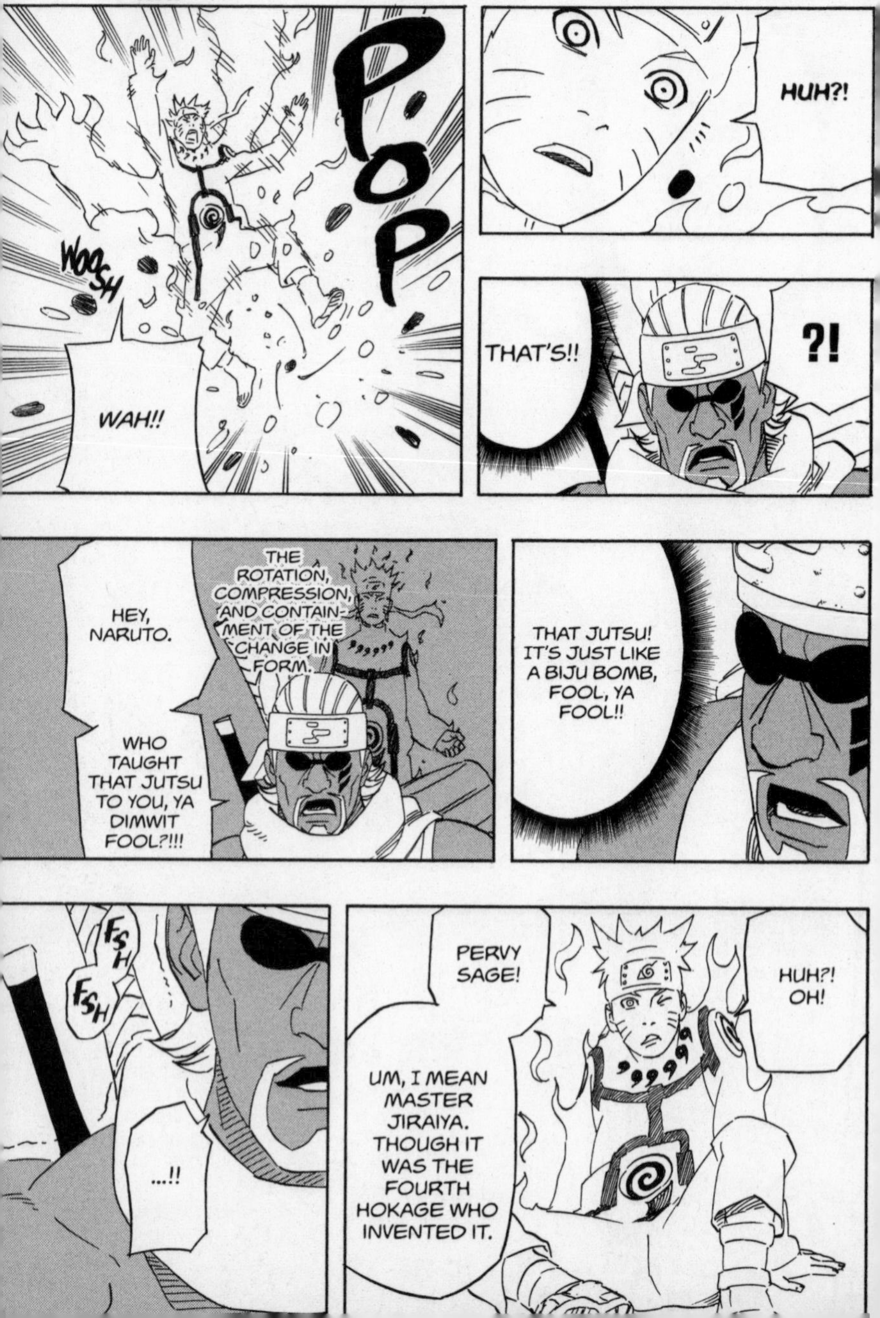
HUH?!
?!
THAT'S!!
POP
WOOSH
WAH!!
THAT JUTSU! IT'S JUST LIKE A BIJU BOMB, FOOL, YA FOOL!!
THE ROTATION, COMPRESSION, AND CONTAINMENT OF THE CHANGE IN FORM.
HEY, NARUTO.
WHO TAUGHT THAT JUTSU TO YOU, YA DIMWIT FOOL?!!!
HUH?! OH!
PERVY SAGE!
UM, I MEAN MASTER JIRAIYA. THOUGH IT WAS THE FOURTH HOKAGE WHO INVENTED IT.
FSH
FSH
...!!

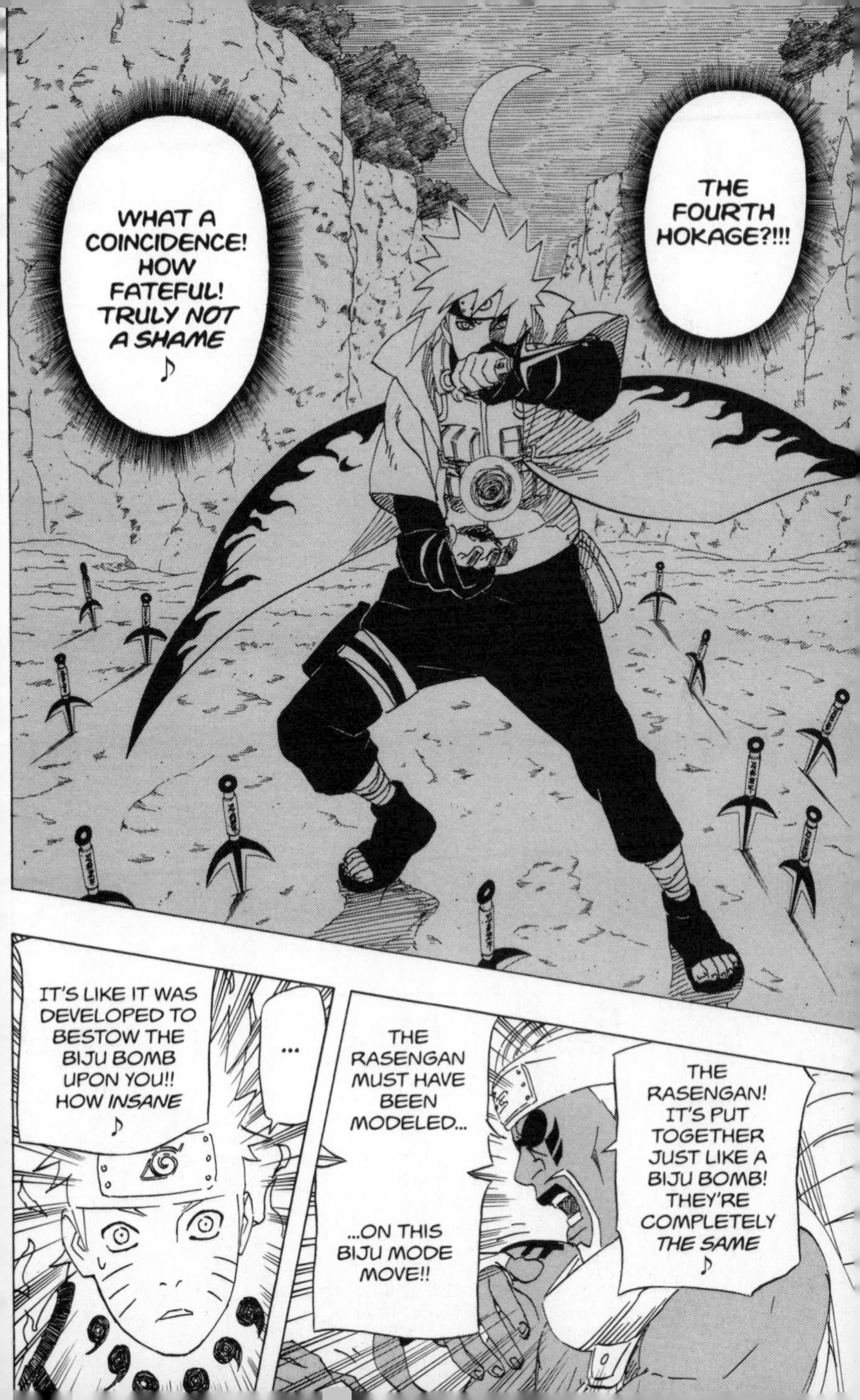
THE FOURTH HOKAGE?!!!
WHAT A COINCIDENCE! HOW FATEFUL! TRULY NOT A SHAME ♪
THE RASENGAN! IT'S PUT TOGETHER JUST LIKE A BIJU BOMB! THEY'RE COMPLETELY THE SAME ♪
THE RASENGAN MUST HAVE BEEN MODELED...
...ON THIS BIJU MODE MOVE!!
...
IT'S LIKE IT WAS DEVELOPED TO BESTOW THE BIJU BOMB UPON YOU!! HOW INSANE ♪

READ THIS WAY

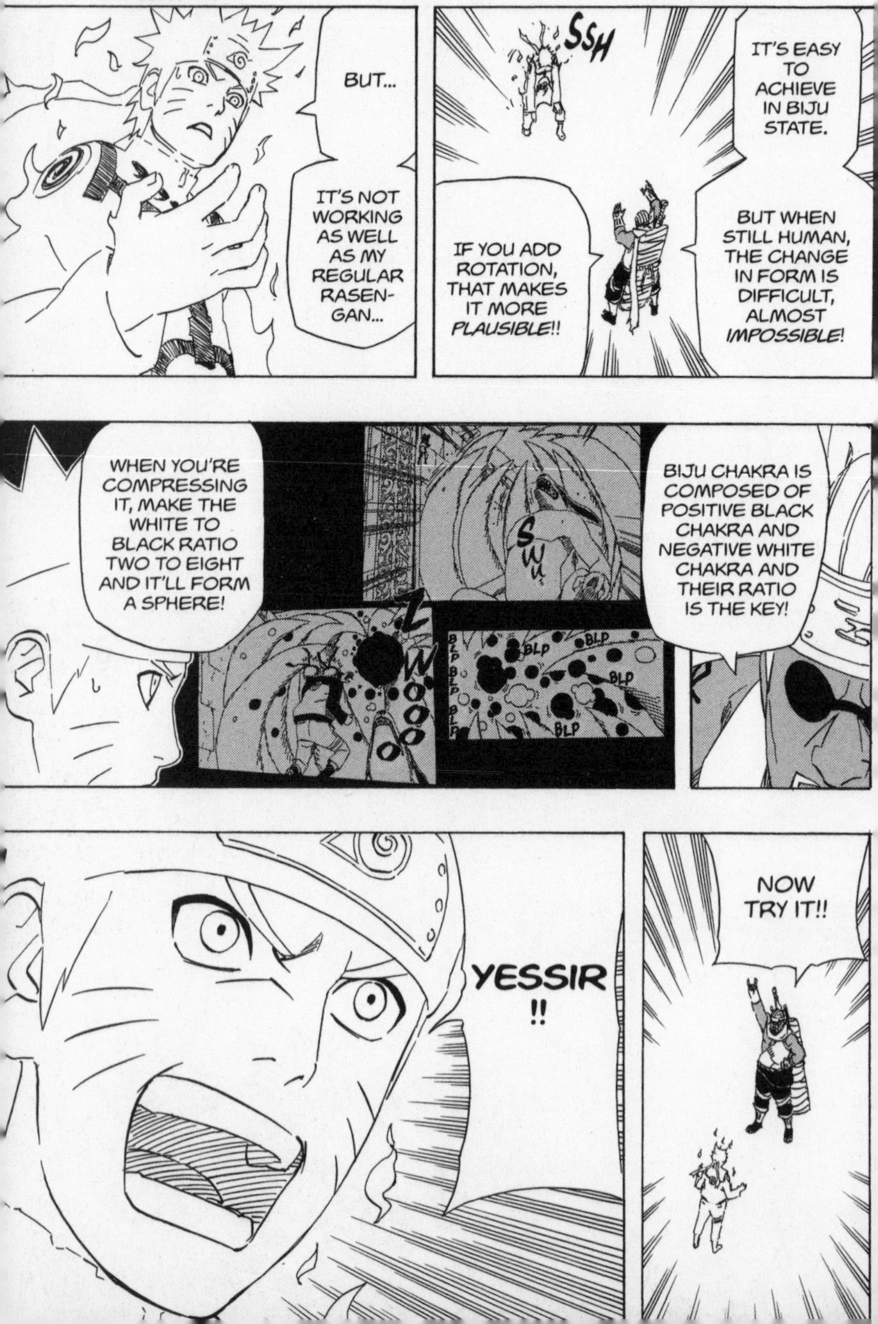

SSH
IT'S EASY TO ACHIEVE IN BIJU STATE.
BUT WHEN STILL HUMAN, THE CHANGE IN FORM IS DIFFICULT, ALMOST *IMPOSSIBLE*!
IF YOU ADD ROTATION, THAT MAKES IT MORE *PLAUSIBLE*!!
BUT...
IT'S NOT WORKING AS WELL AS MY REGULAR RASEN-GAN...
BIJU CHAKRA IS COMPOSED OF POSITIVE BLACK CHAKRA AND NEGATIVE WHITE CHAKRA AND THEIR RATIO IS THE KEY!
SWU
BLP BLP BLP BLP BLP BLP BLP BLP
ZWOOOO
WHEN YOU'RE COMPRESSING IT, MAKE THE WHITE TO BLACK RATIO TWO TO EIGHT AND IT'LL FORM A SPHERE!
NOW TRY IT!!
YESSIR!!

NARUTO

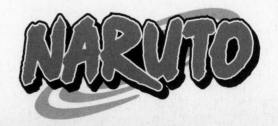

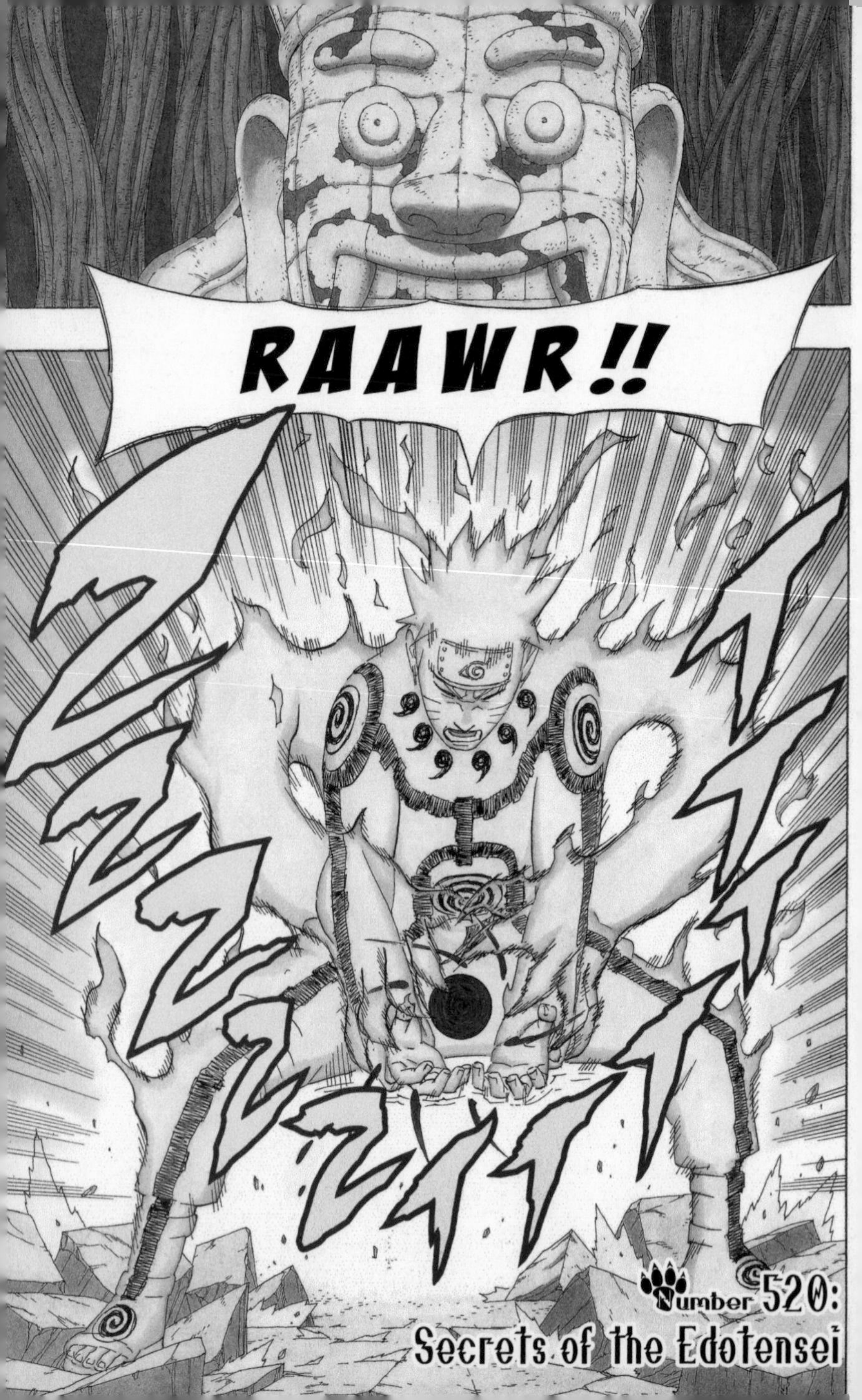
RAAWR!!
Number 520:
Secrets of the Edotensei

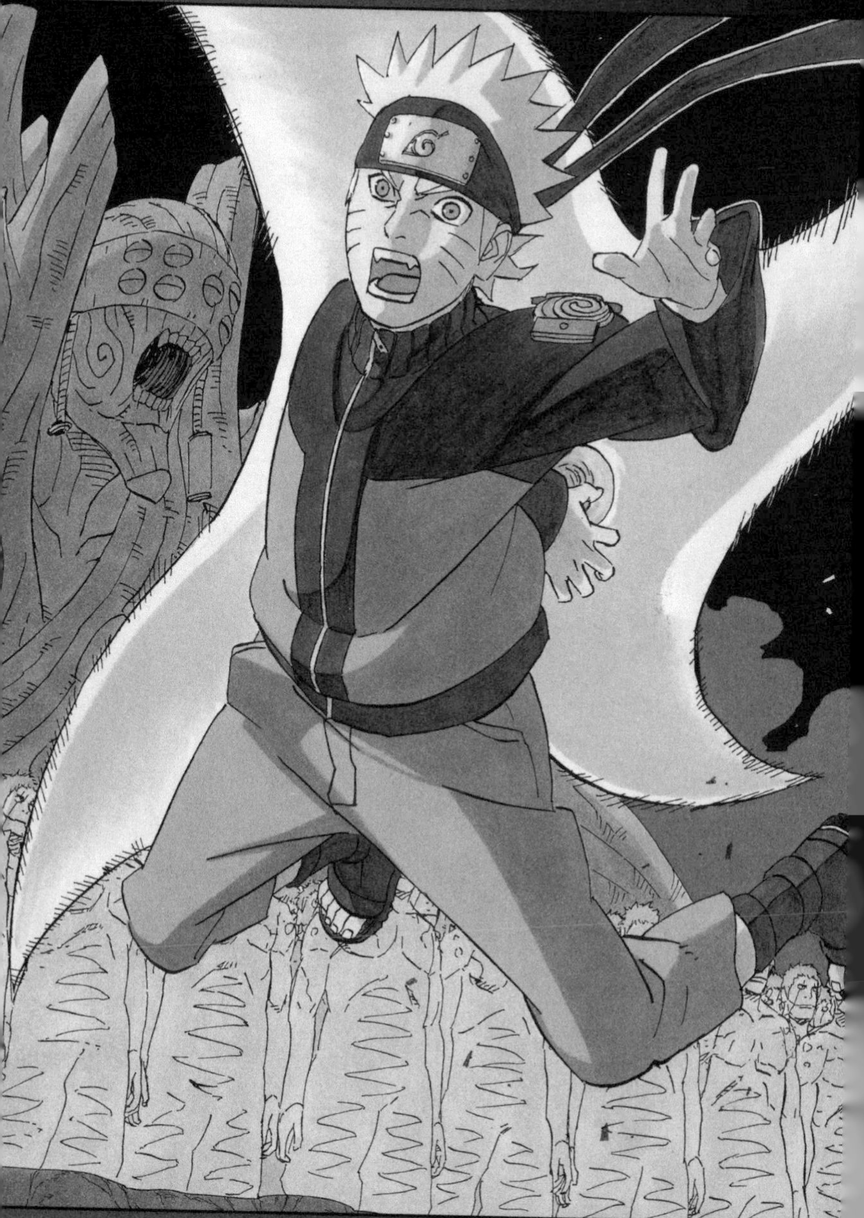

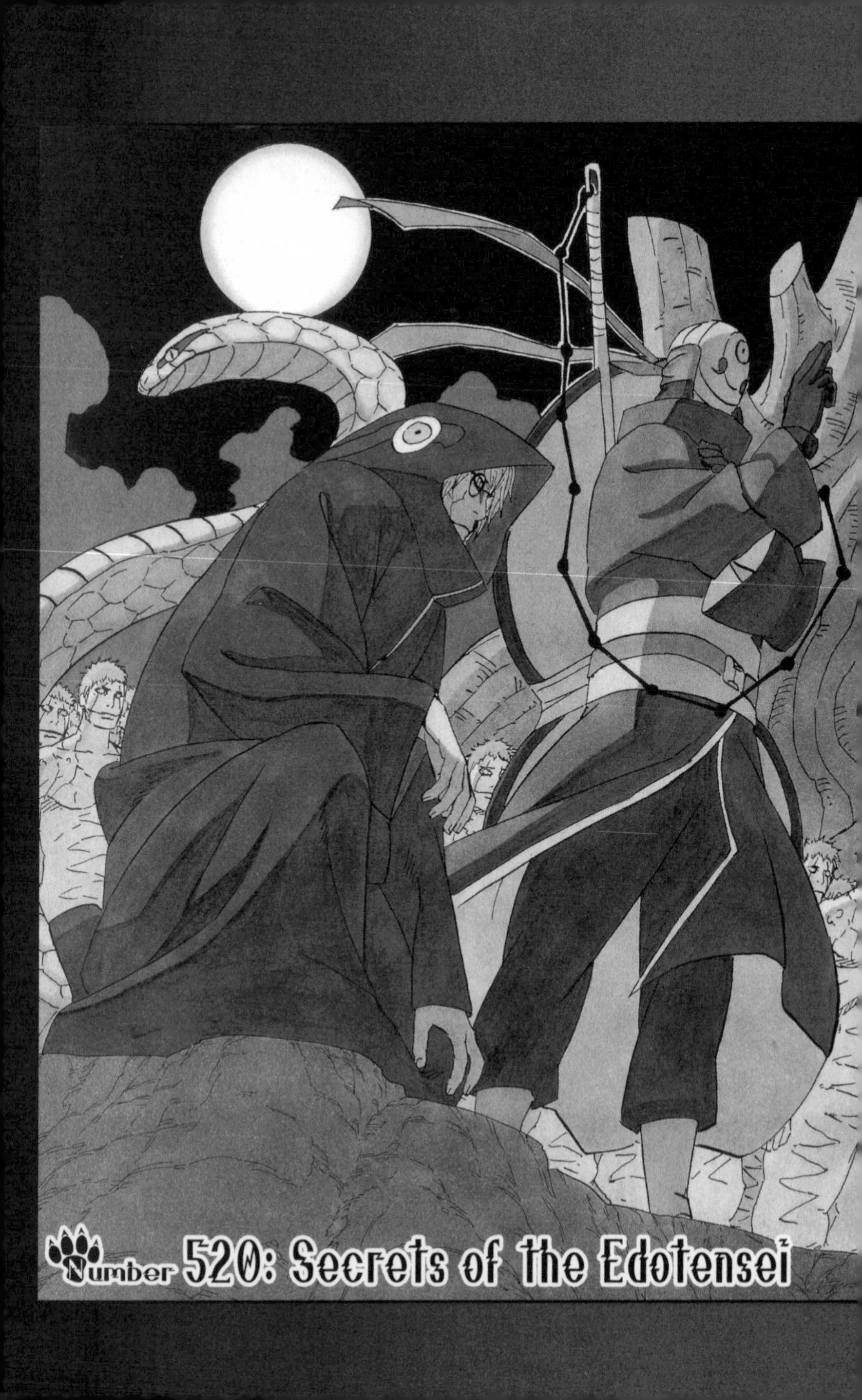

Number 520: Secrets of the Edotensei

NARUTO

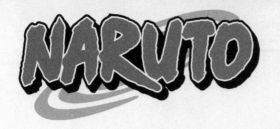

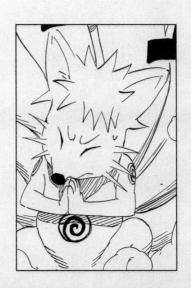

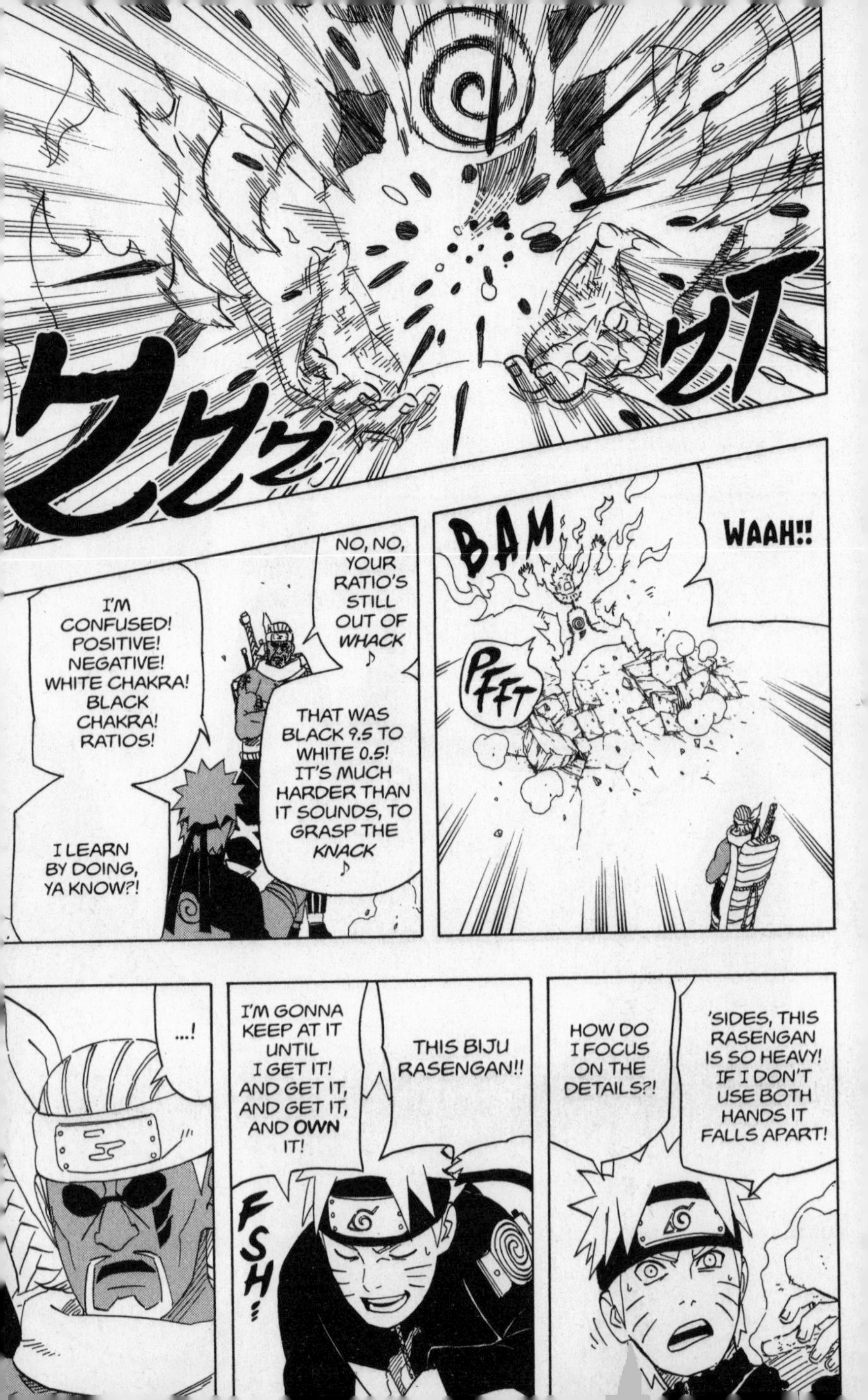
WAAH!!
BAM
PFFT
NO, NO, YOUR RATIO'S STILL OUT OF WHACK ♪
THAT WAS BLACK 9.5 TO WHITE 0.5! IT'S MUCH HARDER THAN IT SOUNDS, TO GRASP THE KNACK ♪
I'M CONFUSED! POSITIVE! NEGATIVE! WHITE CHAKRA! BLACK CHAKRA! RATIOS!
I LEARN BY DOING, YA KNOW?!
'SIDES, THIS RASENGAN IS SO HEAVY! IF I DON'T USE BOTH HANDS IT FALLS APART!
HOW DO I FOCUS ON THE DETAILS?!
THIS BIJU RASENGAN!!
I'M GONNA KEEP AT IT UNTIL I GET IT! AND GET IT, AND GET IT, AND OWN IT!
FSH!!
...!

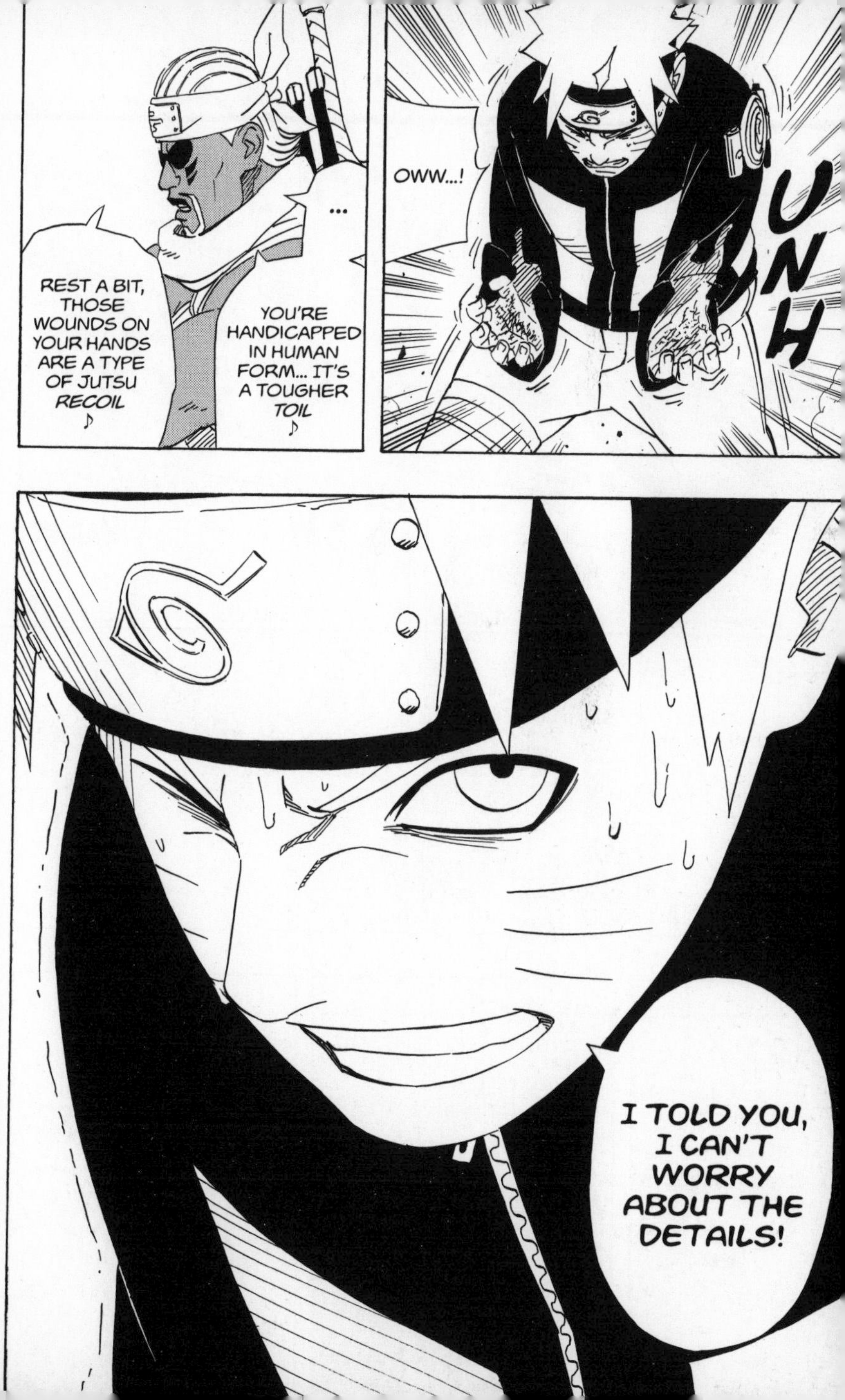

OWW...!
UNH
...
REST A BIT, THOSE WOUNDS ON YOUR HANDS ARE A TYPE OF JUTSU *RECOIL* ♪
YOU'RE HANDICAPPED IN HUMAN FORM... IT'S A TOUGHER *TOIL* ♪
I TOLD YOU, I CAN'T WORRY ABOUT THE DETAILS!

READ THIS WAY

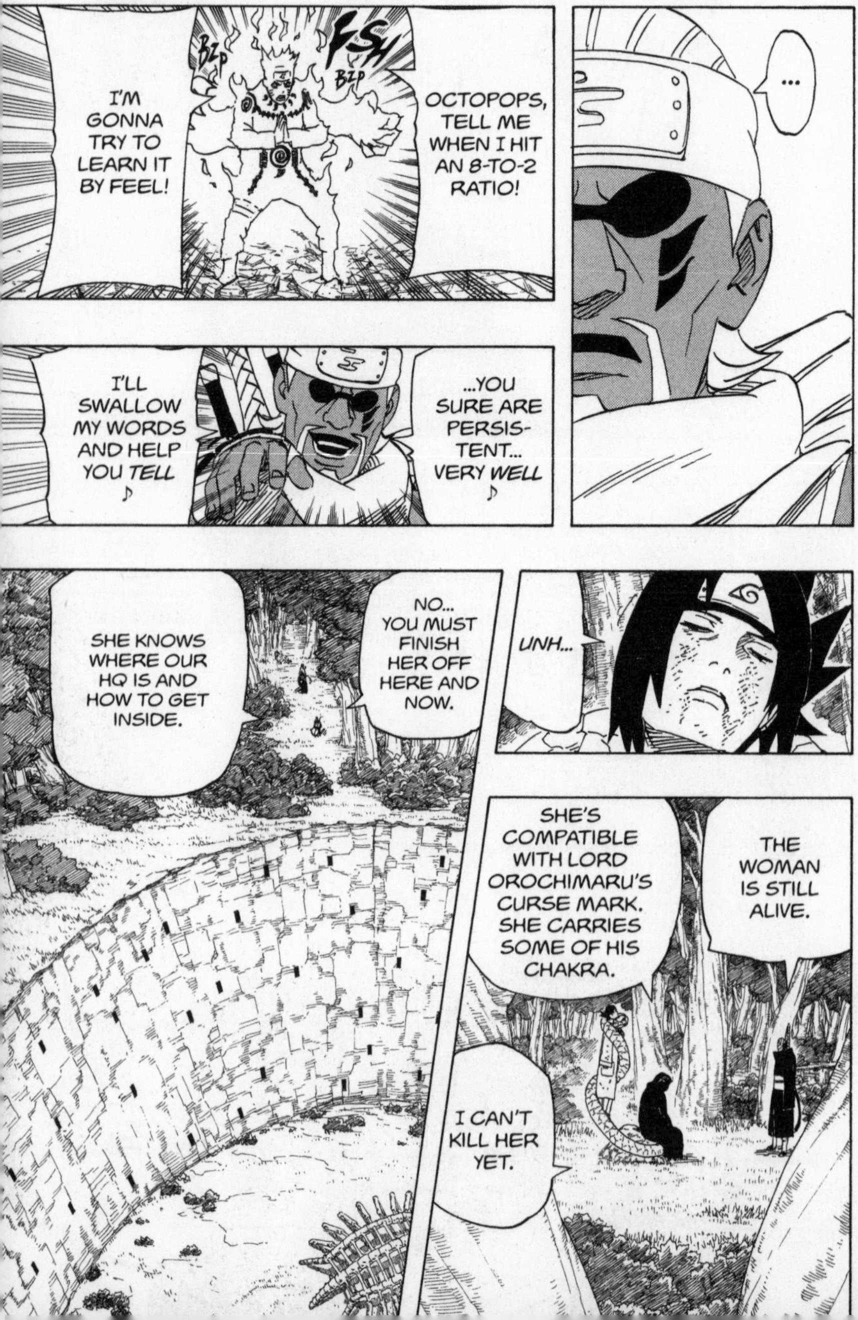
...
OCTOPOPS, TELL ME WHEN I HIT AN 8-TO-2 RATIO!
FSH
BZP
BZP
I'M GONNA TRY TO LEARN IT BY FEEL!
...YOU SURE ARE PERSIS-TENT... VERY WELL ♪
I'LL SWALLOW MY WORDS AND HELP YOU TELL ♪
UNH...
THE WOMAN IS STILL ALIVE.
SHE'S COMPATIBLE WITH LORD OROCHIMARU'S CURSE MARK. SHE CARRIES SOME OF HIS CHAKRA.
I CAN'T KILL HER YET.
NO... YOU MUST FINISH HER OFF HERE AND NOW.
SHE KNOWS WHERE OUR HQ IS AND HOW TO GET INSIDE.

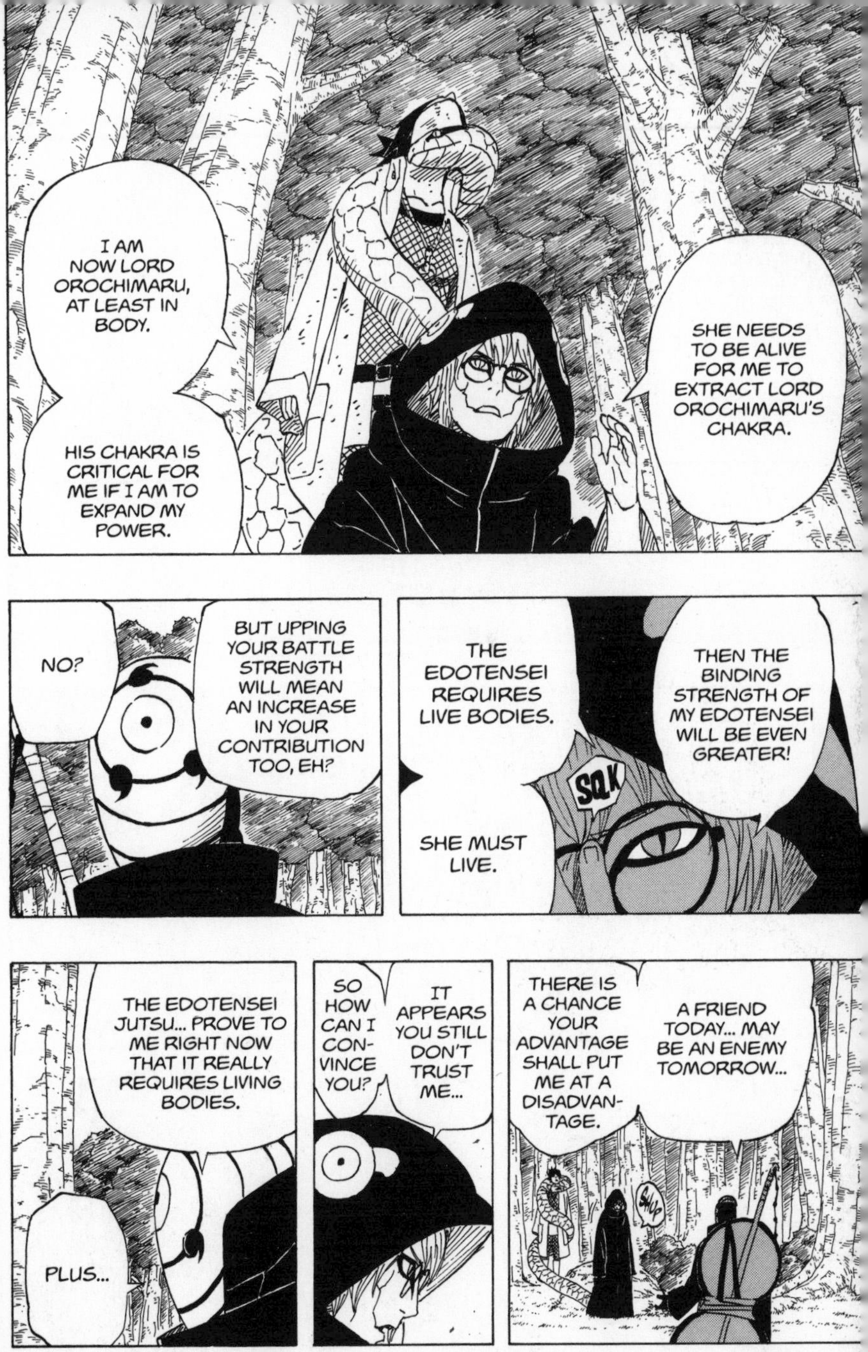
SHE NEEDS TO BE ALIVE FOR ME TO EXTRACT LORD OROCHIMARU'S CHAKRA.
I AM NOW LORD OROCHIMARU, AT LEAST IN BODY.
HIS CHAKRA IS CRITICAL FOR ME IF I AM TO EXPAND MY POWER.
THEN THE BINDING STRENGTH OF MY EDOTENSEI WILL BE EVEN GREATER!
THE EDOTENSEI REQUIRES LIVE BODIES.
SQK
SHE MUST LIVE.
BUT UPPING YOUR BATTLE STRENGTH WILL MEAN AN INCREASE IN YOUR CONTRIBUTION TOO, EH?
NO?
A FRIEND TODAY... MAY BE AN ENEMY TOMORROW...
THERE IS A CHANCE YOUR ADVANTAGE SHALL PUT ME AT A DISADVAN-TAGE.
SHUP
IT APPEARS YOU STILL DON'T TRUST ME...
SO HOW CAN I CON-VINCE YOU?
THE EDOTENSEI JUTSU... PROVE TO ME RIGHT NOW THAT IT REALLY REQUIRES LIVING BODIES.
PLUS...

READ THIS WAY

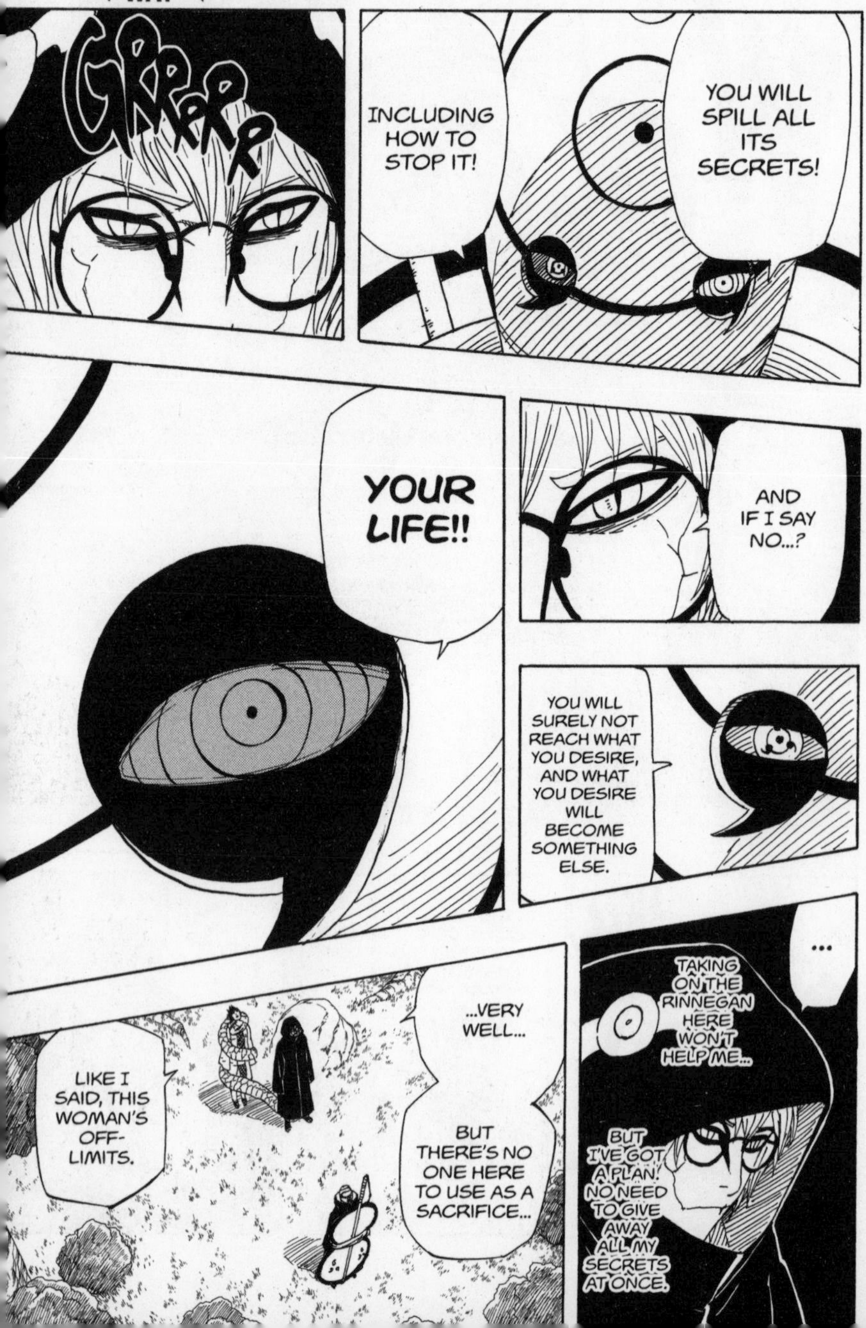
YOU WILL SPILL ALL ITS SECRETS!
INCLUDING HOW TO STOP IT!
GRRRP
AND IF I SAY NO...?
YOU WILL SURELY NOT REACH WHAT YOU DESIRE, AND WHAT YOU DESIRE WILL BECOME SOMETHING ELSE.
YOUR LIFE!!
...
TAKING ON THE RINNEGAN HERE WON'T HELP ME...
BUT I'VE GOT A PLAN! NO NEED TO GIVE AWAY ALL MY SECRETS AT ONCE.
...VERY WELL...
BUT THERE'S NO ONE HERE TO USE AS A SACRIFICE...
LIKE I SAID, THIS WOMAN'S OFF-LIMITS.

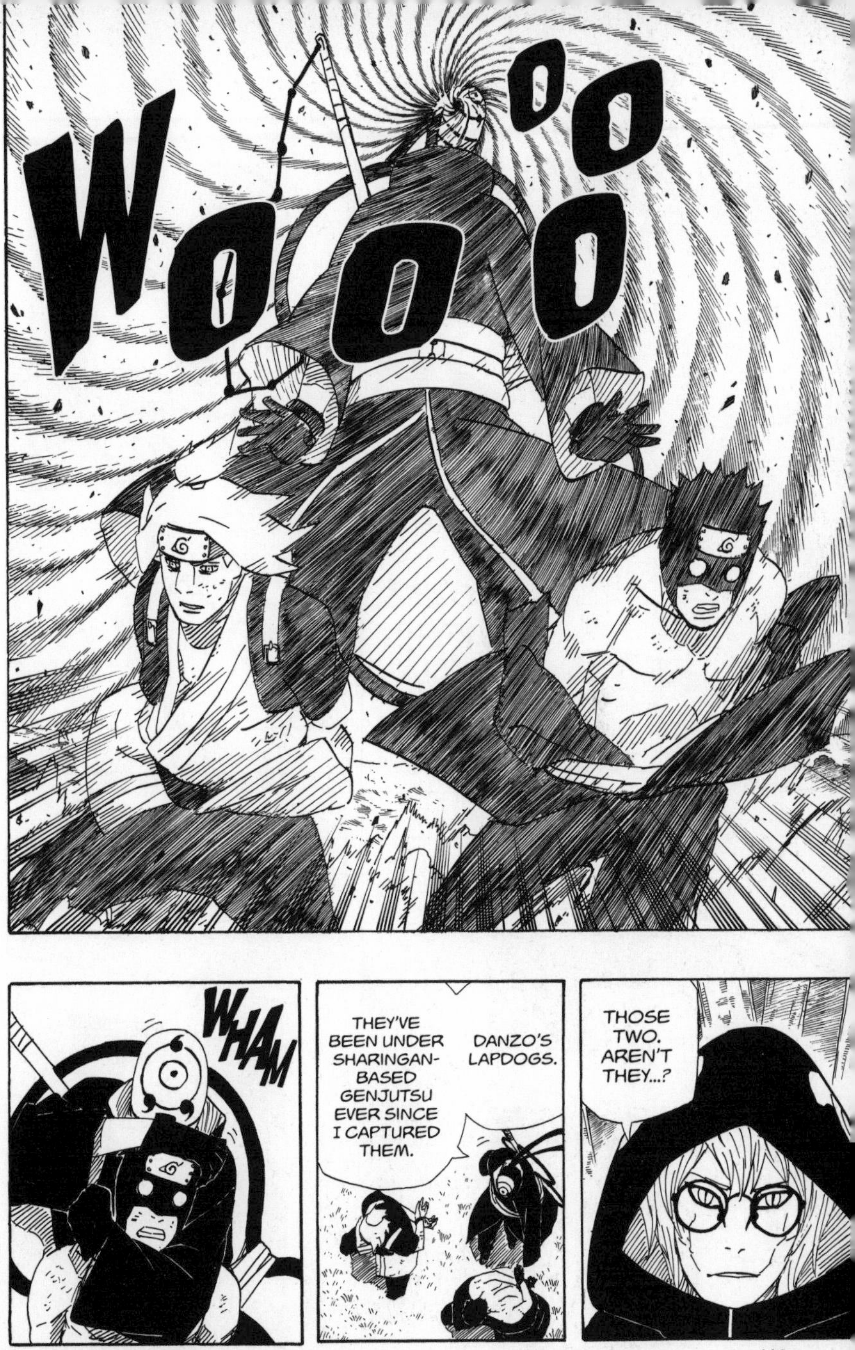
WOOOOO
THOSE TWO. AREN'T THEY...?
DANZO'S LAPDOGS.
THEY'VE BEEN UNDER SHARINGAN-BASED GENJUTSU EVER SINCE I CAPTURED THEM.
WHAM

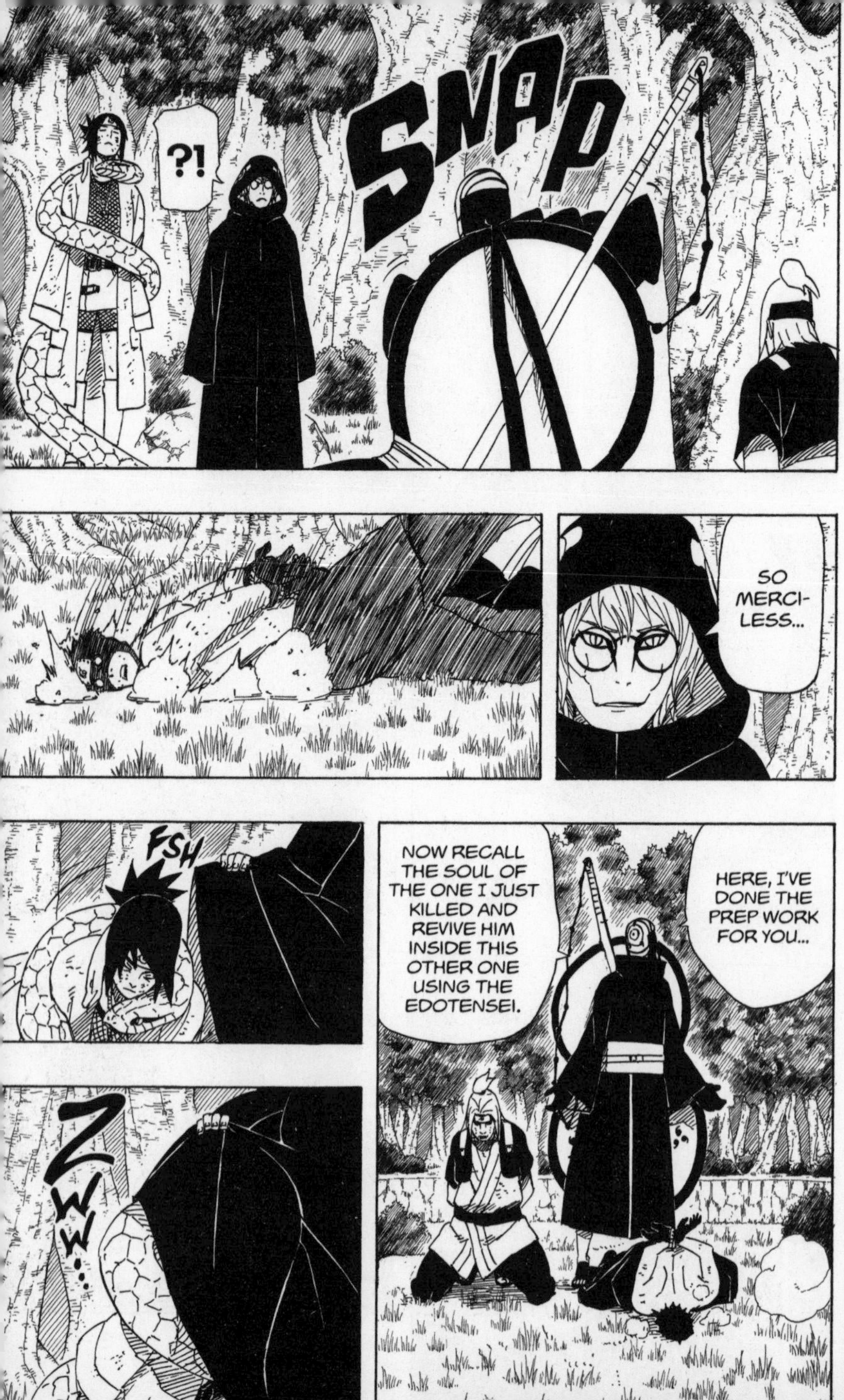
SNAP
?!
SO MERCI-LESS...
HERE, I'VE DONE THE PREP WORK FOR YOU...
NOW RECALL THE SOUL OF THE ONE I JUST KILLED AND REVIVE HIM INSIDE THIS OTHER ONE USING THE EDOTENSEI.
FSH
ZWW...

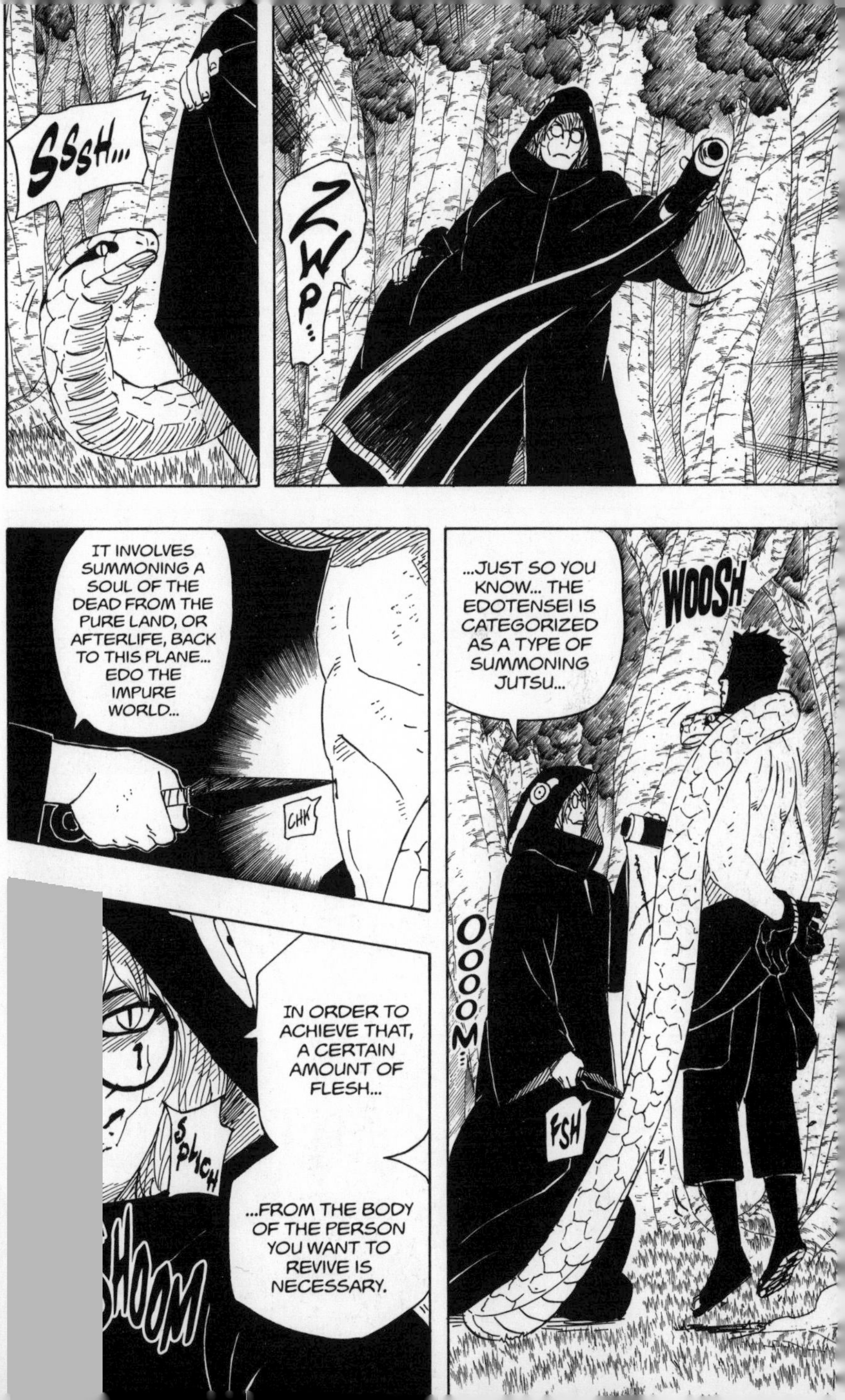
ZWP...
SSSH...
...JUST SO YOU KNOW... THE EDOTENSEI IS CATEGORIZED AS A TYPE OF SUMMONING JUTSU...
WOOSH
OOOOM...
FSH
IT INVOLVES SUMMONING A SOUL OF THE DEAD FROM THE PURE LAND, OR AFTERLIFE, BACK TO THIS PLANE... EDO THE IMPURE WORLD...
CHK
IN ORDER TO ACHIEVE THAT, A CERTAIN AMOUNT OF FLESH...
SPLICH
...FROM THE BODY OF THE PERSON YOU WANT TO REVIVE IS NECESSARY.
SHOOM

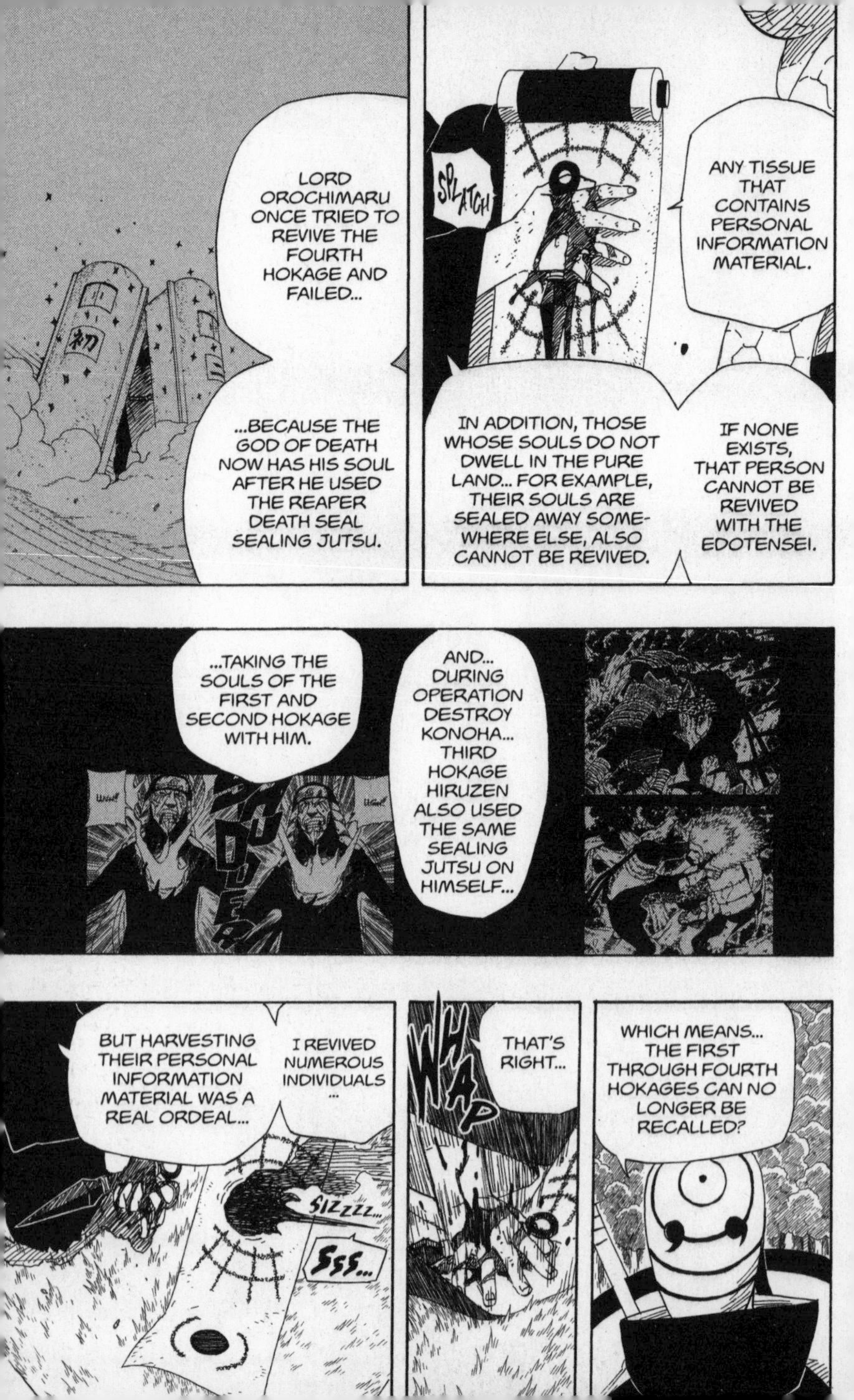
ANY TISSUE THAT CONTAINS PERSONAL INFORMATION MATERIAL.
SPLATCH
IF NONE EXISTS, THAT PERSON CANNOT BE REVIVED WITH THE EDOTENSEI.
IN ADDITION, THOSE WHOSE SOULS DO NOT DWELL IN THE PURE LAND... FOR EXAMPLE, THEIR SOULS ARE SEALED AWAY SOME-WHERE ELSE, ALSO CANNOT BE REVIVED.
LORD OROCHIMARU ONCE TRIED TO REVIVE THE FOURTH HOKAGE AND FAILED...
...BECAUSE THE GOD OF DEATH NOW HAS HIS SOUL AFTER HE USED THE REAPER DEATH SEAL SEALING JUTSU.
AND... DURING OPERATION DESTROY KONOHA... THIRD HOKAGE HIRUZEN ALSO USED THE SAME SEALING JUTSU ON HIMSELF...
...TAKING THE SOULS OF THE FIRST AND SECOND HOKAGE WITH HIM.
WHICH MEANS... THE FIRST THROUGH FOURTH HOKAGES CAN NO LONGER BE RECALLED?
THAT'S RIGHT...
WHAP
I REVIVED NUMEROUS INDIVIDUALS ...
BUT HARVESTING THEIR PERSONAL INFORMATION MATERIAL WAS A REAL ORDEAL...
SIZZZZ...
SSS...

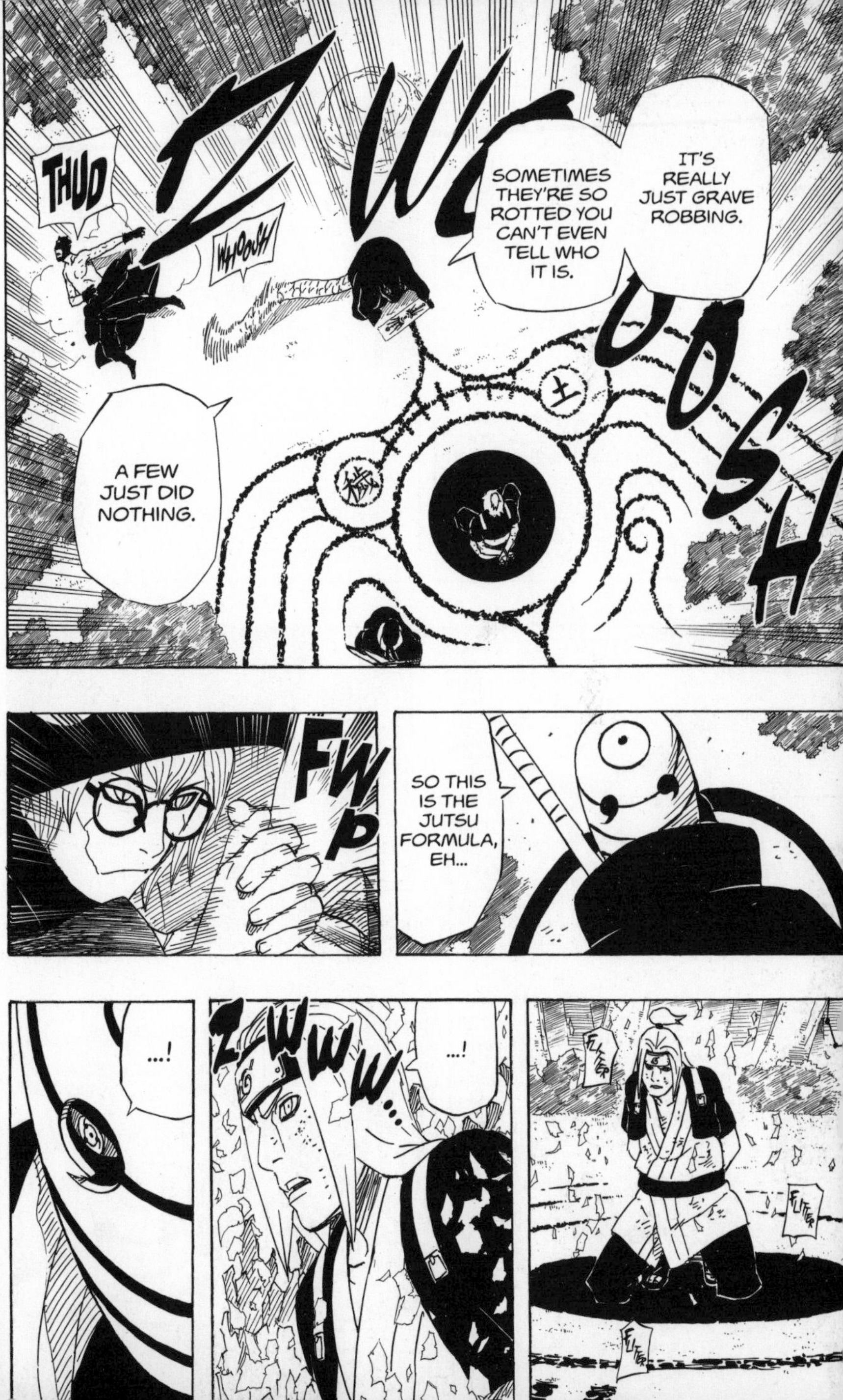
IT'S REALLY JUST GRAVE ROBBING.
SOMETIMES THEY'RE SO ROTTED YOU CAN'T EVEN TELL WHO IT IS.
ZWOOOSH
WHOOSH
THUD
土
穢
A FEW JUST DID NOTHING.
SO THIS IS THE JUTSU FORMULA, EH...
FWP
FLITTER
FLITTER
FLITTER
ZWWW...
...!
...!

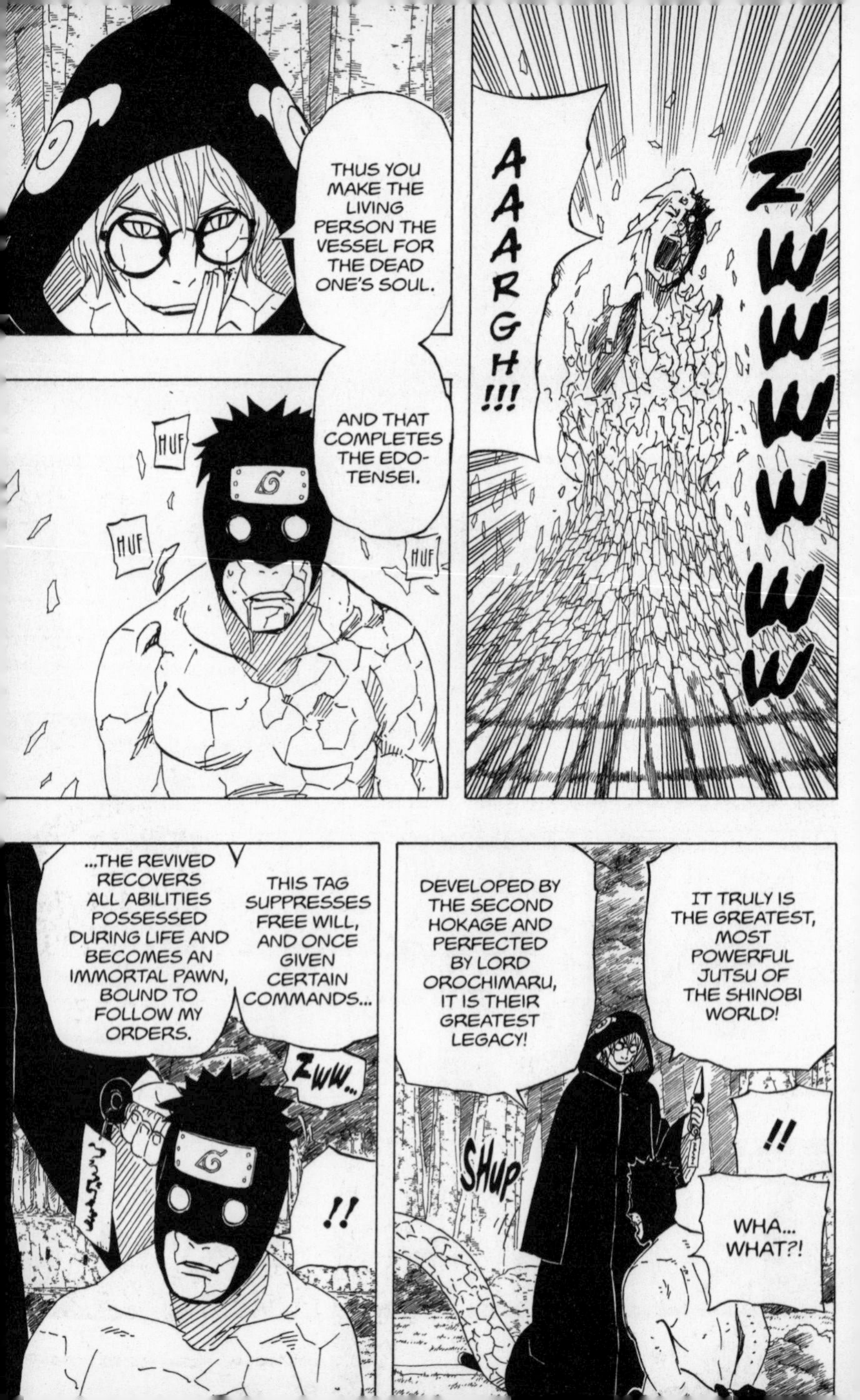
AAAARGH!!!
ZWWWWWW
THUS YOU MAKE THE LIVING PERSON THE VESSEL FOR THE DEAD ONE'S SOUL.
AND THAT COMPLETES THE EDO-TENSEI.
HUF
HUF
HUF
IT TRULY IS THE GREATEST, MOST POWERFUL JUTSU OF THE SHINOBI WORLD!
DEVELOPED BY THE SECOND HOKAGE AND PERFECTED BY LORD OROCHIMARU, IT IS THEIR GREATEST LEGACY!
!!
SHUP
WHA... WHAT?!
THIS TAG SUPPRESSES FREE WILL, AND ONCE GIVEN CERTAIN COMMANDS...
...THE REVIVED RECOVERS ALL ABILITIES POSSESSED DURING LIFE AND BECOMES AN IMMORTAL PAWN, BOUND TO FOLLOW MY ORDERS.
ZWW...
!!

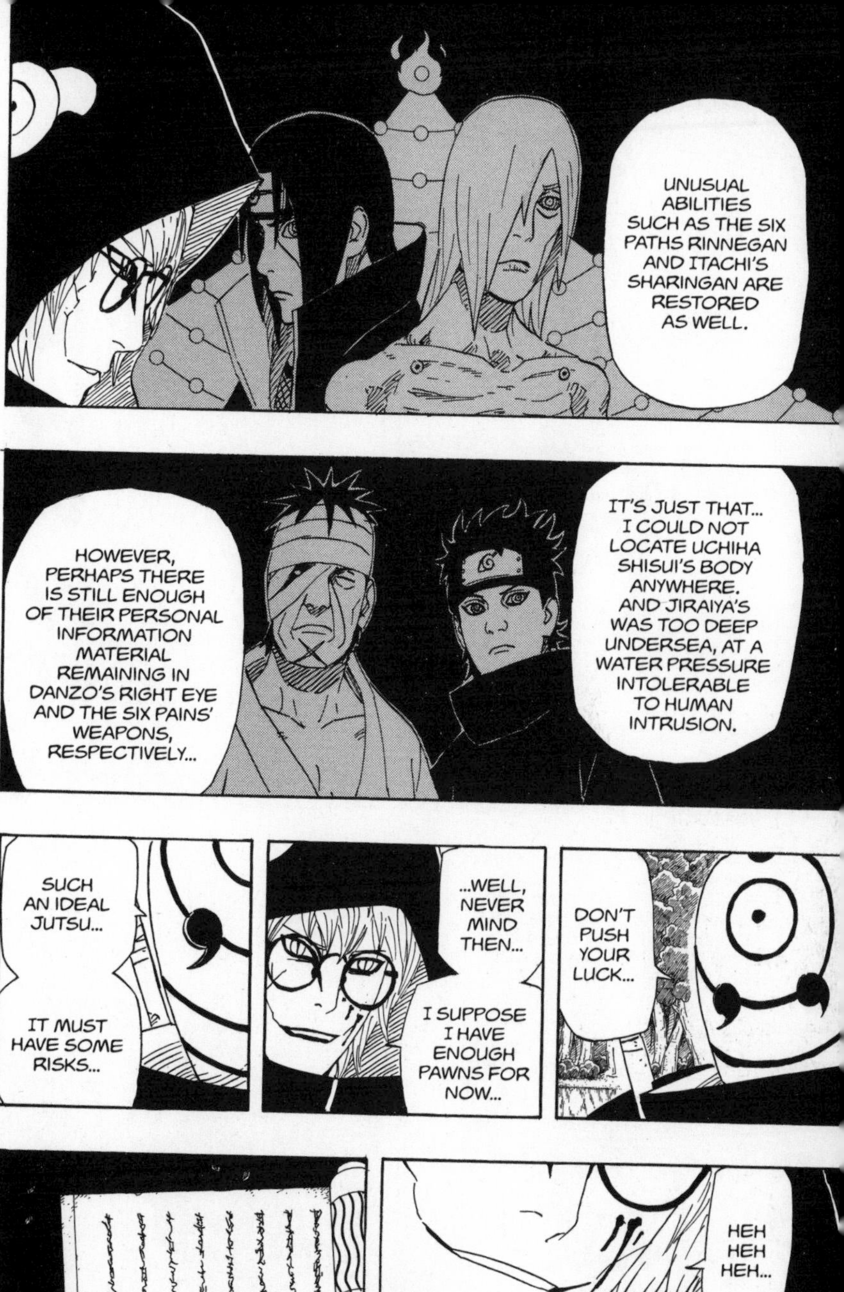
UNUSUAL ABILITIES SUCH AS THE SIX PATHS RINNEGAN AND ITACHI'S SHARINGAN ARE RESTORED AS WELL.
IT'S JUST THAT... I COULD NOT LOCATE UCHIHA SHISUI'S BODY ANYWHERE. AND JIRAIYA'S WAS TOO DEEP UNDERSEA, AT A WATER PRESSURE INTOLERABLE TO HUMAN INTRUSION.
HOWEVER, PERHAPS THERE IS STILL ENOUGH OF THEIR PERSONAL INFORMATION MATERIAL REMAINING IN DANZO'S RIGHT EYE AND THE SIX PAINS' WEAPONS, RESPECTIVELY...
DON'T PUSH YOUR LUCK...
...WELL, NEVER MIND THEN...
I SUPPOSE I HAVE ENOUGH PAWNS FOR NOW...
SUCH AN IDEAL JUTSU...
IT MUST HAVE SOME RISKS...
HEH HEH HEH...

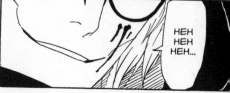

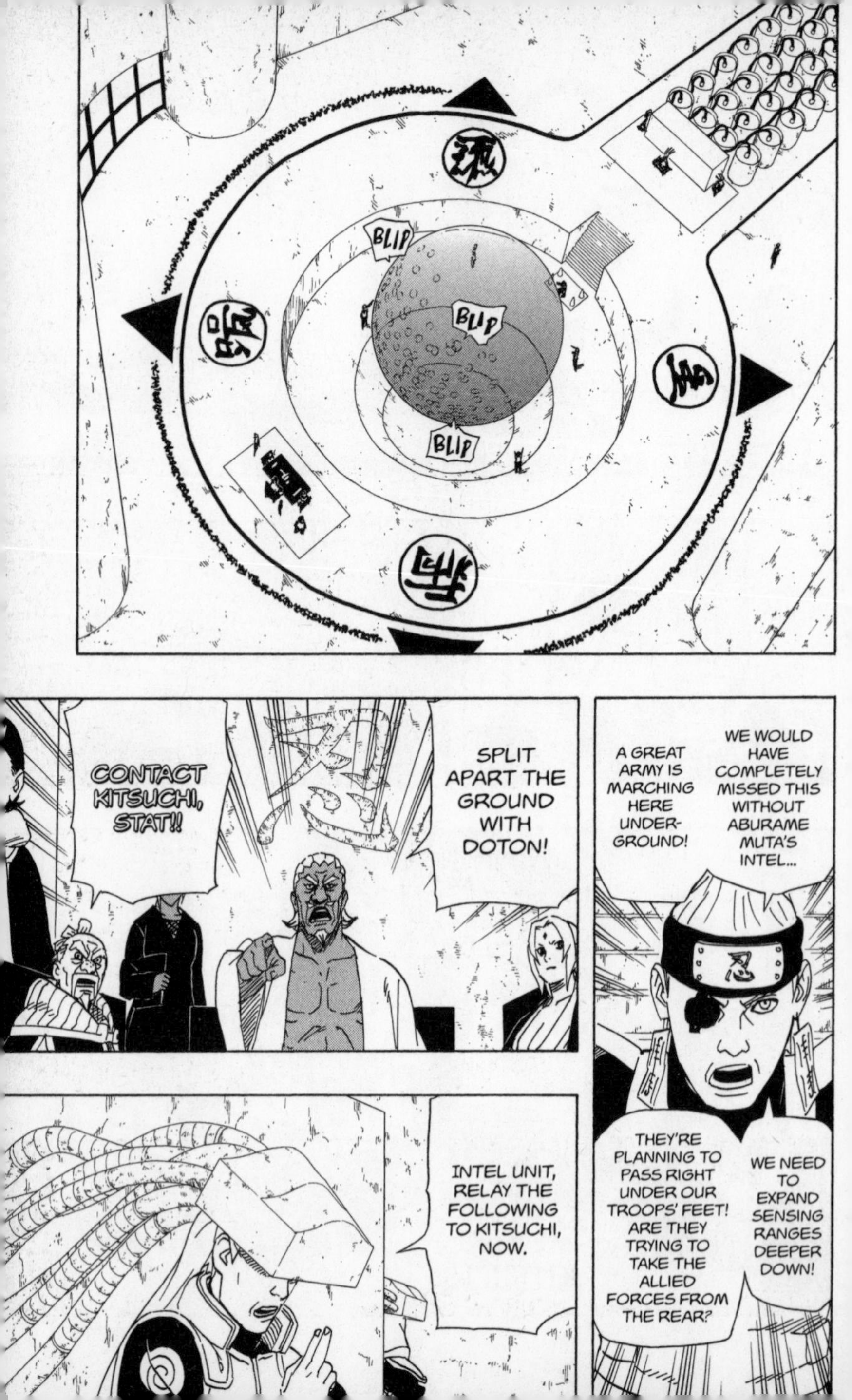
BLIP
BLIP
BLIP
WE WOULD HAVE COMPLETELY MISSED THIS WITHOUT ABURAME MUTA'S INTEL...
A GREAT ARMY IS MARCHING HERE UNDER-GROUND!
WE NEED TO EXPAND SENSING RANGES DEEPER DOWN!
THEY'RE PLANNING TO PASS RIGHT UNDER OUR TROOPS' FEET! ARE THEY TRYING TO TAKE THE ALLIED FORCES FROM THE REAR?
SPLIT APART THE GROUND WITH DOTON!
CONTACT KITSUCHI, STAT!!
INTEL UNIT, RELAY THE FOLLOWING TO KITSUCHI, NOW.

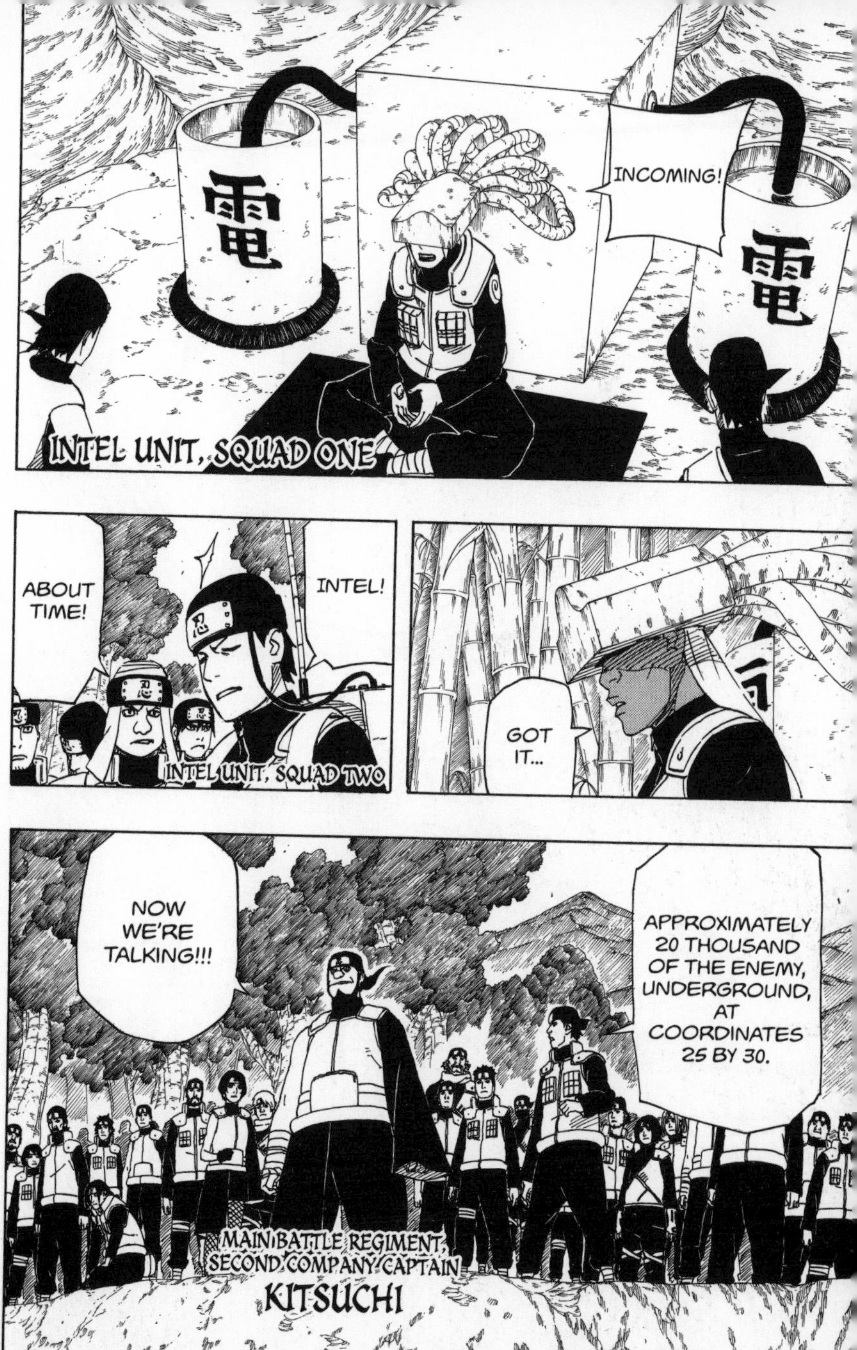
電
電
INCOMING!
INTEL UNIT, SQUAD ONE
GOT IT...
INTEL!
ABOUT TIME!
INTEL UNIT, SQUAD TWO
APPROXIMATELY 20 THOUSAND OF THE ENEMY, UNDERGROUND, AT COORDINATES 25 BY 30.
NOW WE'RE TALKING!!!
MAIN BATTLE REGIMENT, SECOND COMPANY CAPTAIN
KITSUCHI

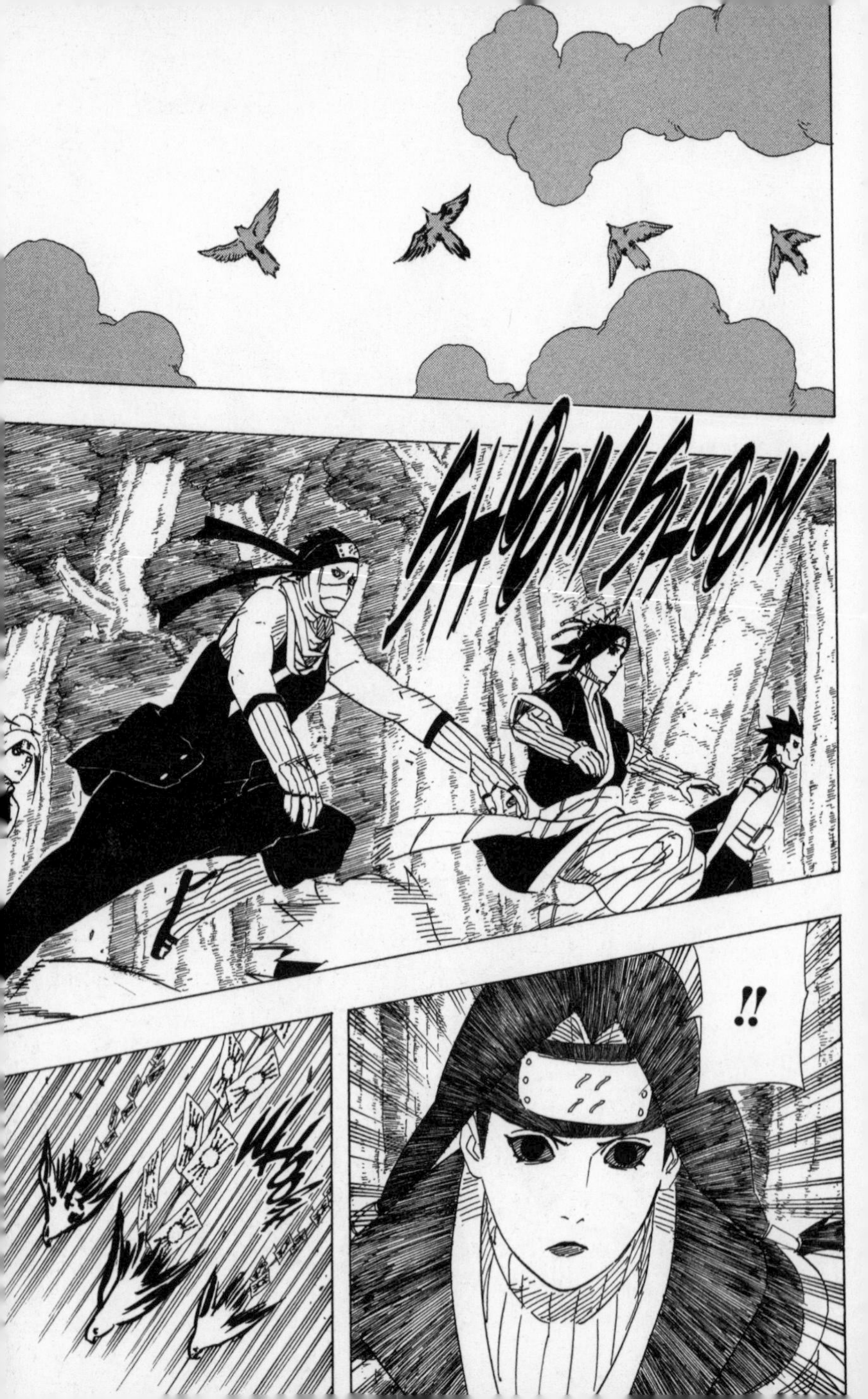
SHOOM SHOOM
!!

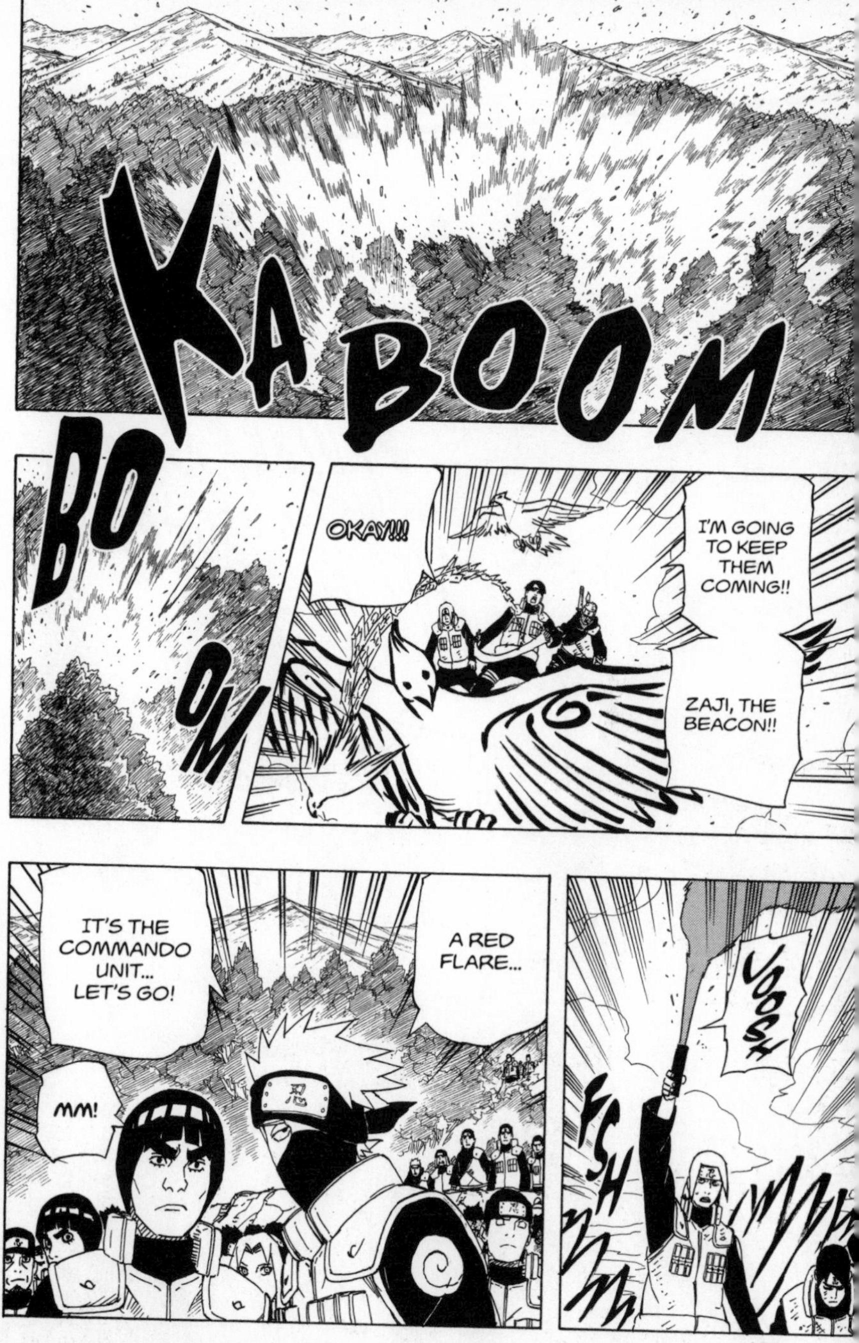
KABOOM
I'M GOING TO KEEP THEM COMING!!
ZAJI, THE BEACON!!
OKAY!!!
BOOM
VOOOSH
FSH
A RED FLARE...
IT'S THE COMMANDO UNIT... LET'S GO!
MM!

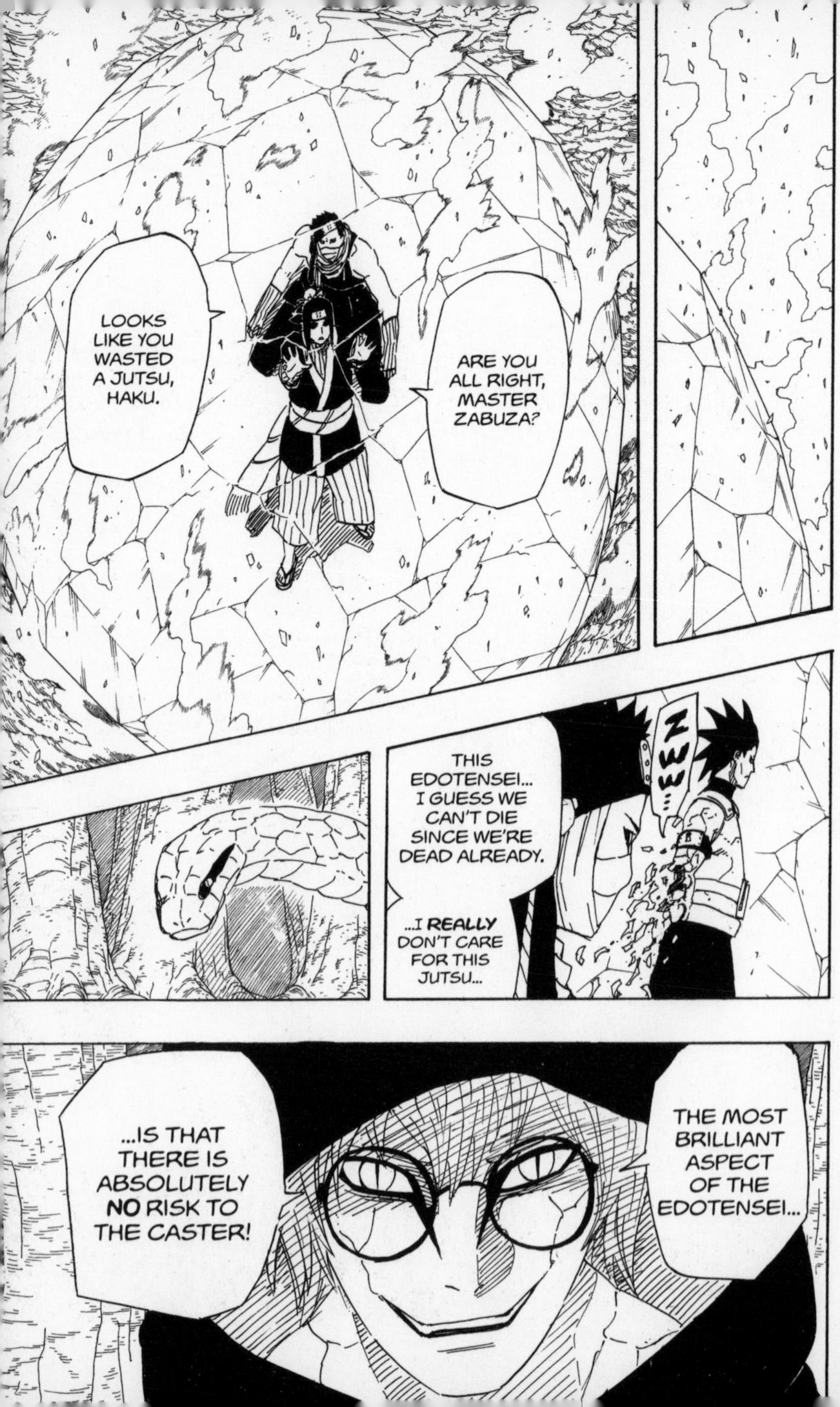
ARE YOU ALL RIGHT, MASTER ZABUZA?
LOOKS LIKE YOU WASTED A JUTSU, HAKU.
NWW...
THIS EDOTENSEI... I GUESS WE CAN'T DIE SINCE WE'RE DEAD ALREADY.
...I **REALLY** DON'T CARE FOR THIS JUTSU...
THE MOST BRILLIANT ASPECT OF THE EDOTENSEI...
...IS THAT THERE IS ABSOLUTELY **NO** RISK TO THE CASTER!

NARUTO

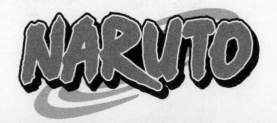

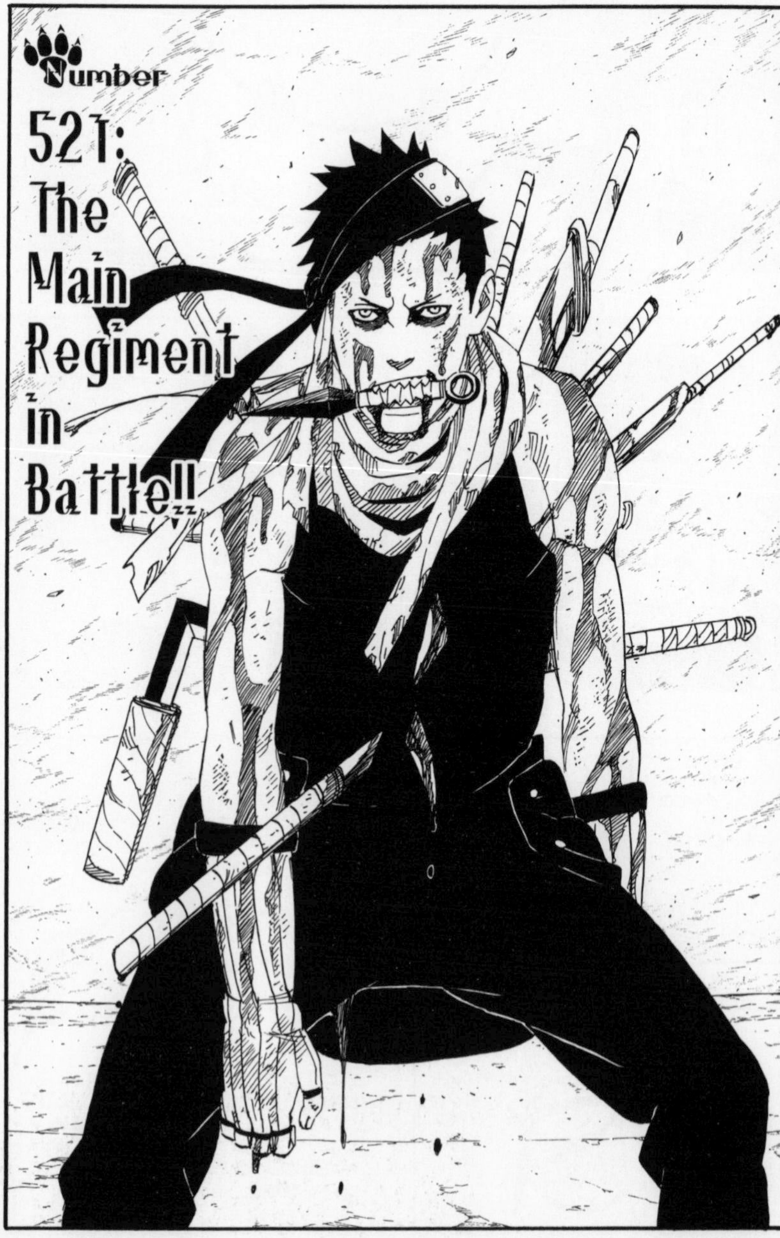
Number
521: The Main Regiment in Battle!!

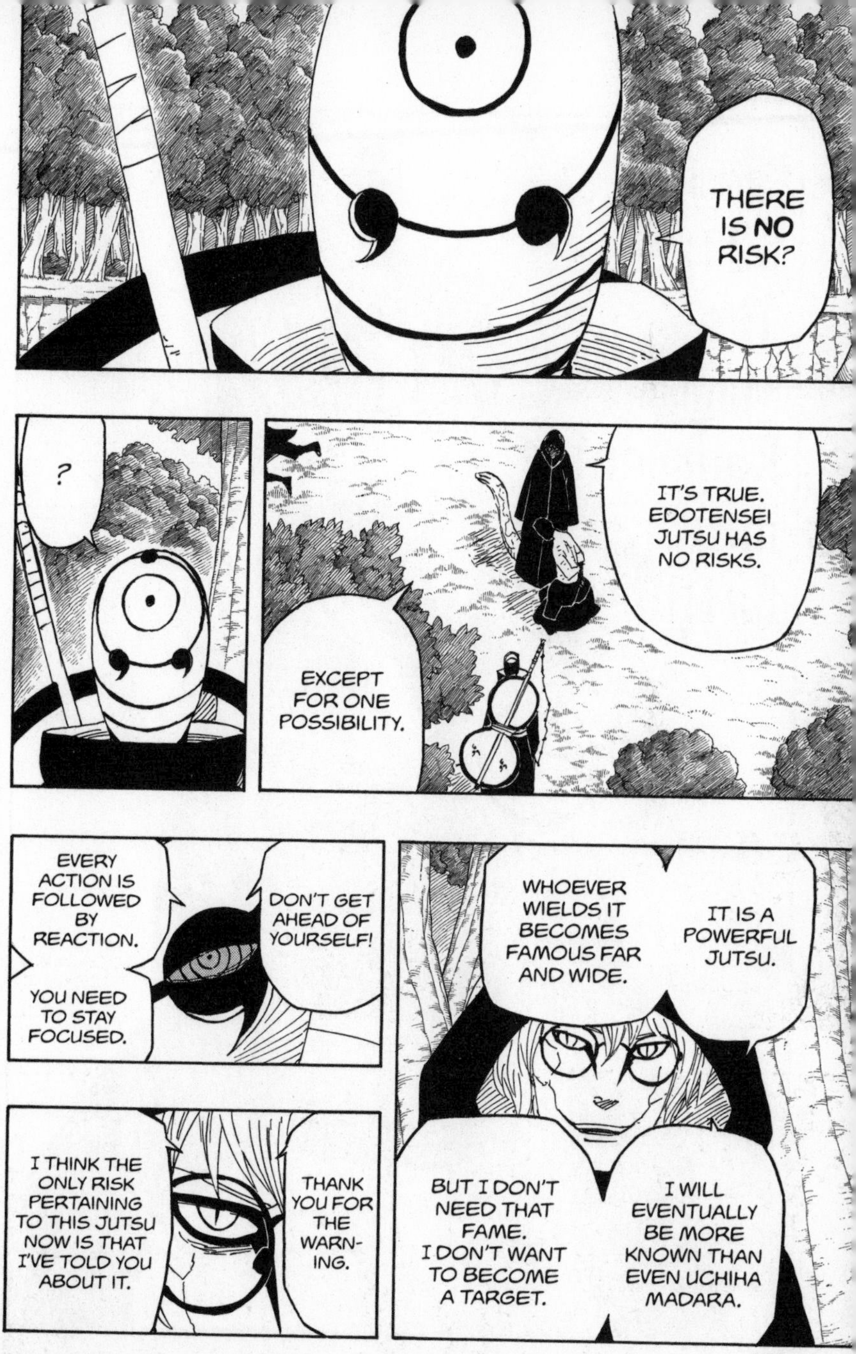
THERE IS NO RISK?
IT'S TRUE. EDOTENSEI JUTSU HAS NO RISKS.
EXCEPT FOR ONE POSSIBILITY.
?
IT IS A POWERFUL JUTSU.
WHOEVER WIELDS IT BECOMES FAMOUS FAR AND WIDE.
I WILL EVENTUALLY BE MORE KNOWN THAN EVEN UCHIHA MADARA.
BUT I DON'T NEED THAT FAME. I DON'T WANT TO BECOME A TARGET.
DON'T GET AHEAD OF YOURSELF!
EVERY ACTION IS FOLLOWED BY REACTION.
YOU NEED TO STAY FOCUSED.
THANK YOU FOR THE WARN-ING.
I THINK THE ONLY RISK PERTAINING TO THIS JUTSU NOW IS THAT I'VE TOLD YOU ABOUT IT.

READ THIS WAY

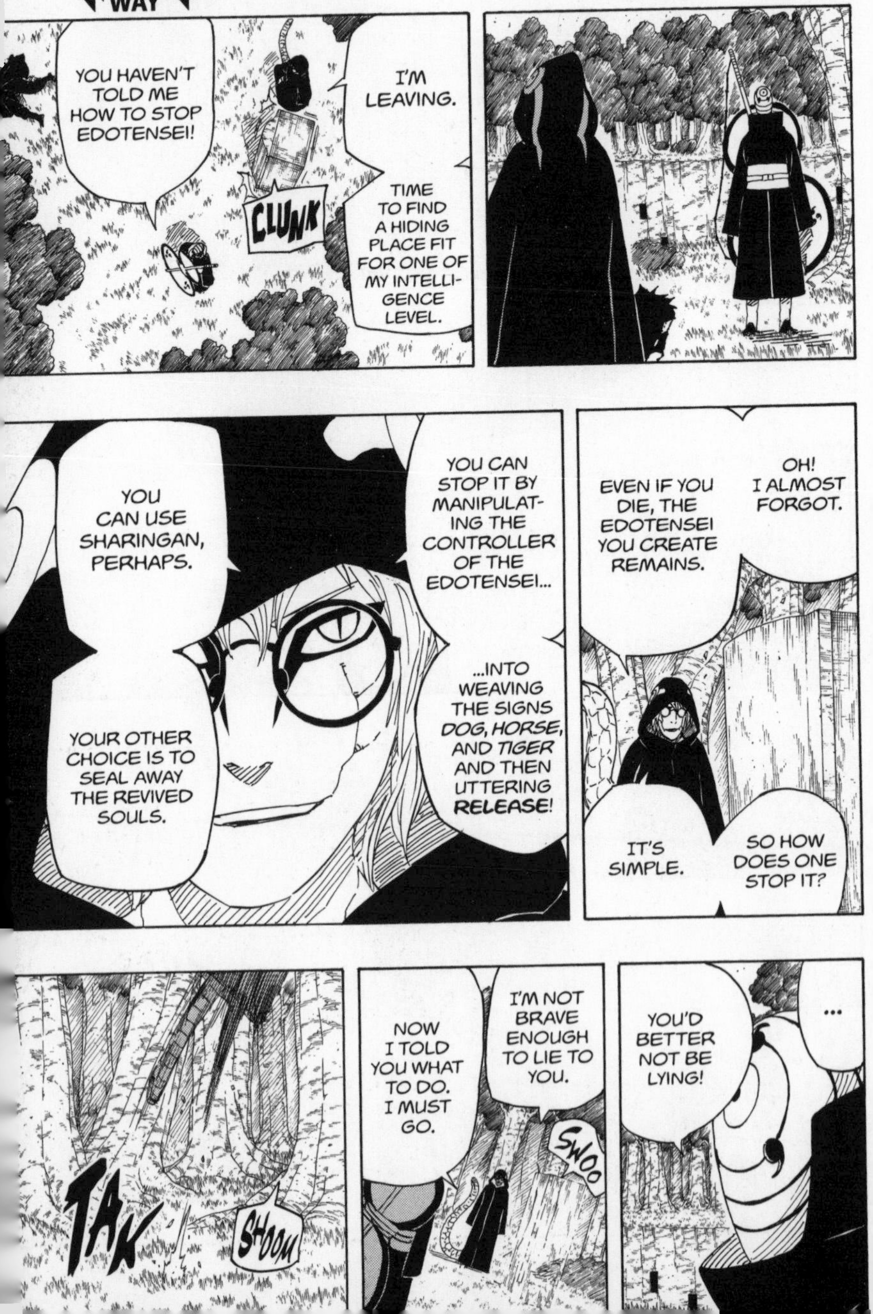
I'M LEAVING.
TIME TO FIND A HIDING PLACE FIT FOR ONE OF MY INTELLIGENCE LEVEL.
YOU HAVEN'T TOLD ME HOW TO STOP EDOTENSEI!
CLUNK
OH! I ALMOST FORGOT.
EVEN IF YOU DIE, THE EDOTENSEI YOU CREATE REMAINS.
SO HOW DOES ONE STOP IT?
IT'S SIMPLE.
YOU CAN STOP IT BY MANIPULATING THE CONTROLLER OF THE EDOTENSEI...
...INTO WEAVING THE SIGNS *DOG, HORSE,* AND *TIGER* AND THEN UTTERING **RELEASE**!
YOU CAN USE SHARINGAN, PERHAPS.
YOUR OTHER CHOICE IS TO SEAL AWAY THE REVIVED SOULS.
...
YOU'D BETTER NOT BE LYING!
I'M NOT BRAVE ENOUGH TO LIE TO YOU.
NOW I TOLD YOU WHAT TO DO. I MUST GO.
SWOO
TAK
SHOOM

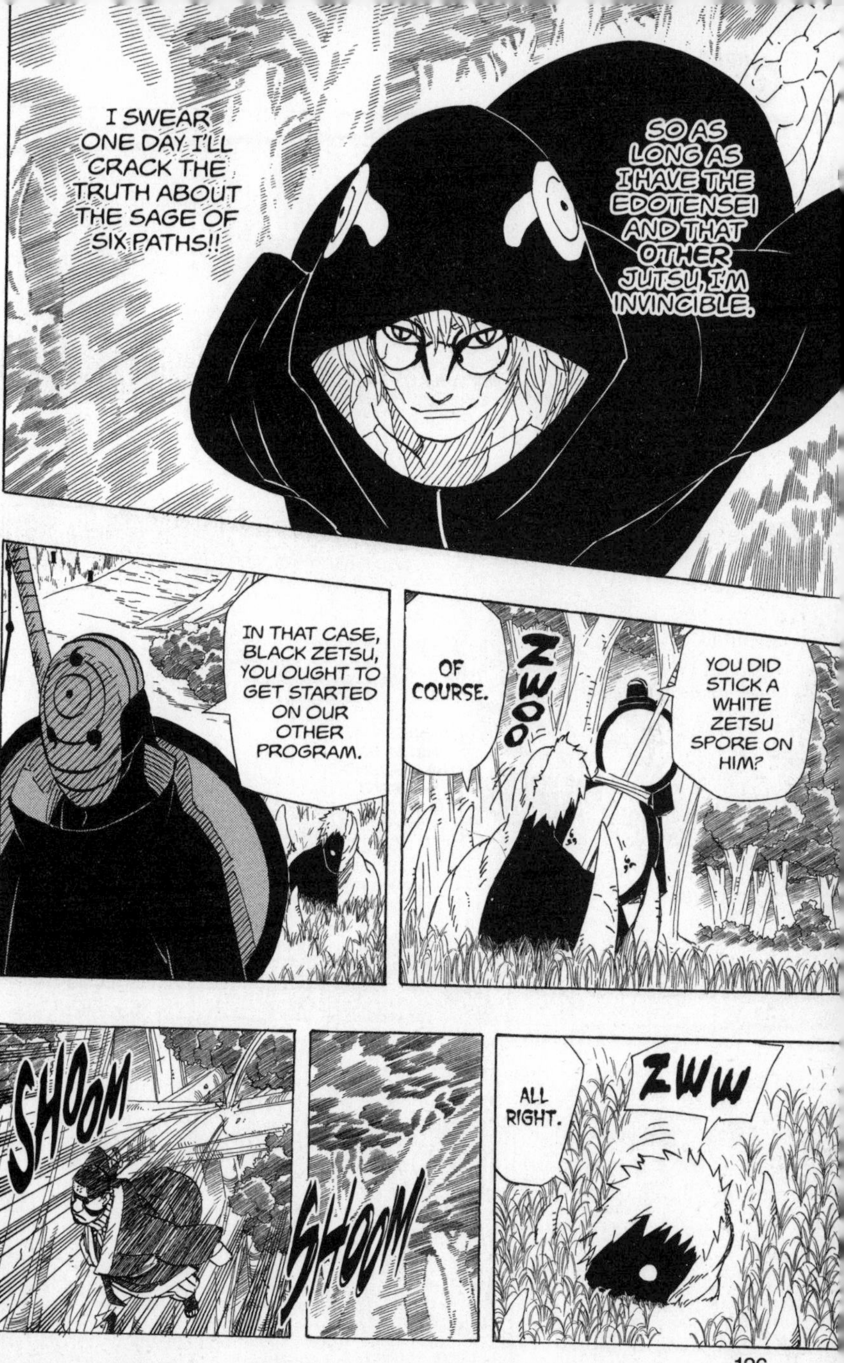
SO AS LONG AS I HAVE THE EDOTENSEI AND THAT OTHER JUTSU, I'M INVINCIBLE.
I SWEAR ONE DAY I'LL CRACK THE TRUTH ABOUT THE SAGE OF SIX PATHS!!
YOU DID STICK A WHITE ZETSU SPORE ON HIM?
ZWOOO
OF COURSE.
IN THAT CASE, BLACK ZETSU, YOU OUGHT TO GET STARTED ON OUR OTHER PROGRAM.
ZWW
ALL RIGHT.
SHOOM
SHOOM

READ THIS WAY

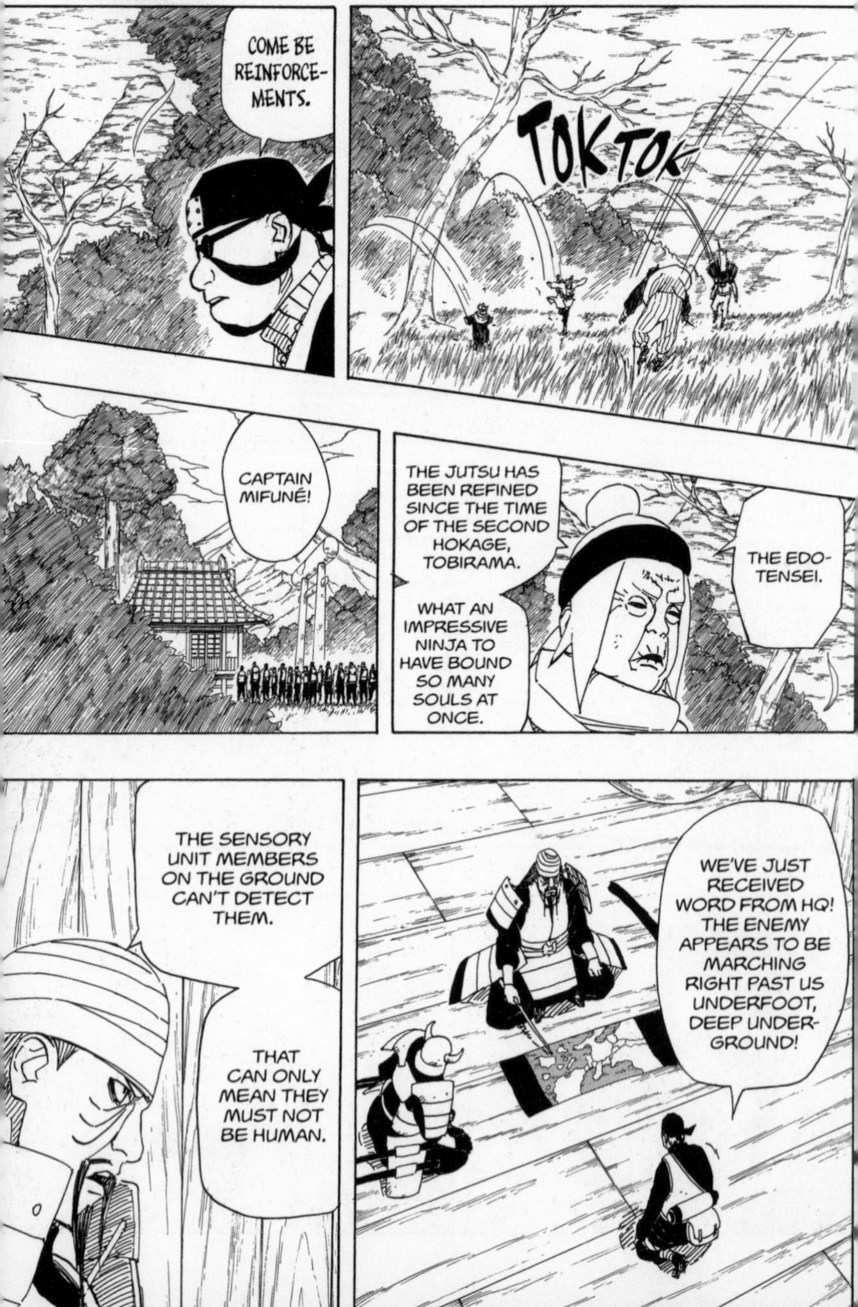
TOKTOK
COME BE REINFORCEMENTS.
THE EDO-TENSEI.
THE JUTSU HAS BEEN REFINED SINCE THE TIME OF THE SECOND HOKAGE, TOBIRAMA.
WHAT AN IMPRESSIVE NINJA TO HAVE BOUND SO MANY SOULS AT ONCE.
CAPTAIN MIFUNÉ!
WE'VE JUST RECEIVED WORD FROM HQ! THE ENEMY APPEARS TO BE MARCHING RIGHT PAST US UNDERFOOT, DEEP UNDERGROUND!
THE SENSORY UNIT MEMBERS ON THE GROUND CAN'T DETECT THEM.
THAT CAN ONLY MEAN THEY MUST NOT BE HUMAN.

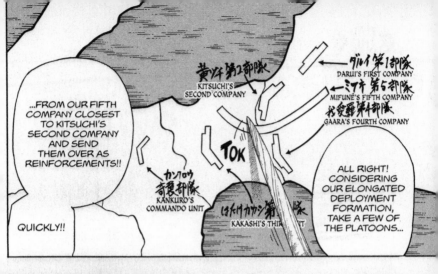

ALL RIGHT! CONSIDERING OUR ELONGATED DEPLOYMENT FORMATION, TAKE A FEW OF THE PLATOONS...
ダルイ第1部隊
DARUI'S FIRST COMPANY
ミフネ第5部隊
MIFUNÉ'S FIFTH COMPANY
我愛羅第4部隊
GAARA'S FOURTH COMPANY
黄ツチ第2部隊
KITSUCHI'S SECOND COMPANY
TOK
KAKASHI'S THIR
カンクロウ奇襲部隊
KANKURO'S COMMANDO UNIT
...FROM OUR FIFTH COMPANY CLOSEST TO KITSUCHI'S SECOND COMPANY AND SEND THEM OVER AS REINFORCEMENTS!!
QUICKLY!!
GOOD CATCH, HAKU.
THAT SPECIES OF GIANT BIRD ACTUALLY DOES FLY IN PAIRS...
...TO ENGAGE IN COOPERATIVE HUNTING.
BUT THAT OCCURS ONLY DURING WINTER, WHEN THEY ARE RAISING YOUNG.
PLUS, THERE IS ALSO THAT BEACON THAT LOOKS LIKE A CLOUD.
OUR ATTACKERS ARE THERE.
PLEASE LEAVE THEM TO ME.

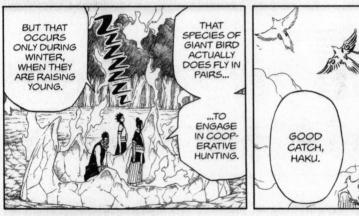

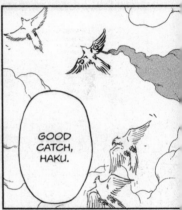

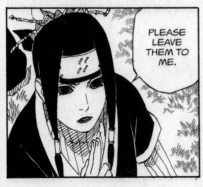

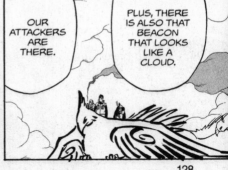

READ THIS WAY

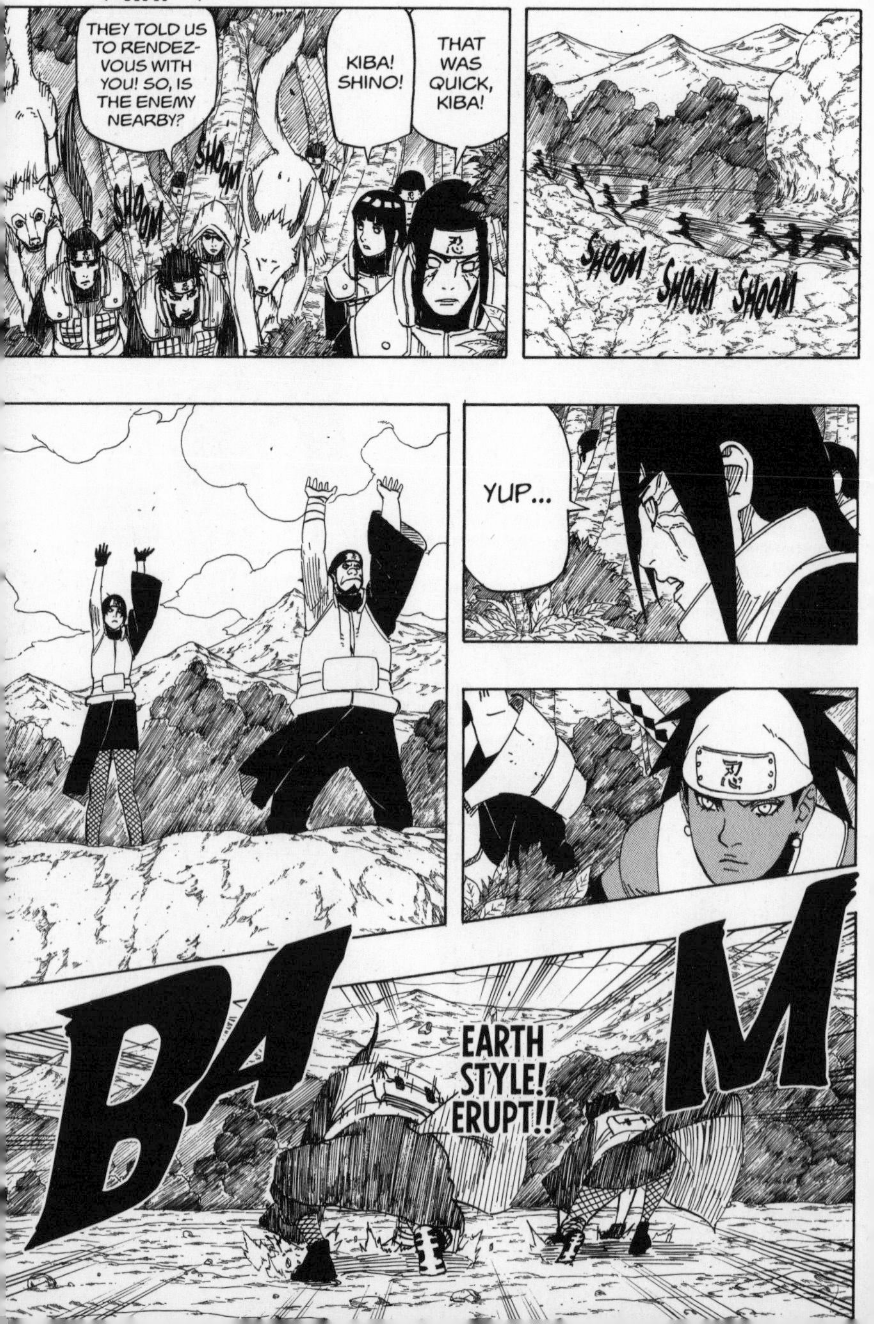
SHOOM
SHOOM
SHOOM
THAT WAS QUICK, KIBA!
KIBA! SHINO!
THEY TOLD US TO RENDEZ-VOUS WITH YOU! SO, IS THE ENEMY NEARBY?
SHOOM
SHOOM
YUP...
BAM
EARTH STYLE! ERUPT!!

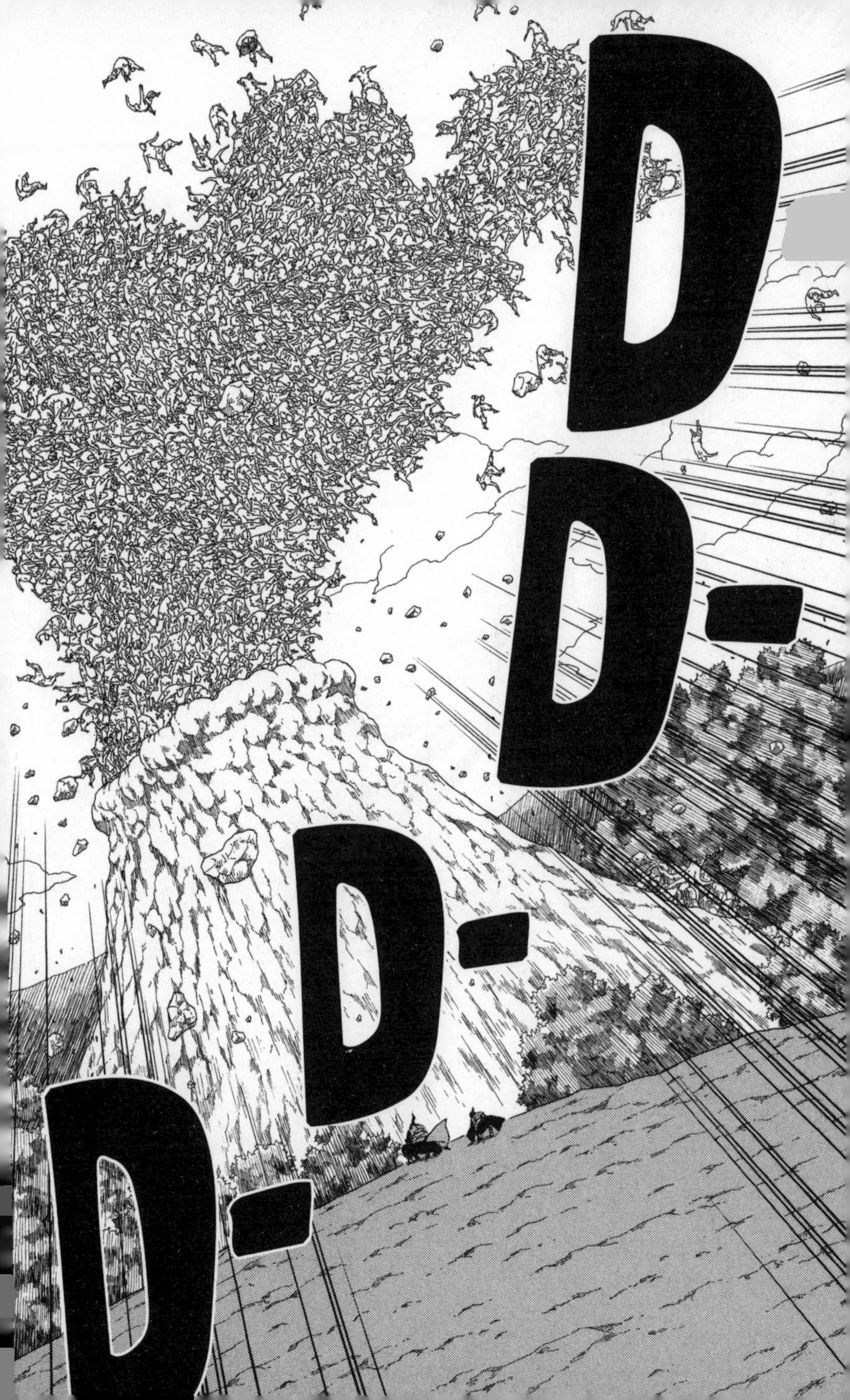
D-D-D-D

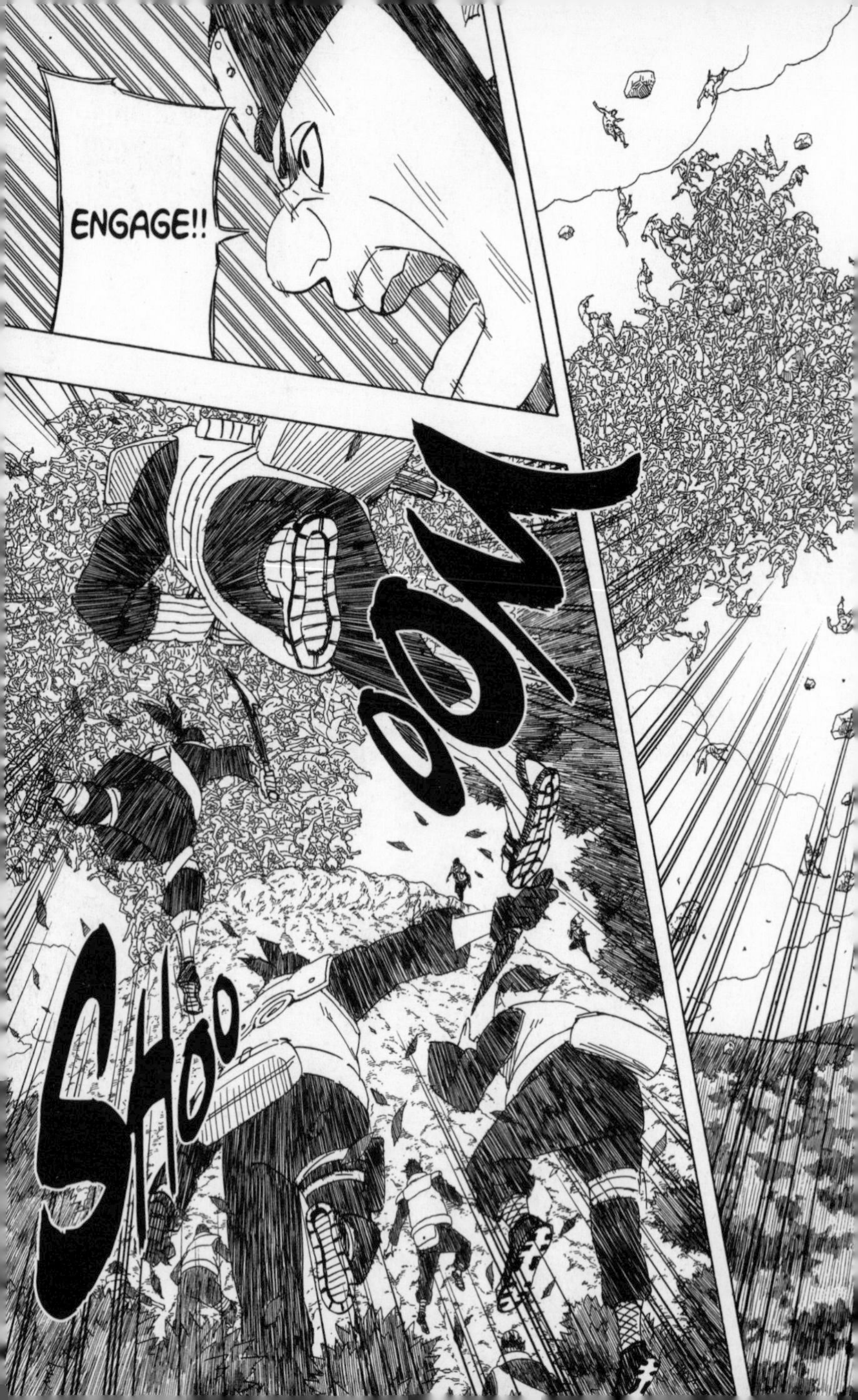
ENGAGE!!
VOOM
SHOO

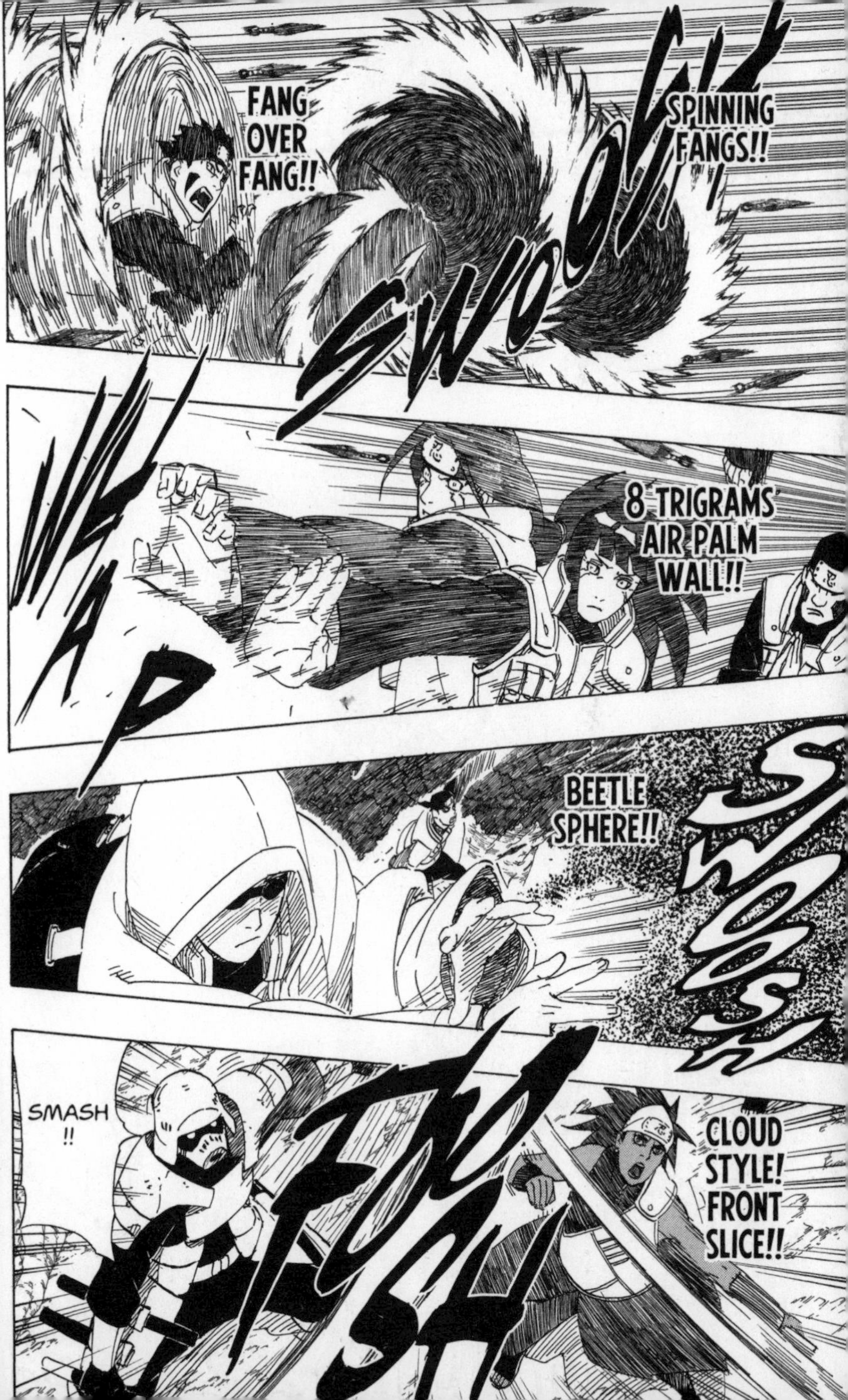
SPINNING FANGS!!
FANG OVER FANG!!
SWOOSH
8 TRIGRAMS AIR PALM WALL!!
WHAP
SWOOSH
BEETLE SPHERE!!
CLOUD STYLE! FRONT SLICE!!
FWASH!
SMASH !!

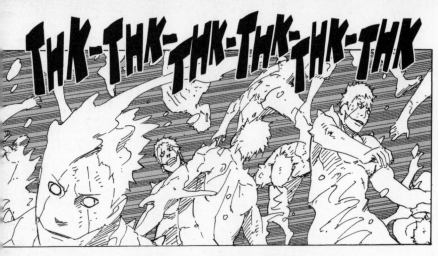

THK-THK-THK-THK-THK-THK

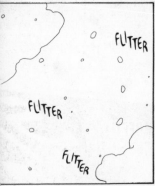

FLITTER

FLITTER

FLITTER

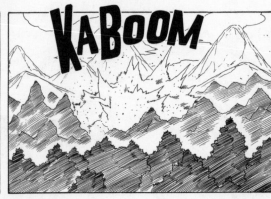

KABOOM

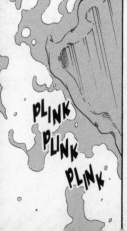

PLINK
PLINK
PLINK

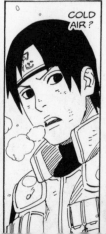

COLD AIR?

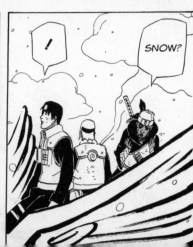

!

SNOW?

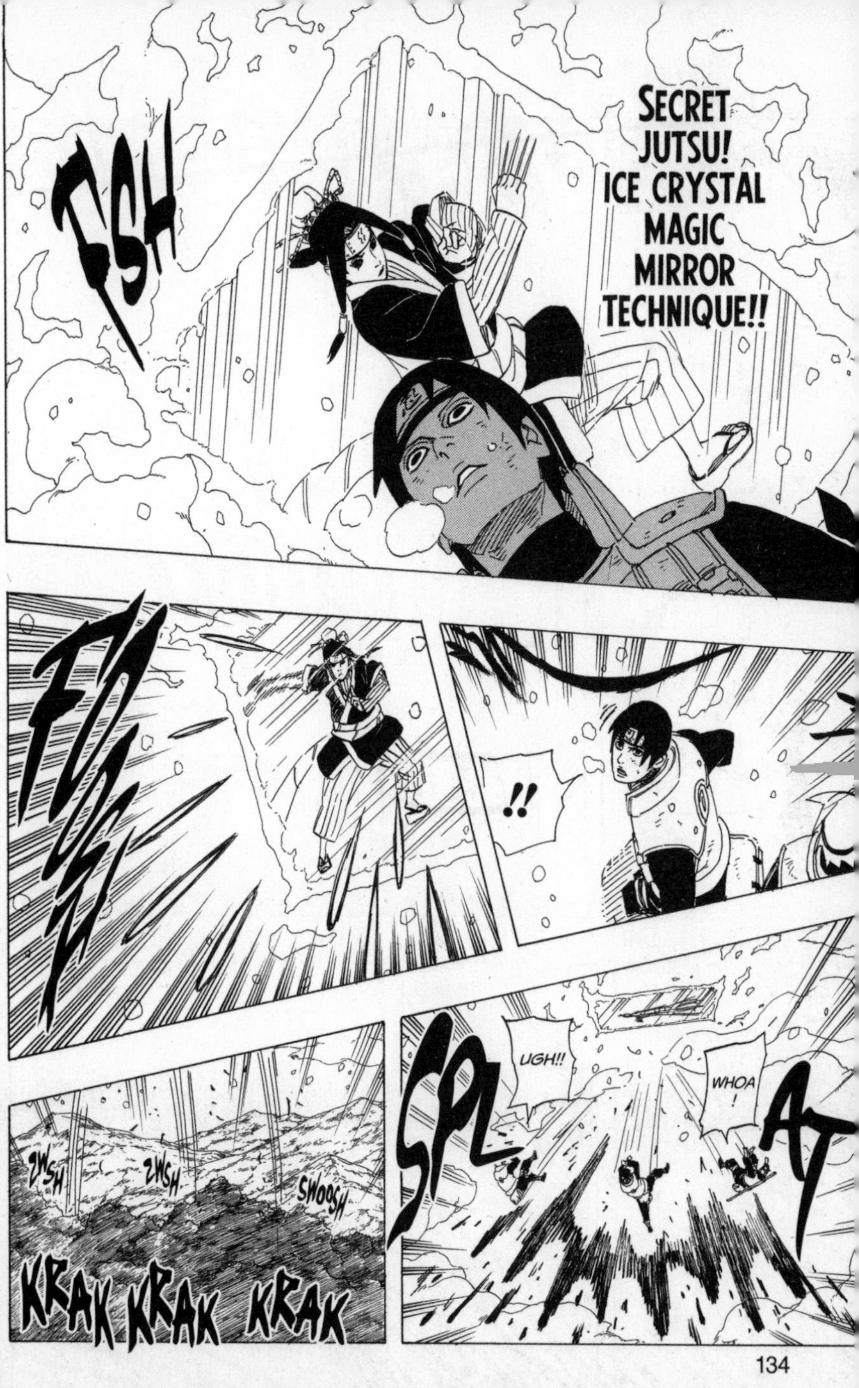
SECRET JUTSU! ICE CRYSTAL MAGIC MIRROR TECHNIQUE!!
FSH
!!
WHOA!
UGH!!
SPLAT
ZWSH
ZWSH
SWOOSH
KRAK KRAK KRAK

READ THIS WAY

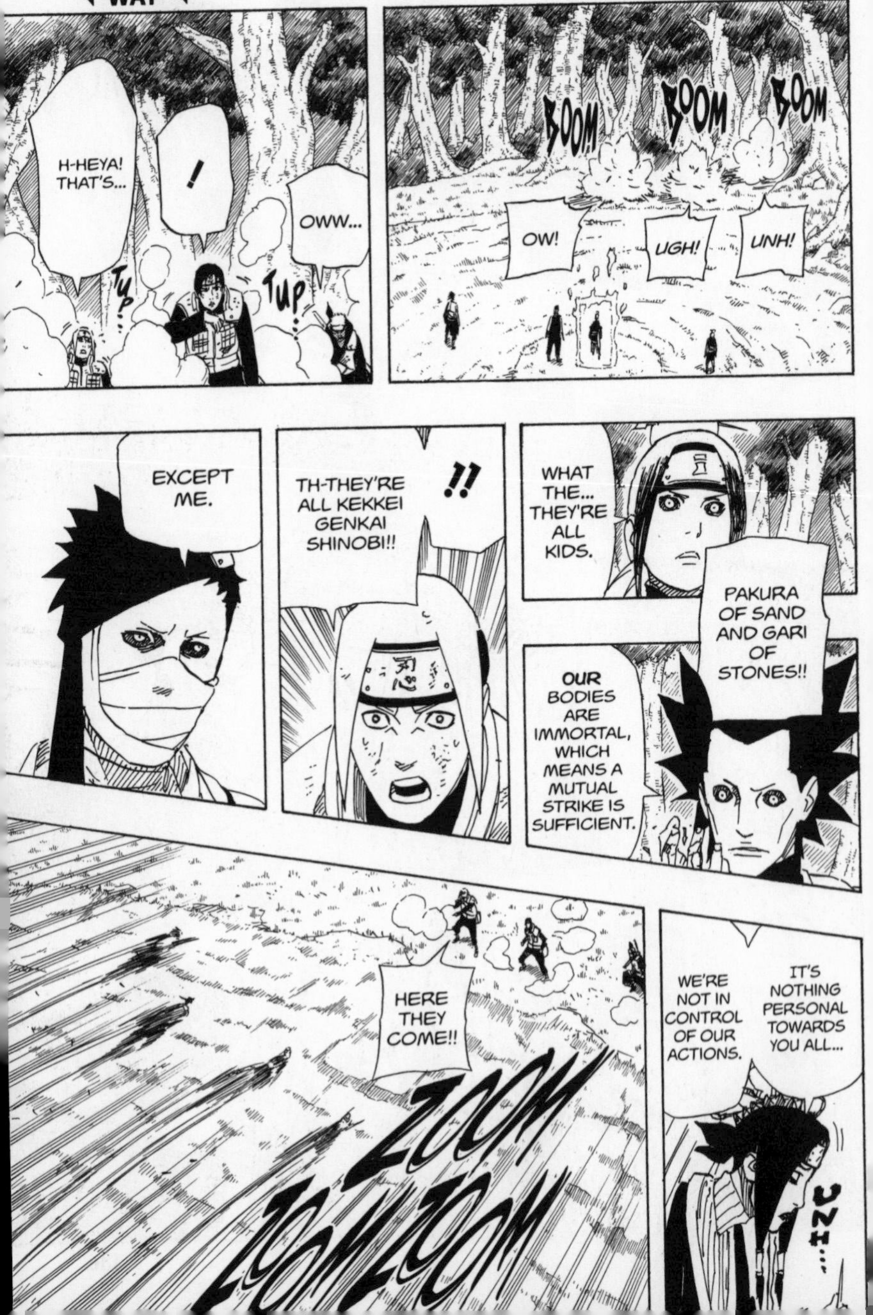
BOOM
BOOM
BOOM
UNH!
UGH!
OW!
OWW...
TUP
TUP
!
H-HEYA! THAT'S...
WHAT THE... THEY'RE ALL KIDS.
PAKURA OF SAND AND GARI OF STONES!!
OUR BODIES ARE IMMORTAL, WHICH MEANS A MUTUAL STRIKE IS SUFFICIENT.
!!
TH-THEY'RE ALL KEKKEI GENKAI SHINOBI!!
EXCEPT ME.
IT'S NOTHING PERSONAL TOWARDS YOU ALL...
WE'RE NOT IN CONTROL OF OUR ACTIONS.
UNH...
HERE THEY COME!!
ZOOM
ZOOM
ZOOM

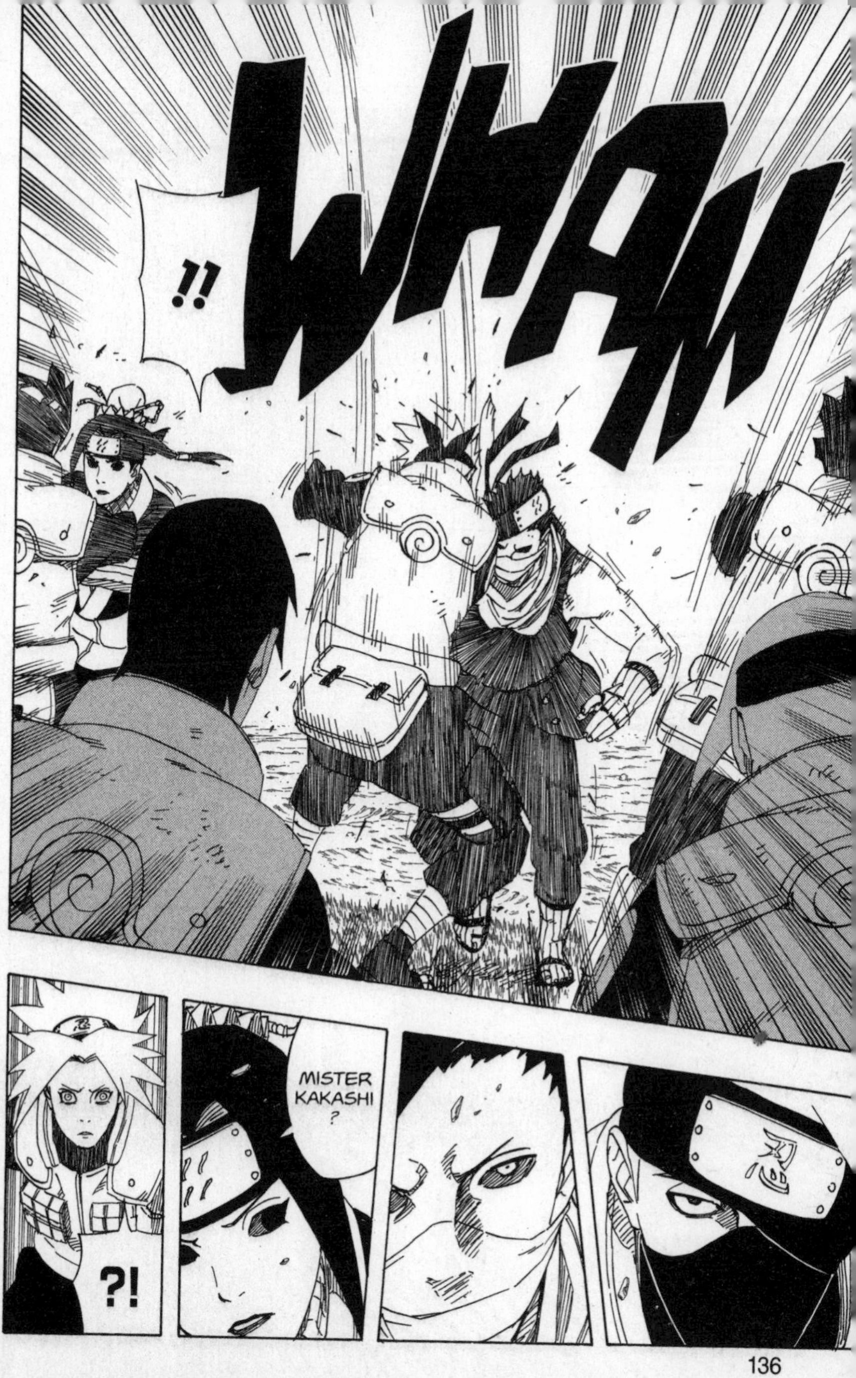
WHAM
!!
MISTER KAKASHI?
?!

READ THIS WAY

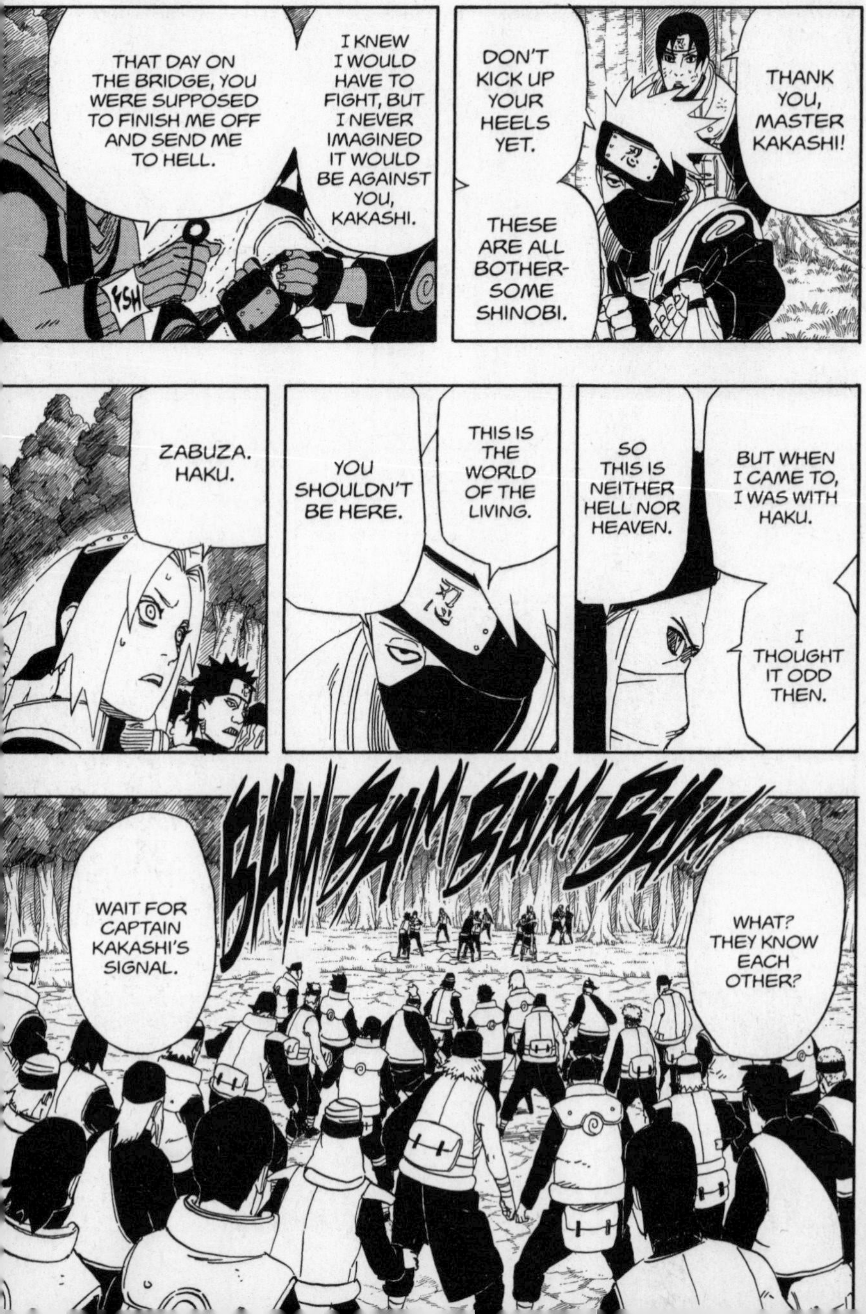
THANK YOU, MASTER KAKASHI!
DON'T KICK UP YOUR HEELS YET.
THESE ARE ALL BOTHERSOME SHINOBI.
I KNEW I WOULD HAVE TO FIGHT, BUT I NEVER IMAGINED IT WOULD BE AGAINST YOU, KAKASHI.
THAT DAY ON THE BRIDGE, YOU WERE SUPPOSED TO FINISH ME OFF AND SEND ME TO HELL.
FSH
BUT WHEN I CAME TO, I WAS WITH HAKU.
I THOUGHT IT ODD THEN.
SO THIS IS NEITHER HELL NOR HEAVEN.
THIS IS THE WORLD OF THE LIVING.
YOU SHOULDN'T BE HERE.
ZABUZA. HAKU.
WHAT? THEY KNOW EACH OTHER?
BAM BAM BAM BAM
WAIT FOR CAPTAIN KAKASHI'S SIGNAL.

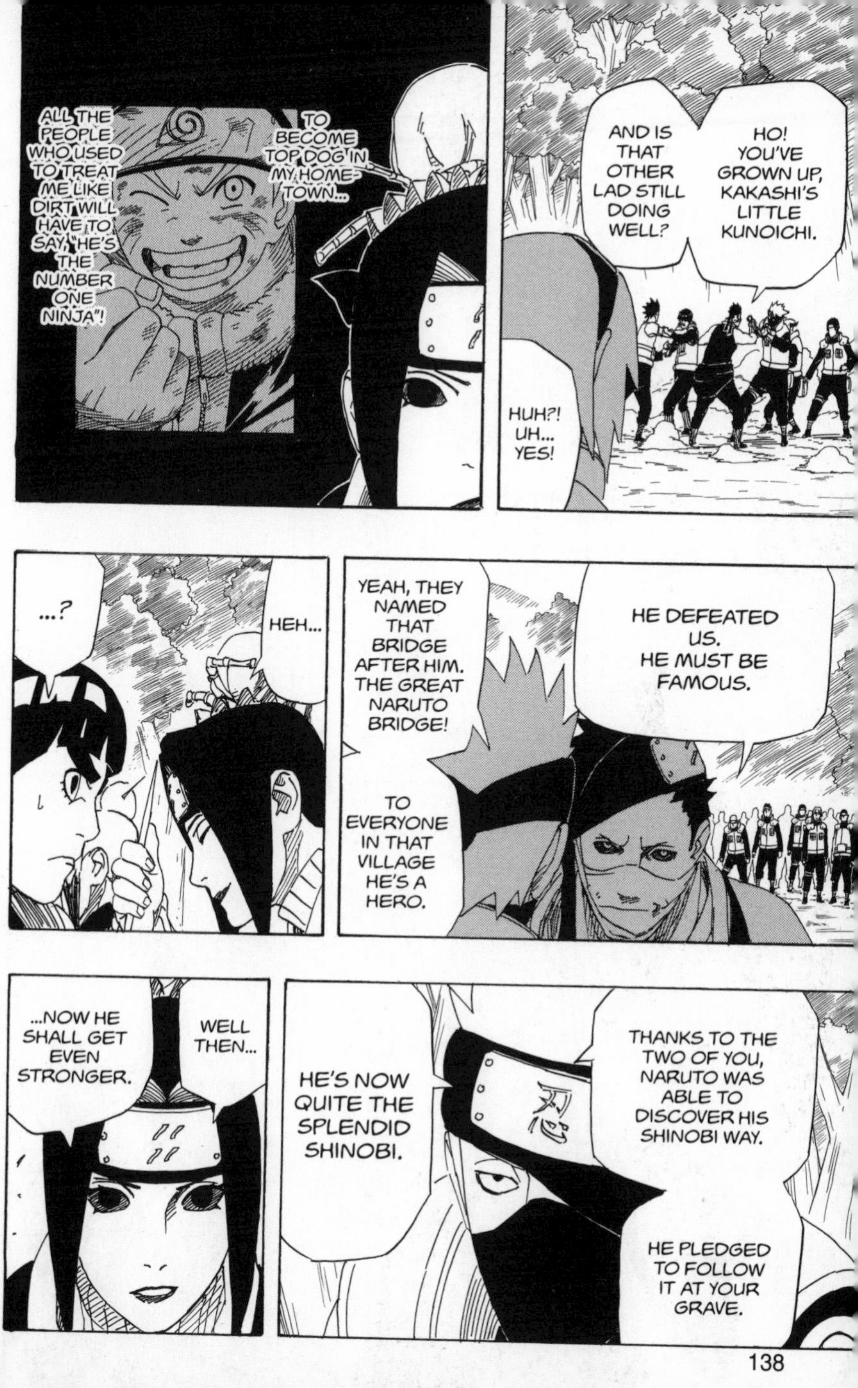
HO! YOU'VE GROWN UP, KAKASHI'S LITTLE KUNOICHI.
AND IS THAT OTHER LAD STILL DOING WELL?
HUH?! UH... YES!
TO BECOME TOP DOG IN MY HOME-TOWN...
ALL THE PEOPLE WHO USED TO TREAT ME LIKE DIRT WILL HAVE TO SAY, "HE'S THE NUMBER ONE NINJA"!
HE DEFEATED US. HE MUST BE FAMOUS.
YEAH, THEY NAMED THAT BRIDGE AFTER HIM. THE GREAT NARUTO BRIDGE!
TO EVERYONE IN THAT VILLAGE HE'S A HERO.
HEH...
...?
THANKS TO THE TWO OF YOU, NARUTO WAS ABLE TO DISCOVER HIS SHINOBI WAY.
HE PLEDGED TO FOLLOW IT AT YOUR GRAVE.
HE'S NOW QUITE THE SPLENDID SHINOBI.
WELL THEN...
...NOW HE SHALL GET EVEN STRONGER.

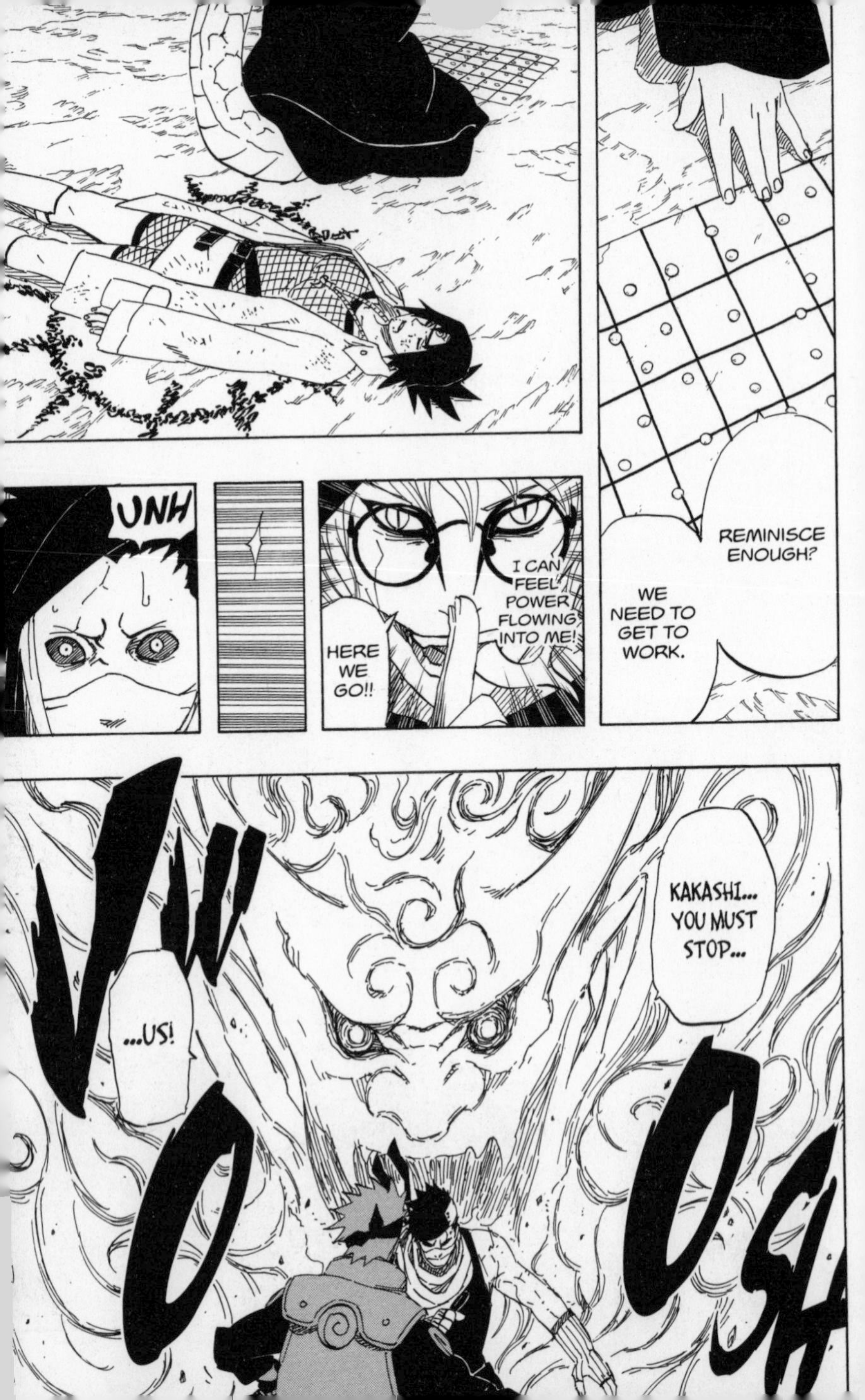
REMINISCE ENOUGH?
WE NEED TO GET TO WORK.
I CAN FEEL POWER FLOWING INTO ME!
HERE WE GO!!
UNH
KAKASHI... YOU MUST STOP...
...US!
VWOOSH

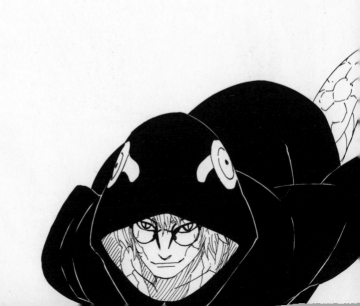

Number 522: We Died.

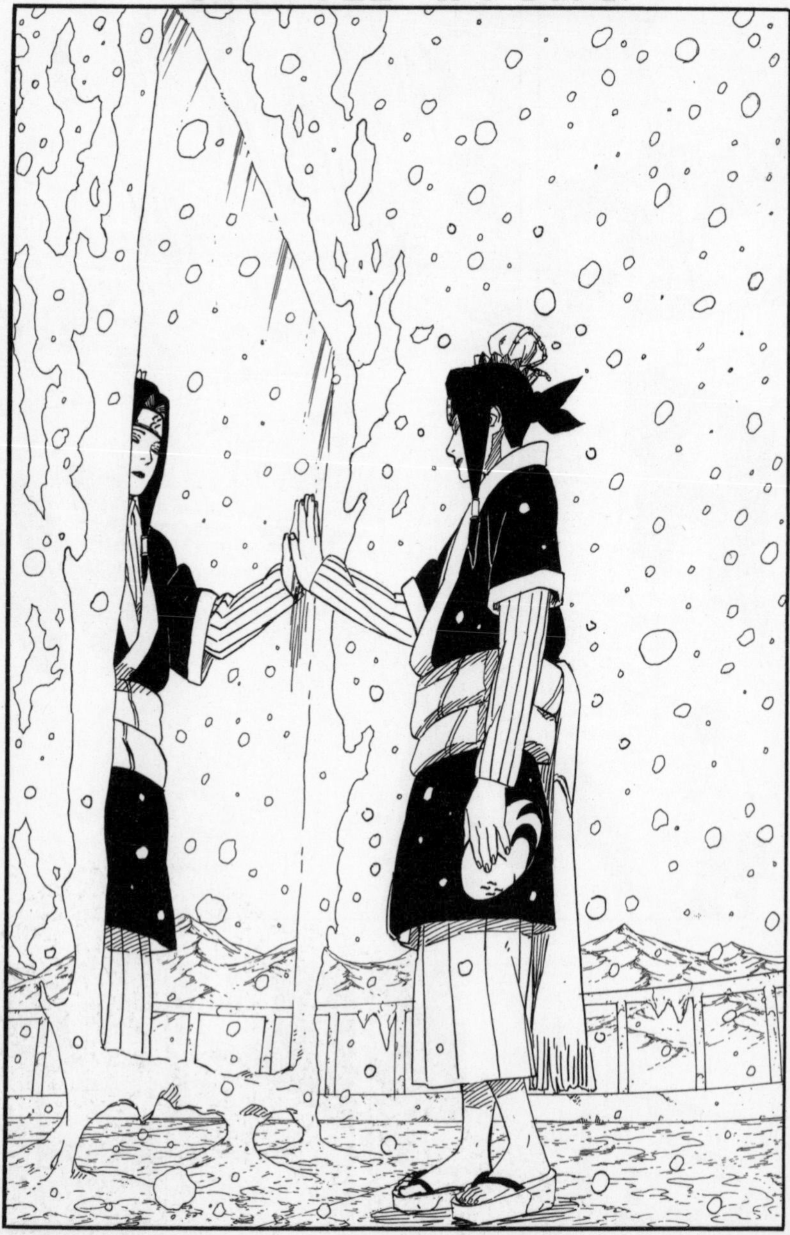

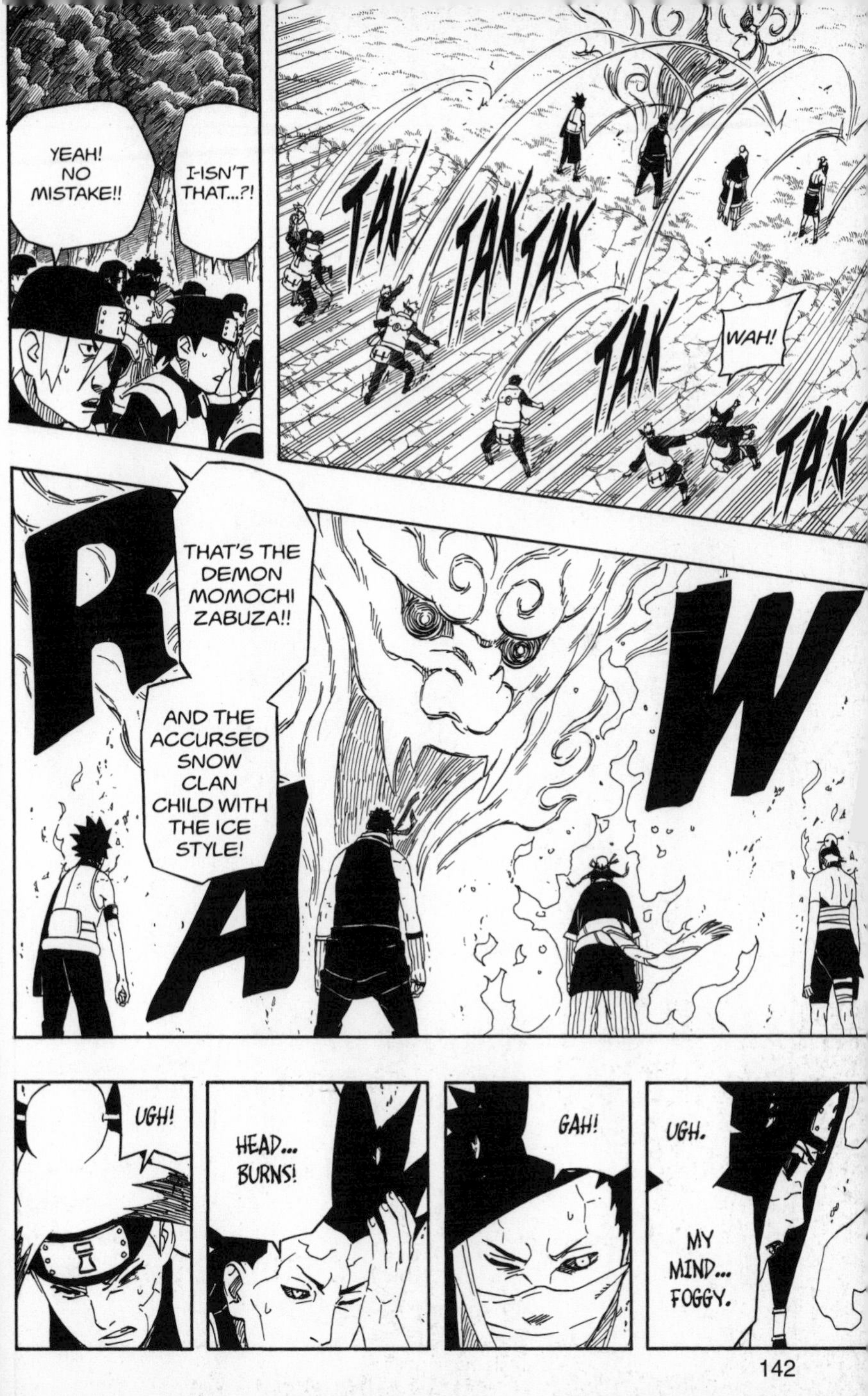
WAH!
TAK
TAKTAK
TAK
TAK
I-ISN'T THAT...?!
YEAH! NO MISTAKE!!
RAAW
THAT'S THE DEMON MOMOCHI ZABUZA!!
AND THE ACCURSED SNOW CLAN CHILD WITH THE ICE STYLE!
UGH.
MY MIND... FOGGY.
GAH!
HEAD... BURNS!
UGH!

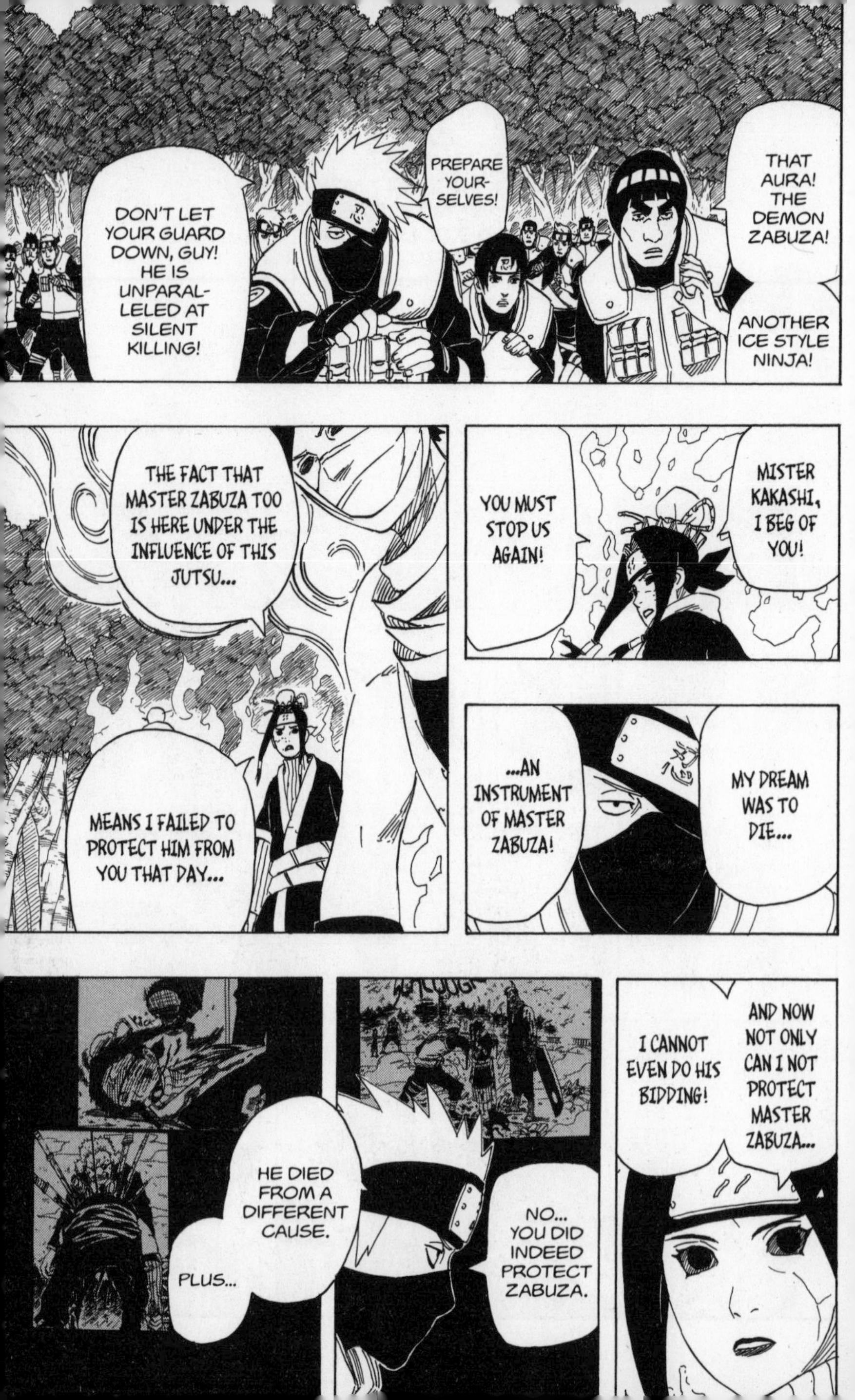
THAT AURA! THE DEMON ZABUZA!
ANOTHER ICE STYLE NINJA!
PREPARE YOUR-SELVES!
DON'T LET YOUR GUARD DOWN, GUY! HE IS UNPARAL-LELED AT SILENT KILLING!
MISTER KAKASHI, I BEG OF YOU!
YOU MUST STOP US AGAIN!
MY DREAM WAS TO DIE...
...AN INSTRUMENT OF MASTER ZABUZA!
THE FACT THAT MASTER ZABUZA TOO IS HERE UNDER THE INFLUENCE OF THIS JUTSU...
MEANS I FAILED TO PROTECT HIM FROM YOU THAT DAY...
AND NOW NOT ONLY CAN I NOT PROTECT MASTER ZABUZA...
I CANNOT EVEN DO HIS BIDDING!
NO... YOU DID INDEED PROTECT ZABUZA.
HE DIED FROM A DIFFERENT CAUSE.
PLUS...

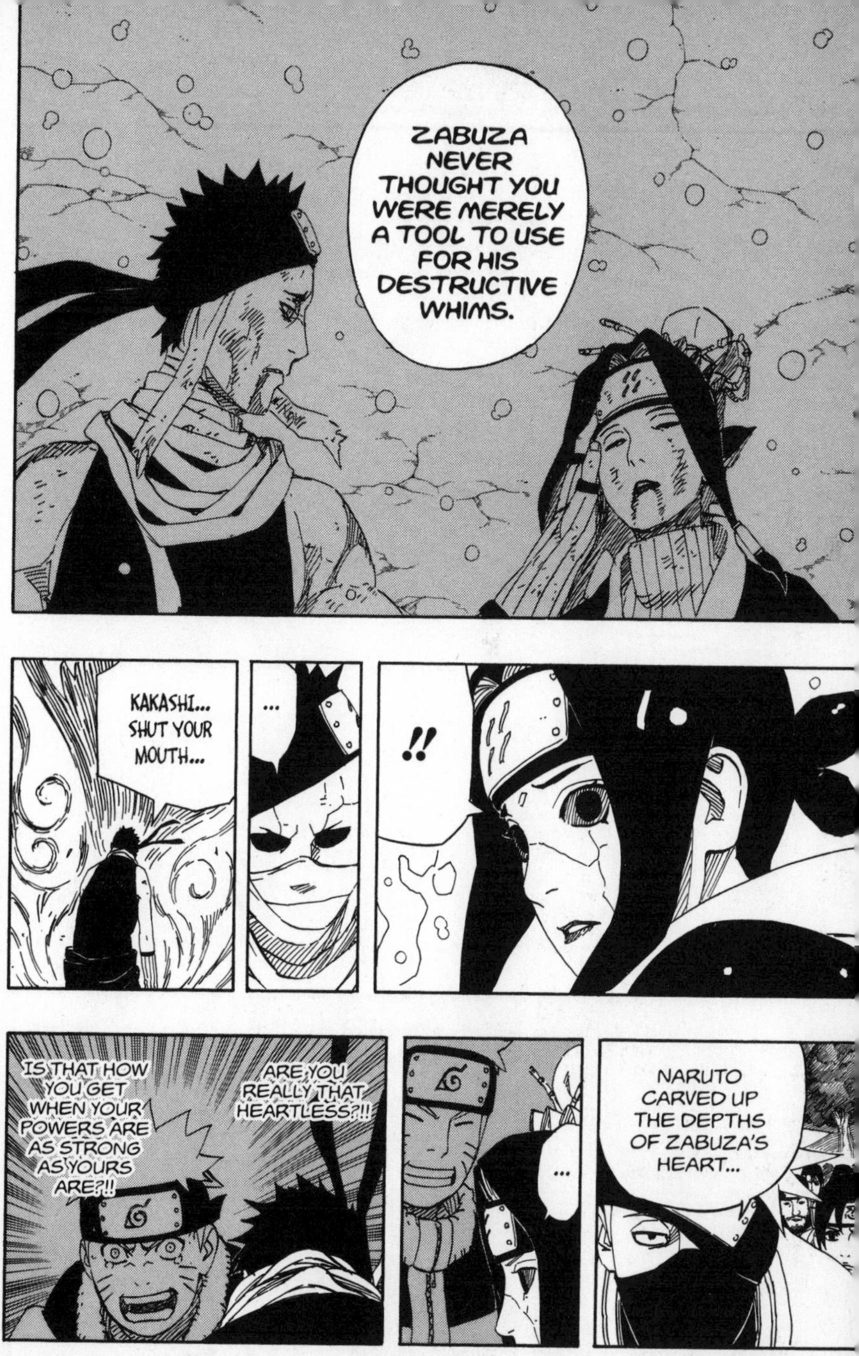
ZABUZA NEVER THOUGHT YOU WERE MERELY A TOOL TO USE FOR HIS DESTRUCTIVE WHIMS.
!!
...
KAKASHI... SHUT YOUR MOUTH...
NARUTO CARVED UP THE DEPTHS OF ZABUZA'S HEART...
...
ARE YOU REALLY THAT HEARTLESS?!!
IS THAT HOW YOU GET WHEN YOUR POWERS ARE AS STRONG AS YOURS ARE?!!

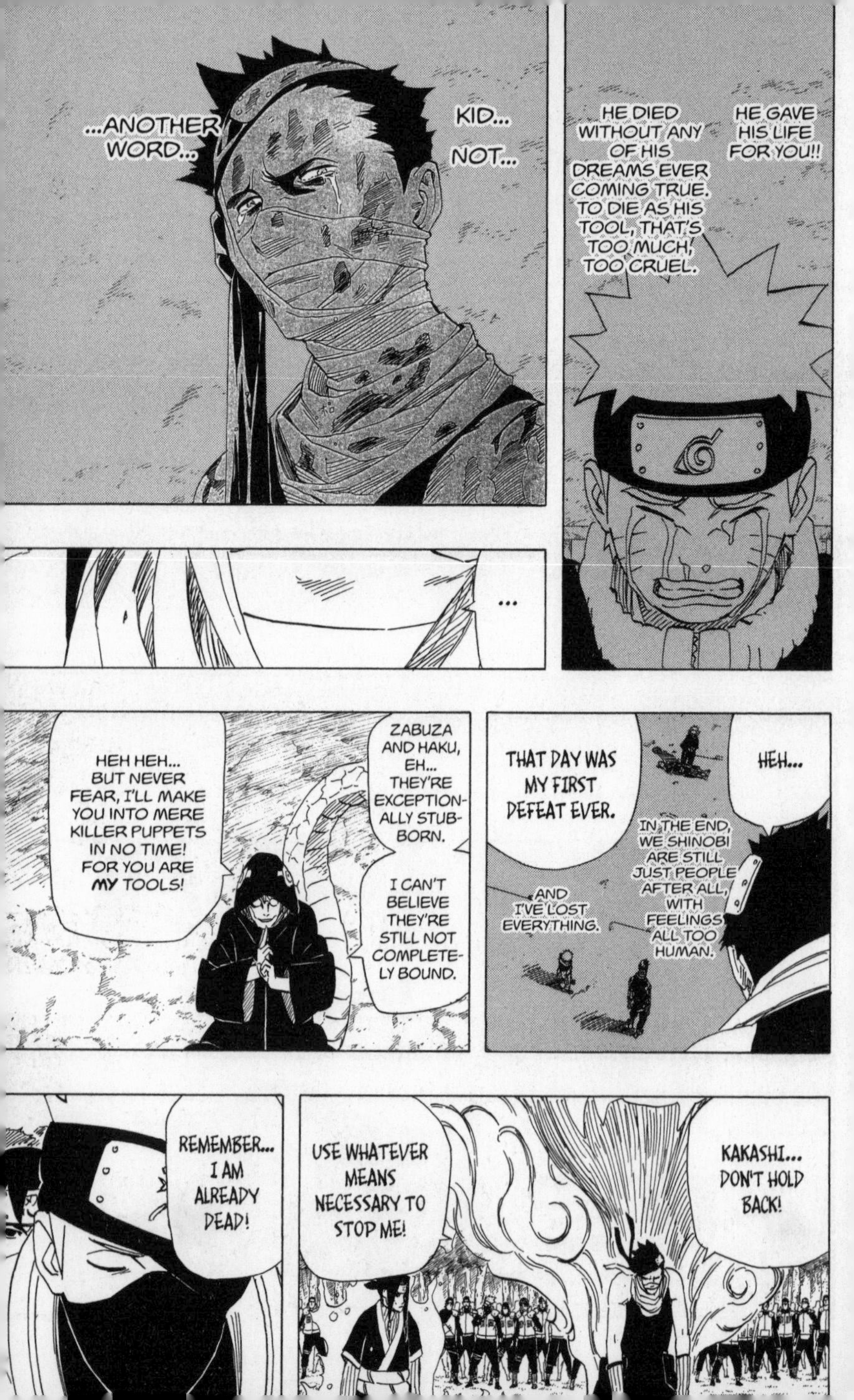
HE GAVE HIS LIFE FOR YOU!!
HE DIED WITHOUT ANY OF HIS DREAMS EVER COMING TRUE. TO DIE AS HIS TOOL, THAT'S TOO MUCH, TOO CRUEL.
KID... NOT...
...ANOTHER WORD...
...
HEH...
THAT DAY WAS MY FIRST DEFEAT EVER.
IN THE END, WE SHINOBI ARE STILL JUST PEOPLE AFTER ALL, WITH FEELINGS ALL TOO HUMAN.
AND I'VE LOST EVERYTHING.
ZABUZA AND HAKU, EH... THEY'RE EXCEPTION-ALLY STUB-BORN.
I CAN'T BELIEVE THEY'RE STILL NOT COMPLETE-LY BOUND.
HEH HEH... BUT NEVER FEAR, I'LL MAKE YOU INTO MERE KILLER PUPPETS IN NO TIME! FOR YOU ARE MY TOOLS!
KAKASHI... DON'T HOLD BACK!
USE WHATEVER MEANS NECESSARY TO STOP ME!
REMEMBER... I AM ALREADY DEAD!

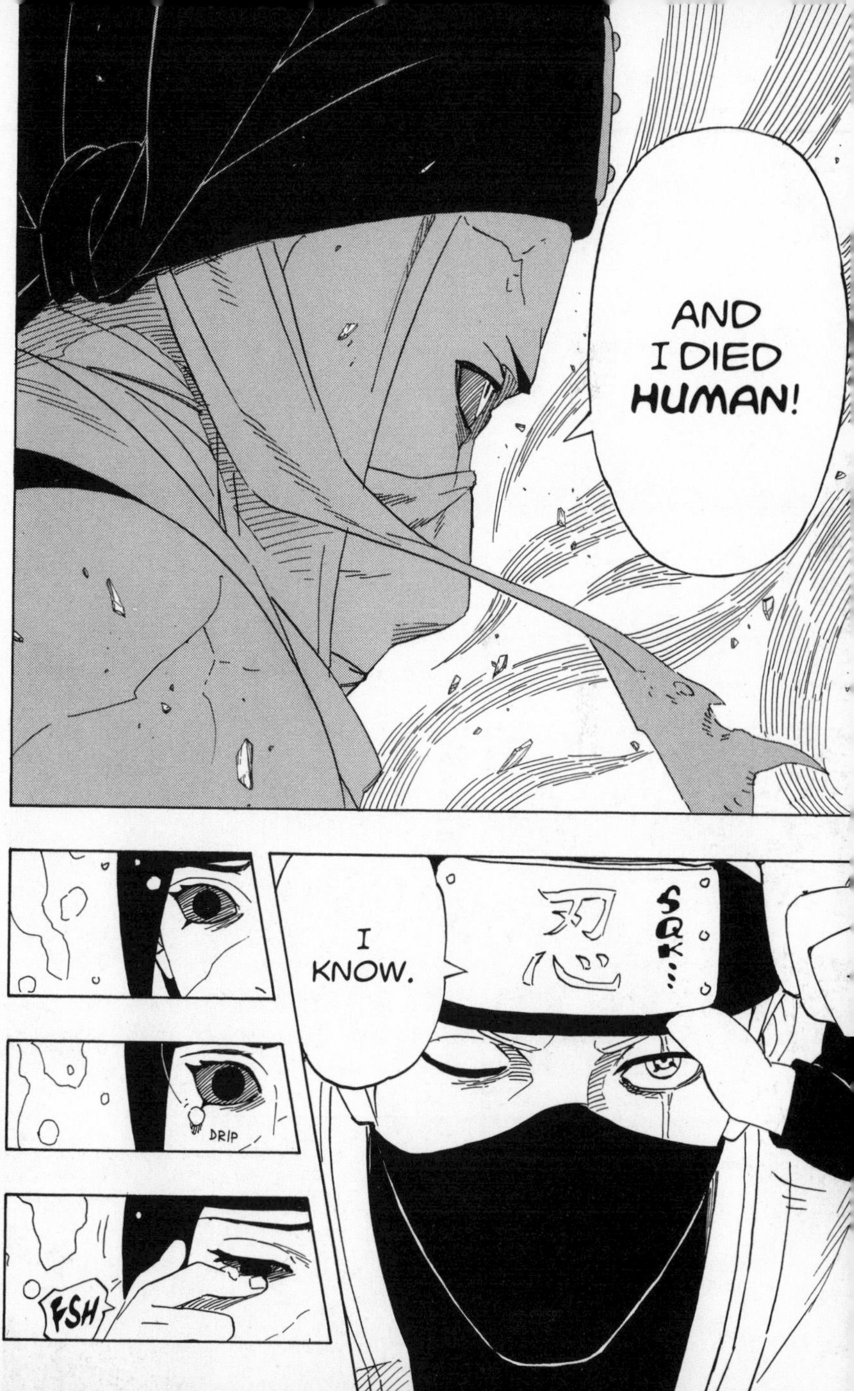
AND I DIED HUMAN!
SQK...
I KNOW.
DRIP
FSH

READ THIS WAY

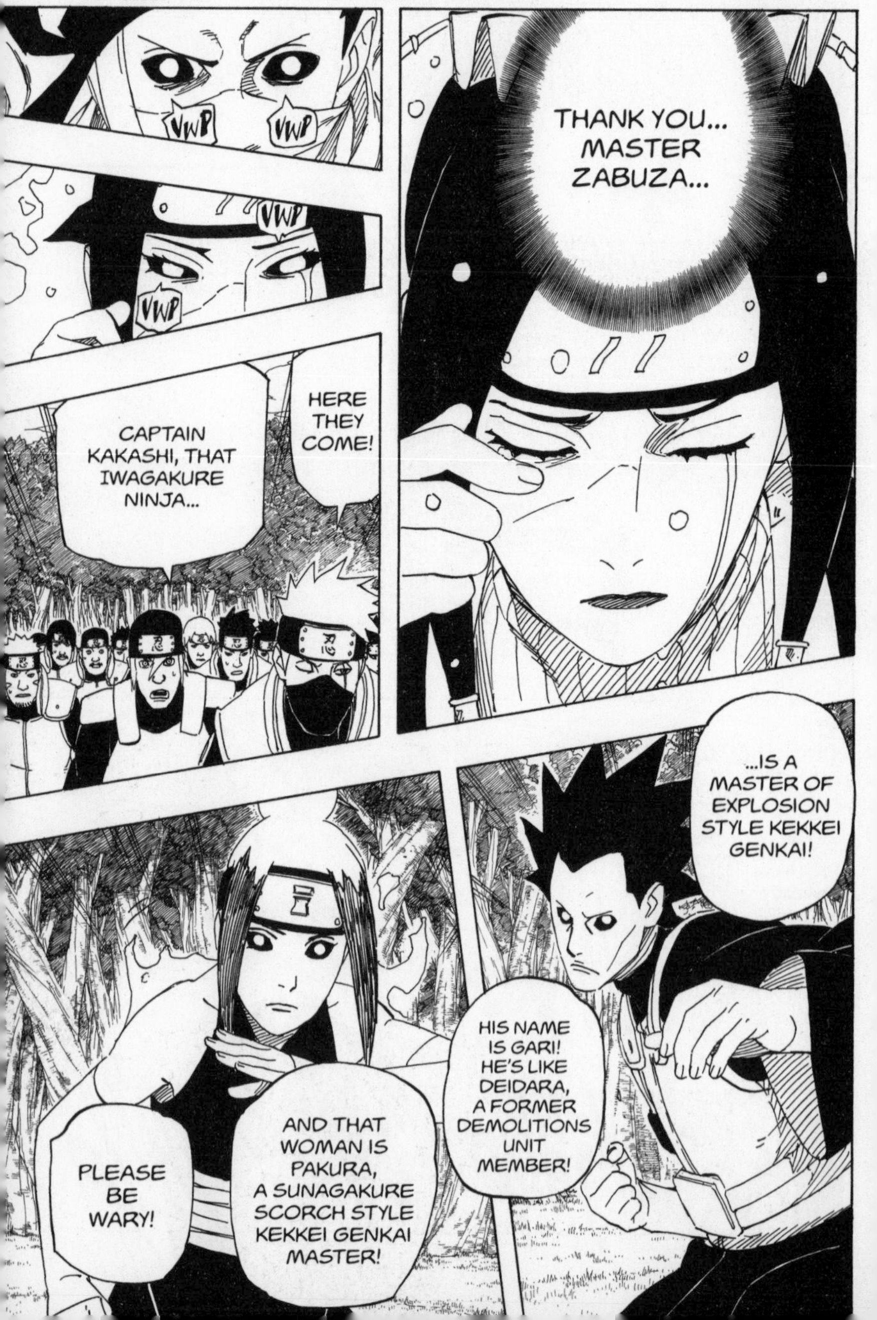
THANK YOU... MASTER ZABUZA...
VWP
VWP
VWP
VWP
HERE THEY COME!
CAPTAIN KAKASHI, THAT IWAGAKURE NINJA...
...IS A MASTER OF EXPLOSION STYLE KEKKEI GENKAI!
HIS NAME IS GARI! HE'S LIKE DEIDARA, A FORMER DEMOLITIONS UNIT MEMBER!
AND THAT WOMAN IS PAKURA, A SUNAGAKURE SCORCH STYLE KEKKEI GENKAI MASTER!
PLEASE BE WARY!

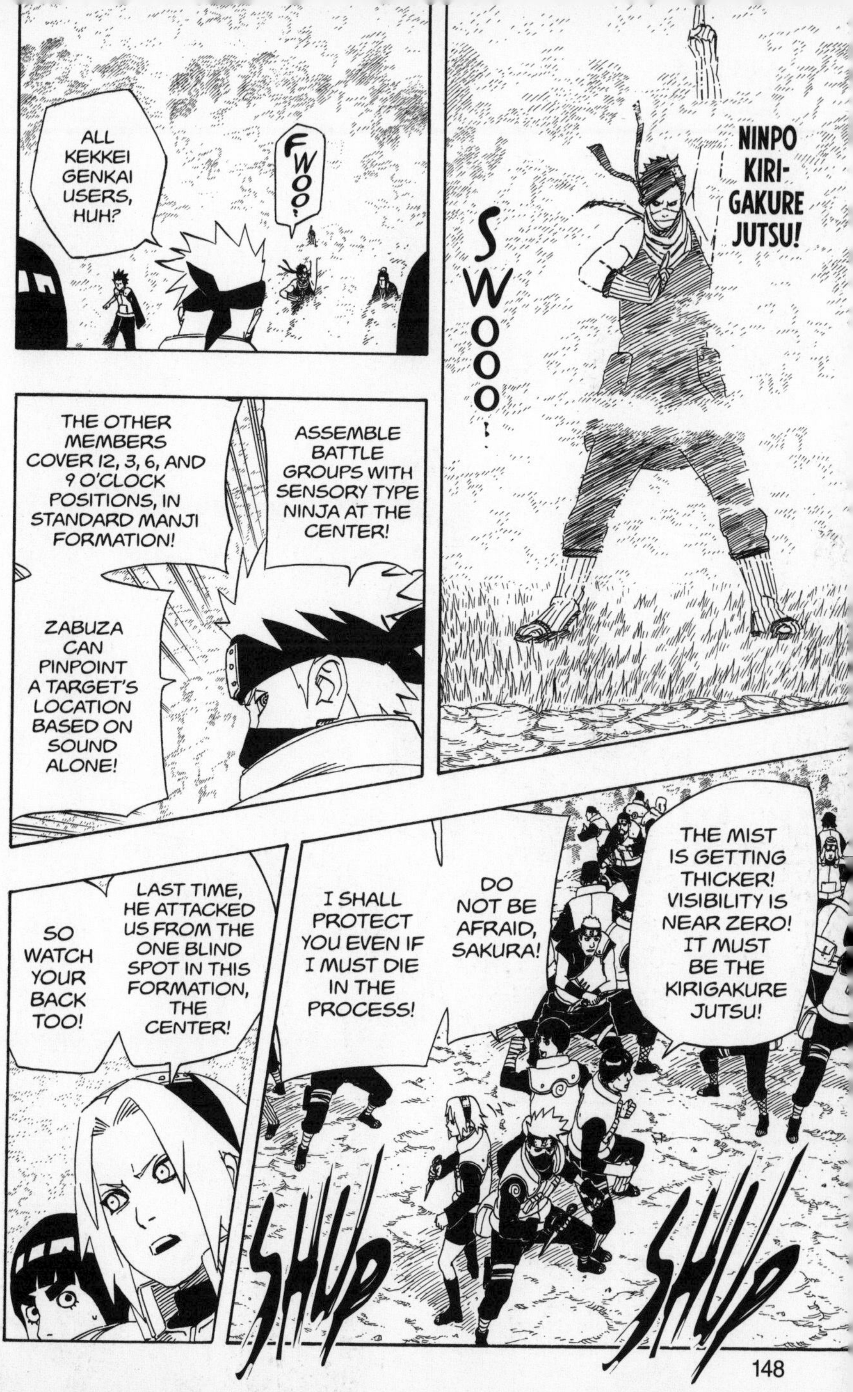
NINPO KIRI-GAKURE JUTSU!
SWOOO
ALL KEKKEI GENKAI USERS, HUH?
FWOO
ASSEMBLE BATTLE GROUPS WITH SENSORY TYPE NINJA AT THE CENTER!
THE OTHER MEMBERS COVER 12, 3, 6, AND 9 O'CLOCK POSITIONS, IN STANDARD MANJI FORMATION!
ZABUZA CAN PINPOINT A TARGET'S LOCATION BASED ON SOUND ALONE!
THE MIST IS GETTING THICKER! VISIBILITY IS NEAR ZERO! IT MUST BE THE KIRIGAKURE JUTSU!
DO NOT BE AFRAID, SAKURA!
I SHALL PROTECT YOU EVEN IF I MUST DIE IN THE PROCESS!
SHUP
SHUP
LAST TIME, HE ATTACKED US FROM THE ONE BLIND SPOT IN THIS FORMATION, THE CENTER!
SO WATCH YOUR BACK TOO!

READ THIS WAY

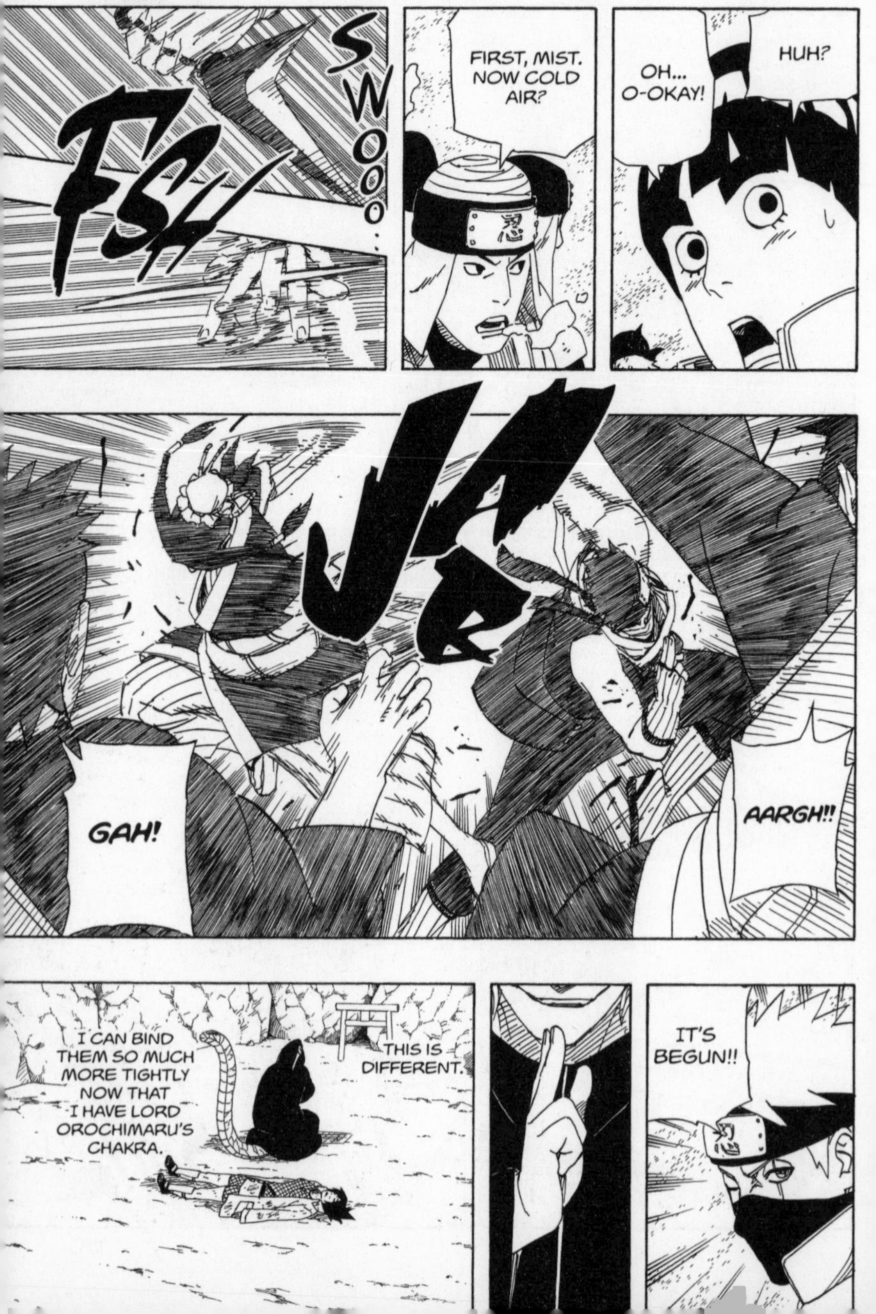
HUH?
OH... O-OKAY!
FIRST, MIST. NOW COLD AIR?
SWOOO...
FSH
JAB
AARGH!!
GAH!
IT'S BEGUN!!
THIS IS DIFFERENT.
I CAN BIND THEM SO MUCH MORE TIGHTLY NOW THAT I HAVE LORD OROCHIMARU'S CHAKRA.

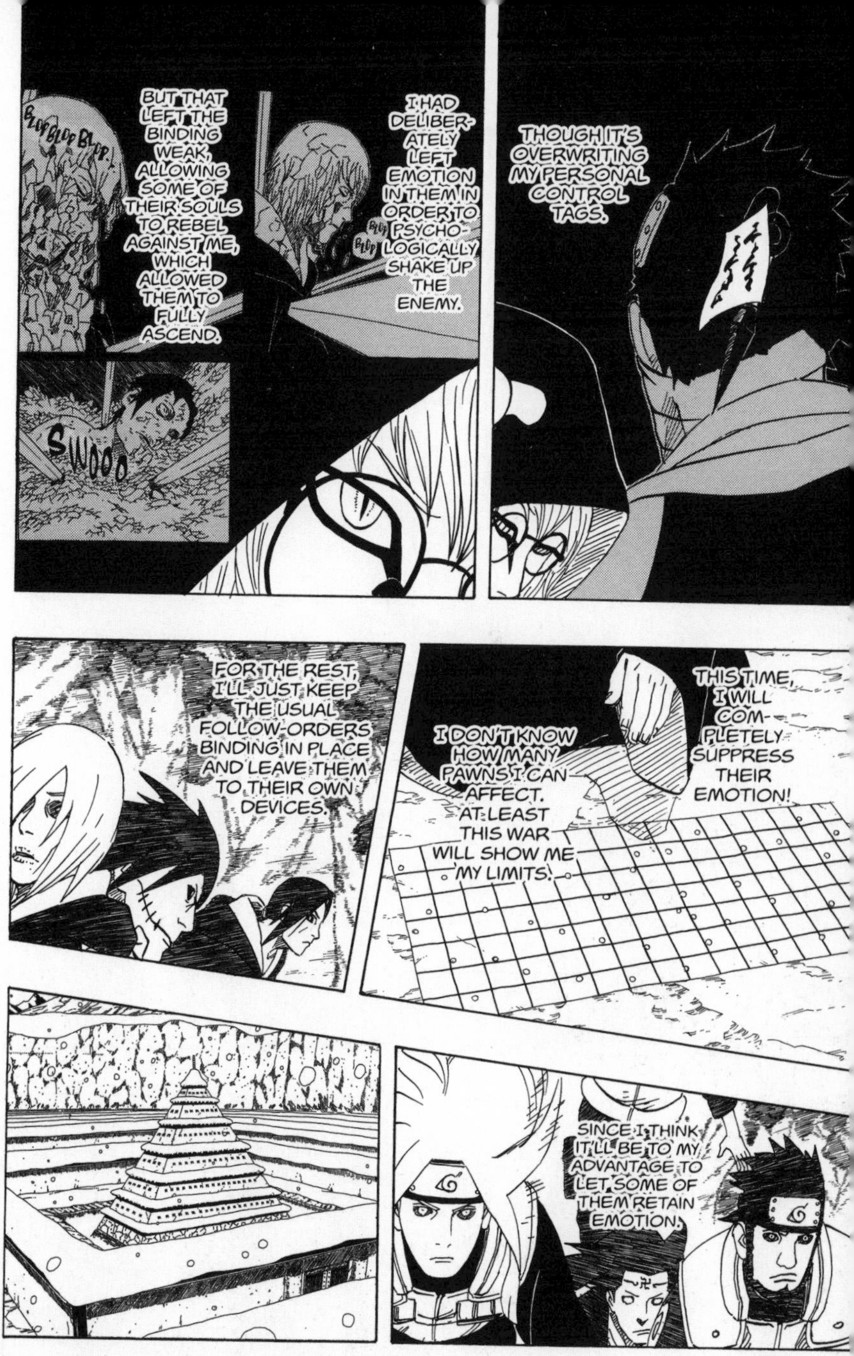
THOUGH IT'S OVERWRITING MY PERSONAL CONTROL TAGS.
I HAD DELIBERATELY LEFT EMOTION IN THEM IN ORDER TO PSYCHOLOGICALLY SHAKE UP THE ENEMY.
BLOP BLOP
BUT THAT LEFT THE BINDING WEAK, ALLOWING SOME OF THEIR SOULS TO REBEL AGAINST ME, WHICH ALLOWED THEM TO FULLY ASCEND.
BLOP BLOP BLOP
SWOOO
THIS TIME, I WILL COMPLETELY SUPPRESS THEIR EMOTION!
I DON'T KNOW HOW MANY PAWNS I CAN AFFECT. AT LEAST THIS WAR WILL SHOW ME MY LIMITS.
FOR THE REST, I'LL JUST KEEP THE USUAL FOLLOW-ORDERS BINDING IN PLACE AND LEAVE THEM TO THEIR OWN DEVICES.
SINCE I THINK IT'LL BE TO MY ADVANTAGE TO LET SOME OF THEM RETAIN EMOTION.

READ THIS WAY

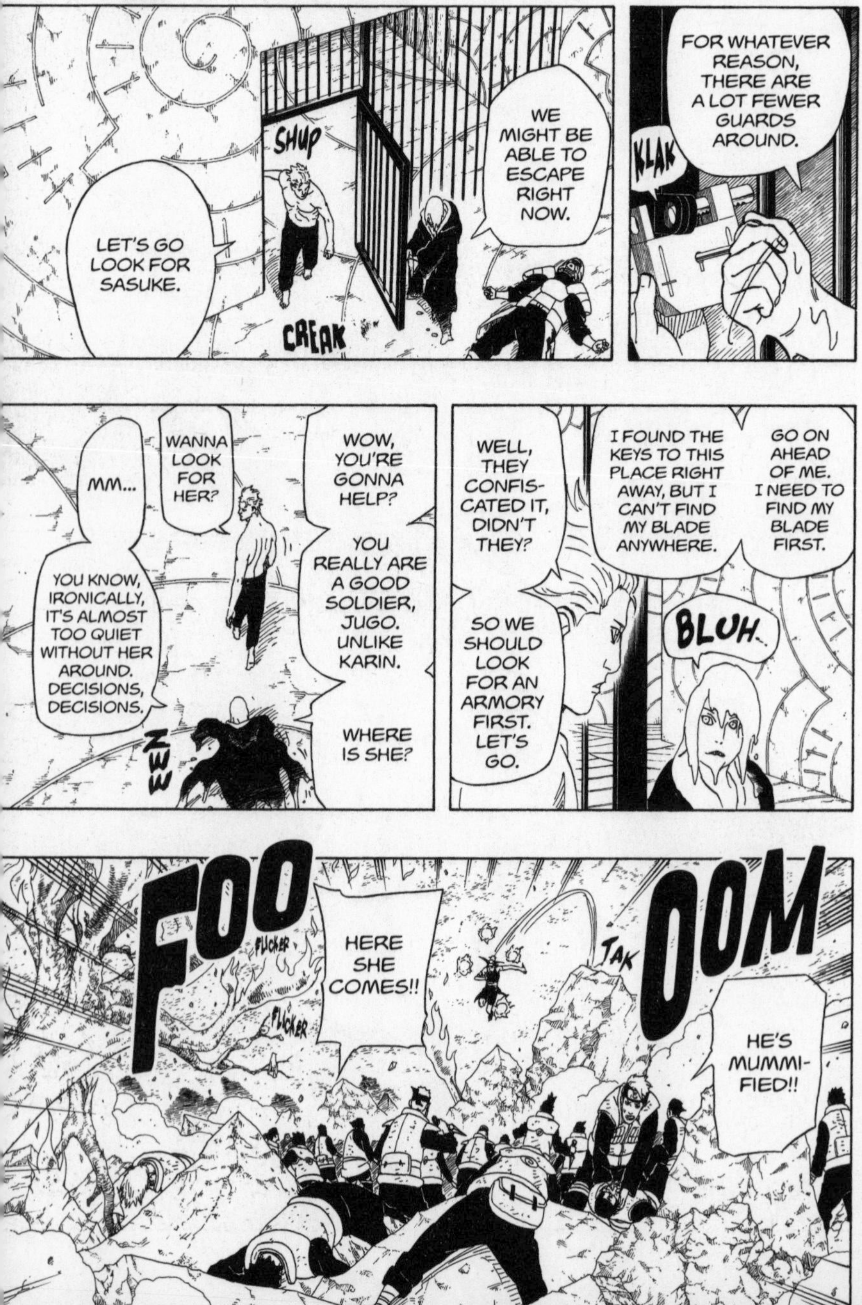
FOR WHATEVER REASON, THERE ARE A LOT FEWER GUARDS AROUND.
KLAK
WE MIGHT BE ABLE TO ESCAPE RIGHT NOW.
SHUP
CREAK
LET'S GO LOOK FOR SASUKE.
GO ON AHEAD OF ME. I NEED TO FIND MY BLADE FIRST.
I FOUND THE KEYS TO THIS PLACE RIGHT AWAY, BUT I CAN'T FIND MY BLADE ANYWHERE.
BLUH...
WELL, THEY CONFISCATED IT, DIDN'T THEY?
SO WE SHOULD LOOK FOR AN ARMORY FIRST. LET'S GO.
WOW, YOU'RE GONNA HELP?
YOU REALLY ARE A GOOD SOLDIER, JUGO. UNLIKE KARIN.
WHERE IS SHE?
WANNA LOOK FOR HER?
MM...
YOU KNOW, IRONICALLY, IT'S ALMOST TOO QUIET WITHOUT HER AROUND. DECISIONS, DECISIONS.
ZWW
FOO OOM
HE'S MUMMIFIED!!
TAK
HERE SHE COMES!!
FLICKER
FLICKER

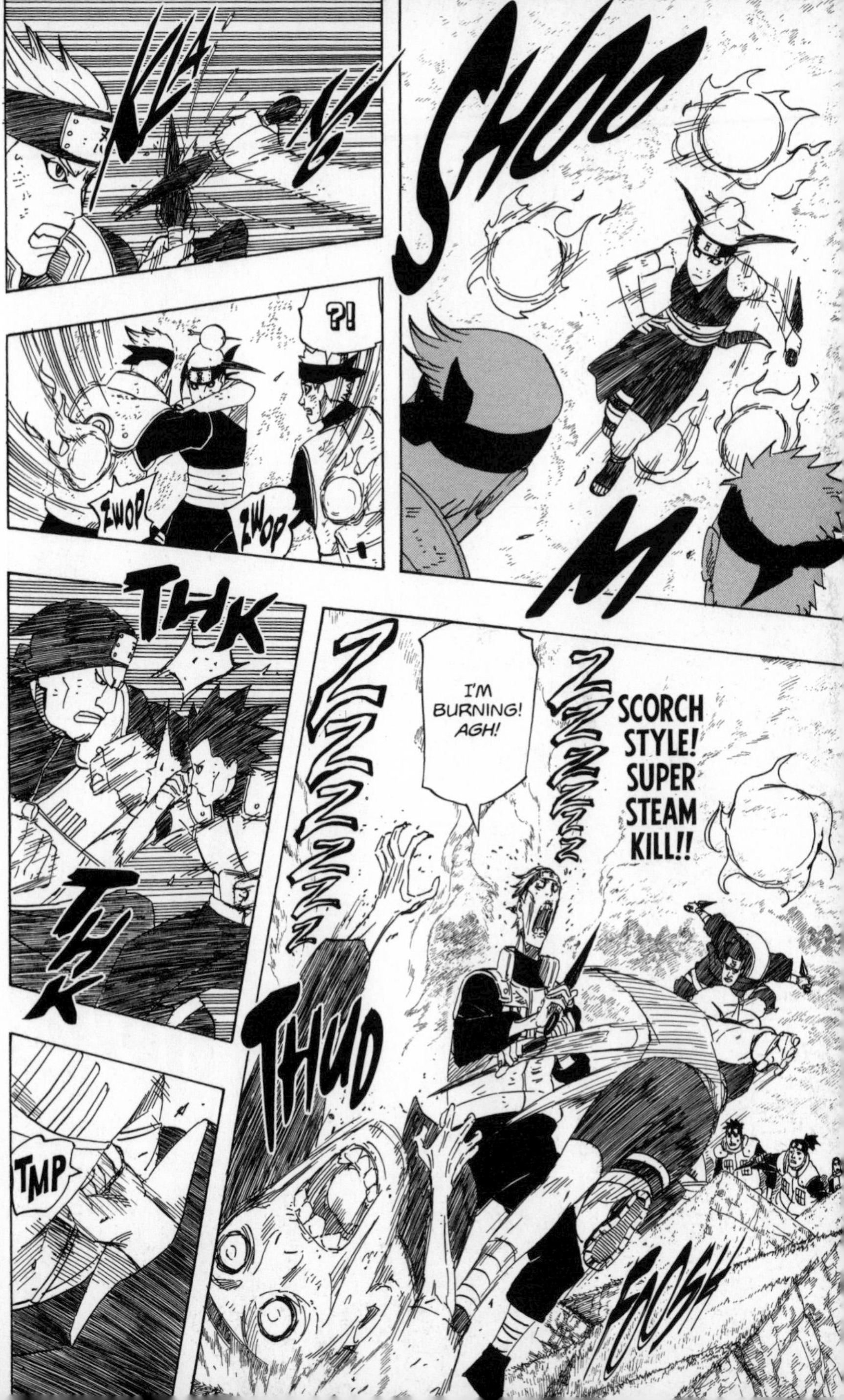
SHOO
M
KLANG
?!
ZWOP
ZWOP
ZZZZZZZZZ
I'M BURNING! AGH!
ZZZZZZZZ
SCORCH STYLE! SUPER STEAM KILL!!
THUD
THK
THK
TMP

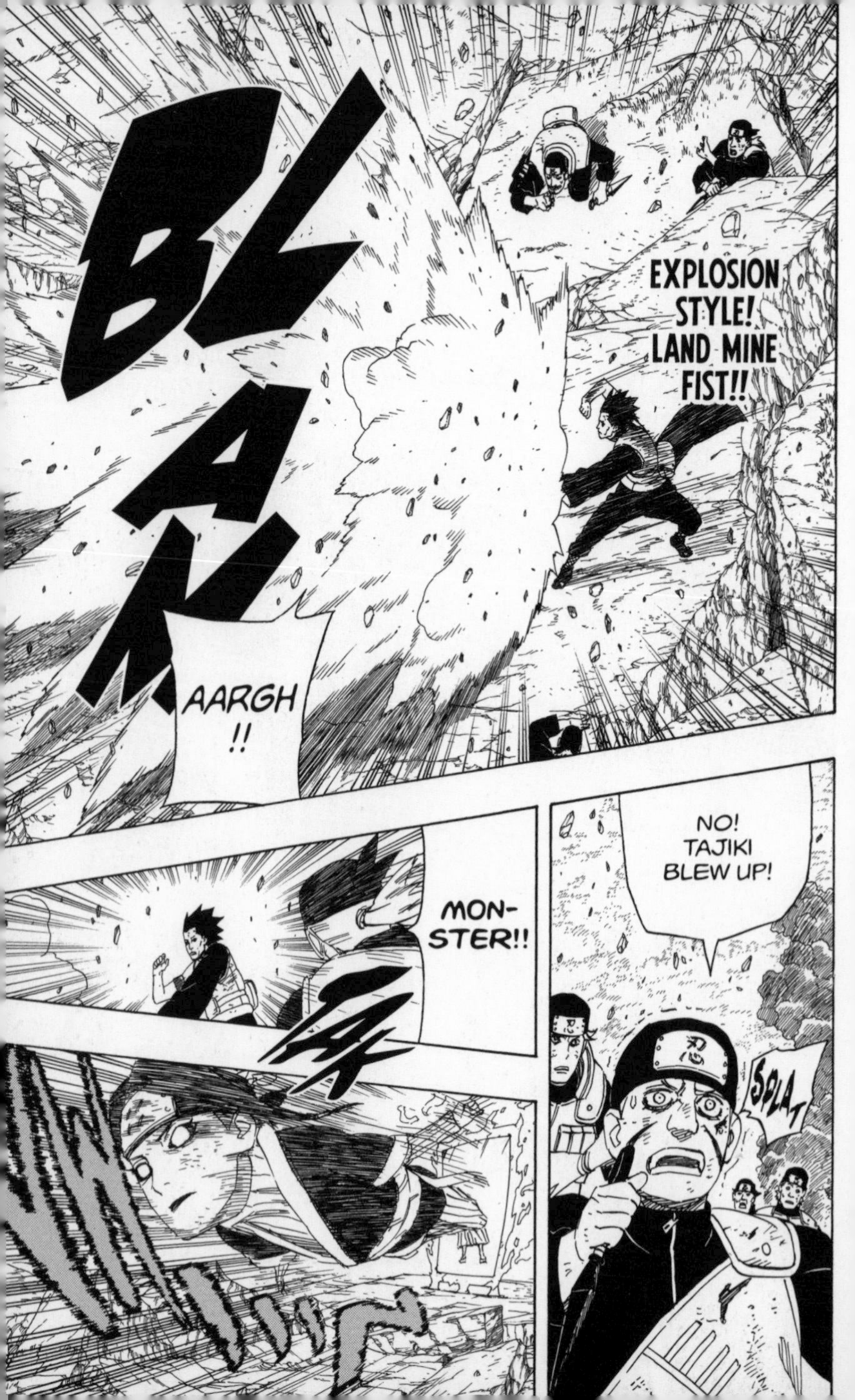
EXPLOSION STYLE! LAND MINE FIST!!
BLAM
AARGH !!
NO! TAJIKI BLEW UP!
SPLAT
MON-STER!!
TAK

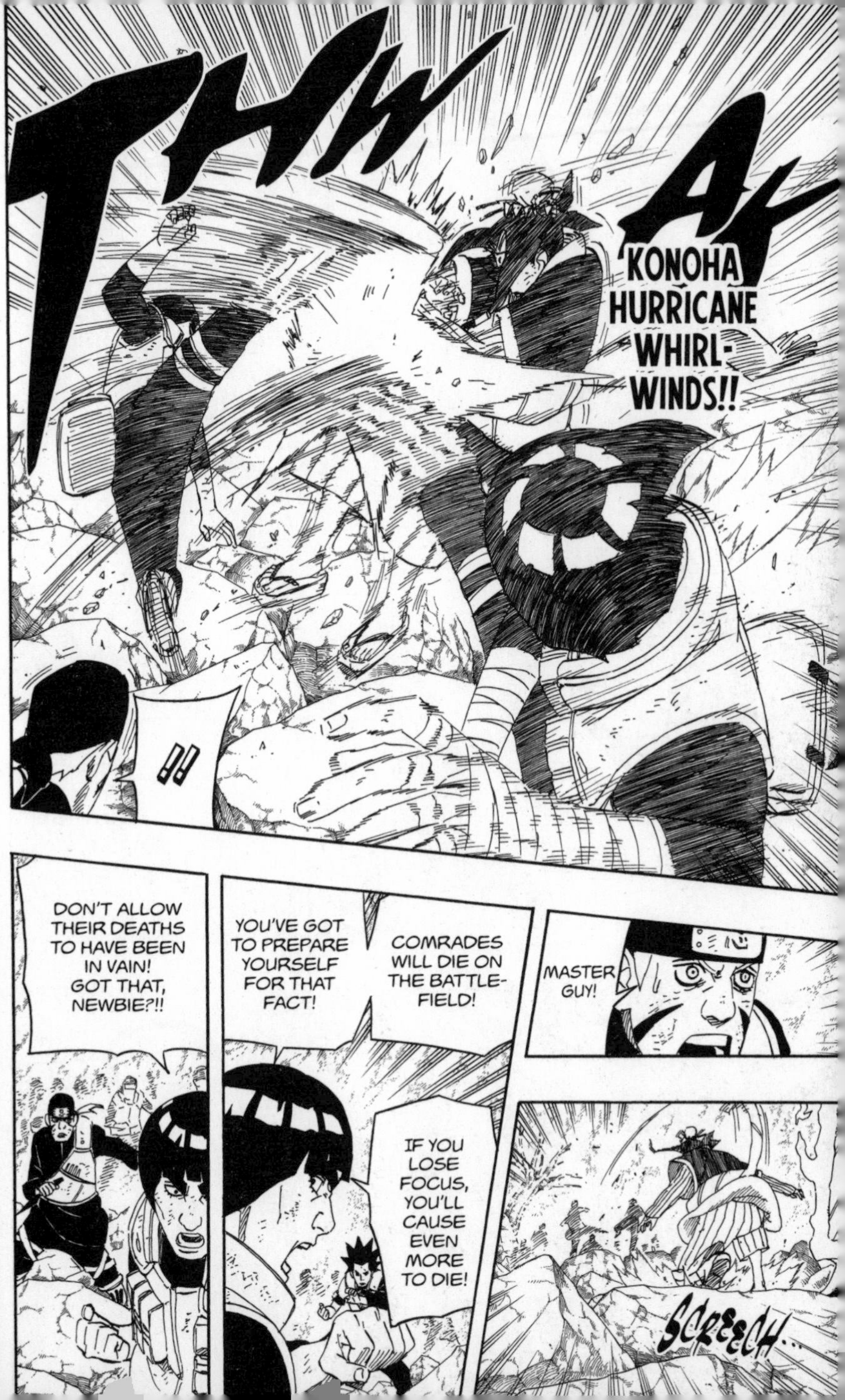
THWAK
KONOHA HURRICANE WHIRL-WINDS!!
!!
MASTER GUY!
COMRADES WILL DIE ON THE BATTLE-FIELD!
YOU'VE GOT TO PREPARE YOURSELF FOR THAT FACT!
DON'T ALLOW THEIR DEATHS TO HAVE BEEN IN VAIN! GOT THAT, NEWBIE?!!
SCREECH...
IF YOU LOSE FOCUS, YOU'LL CAUSE EVEN MORE TO DIE!

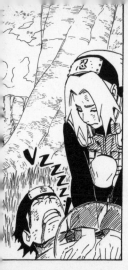

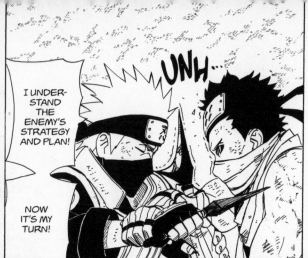

UNH...
I UNDERSTAND THE ENEMY'S STRATEGY AND PLAN!
NOW IT'S MY TURN!
VZZZZ
HEH HEH... I AM NOT SO NAÏVE AS TO LET MY OPPONENT...
...CATCH THEIR BREATH!
CHAK
KUCHIYOSE SUMMONING!!
BAM

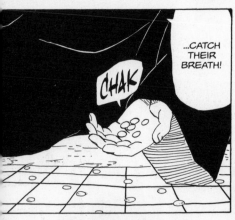

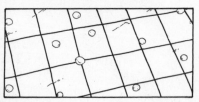

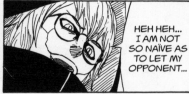

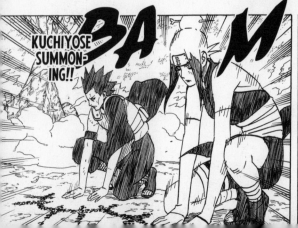

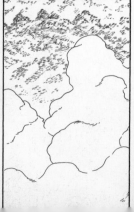

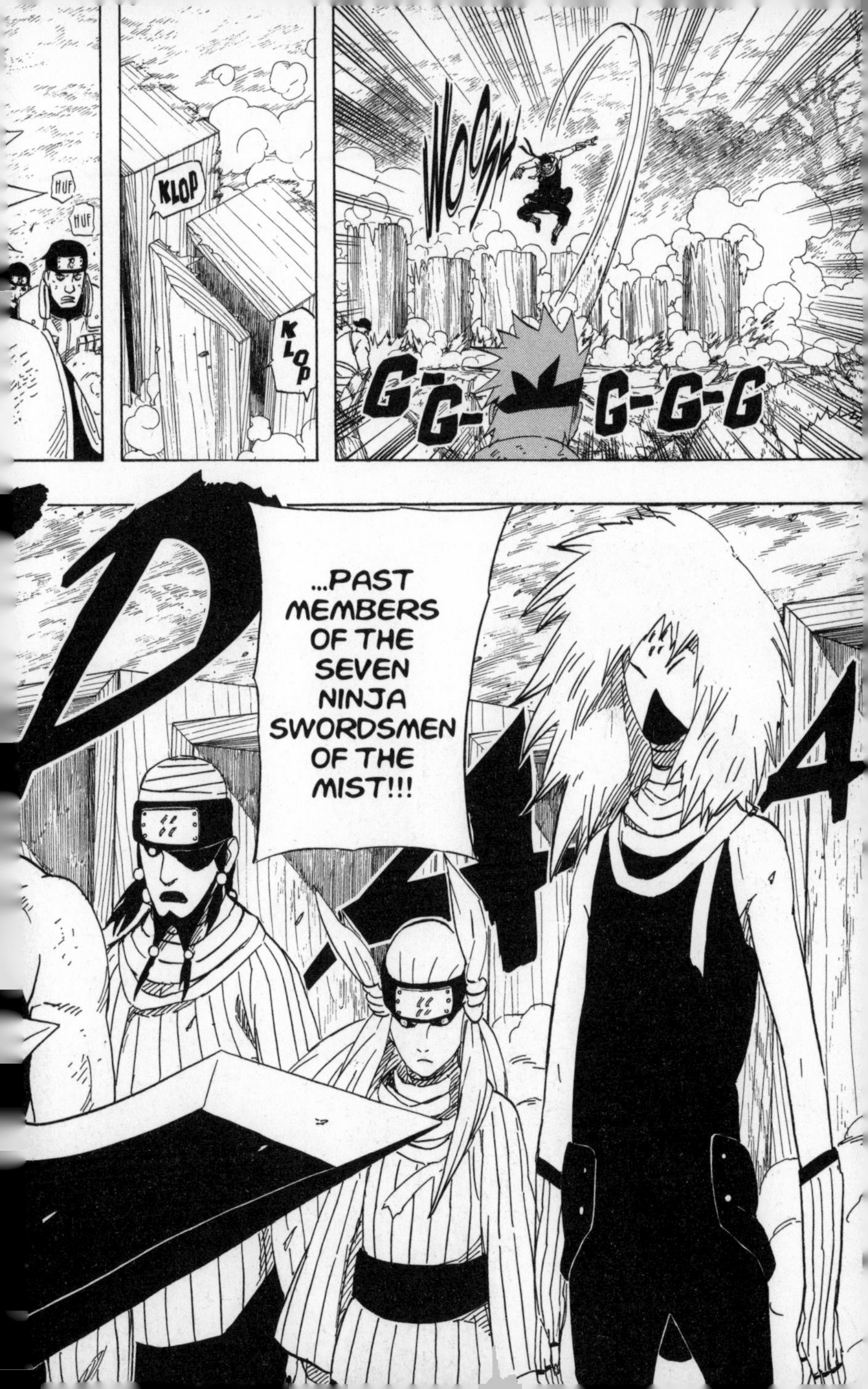
WOOSH
GG-G-G-G
KLOP
KLOP
HUF
HUF
...PAST MEMBERS OF THE SEVEN NINJA SWORDSMEN OF THE MIST!!!

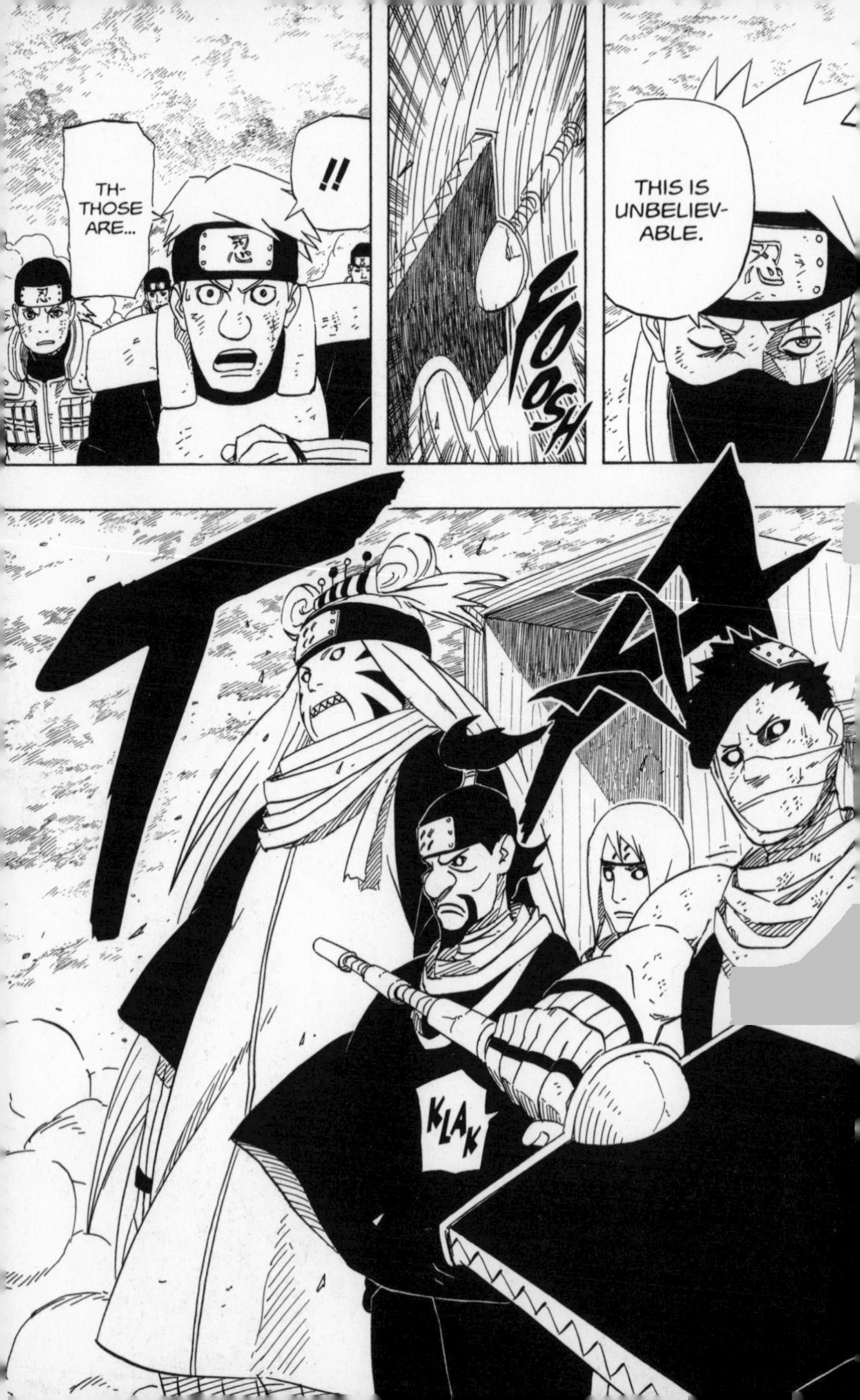
THIS IS UNBELIEVABLE.
FOOSH
!!
TH- THOSE ARE...
KLAK

NARUTO

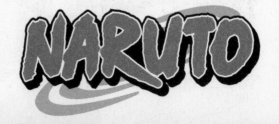

Number 523: The Legendary Seven Swordsmen of the Mist!!

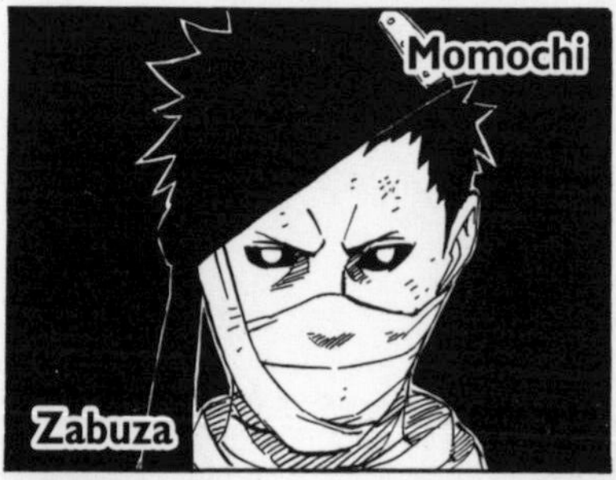
Momochi
Zabuza

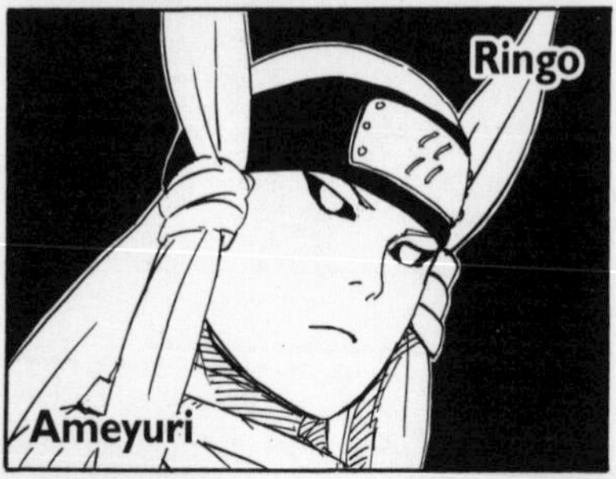
Ringo
Ameyuri

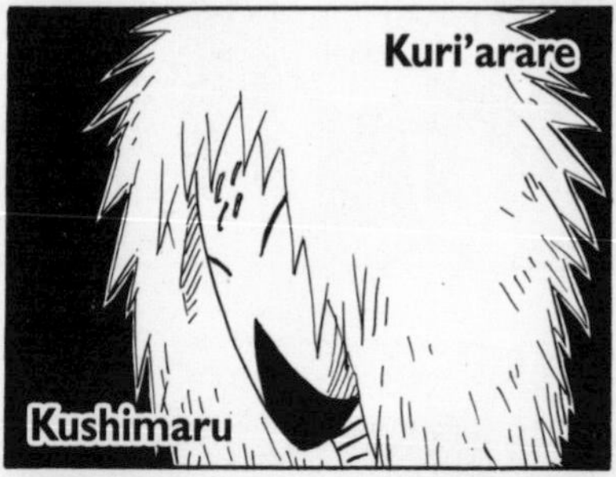
Kuri'arare
Kushimaru

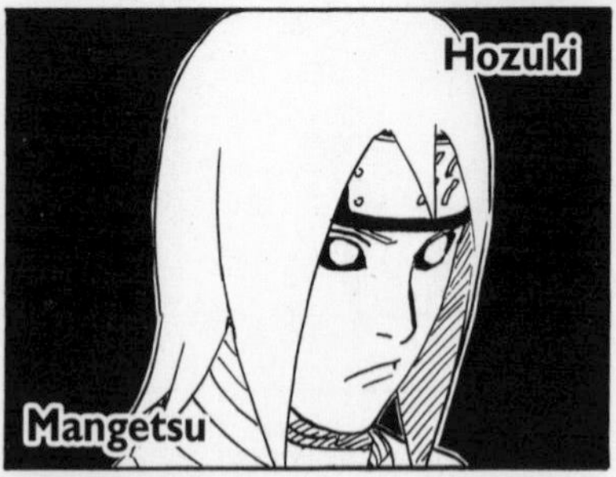
Hozuki
Mangetsu

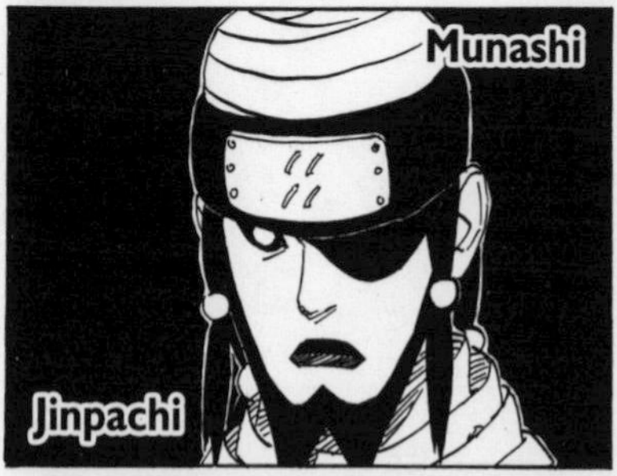
Munashi
Jinpachi

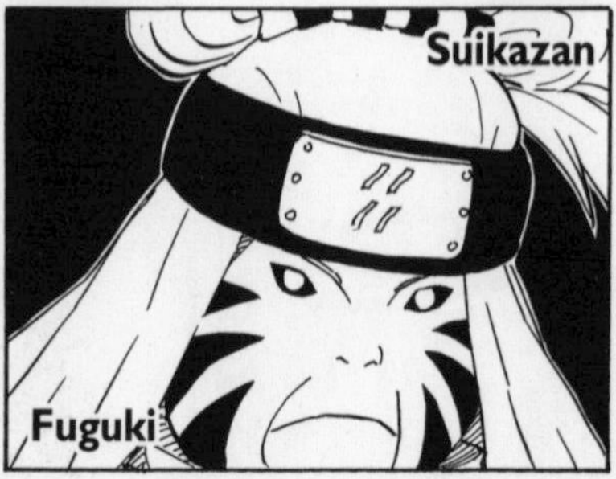
Suikazan
Fuguki

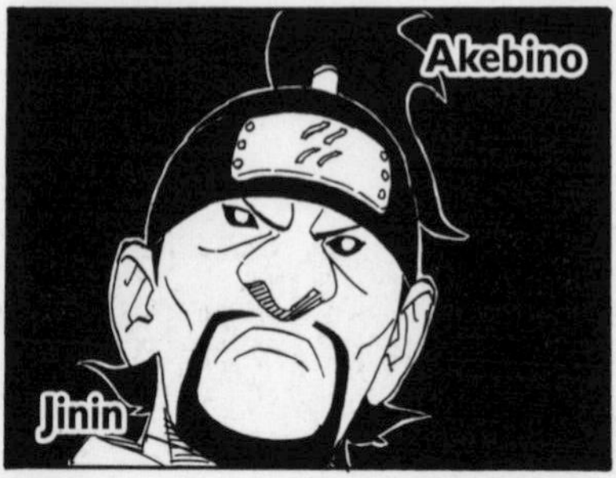
Akebino
Jinin

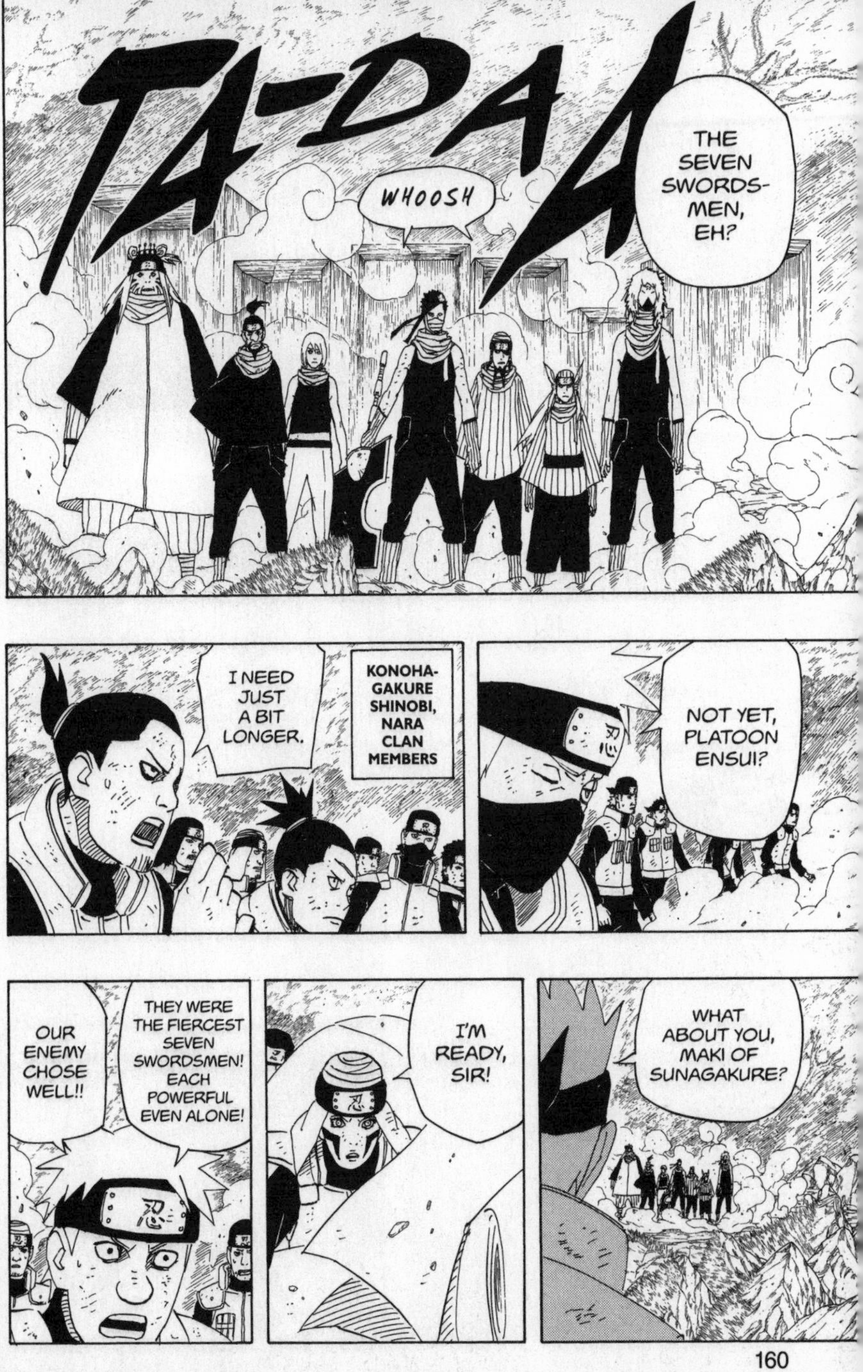
THE SEVEN SWORDS-MEN, EH?
TA-DAA
WHOOSH
NOT YET, PLATOON ENSUI?
KONOHA-GAKURE SHINOBI, NARA CLAN MEMBERS
I NEED JUST A BIT LONGER.
WHAT ABOUT YOU, MAKI OF SUNAGAKURE?
I'M READY, SIR!
THEY WERE THE FIERCEST SEVEN SWORDSMEN! EACH POWERFUL EVEN ALONE!
OUR ENEMY CHOSE WELL!!

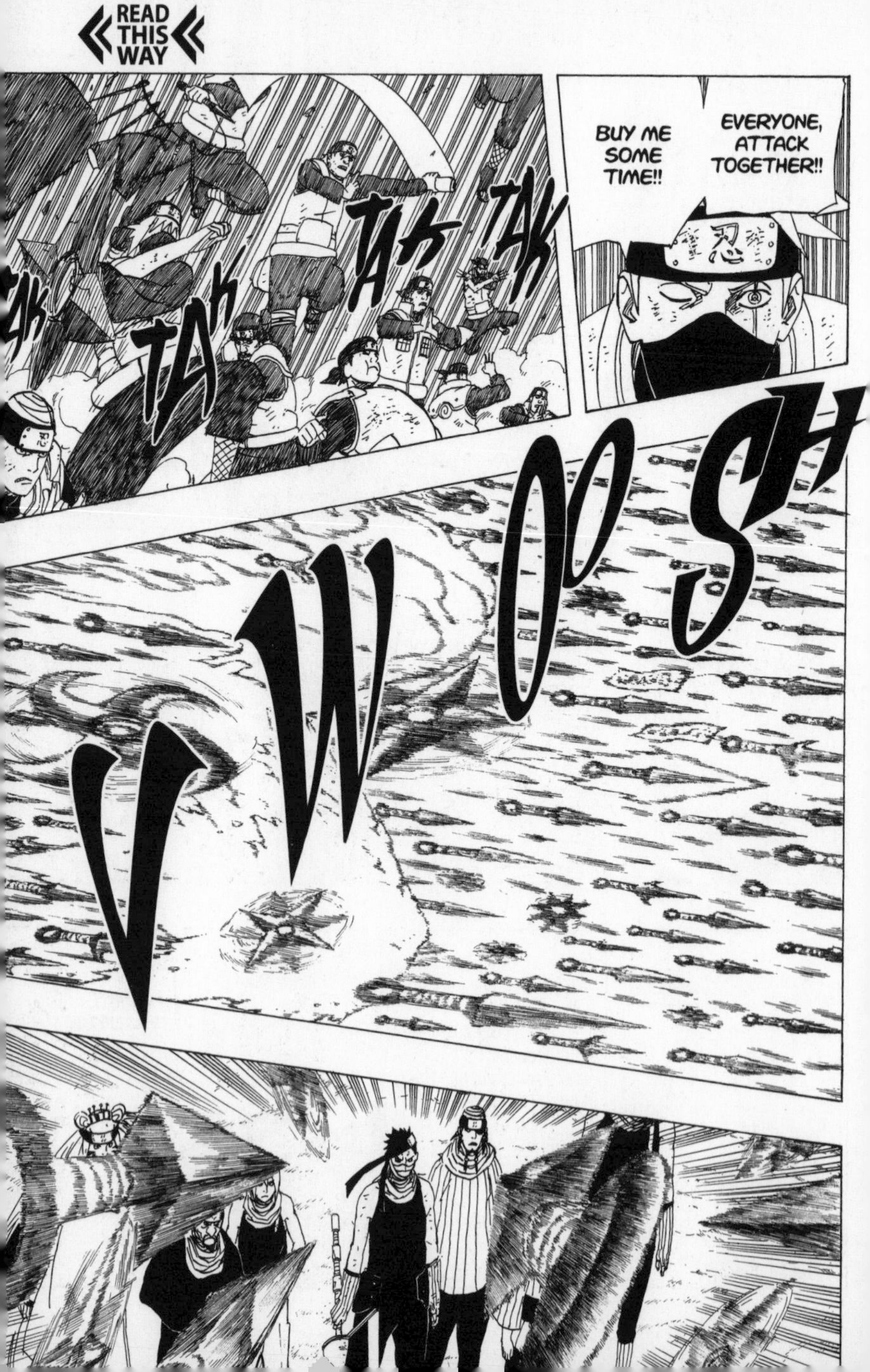
READ THIS WAY
EVERYONE, ATTACK TOGETHER!!
BUY ME SOME TIME!!
TAK TAK TAK TAK TAK
VWOOOSH

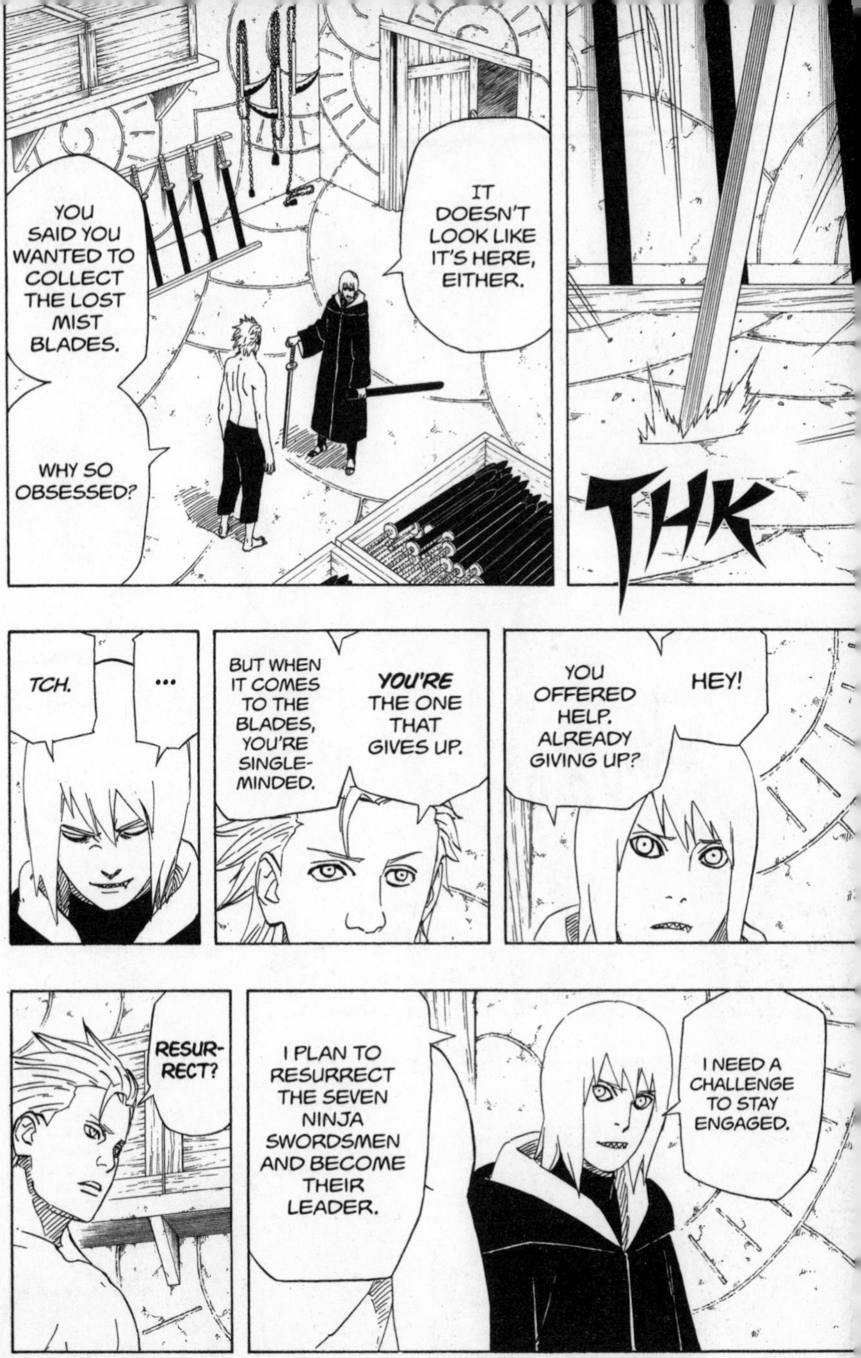
THK
IT DOESN'T LOOK LIKE IT'S HERE, EITHER.
YOU SAID YOU WANTED TO COLLECT THE LOST MIST BLADES.
WHY SO OBSESSED?
HEY!
YOU OFFERED HELP. ALREADY GIVING UP?
YOU'RE THE ONE THAT GIVES UP.
BUT WHEN IT COMES TO THE BLADES, YOU'RE SINGLE-MINDED.
...
TCH.
I NEED A CHALLENGE TO STAY ENGAGED.
I PLAN TO RESURRECT THE SEVEN NINJA SWORDSMEN AND BECOME THEIR LEADER.
RESUR-RECT?

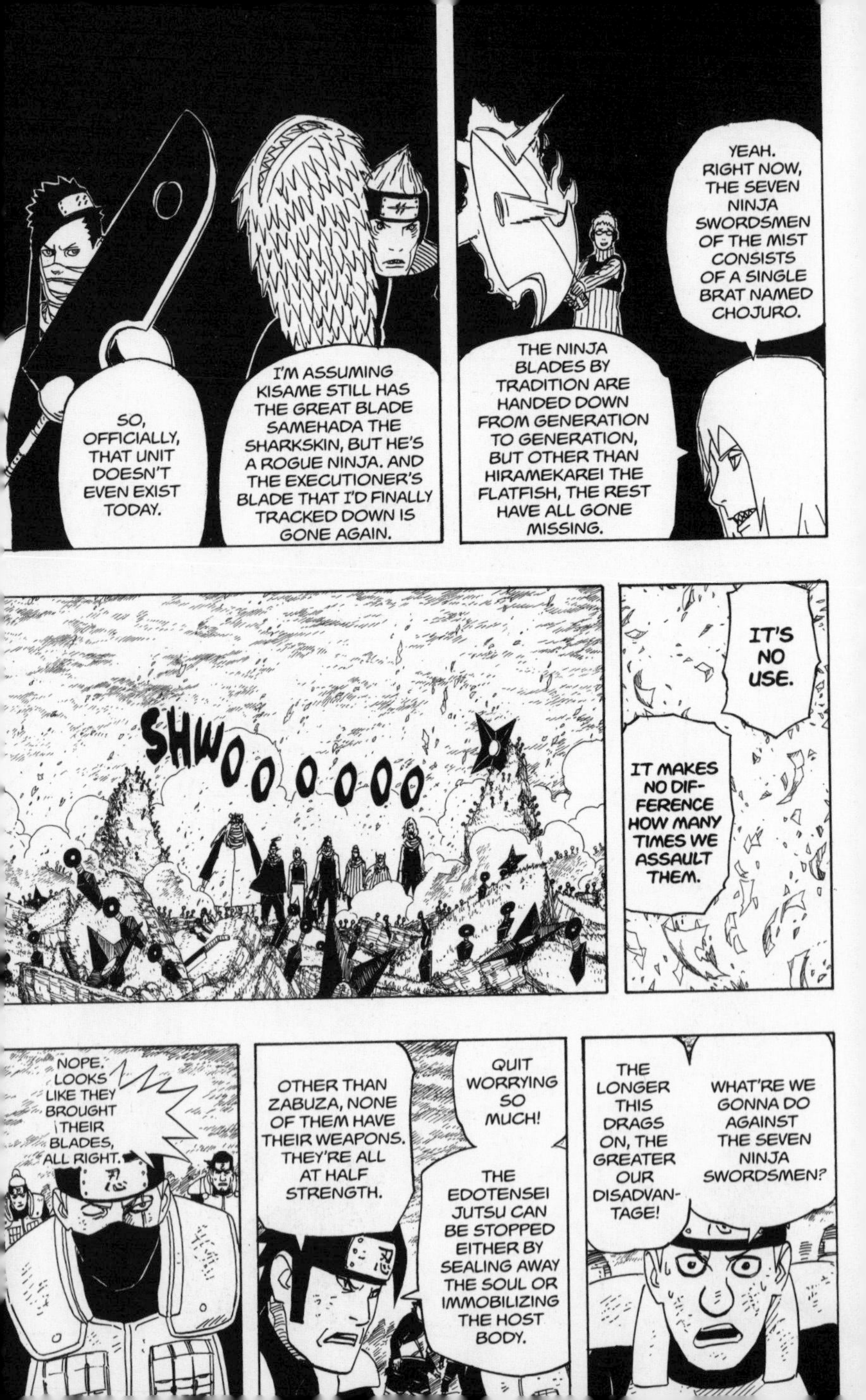
YEAH. RIGHT NOW, THE SEVEN NINJA SWORDSMEN OF THE MIST CONSISTS OF A SINGLE BRAT NAMED CHOJURO.
THE NINJA BLADES BY TRADITION ARE HANDED DOWN FROM GENERATION TO GENERATION, BUT OTHER THAN HIRAMEKAREI THE FLATFISH, THE REST HAVE ALL GONE MISSING.
I'M ASSUMING KISAME STILL HAS THE GREAT BLADE SAMEHADA THE SHARKSKIN, BUT HE'S A ROGUE NINJA. AND THE EXECUTIONER'S BLADE THAT I'D FINALLY TRACKED DOWN IS GONE AGAIN.
SO, OFFICIALLY, THAT UNIT DOESN'T EVEN EXIST TODAY.
IT'S NO USE.
IT MAKES NO DIFFERENCE HOW MANY TIMES WE ASSAULT THEM.
SHWOOOOOOO
WHAT'RE WE GONNA DO AGAINST THE SEVEN NINJA SWORDSMEN?
THE LONGER THIS DRAGS ON, THE GREATER OUR DISADVANTAGE!
QUIT WORRYING SO MUCH!
THE EDOTENSEI JUTSU CAN BE STOPPED EITHER BY SEALING AWAY THE SOUL OR IMMOBILIZING THE HOST BODY.
OTHER THAN ZABUZA, NONE OF THEM HAVE THEIR WEAPONS. THEY'RE ALL AT HALF STRENGTH.
NOPE. LOOKS LIKE THEY BROUGHT THEIR BLADES, ALL RIGHT.

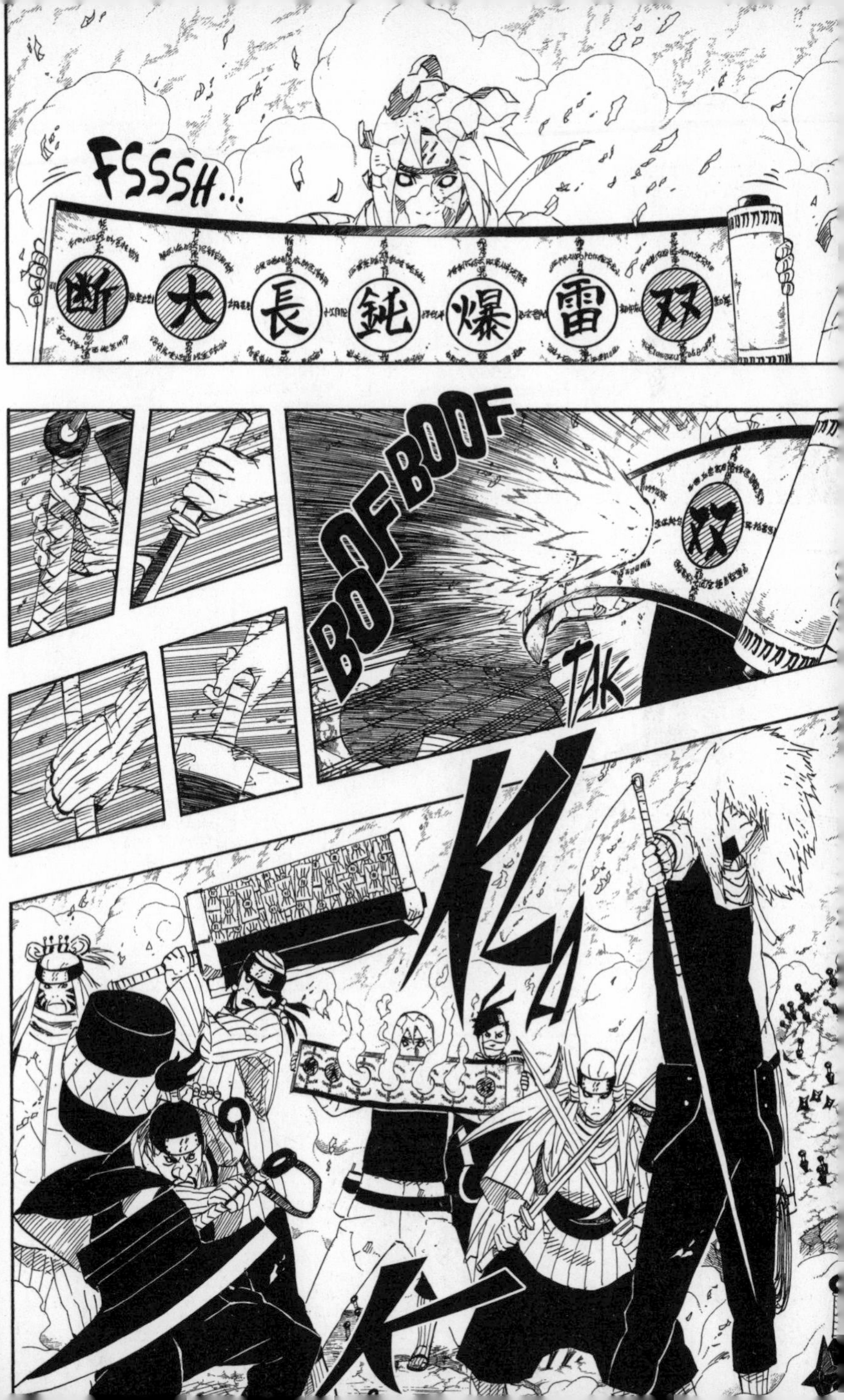
FSSSH...
断 大 長 鈍 爆 雷 双
BOOFBOOF
双
TAK
KLAK

READ THIS WAY

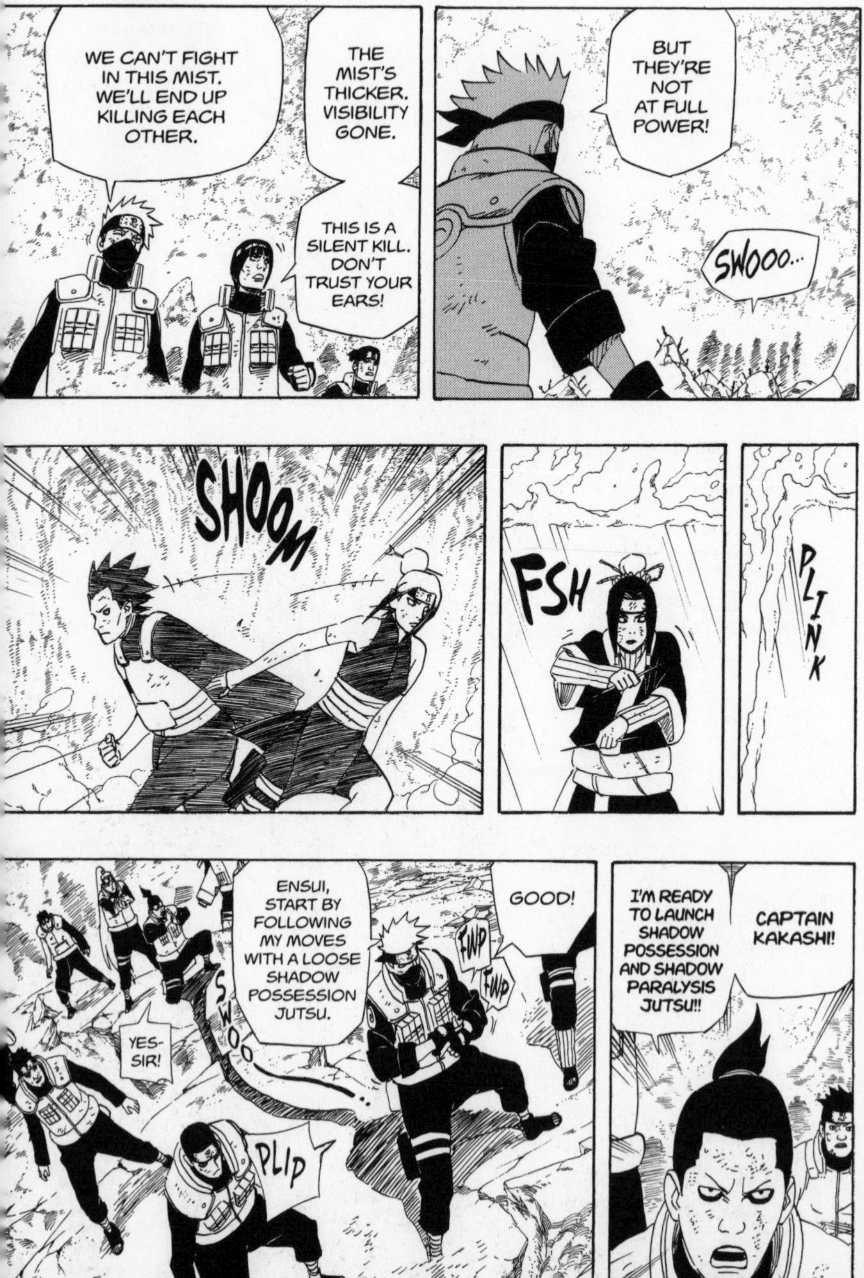
BUT THEY'RE NOT AT FULL POWER!
SWOOO...
THE MIST'S THICKER. VISIBILITY GONE.
WE CAN'T FIGHT IN THIS MIST. WE'LL END UP KILLING EACH OTHER.
THIS IS A SILENT KILL. DON'T TRUST YOUR EARS!
PLINK
FSH
SHOOM
CAPTAIN KAKASHI!
I'M READY TO LAUNCH SHADOW POSSESSION AND SHADOW PARALYSIS JUTSU!!
GOOD!
FWIP
FWIP
ENSUI, START BY FOLLOWING MY MOVES WITH A LOOSE SHADOW POSSESSION JUTSU.
SWOOO
YES-SIR!
PLIP

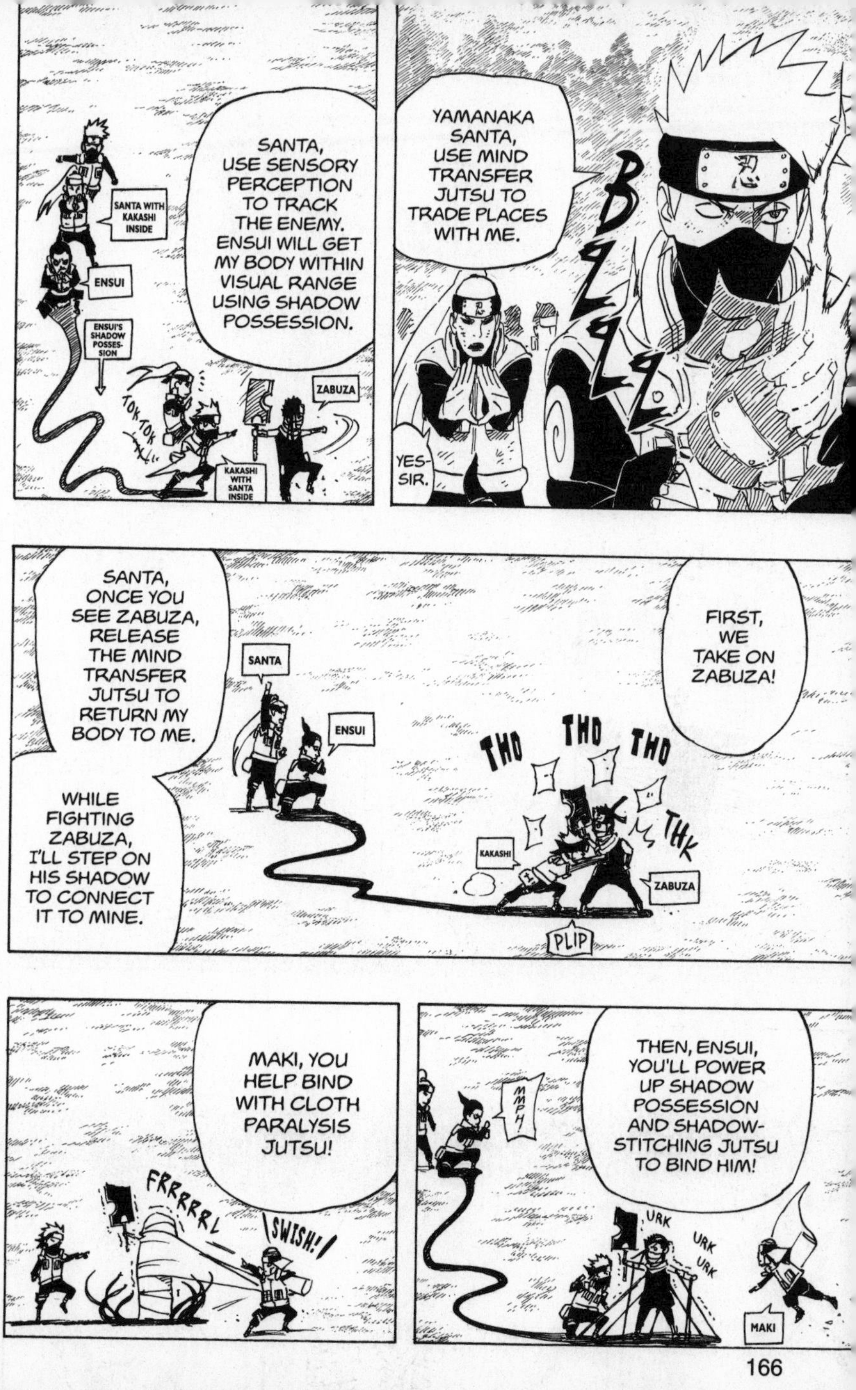
YAMANAKA SANTA, USE MIND TRANSFER JUTSU TO TRADE PLACES WITH ME.
YES-SIR.
SANTA, USE SENSORY PERCEPTION TO TRACK THE ENEMY. ENSUI WILL GET MY BODY WITHIN VISUAL RANGE USING SHADOW POSSESSION.
SANTA WITH KAKASHI INSIDE
ENSUI
ENSUI'S SHADOW POSSES-SION
ZABUZA
TOK TOK
KAKASHI WITH SANTA INSIDE
FIRST, WE TAKE ON ZABUZA!
SANTA, ONCE YOU SEE ZABUZA, RELEASE THE MIND TRANSFER JUTSU TO RETURN MY BODY TO ME.
WHILE FIGHTING ZABUZA, I'LL STEP ON HIS SHADOW TO CONNECT IT TO MINE.
SANTA
ENSUI
THD THD THD
THK
KAKASHI
ZABUZA
PLIP
THEN, ENSUI, YOU'LL POWER UP SHADOW POSSESSION AND SHADOW-STITCHING JUTSU TO BIND HIM!
MMPH!
URK
URK
URK
MAKI
MAKI, YOU HELP BIND WITH CLOTH PARALYSIS JUTSU!
FRRRRRL
SWISH!

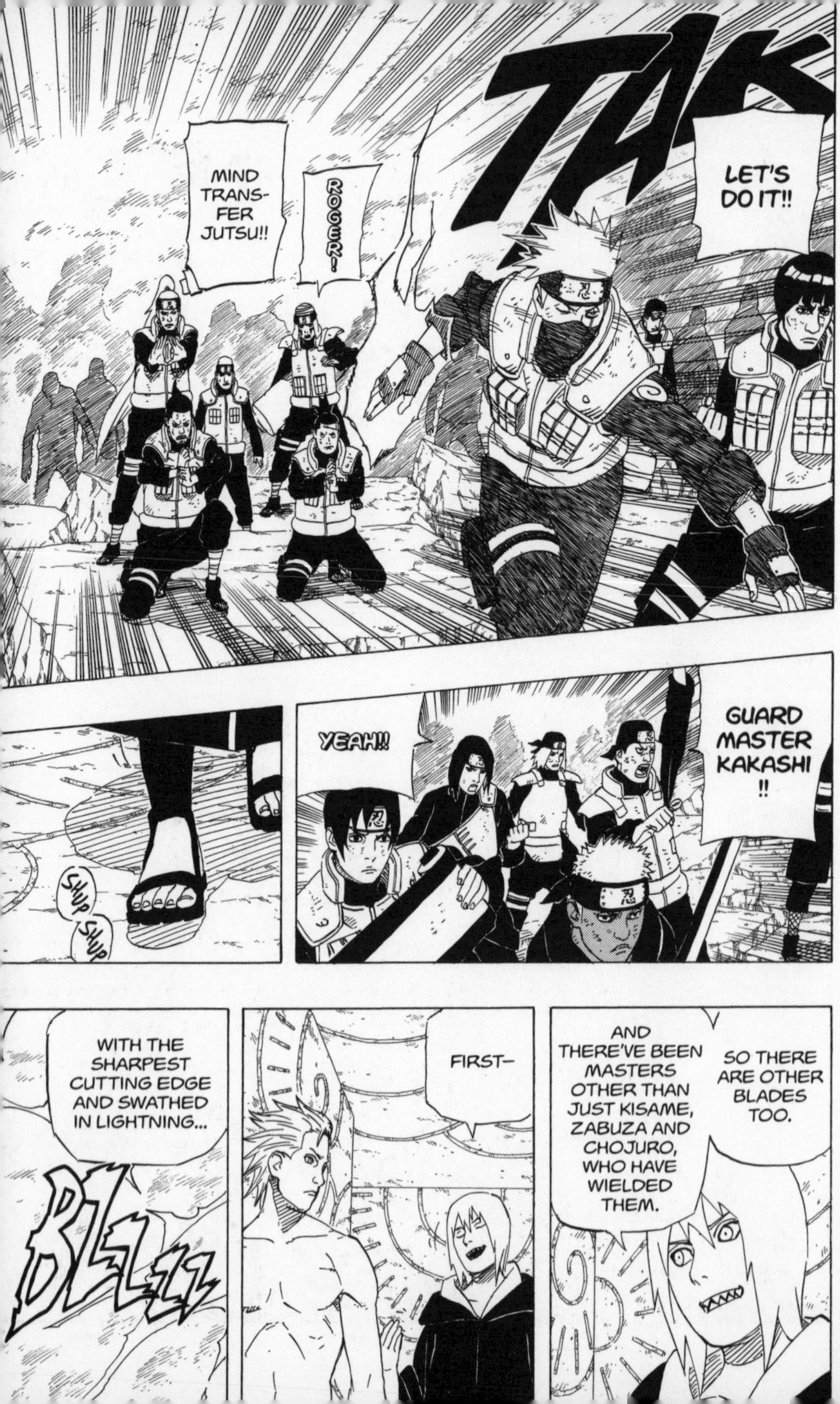
TAK
LET'S DO IT!!
ROGER!
MIND TRANS-FER JUTSU!!
GUARD MASTER KAKASHI !!
YEAH!!
SHUP SHUP
SO THERE ARE OTHER BLADES TOO.
AND THERE'VE BEEN MASTERS OTHER THAN JUST KISAME, ZABUZA AND CHOJURO, WHO HAVE WIELDED THEM.
FIRST—
WITH THE SHARPEST CUTTING EDGE AND SWATHED IN LIGHTNING...

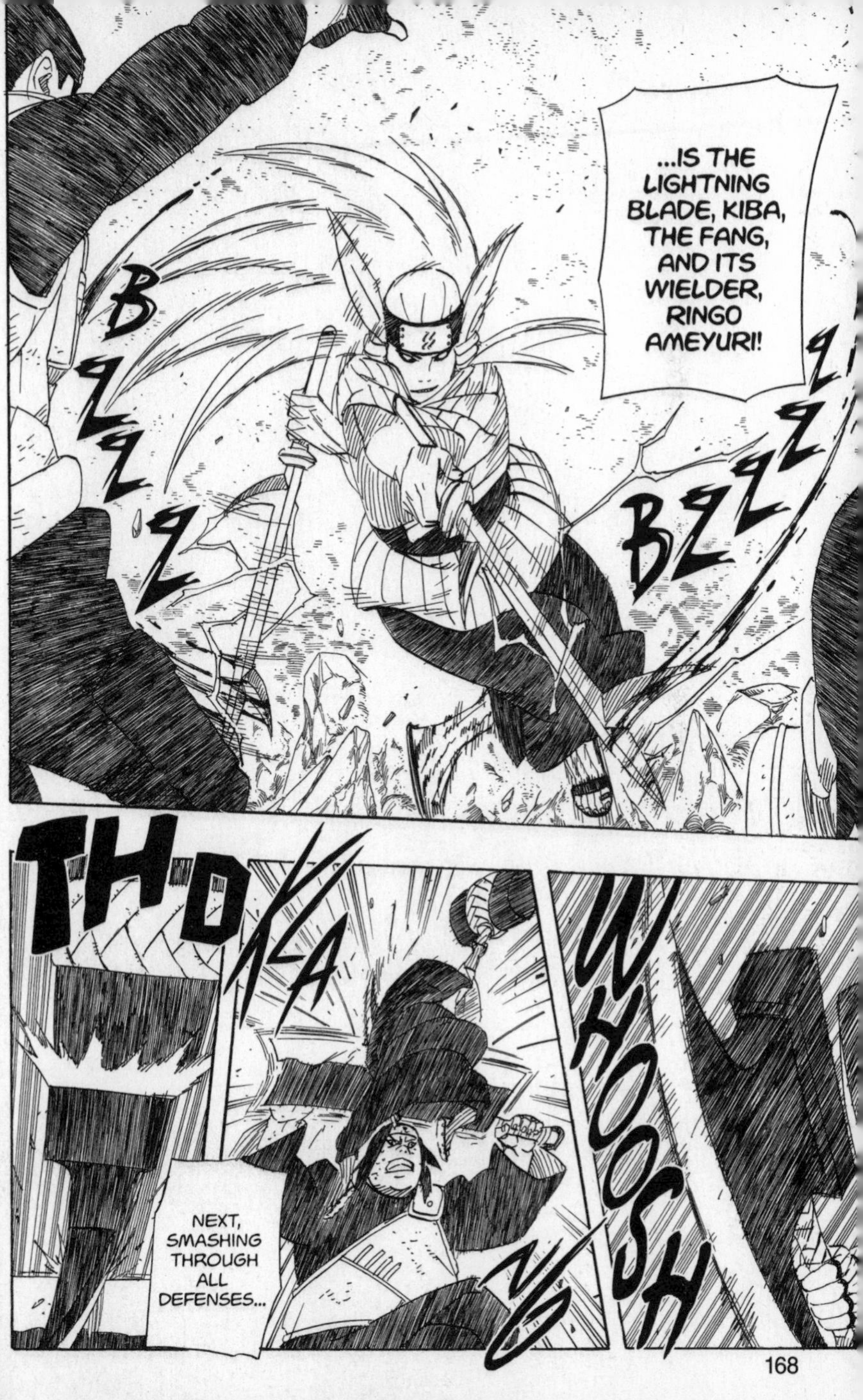
...IS THE LIGHTNING BLADE, KIBA, THE FANG, AND ITS WIELDER, RINGO AMEYURI!
BZZZZ
BZZZZ
WHOOSH
KA
THD
NEXT, SMASHING THROUGH ALL DEFENSES...

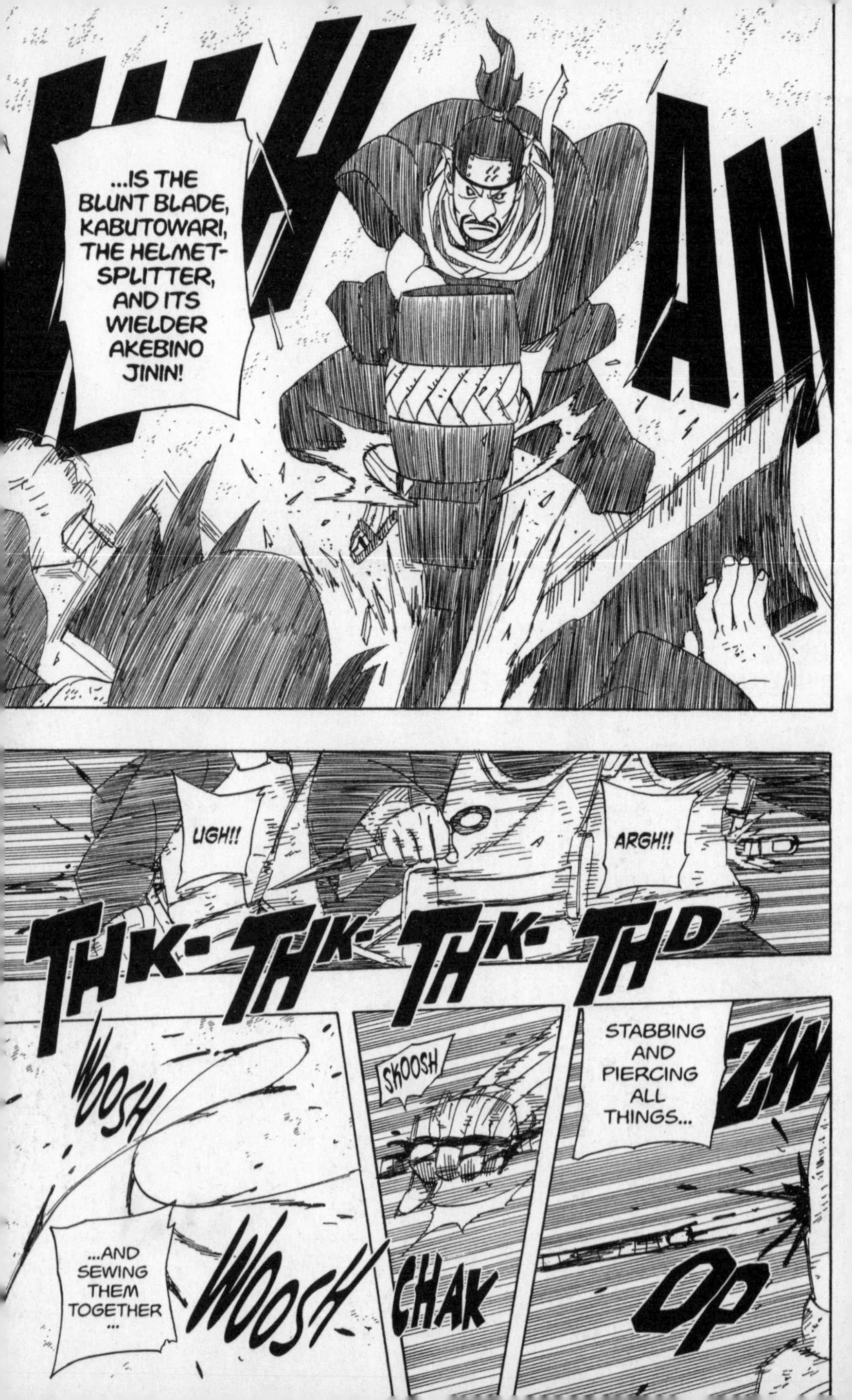
...IS THE BLUNT BLADE, KABUTOWARI, THE HELMET-SPLITTER, AND ITS WIELDER AKEBINO JININ!
ARGH!!
UGH!!
THK-THK-THK-THD
STABBING AND PIERCING ALL THINGS...
ZWOP
SKOOSH
CHAK
WOOSH
...AND SEWING THEM TOGETHER ...
WOOSH

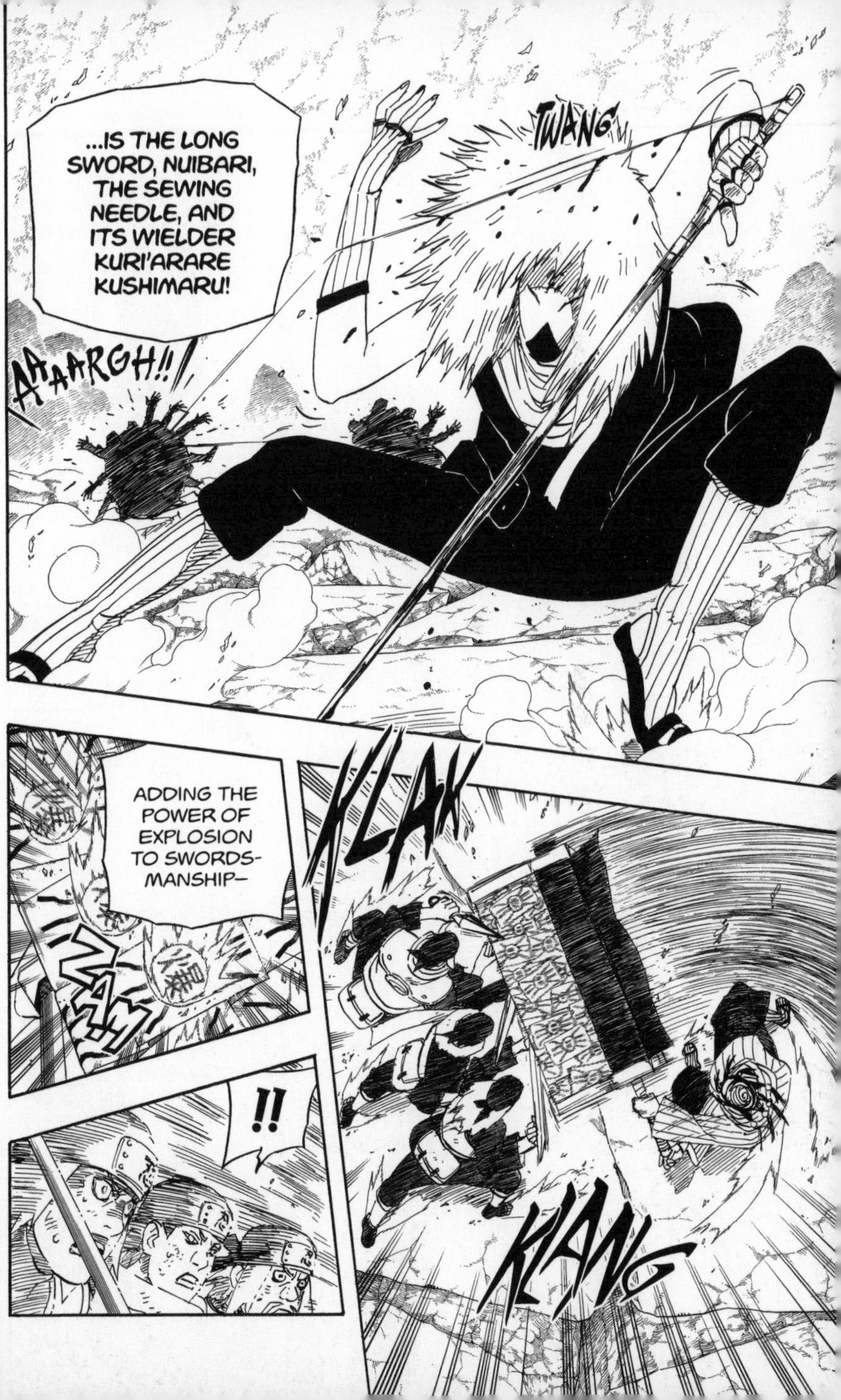
...IS THE LONG SWORD, NUIBARI, THE SEWING NEEDLE, AND ITS WIELDER KURI'ARARE KUSHIMARU!
TWANG
AAAARGH!!
KLAK
KLANG
ADDING THE POWER OF EXPLOSION TO SWORDS-MANSHIP–
ZAAM
!!

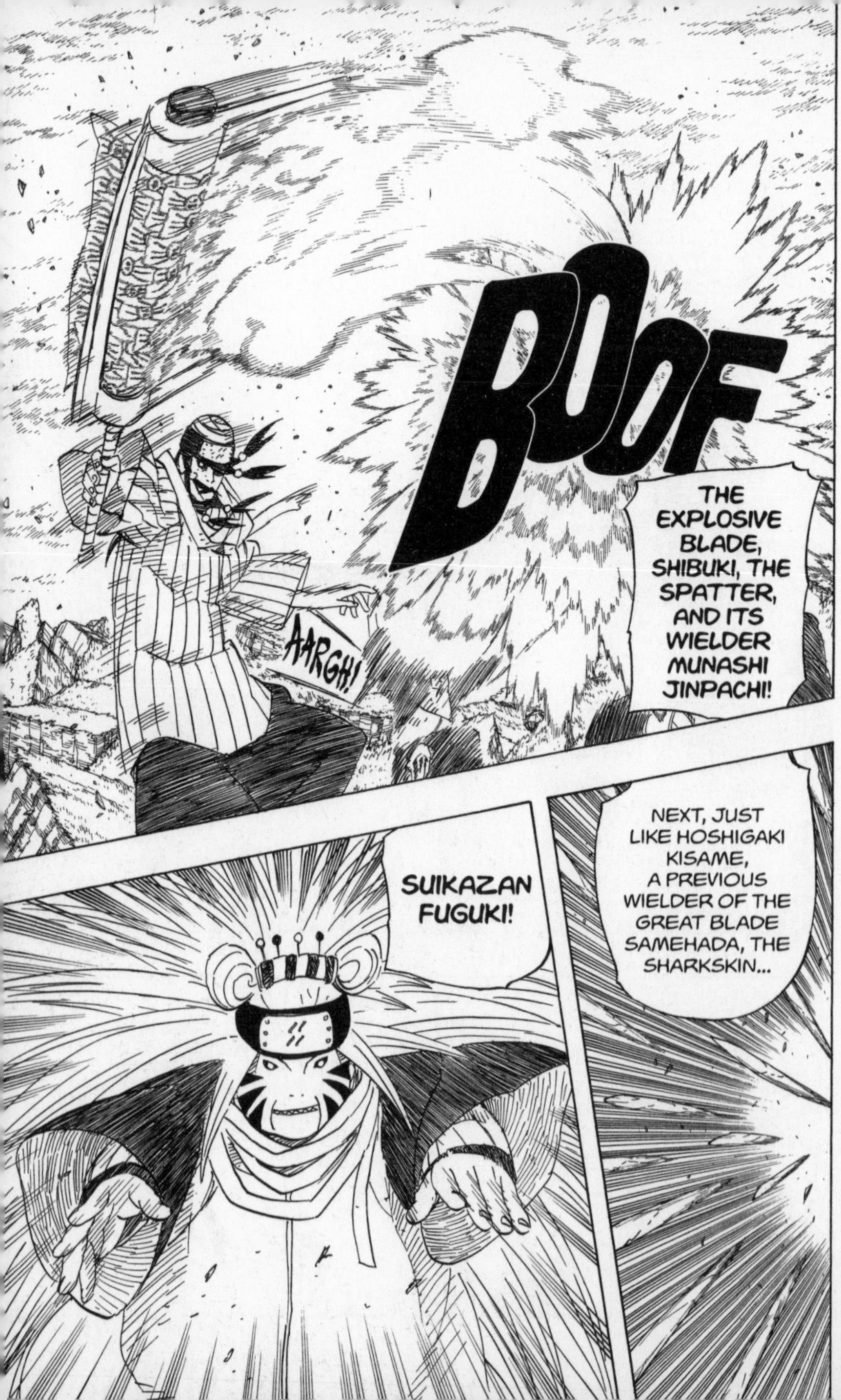
BOOF
THE EXPLOSIVE BLADE, SHIBUKI, THE SPATTER, AND ITS WIELDER MUNASHI JINPACHI!
AARGH!
NEXT, JUST LIKE HOSHIGAKI KISAME, A PREVIOUS WIELDER OF THE GREAT BLADE SAMEHADA, THE SHARKSKIN...
SUIKAZAN FUGUKI!

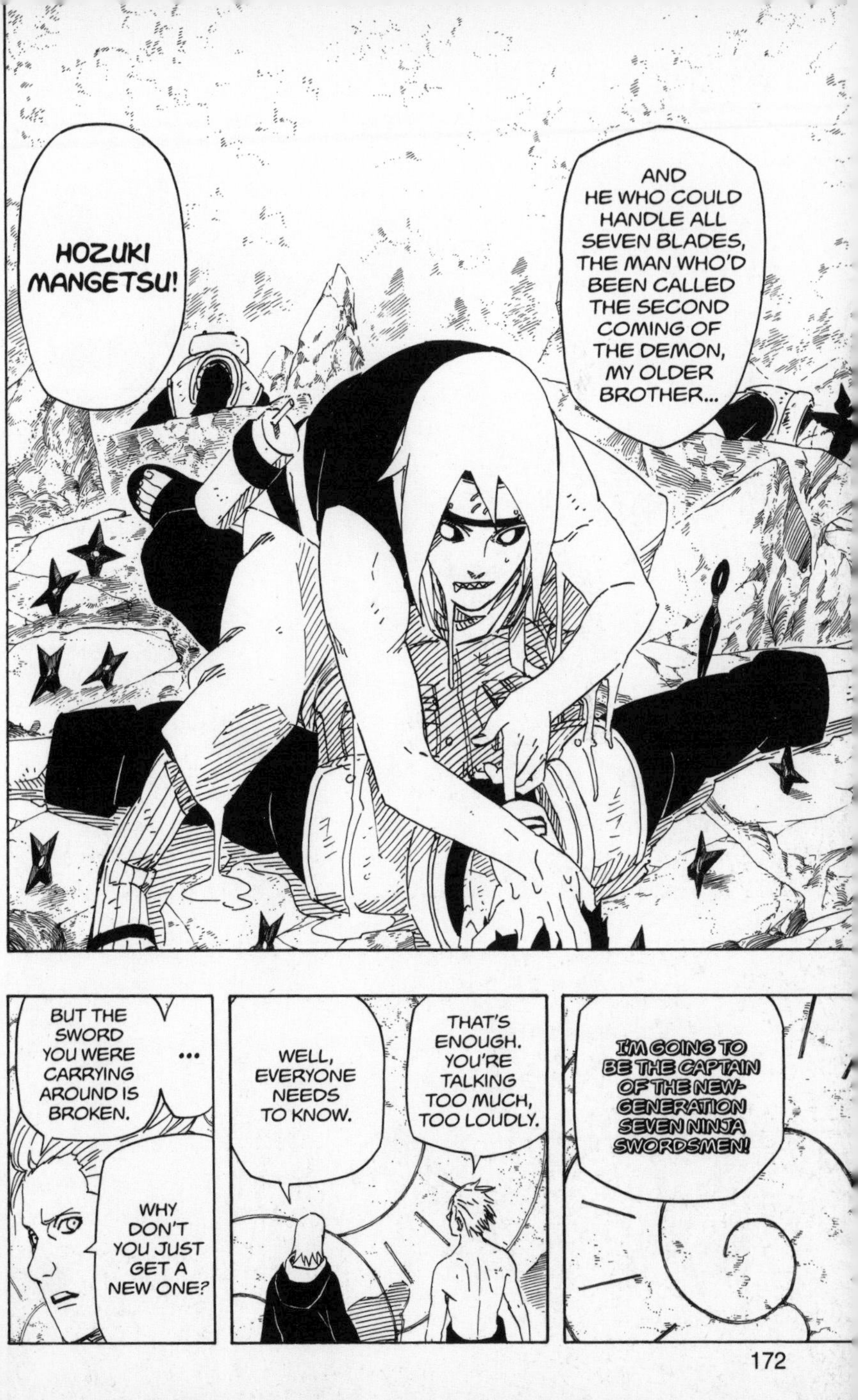
AND HE WHO COULD HANDLE ALL SEVEN BLADES, THE MAN WHO'D BEEN CALLED THE SECOND COMING OF THE DEMON, MY OLDER BROTHER...
HOZUKI MANGETSU!
I'M GOING TO BE THE CAPTAIN OF THE NEW-GENERATION SEVEN NINJA SWORDSMEN!
THAT'S ENOUGH. YOU'RE TALKING TOO MUCH, TOO LOUDLY.
WELL, EVERYONE NEEDS TO KNOW.
BUT THE SWORD YOU WERE CARRYING AROUND IS BROKEN.
...
WHY DON'T YOU JUST GET A NEW ONE?

READ THIS WAY

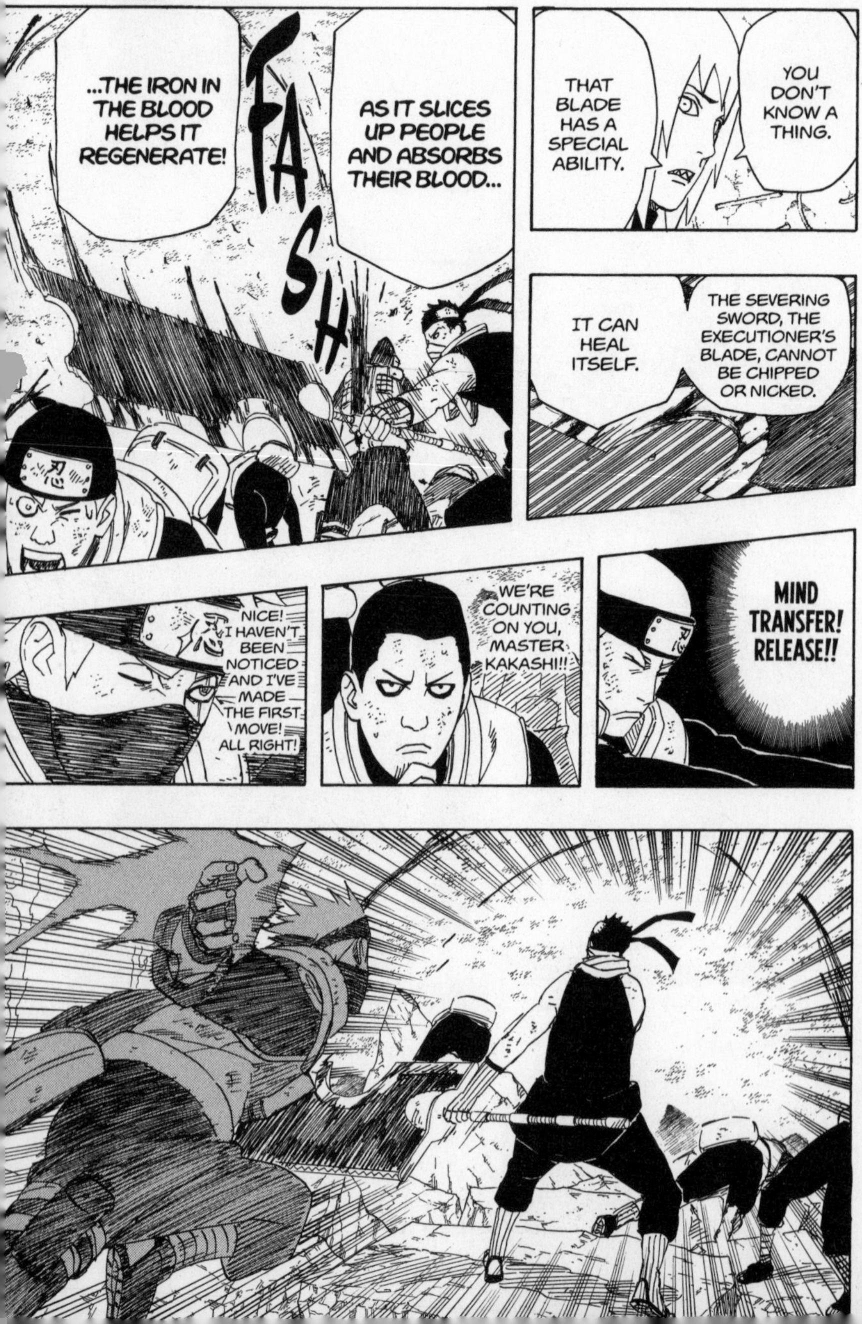

YOU DON'T KNOW A THING.
THAT BLADE HAS A SPECIAL ABILITY.
THE SEVERING SWORD, THE EXECUTIONER'S BLADE, CANNOT BE CHIPPED OR NICKED.
IT CAN HEAL ITSELF.
AS IT SLICES UP PEOPLE AND ABSORBS THEIR BLOOD...
FASH
...THE IRON IN THE BLOOD HELPS IT REGENERATE!
MIND TRANSFER! RELEASE!!
WE'RE COUNTING ON YOU, MASTER KAKASHI!!!
NICE! I HAVEN'T BEEN NOTICED AND I'VE MADE THE FIRST MOVE! ALL RIGHT!

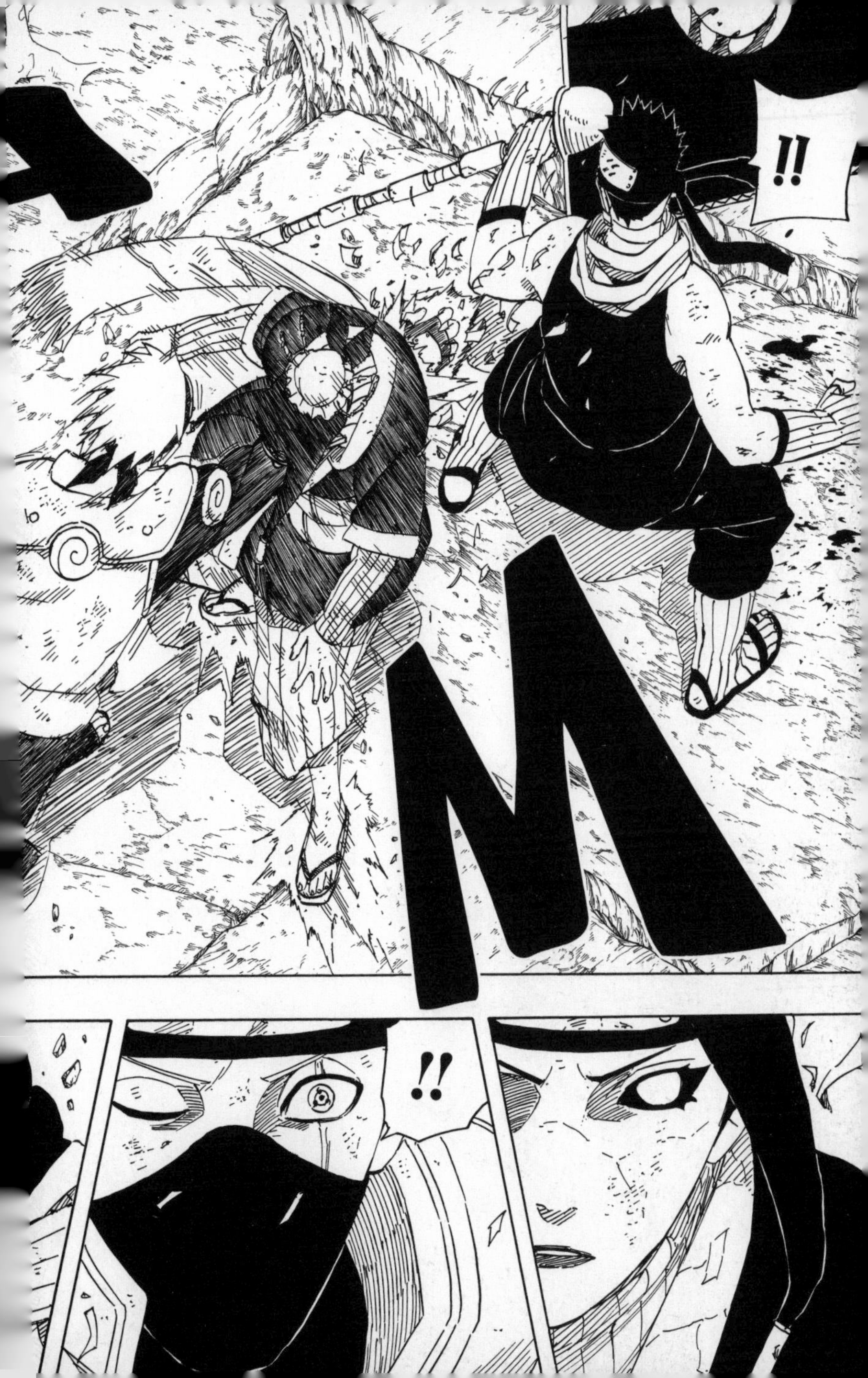
!!
M
!!

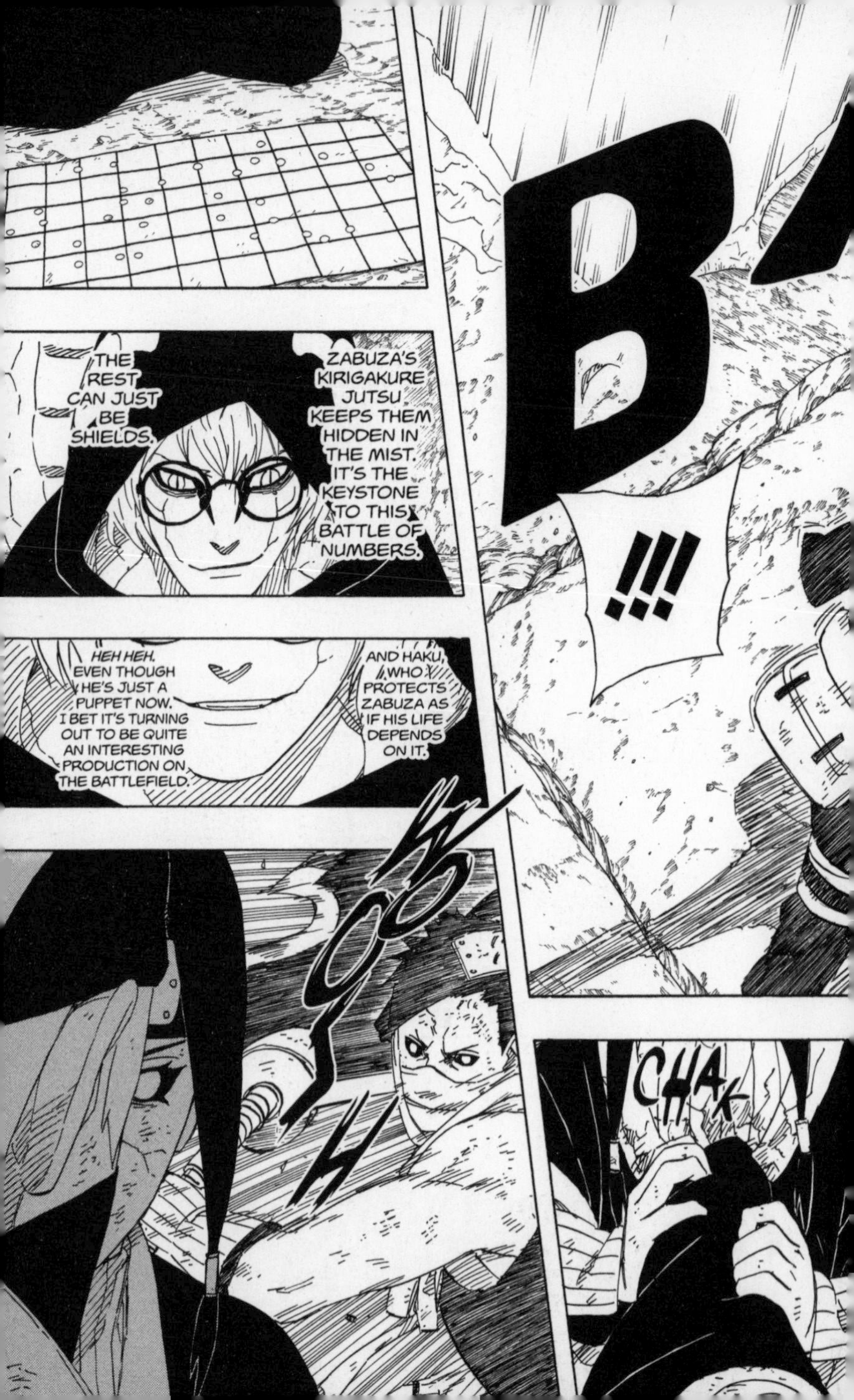
B
!!!
CHAK
THE REST CAN JUST BE SHIELDS.
ZABUZA'S KIRIGAKURE JUTSU KEEPS THEM HIDDEN IN THE MIST. IT'S THE KEYSTONE TO THIS BATTLE OF NUMBERS.
AND HAKU, WHO PROTECTS ZABUZA AS IF HIS LIFE DEPENDS ON IT.
HEH HEH. EVEN THOUGH HE'S JUST A PUPPET NOW. I BET IT'S TURNING OUT TO BE QUITE AN INTERESTING PRODUCTION ON THE BATTLEFIELD.
WHOOSH

NARUTO

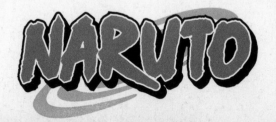

Number 524: That Which Ought to Be Protected

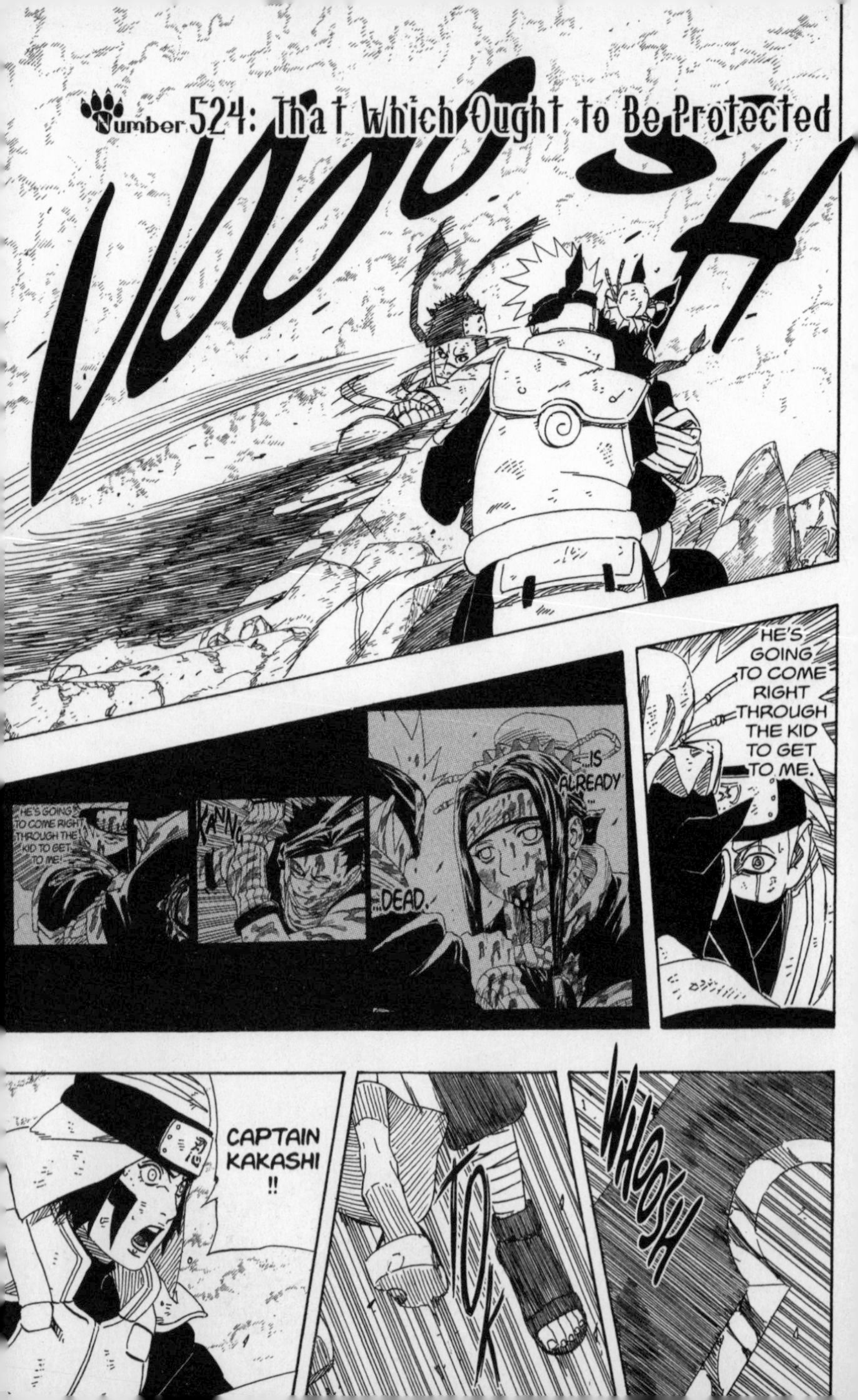
VOOOSH
HE'S GOING TO COME RIGHT THROUGH THE KID TO GET TO ME.
...IS ALREADY...
...DEAD.
KANNG
HE'S GOING TO COME RIGHT THROUGH THE KID TO GET TO ME!
WHOOSH
TOK
CAPTAIN KAKASHI!!

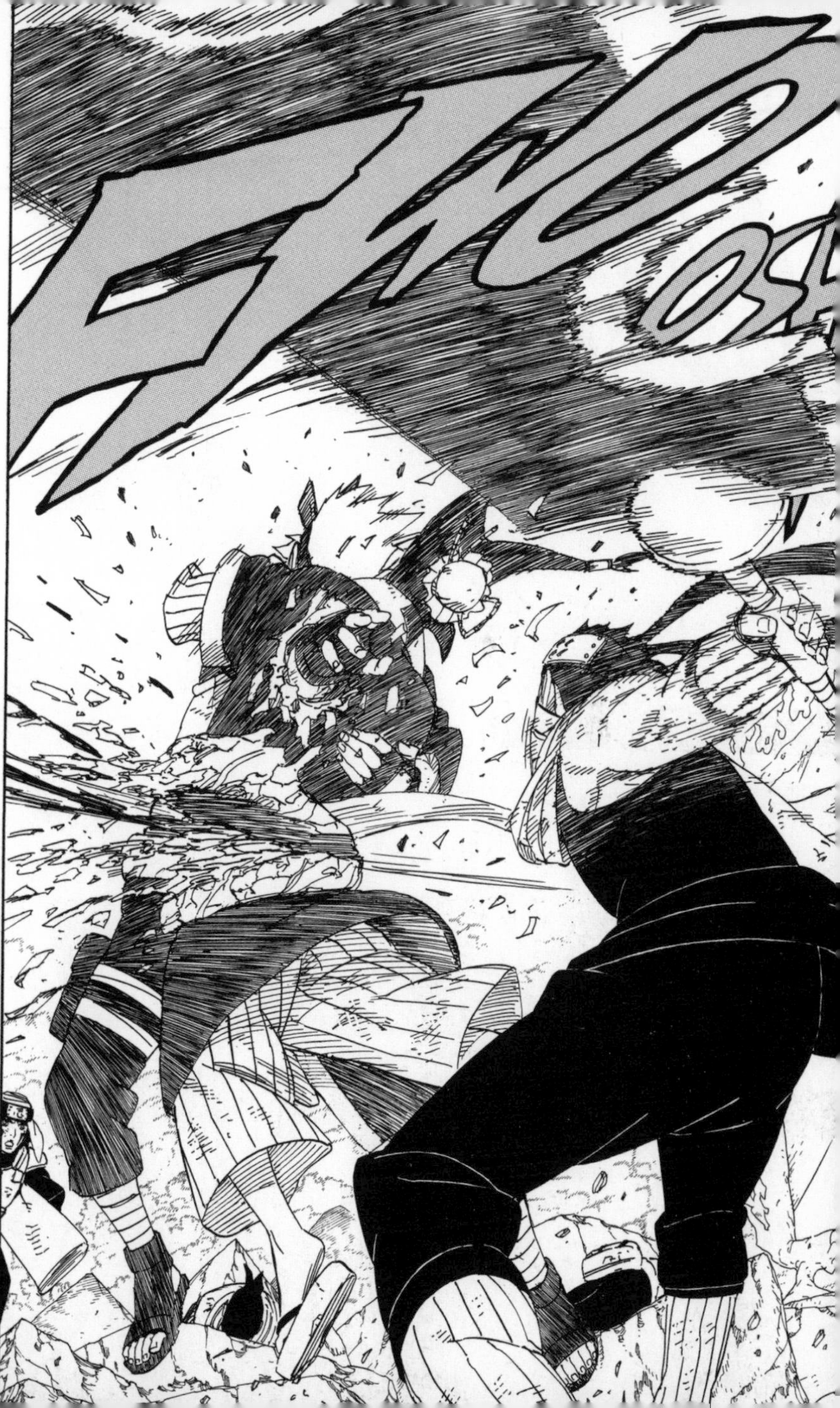
SHO
OSH

READ THIS WAY

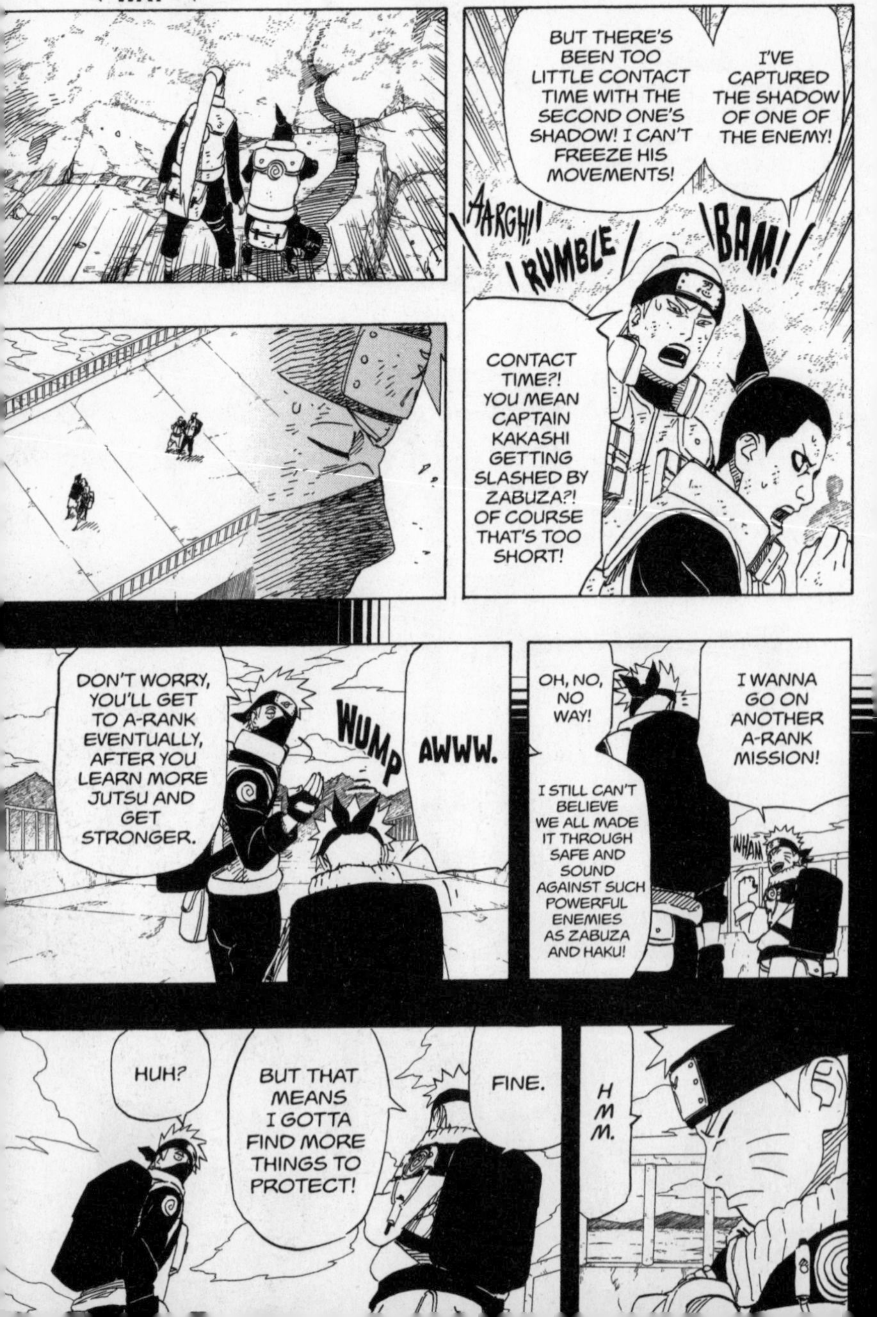
I'VE CAPTURED THE SHADOW OF ONE OF THE ENEMY!
BUT THERE'S BEEN TOO LITTLE CONTACT TIME WITH THE SECOND ONE'S SHADOW! I CAN'T FREEZE HIS MOVEMENTS!
BAM!
RUMBLE
AARGH!!
CONTACT TIME?! YOU MEAN CAPTAIN KAKASHI GETTING SLASHED BY ZABUZA?! OF COURSE THAT'S TOO SHORT!
I WANNA GO ON ANOTHER A-RANK MISSION!
WHAM
OH, NO, NO WAY!
I STILL CAN'T BELIEVE WE ALL MADE IT THROUGH SAFE AND SOUND AGAINST SUCH POWERFUL ENEMIES AS ZABUZA AND HAKU!
AWWW.
WUMP
DON'T WORRY, YOU'LL GET TO A-RANK EVENTUALLY, AFTER YOU LEARN MORE JUTSU AND GET STRONGER.
HMM.
FINE.
BUT THAT MEANS I GOTTA FIND MORE THINGS TO PROTECT!
HUH?

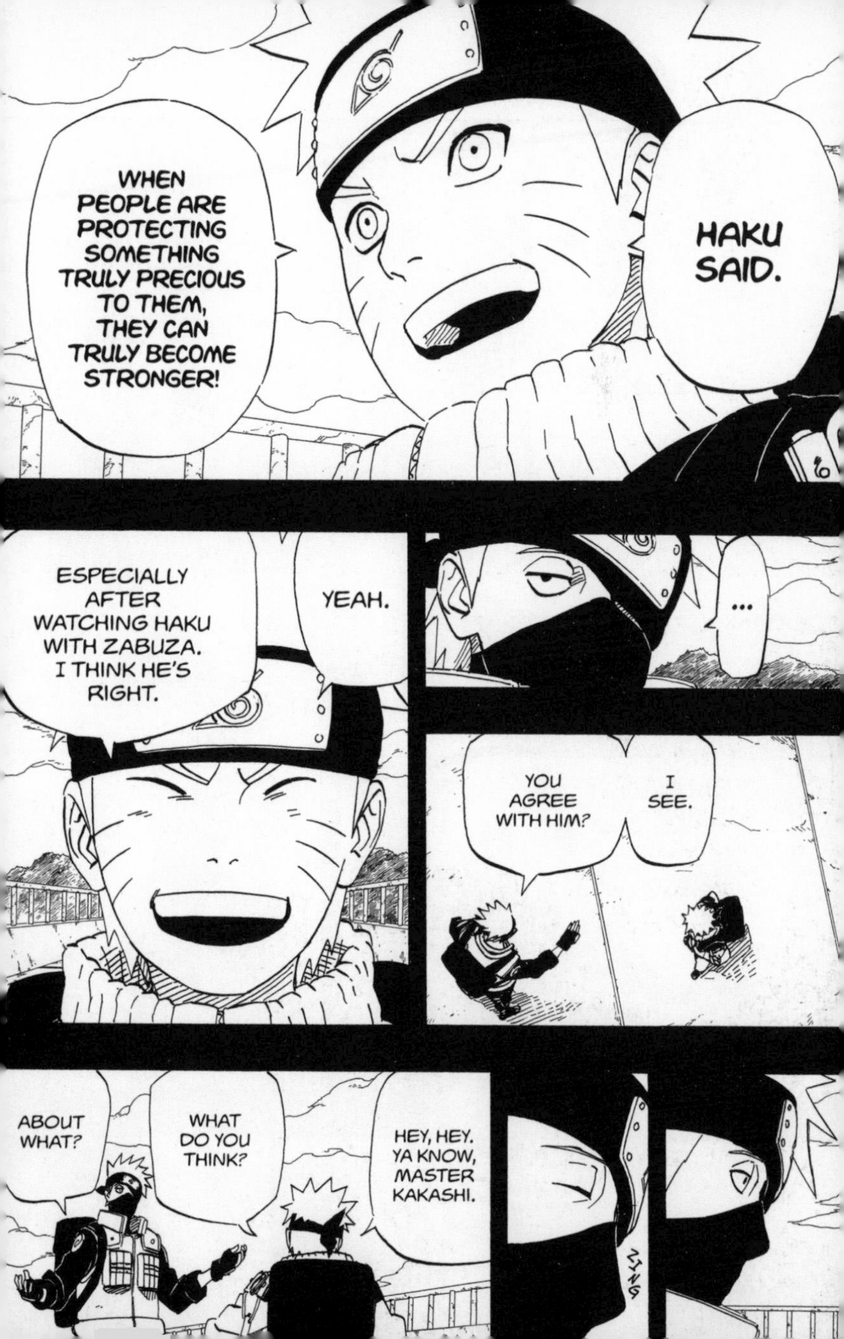
HAKU SAID.
WHEN PEOPLE ARE PROTECTING SOMETHING TRULY PRECIOUS TO THEM, THEY CAN TRULY BECOME STRONGER!
...
I SEE.
YOU AGREE WITH HIM?
YEAH.
ESPECIALLY AFTER WATCHING HAKU WITH ZABUZA. I THINK HE'S RIGHT.
ZING
HEY, HEY. YA KNOW, MASTER KAKASHI.
WHAT DO YOU THINK?
ABOUT WHAT?

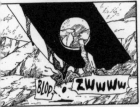

BLOP. · ZWWW

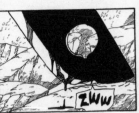

ZWW

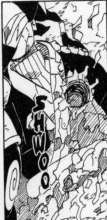

SHWOO

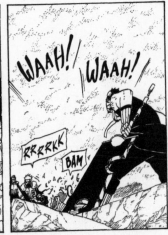

WAAH! WAAH!

RRRKK

BAM

I'M GLAD YOU WERE NARUTO'S FIRST ADVER-SARIES.

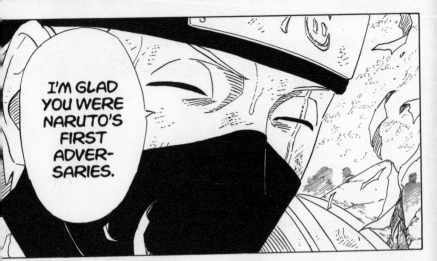

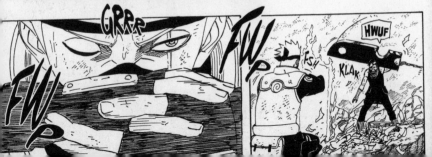

GRRR

FWP

FWP

FSH

KLAK

HWUF

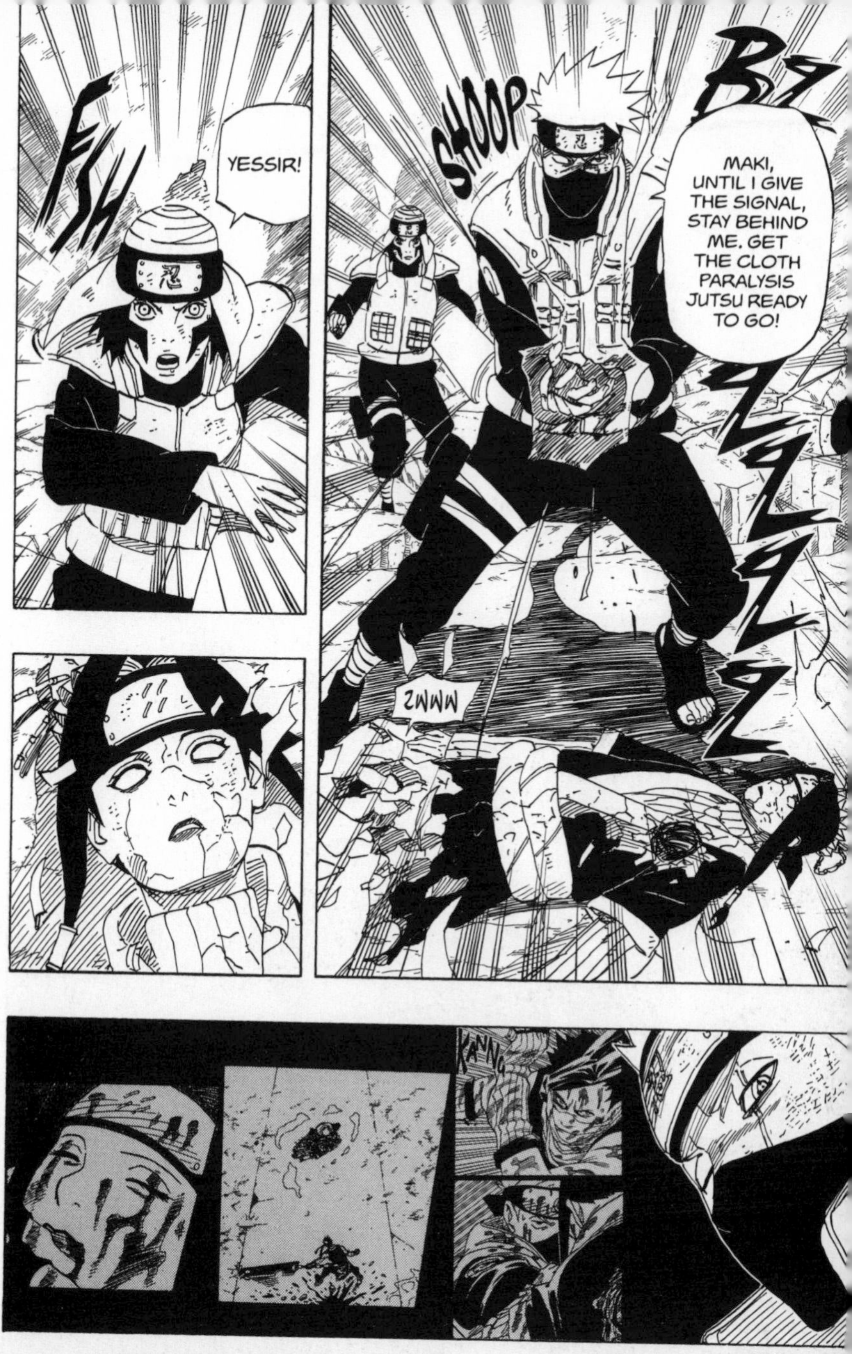
SHOOP
MAKI, UNTIL I GIVE THE SIGNAL, STAY BEHIND ME. GET THE CLOTH PARALYSIS JUTSU READY TO GO!
FSH
YESSIR!
KANNG

READ THIS WAY

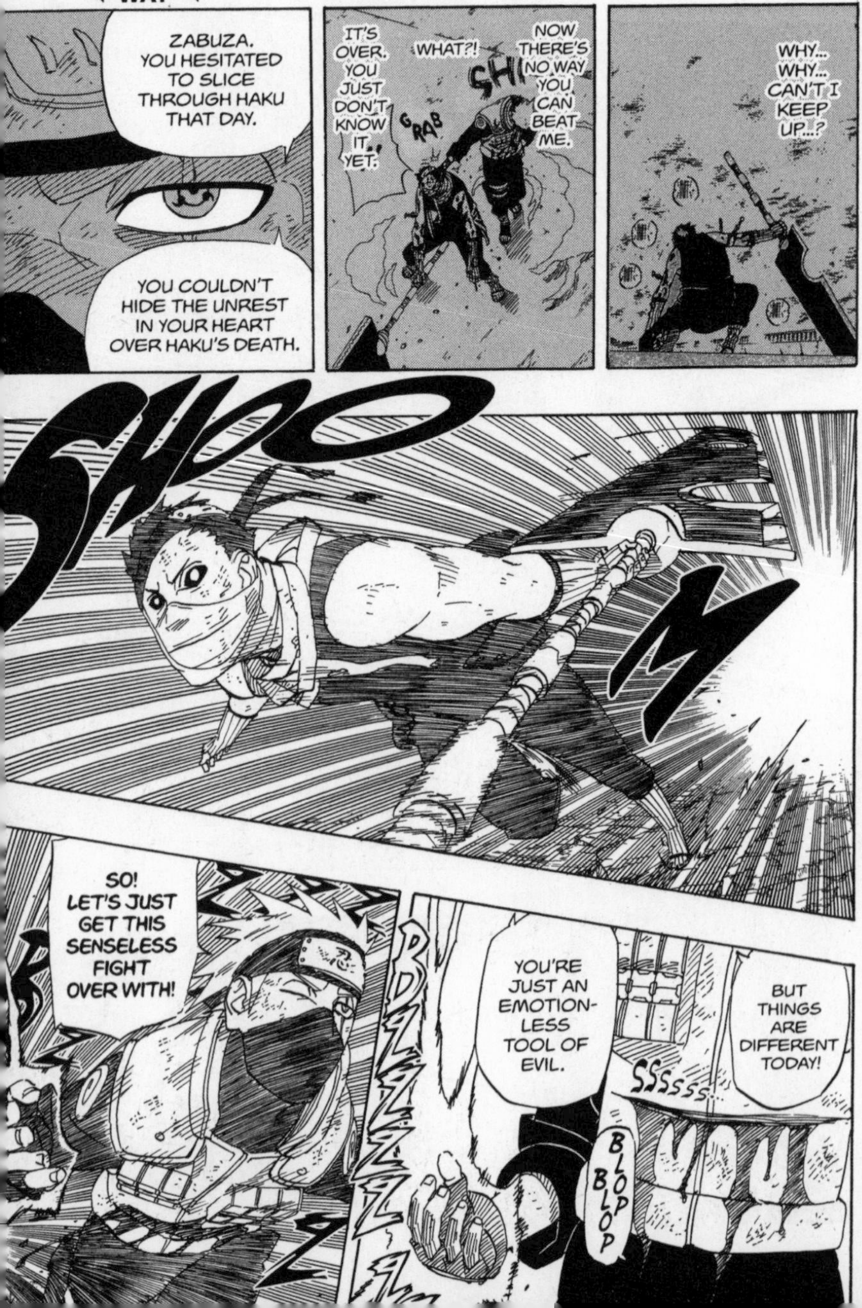
WHY... WHY... CAN'T I KEEP UP...?
NOW THERE'S NO WAY YOU CAN BEAT ME.
SHI
WHAT?!
GRAB
IT'S OVER. YOU JUST DON'T KNOW IT... YET.
ZABUZA. YOU HESITATED TO SLICE THROUGH HAKU THAT DAY.
YOU COULDN'T HIDE THE UNREST IN YOUR HEART OVER HAKU'S DEATH.
SHOOM
BUT THINGS ARE DIFFERENT TODAY!
YOU'RE JUST AN EMOTION-LESS TOOL OF EVIL.
SSSSSS...
BLOP BLOP
SO! LET'S JUST GET THIS SENSELESS FIGHT OVER WITH!

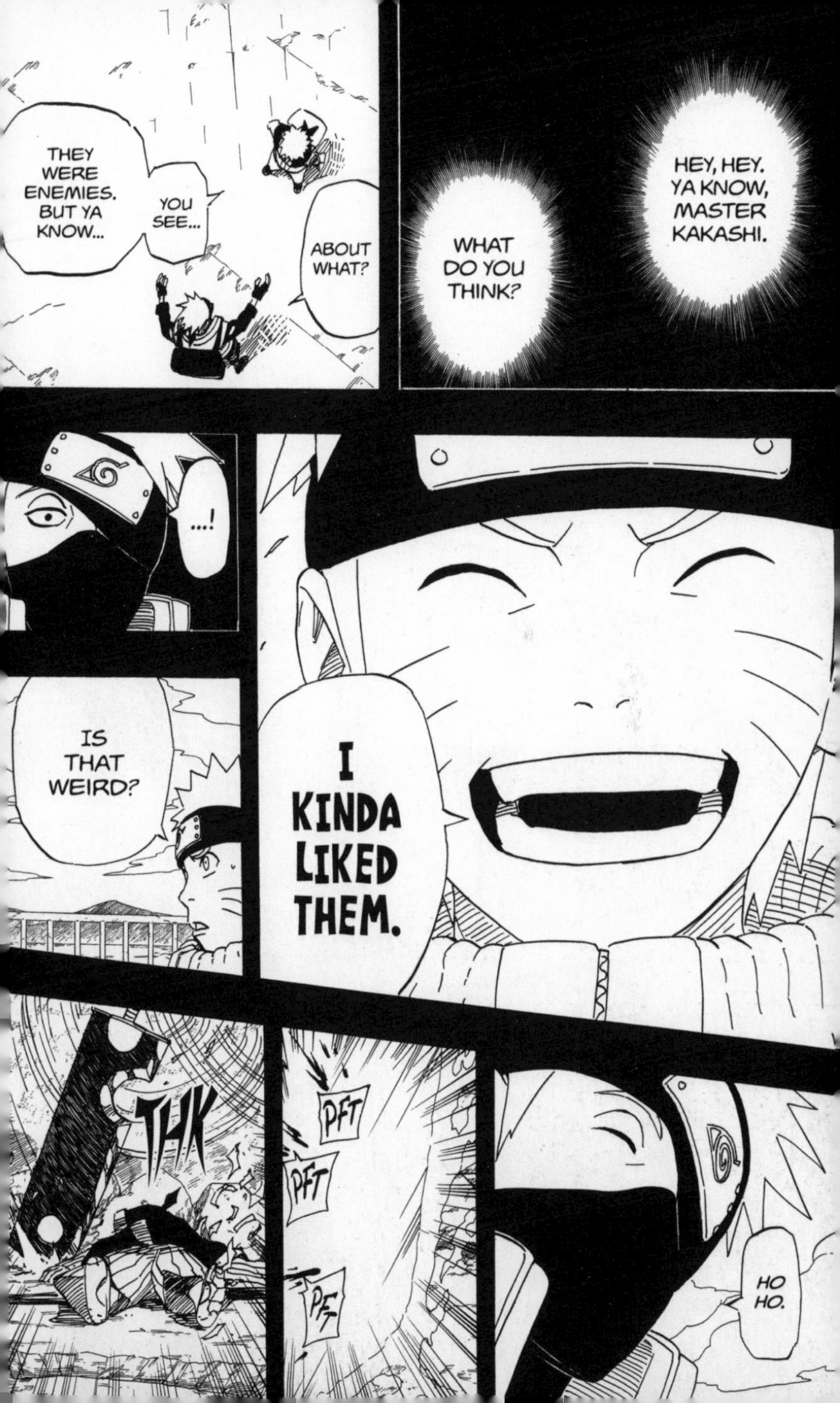
HEY, HEY. YA KNOW, MASTER KAKASHI.
WHAT DO YOU THINK?
ABOUT WHAT?
YOU SEE...
THEY WERE ENEMIES. BUT YA KNOW...
I KINDA LIKED THEM.
...!
IS THAT WEIRD?
HO HO.
PFT
PFT
PFT
THK

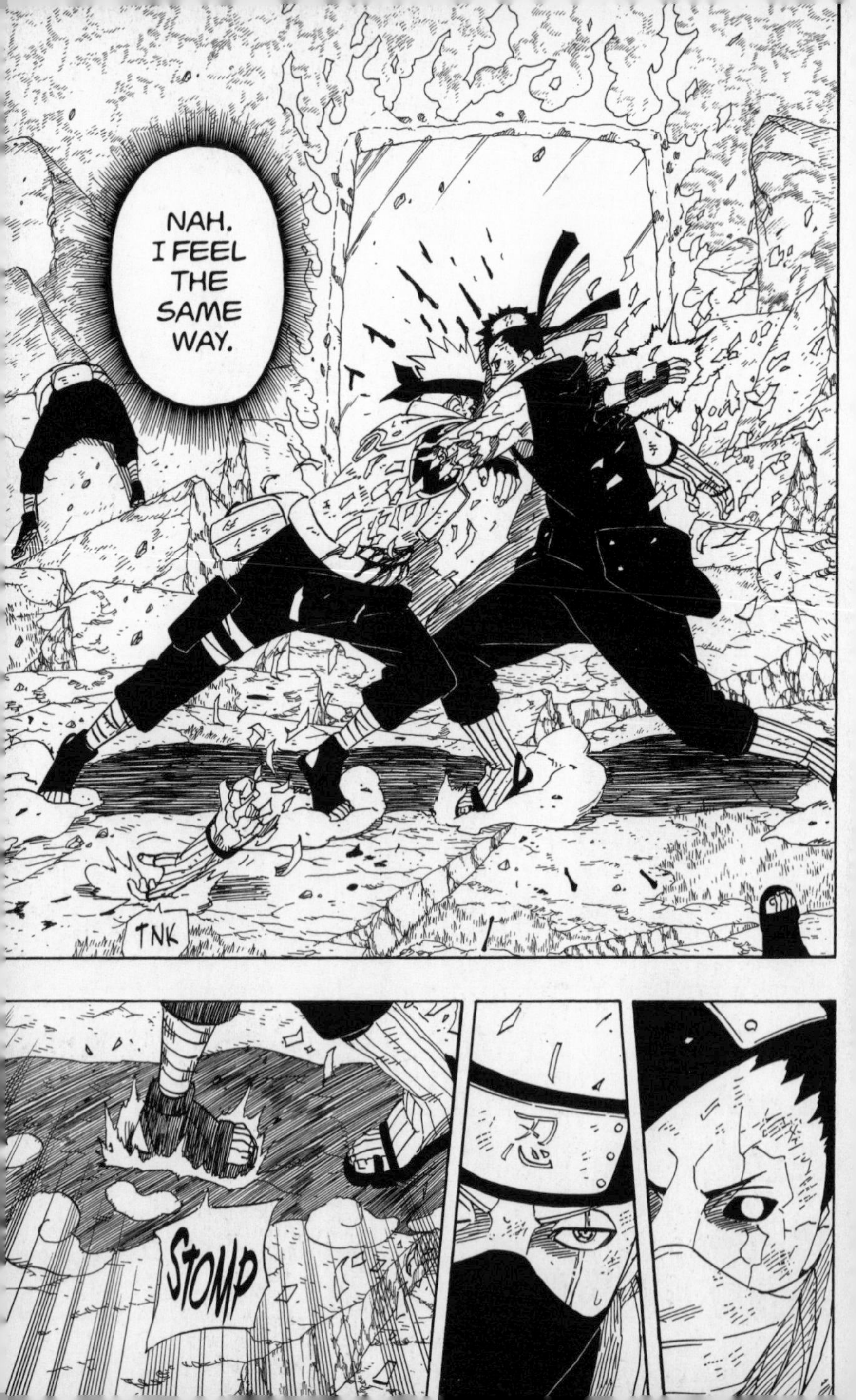
NAH. I FEEL THE SAME WAY.
TNK
STOMP

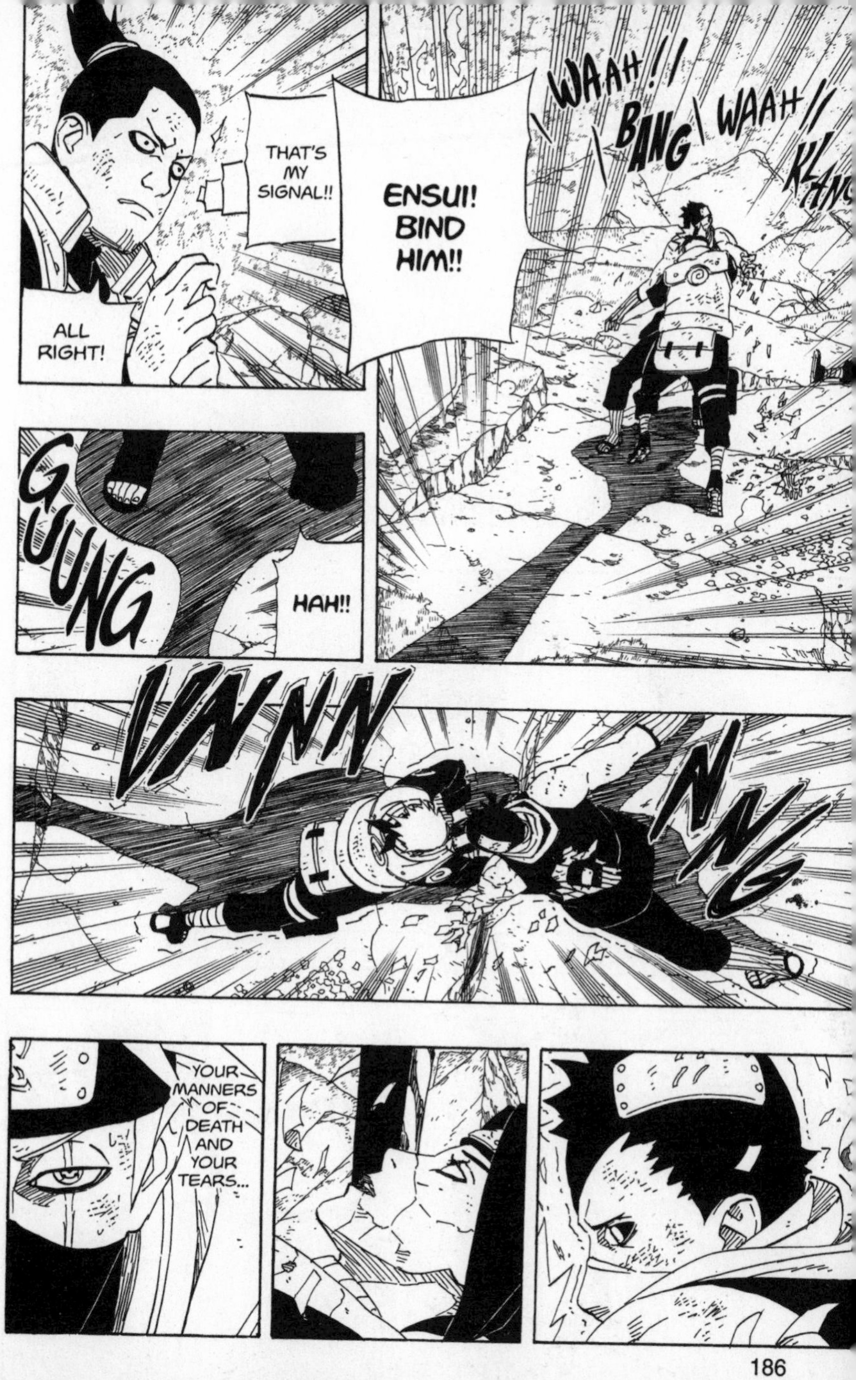

WAAH!!
BANG
WAAH!!
KLAN
ENSUI! BIND HIM!!
THAT'S MY SIGNAL!!
ALL RIGHT!
GUUNG
HAH!!
VNNN
NNG
YOUR MANNERS OF DEATH AND YOUR TEARS...

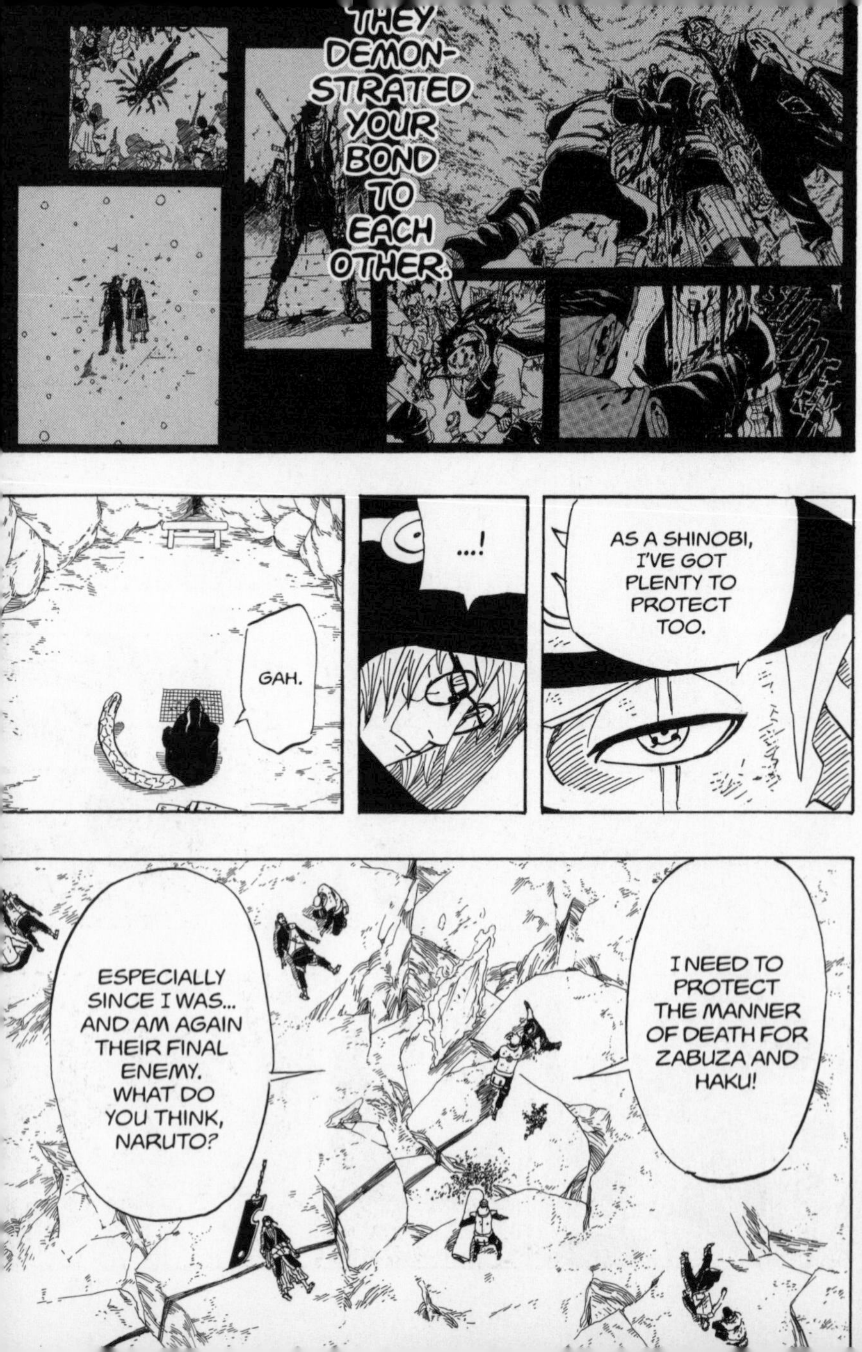
THEY DEMON-STRATED YOUR BOND TO EACH OTHER.
AS A SHINOBI, I'VE GOT PLENTY TO PROTECT TOO.
...!
GAH.
I NEED TO PROTECT THE MANNER OF DEATH FOR ZABUZA AND HAKU!
ESPECIALLY SINCE I WAS... AND AM AGAIN THEIR FINAL ENEMY. WHAT DO YOU THINK, NARUTO?

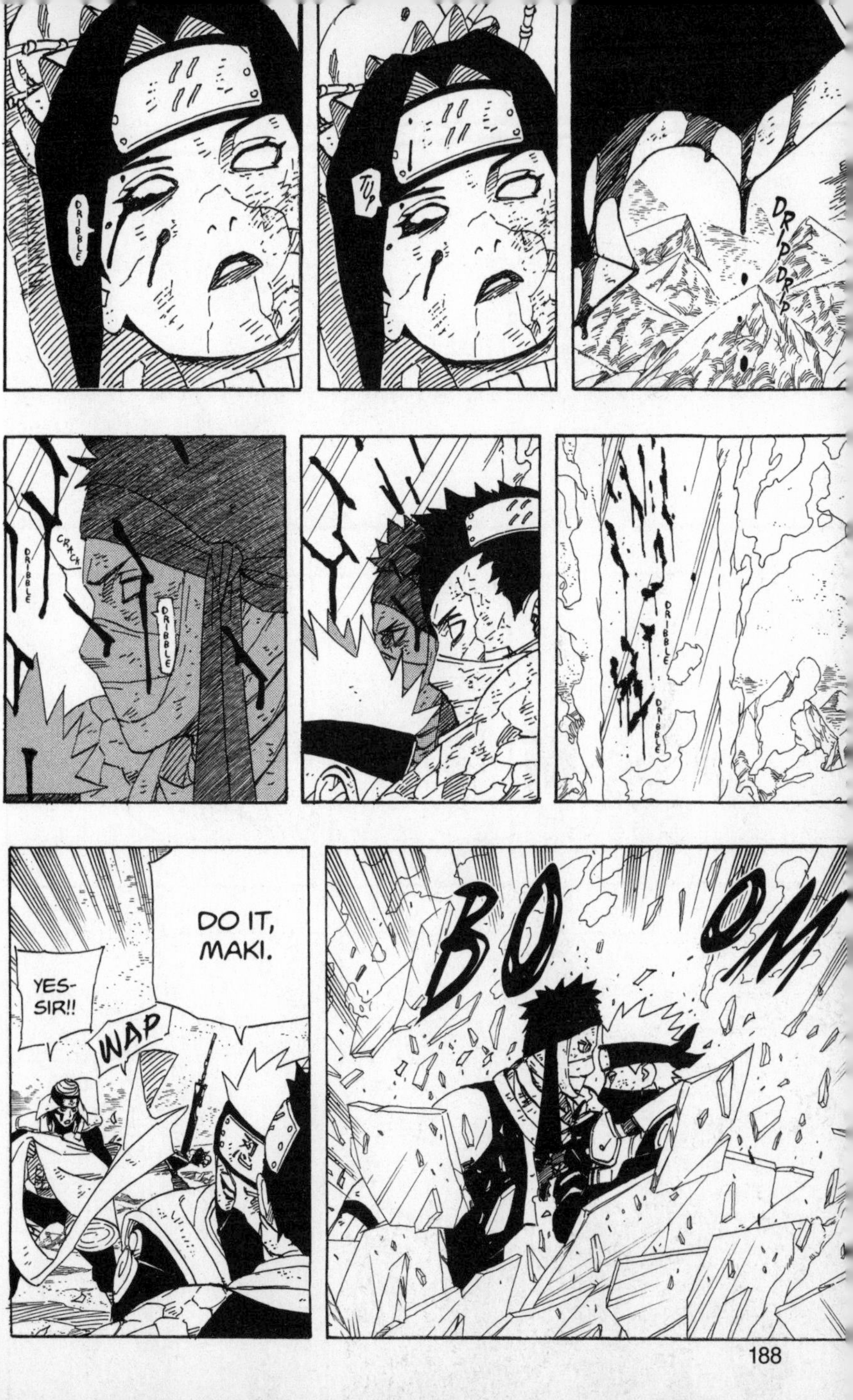
DRIP DRIP
TUP
DRIBBLE
DRIBBLE
DRIBBLE
CRACK
DRIBBLE
DRIBBLE
BOOM
DO IT, MAKI.
YES-SIR!!
WAP

READ THIS WAY

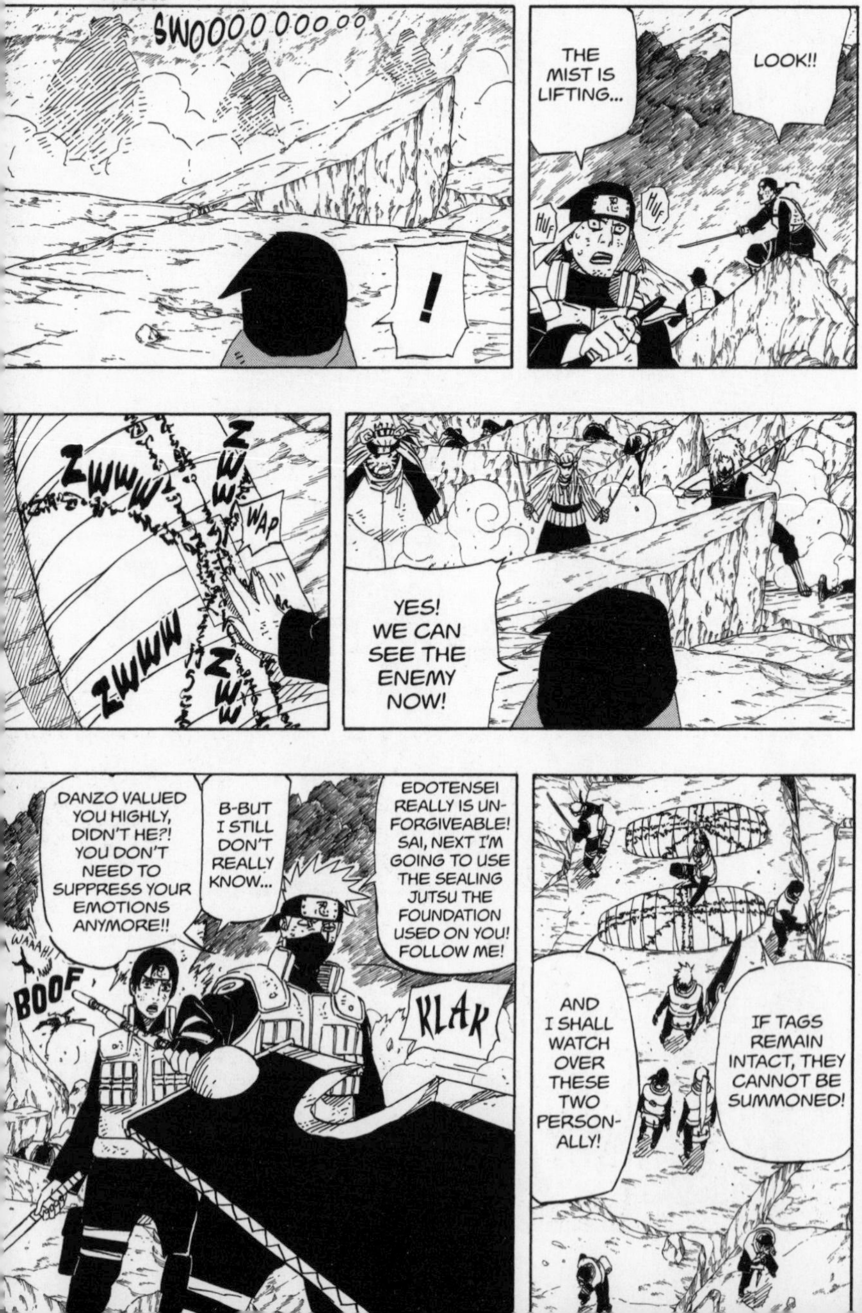
LOOK!!
THE MIST IS LIFTING...
HUF
HUF
SWOOOOOOOOO
!
YES! WE CAN SEE THE ENEMY NOW!
ZWWW
WAP
ZWWW
ZWWW
ZWWW
IF TAGS REMAIN INTACT, THEY CANNOT BE SUMMONED!
AND I SHALL WATCH OVER THESE TWO PERSONALLY!
EDOTENSEI REALLY IS UNFORGIVEABLE! SAI, NEXT I'M GOING TO USE THE SEALING JUTSU THE FOUNDATION USED ON YOU! FOLLOW ME!
B-BUT I STILL DON'T REALLY KNOW...
DANZO VALUED YOU HIGHLY, DIDN'T HE?! YOU DON'T NEED TO SUPPRESS YOUR EMOTIONS ANYMORE!!
KLAK
WAAAH!
BOOF

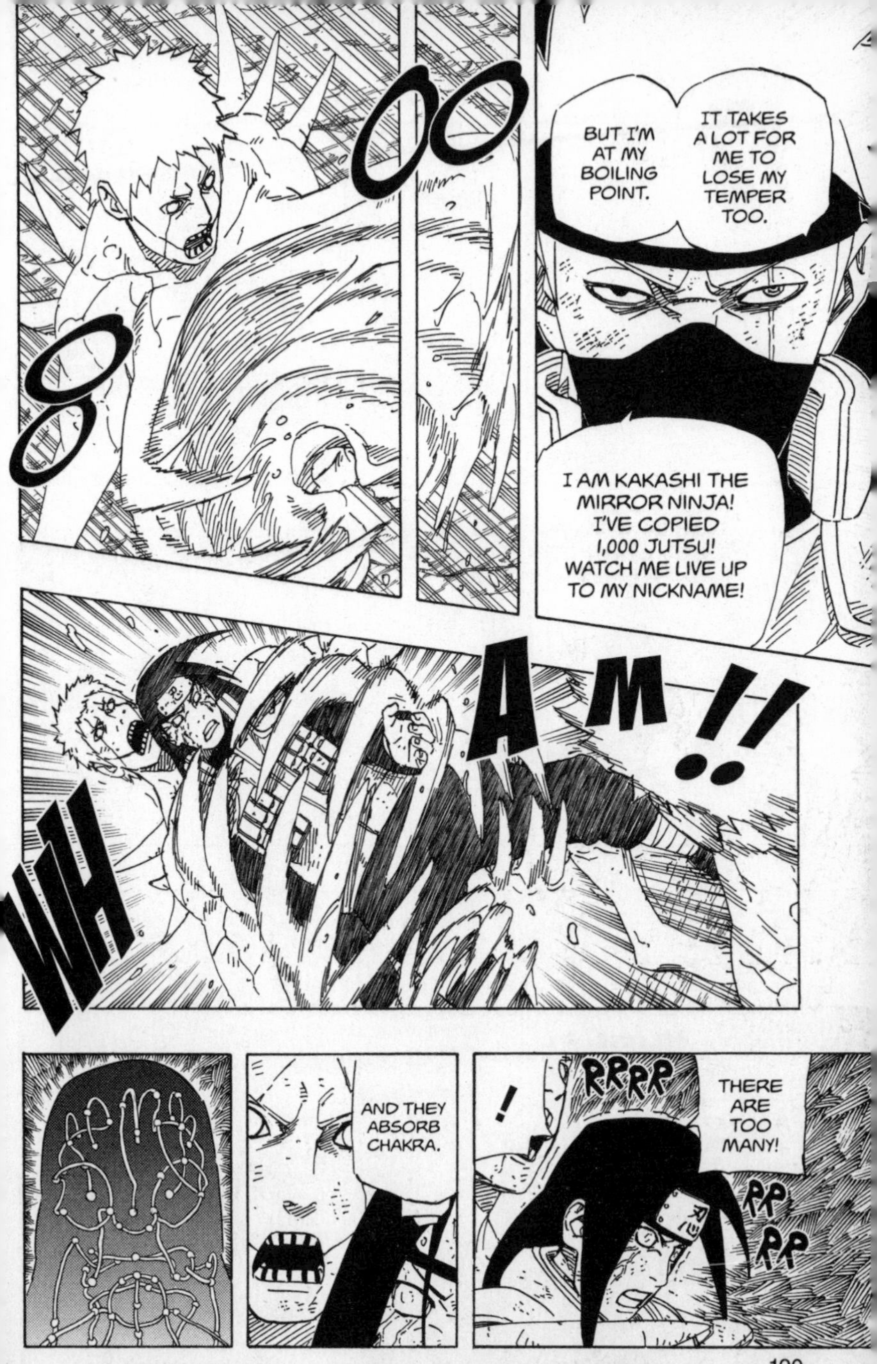
IT TAKES A LOT FOR ME TO LOSE MY TEMPER TOO.
BUT I'M AT MY BOILING POINT.
I AM KAKASHI THE MIRROR NINJA! I'VE COPIED 1,000 JUTSU! WATCH ME LIVE UP TO MY NICKNAME!
OO
O
WHAM!!
THERE ARE TOO MANY!
RRRR
!
RR
RR
AND THEY ABSORB CHAKRA.

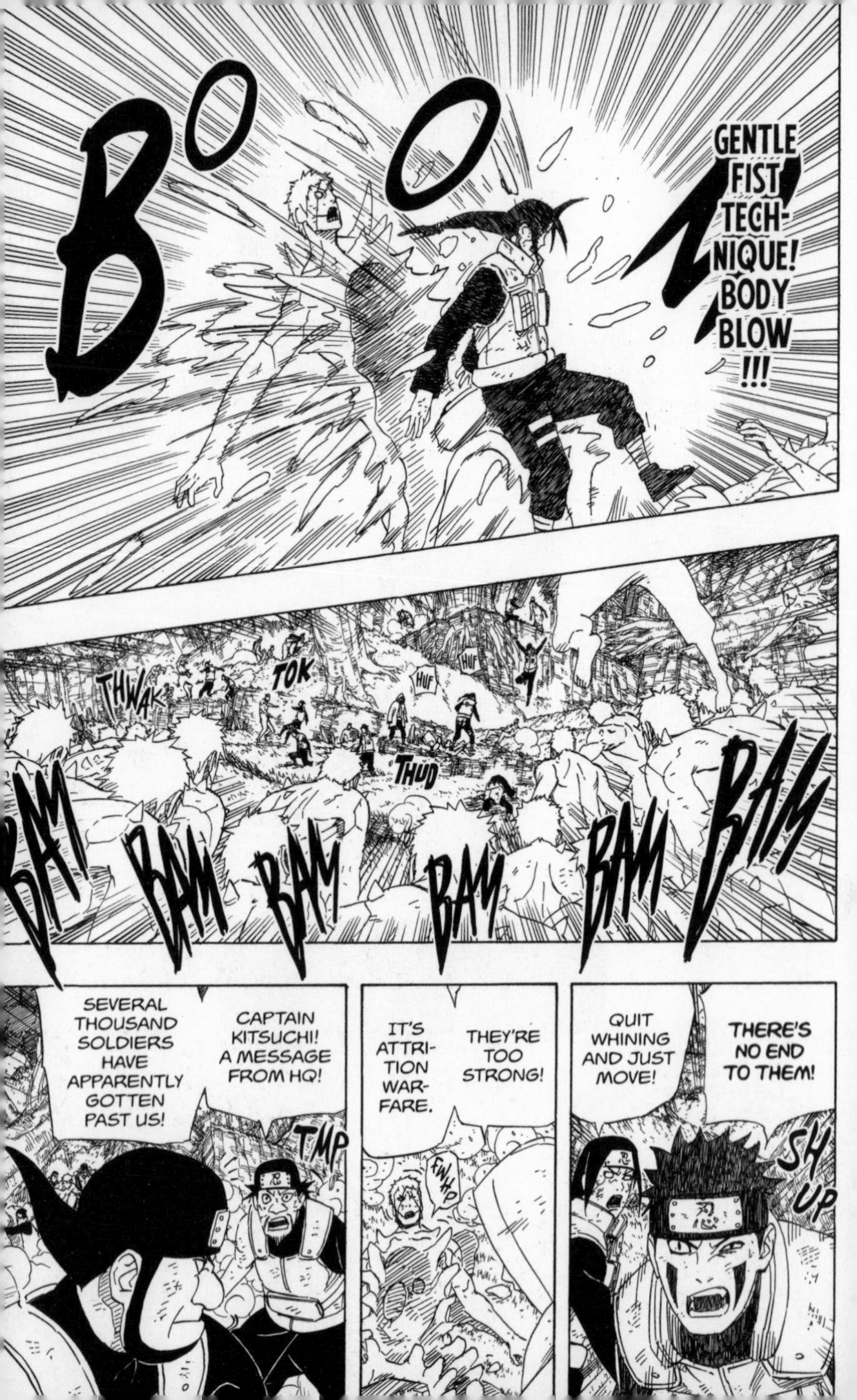
GENTLE FIST TECHNIQUE! BODY BLOW!!!
BOO
BAM
BAM
BAM
BAM
BAM
BAM
HUF
HUF
THUD
TOK
THWAK
THERE'S NO END TO THEM!
QUIT WHINING AND JUST MOVE!
SHUP
THEY'RE TOO STRONG!
IT'S ATTRITION WARFARE.
FWHP
CAPTAIN KITSUCHI! A MESSAGE FROM HQ!
SEVERAL THOUSAND SOLDIERS HAVE APPARENTLY GOTTEN PAST US!
TMP

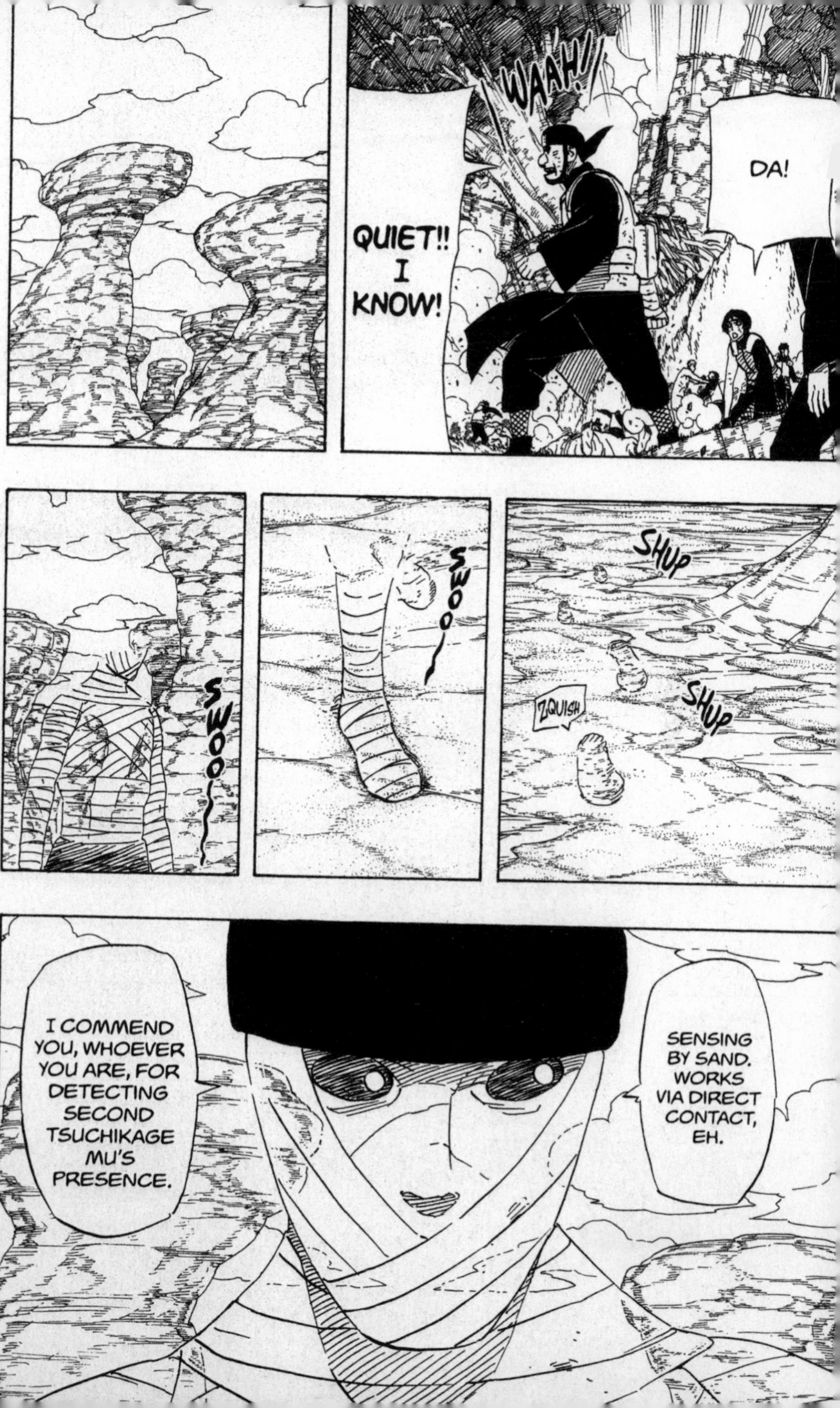
DA!
WAAH!!
QUIET!! I KNOW!
SHUP
ZQUISH
SHUP
SWOO
SWOO
SENSING BY SAND. WORKS VIA DIRECT CONTACT, EH.
I COMMEND YOU, WHOEVER YOU ARE, FOR DETECTING SECOND TSUCHIKAGE MU'S PRESENCE.

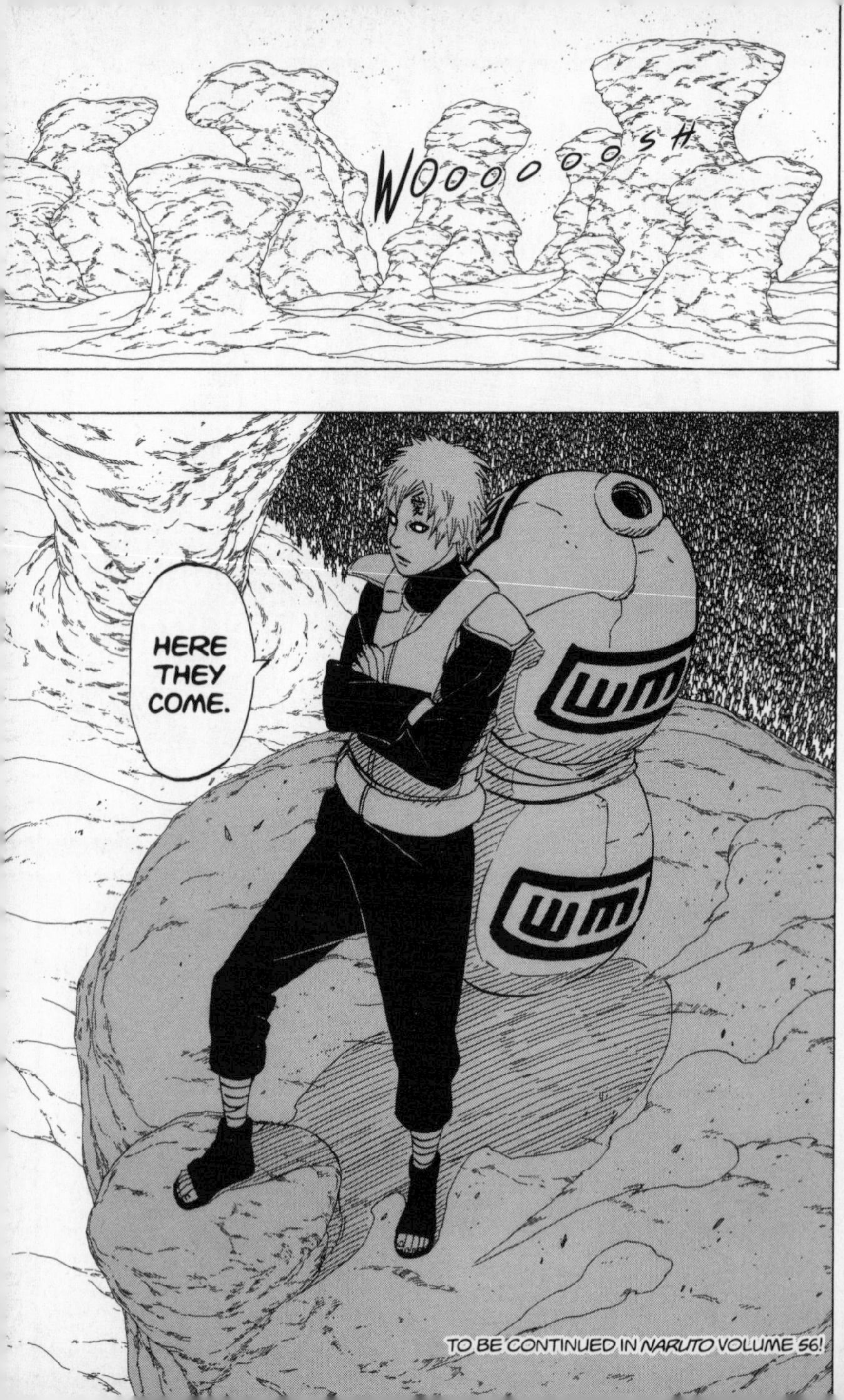
WOOOOOOSH
HERE THEY COME.
TO BE CONTINUED IN NARUTO VOLUME 56!

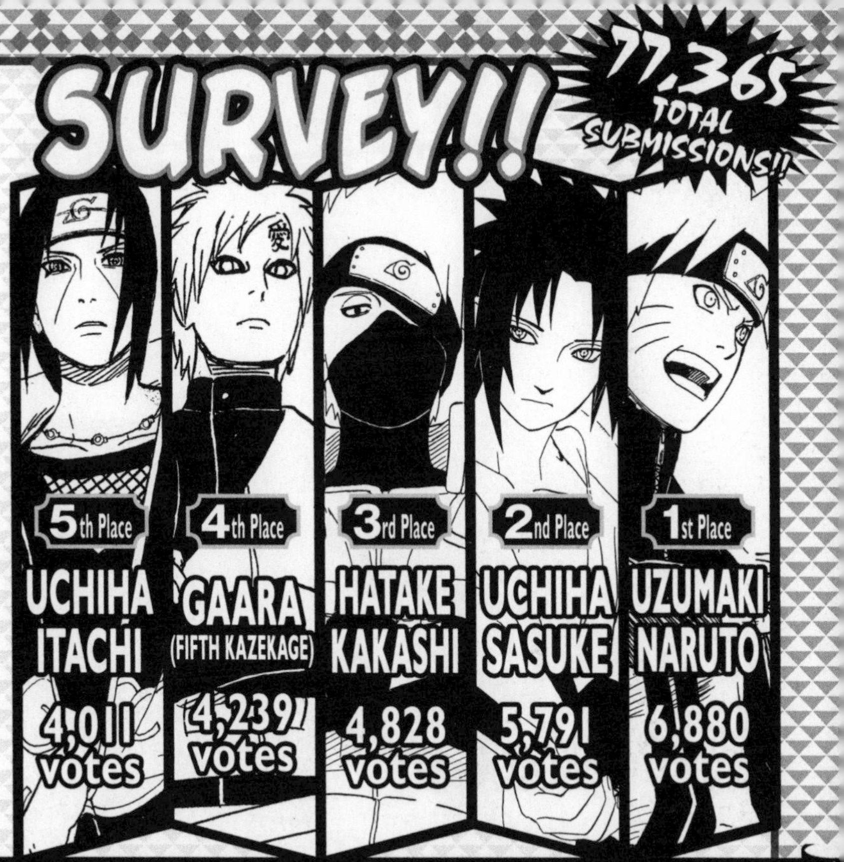
SURVEY!!
77,365 TOTAL SUBMISSIONS!!
1st Place
UZUMAKI NARUTO
6,880 votes
2nd Place
UCHIHA SASUKE
5,791 votes
3rd Place
HATAKE KAKASHI
4,828 votes
4th Place
GAARA (FIFTH KAZEKAGE)
4,239 votes
5th Place
UCHIHA ITACHI
4,011 votes

53rd Place Chikushodo [Pain] 15 votes
Tayuya 15 votes
Sarutobi Asuma 15 votes
56th Place Eight Tails 12 votes
Omoi 12 votes
58th Place Rin 9 votes
Senju Tobirama (Second Hokage) 9 votes
Kishimoto Masashi 9 votes
Yahiko 9 votes
62nd Place Terumii Mei (Fifth Mizukage) 8 votes
Gekko Hayate 8 votes
Shiranui Genma 8 votes
Akimichi Choji 8 votes
Jugo 8 votes
Mitarashi Anko 8 votes
68th Place Uchiha Shisui 7 votes
Darui 7 votes
Ao 7 votes
Yagura 7 votes
Konohamaru 7 votes
Shee 7 votes
Shizune 7 votes
Senju Hashirama (First Hokage) 7 votes
76th Place Sage of Six Paths 6 votes
Pakkun 6 votes
Shin 6 votes
'Ay (Fourth Raikage) 6 votes
Chojuro 6 votes
Hyuga Tokuma 6 votes
Akamaru 6 votes
Yuhi Kurenai 6 votes
Captain Yamato's head gear 6 votes
Sarutobi Hiruzen (Third Hokage) 6 votes
Amaru 6 votes
Fu 6 votes
Etc. (1 vote each) 26 names total

(This poll conducted in Japan.)

7TH CHARACTER POPULARITY

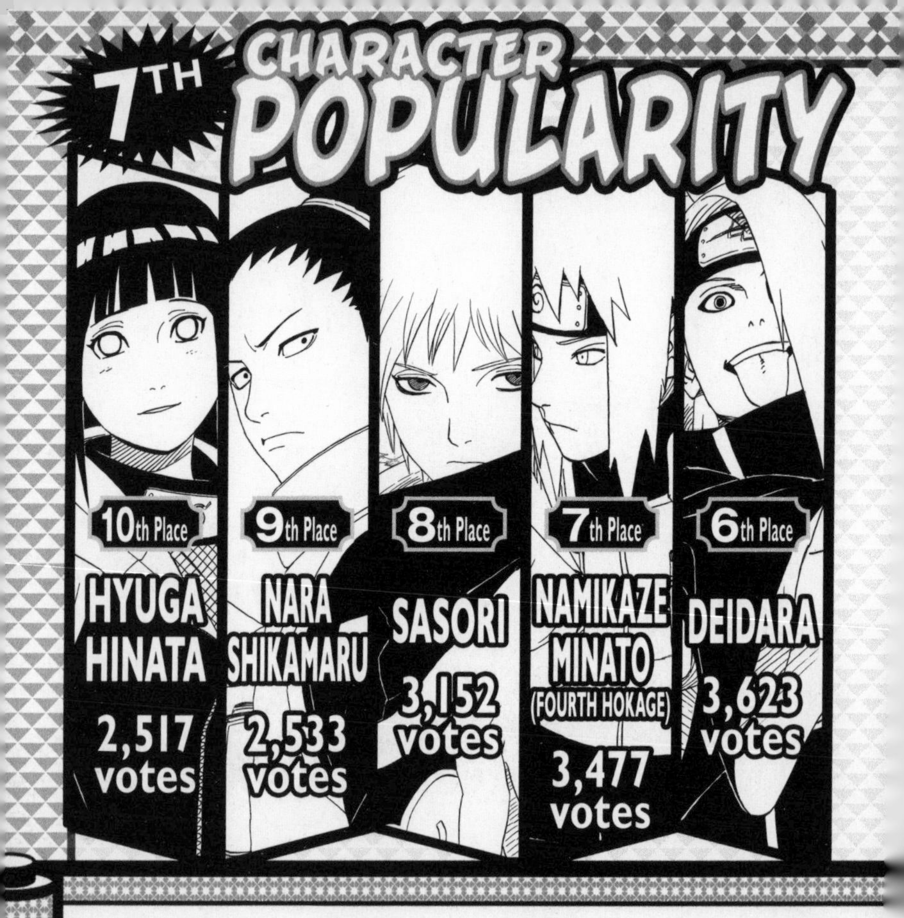
6th Place
DEIDARA
3,623 votes
7th Place
NAMIKAZE MINATO (FOURTH HOKAGE)
3,477 votes
8th Place
SASORI
3,152 votes
9th Place
NARA SHIKAMARU
2,533 votes
10th Place
HYUGA HINATA
2,517 votes

11th Place Umino Iruka 2,494 votes
12th Place Haruno Sakura 2,188 votes
Sai 2,188 votes
14th Place Yamato 1,925 votes
15th Place Hyuga Neji 1,794 votes
16th Place Jiraiya 1,723 votes
17th Place Hidan 1,635 votes
18th Place Temari 1,628 votes
19th Place Uchiha Madara (Tobi) 1,621 votes
20th Place Rock Lee 1,597 votes
21st Place Uzumaki Kushina 1,338 votes
22nd Place Hoshigaki Kisame 1,320 votes
Pain 1,320 votes
Konan 1,320 votes
25th Place Killer Bee 1,312 votes
26th Place Might Guy 1,299 votes
27th Place Kankuro 1,214 votes
28th Place Inuzuka Kiba 1,079 votes
29th Place Aburame Shino 989 votes
Yamanaka Ino 989 votes
31st Place Karin 862 votes
32nd Place Tenten 723 votes
33rd Place Tsunade (Fifth Hokage) 667 votes
34th Place Hozuki Suigetsu 539 votes
Toruné 539 votes
36th Place Kakuzu 381 votes
37th Place Foo 212 votes
Hagane Kotetsu 212 votes
Haku 212 votes
Yakushi Kabuto 212 votes
41st Place Kamizuki Izumo 813 votes
42nd Place Momochi Zabuza 72 votes
43rd Place Shimura Danzo 54 votes
44th Place Orochimaru 27 votes
Zetsu 27 votes
Utakata 27 votes
Inomatsu 27 votes
Samui 27 votes
49th Place Kimimaro 19 votes
Nagato 19 votes
Uchiha Obito 19 votes
Nine Tails 19 votes

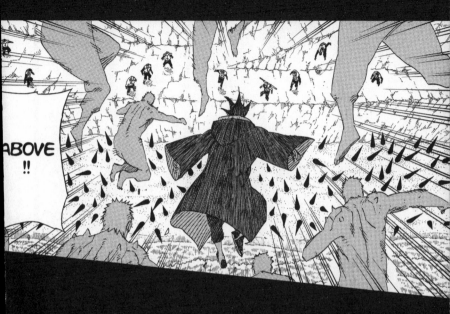

IN THE NEXT VOLUME...

TEAM ASUMA, REUNITED

Naruto and the Allied Shinobi Forces battle Kabuto's hordes of reanimated ninja soldiers. In the process, they come face-to-face with old friends brought back from the dead...plus enemies and weapons more fearsome than any they could have imagined!

AVAILABLE MARCH 2012!

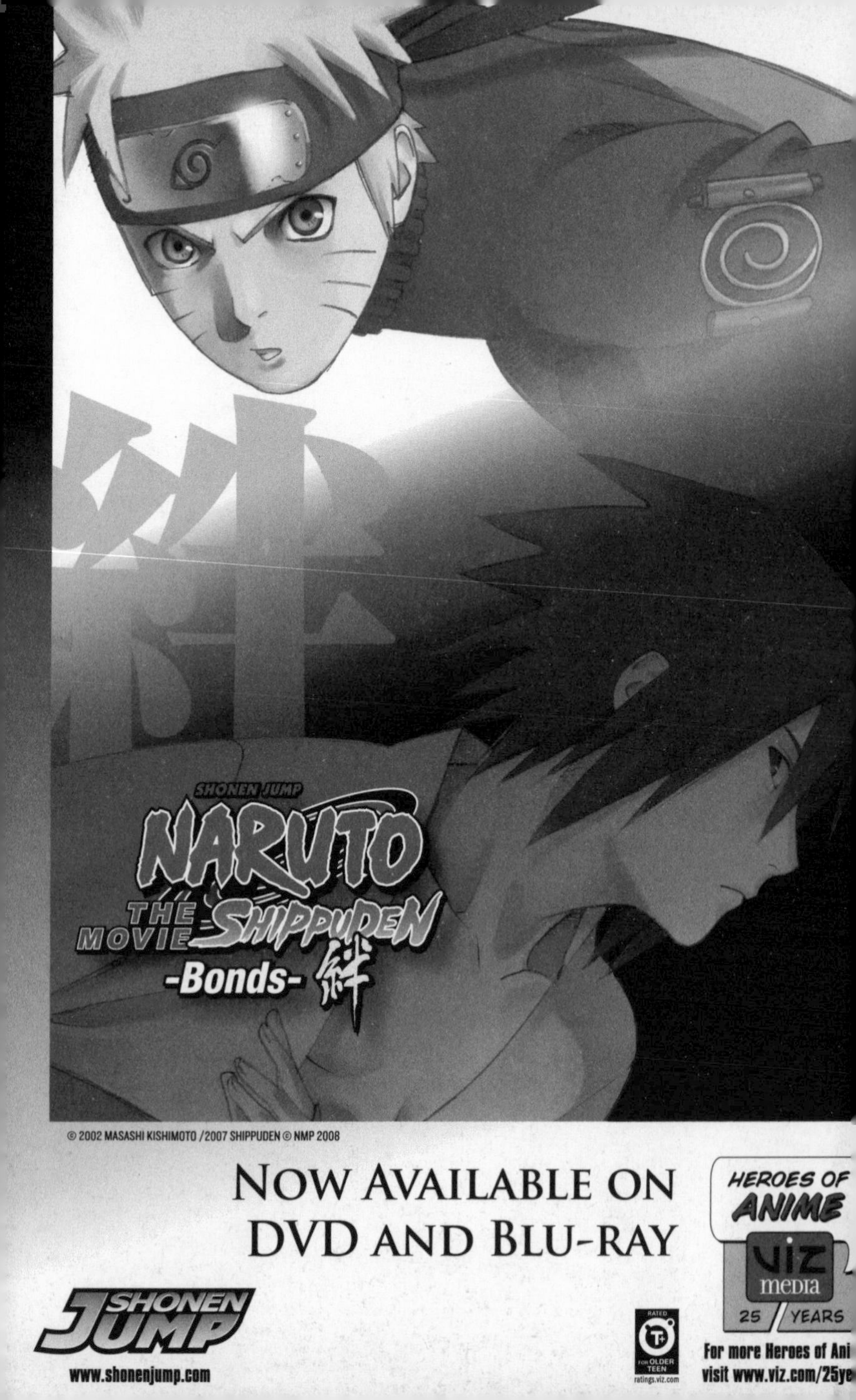
SHONEN JUMP
NARUTO
THE MOVIE SHIPPUDEN
-Bonds- 絆

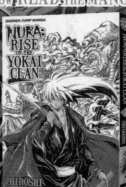

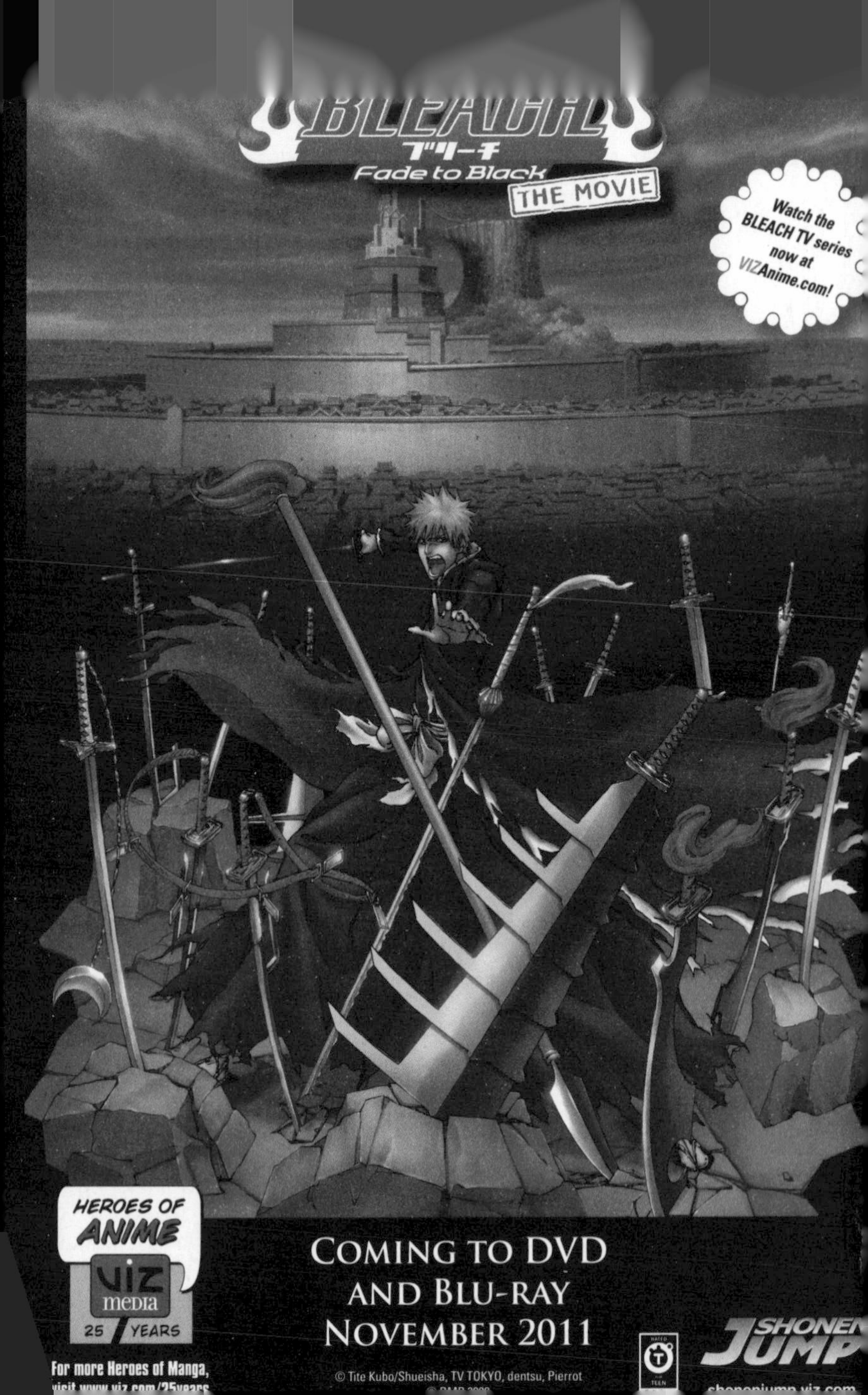
BLEACH
ブリーチ
Fade to Black
THE MOVIE
Watch the BLEACH TV series now at VIZAnime.com!
HEROES OF ANIME
VIZ media
25 YEARS
COMING TO DVD AND BLU-RAY NOVEMBER 2011
SHONEN JUMP
For more Heroes of Manga,
© Tite Kubo/Shueisha, TV TOKYO, dentsu, Pierrot

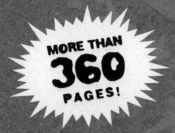
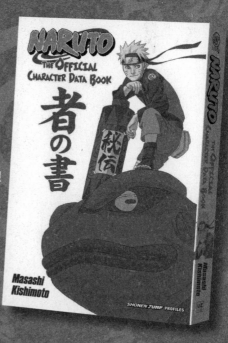